NOBLE'S

Wedding Venues Guide

1997

Copyright ©
The Noble Publishing Company
Pavillon (Publishing) Ltd
Goudhurst, Kent

First published 1996

This edition 1997

Editor: Janet Simpson
Assistant Editor: Lynn Lewis
Production: Joe Brinley

The publishers have made every effort to ensure that the information
contained in this book is correct at the time of going to press.
They cannot, however, accept responsibility for any errors
or inaccuracies contained herein.

ISBN: 0 9528144-5-5

Concept and design by Pavillon (Publishing) Ltd
Front cover concept by Ken Bentley
Illustration by Camilla Dowse
Colour reproduction by Latent Image West
Printed in the UK by Butler & Tanner

*T*his book will not only save you time, it will save you several headaches, possibly a few arguments and will certainly avoid chasing wild geese. You hold in your hand 18 months of research, lots of computer space, thousands of telephone calls and several weeks of printing and binding.

This is the second edition of Noble's Wedding Venues Guide. We produced the first edition because there was no easy way for couples to find out which venues held civil wedding licences and what facilities those venues offered. This edition not only updates those entries, but adds venues which gained their licences throughout 1996.

We aim to be as comprehensive as possible and to provide the information you want in a format that is easy to find your way around. Sadly we don't have complete entries on some venues; but not for lack of trying. Every venue in this book has been written to, phoned and faxed at least twice - and remember we are providing a free entry for all venues. For some this appears not be be enough, and one would hope that if you were likely to give them money (ie. if you book your wedding there), they would be more responsive - and in some cases more polite - but I wouldn't bank on it. In our experience the venues that are helpful and courteous to you from the moment you first make contact are the ones that will make sure that you wedding day is special. After all, they don't get a dress rehearsal for your wedding; if something isn't right you can't wind back the clock and do it all over again.

If you want any advice, (and I'm sure friends and relatives will be offering you plenty), it's 'stick to what you want for your wedding'. It is your day after all. The venues in these pages prove that most things are possible, whether it's marriage in a fairytale castle, in underground caves, in a zoo, on a boat, at your favourite football club, or at the races. There are venues for an intimate private house party or a major bash for a thousand. You can get married at the pub with a pie and a pint to follow, or take over a stately home Great Gatsby style, with full silver service. It's all here.

Happy hunting and have a great day!

Janet Simpson
Editor

Finding the right county

Entries in Noble's Wedding Venues Guide have been listed alphabetically by county and alphabetically within each county. We have taken current physical county boundaries to define where a venue is located although some may have a different county in their postal address, or may still be using old county names. Much to many people's surprise Middlesex no longer exisits, for example, and many places that were once in Surrey, Essex, or Kent are now in Greater London. Similarly places that were once in Cheshire or Lancashire are now in Greater Manchester. To add to the confusion, new counties were introduced in April 1996, while several disappeared. For entries formerly in North Humberside, for instance, you should now look up East Riding of Yorkshire or Kingston Upon Hull. Avon has now been divided into Bath and North East Somerset, North Somerset and South Gloucestershire. Wales has also changed considerably with several old county names returning.

A few facts on civil ceremonies

All venues in England and Wales that can hold a civil wedding ceremony on their premises have a licence for a room or rooms which have been deemed acceptable by the local registrar. They will not be able to marry you anywhere else on the premises. By law licensed premises must have a roof and be permanent structure. You can therefore get married on a permanently moored boat, but not one that cruises up and down the river. Similarly, you can get married in a football club boardroom, but never on the pitch (although you can usually have photos taken there). The nearest you will get to a ceremony outside is one held in a conservatory or orangery, or a permanent garden gazebo (not many of these are licensed).
It is the registrar local to the venue who will perform your wedding ceremony, and he/she must be booked by you, along with the venue (who will tell you who to contact). You must also notify the registrar where you live that you intend to marry and where.

Tips for your search

•Assuming that you want to be the only wedding taking place at your chosen venue, it is wise to get confirmation that this will be the case. Some of the larger venues may host several weddings in one day and although, in many cases, this poses no problem, it can be embarrasing and upsetting if certain facilities, such as the garden or the toilets, are shared (no bride wants to meet another bride in the ladies).
•If you are limited to wines offered by the venue ask for a wine tasting session so that you can chose the wines you want.
•If you or your guests are likely to want to stay overnight on the premises or nearby, ask about preferential rates for accommodation. Where possible we have included this information in our details on each venue.
•In order to make it easier for your guests to find your wedding venue, ask if maps can be provided which you can send out with your invitations, along with details of parking and, of course, local accommodation.

CONTENTS

Ceremony Facilities

 Building of historic interest

 Capacity sitting

 Capacity standing

 Wheelchair access

 Area suitable for indoor photography

 Area suitable for outdoor photography

Price guide: This is the starting price for hiring the venue for a ceremony. This price does not include registrar's fees, which are usually around £150.

Reception Facilities

 Capacity - waited service

 Capacity - buffet

 Marquee possible & capacity

 In-house catering

 Contract catering - could use own

 Contract catering - approved list only

 Liquor licence

 Late night liquor licence

 Area for displaying wedding gifts

 Changing room available

 Flowers for venue can be provided

 Cake can be provided

 Cakes stand & knife can be provided

 Toastmaster can be arranged

 Photographer/videographer can be arranged

 Dancing/disco can be arranged

 Piped music can be arranged

 Live Music can be arranged

 Entertainment or stage can be arranged

 Accommodation on premises and number of rooms

Catering: This is the starting price for catering (food only) per head at this venue. Where possible we have given starting prices for buffets and sit down meals

6

Assembly Rooms & Museum of Costume
Bennett Street, Bath, BA1 2QH
Tel: 01225 477783 Fax: 01225 477709
Contact: Christina Scott, Sales Manager

Ceremony

This building (now National Trust) was built in 1771 to house Georgian Assemblies. Its suite of rooms, Ballroom, Octagon and Tea Room, was restored in 1991. They are linked in sequence, as well as to the central vestibule. Furnishings include paintings by Gainsborough and Hoare and 18th Century crystal chandeliers. Private tours can be arranged. Up to three ceremonies are allowed per day, every day except Sunday and Christmas Day.
Price guide: £50

Reception

While no accommodation is available on the premises, the Assembly Rooms has arranged preferential rates with local hostelries. If required, the appointed contract caterers will provide themed meals.
Catering: £7 to £35pp.

Combe Grove Manor Hotel & Country Club
Brassknocker Hill
Monkton Combe, Bath BA2 7HS
Tel: 01225 834644 Fax: 01225 834961
Contact: Cathy Cox, Conference & Banqueting Co-ordinator

Ceremony

This elegant manor house, set in 82 acres of gardens and woodland, was built in 1698 and is now a hotel and country club. Five rooms are licensed for wedding ceremonies; the largest housing 100, while the smallest (the Library and the Roman Room), take just 25. Some rooms are located within the manor house itself, others are in the more recently built Garden Lodge. There is limited wheelchair access.
Price guide: from £100

Reception

The hotel can arrange everything from horses and carriage to fireworks and hot air balloons. Both helicopters and hot air balloons can land on site. For those who can't resist the water, the canal is a mere half a mile away.
Leisure facilities on site include tennis, swimming and golf. couples booking their reception at Combe Grove receive complimentary accommodation in a standard room on their wedding night. The hotel also offers a honeymoon package, and special bridal beauty treatments.
Catering: Buffets from 6.25pp Sit down from £19.50pp

Guildhall
High Street,
Bath, BA1 5AW
Tel: 01225 477783 Fax: 01225 477709
Contact: Christina Scott, Sales Manager

Ceremony

This National Trust, listed building (completed 1778), houses a famous banqueting room featuring 18th Century chandeliers and neo-classical decoration; including plasterwork and gilding. This, and the adjoining Aix-en-Provence Room, are found on the first floor. Both rooms are reached via the Adam-style Grand Staircase. There are smaller rooms on the ground floor.
Price guide: £20

Reception

You may have a choice of caterer, which does not have to be from an approved list. Accommodation is not available on the premises, but preferential rates have been agreed with local establishments.
Catering: £7.35pp

Pump Room & Roman Baths
Stall Street, Bath, BA1 1LZ
Tel: 01225 477783 Fax: 01225 477709
Contact: Christina Scott, Sales Manager

Ceremony

The 2000 year old torch-lit Roman Baths, and world-famous Georgian Pump Room (completed in 1795), is now owned by the National Trust. The complex includes the Concert Room, Drawing Room, Smoking Room, Terrace and Roman Baths. As few as 20 and as many as 400 can be accommodated for the wedding ceremony. Three ceremonies per day is the maximum number allowed, and on any day except Christmas Day. Special features can include guided tours of the Roman Baths lit by flares.
Price guide: £30

Reception

Catering specialities by the appointed contract caterers include themed dinners; Georgian, Roman, etc. Overnight accommodation is not available on the premises, but the Pump Room has preferential rates with local establishments.
Catering: £7 - £45 pp

Theatre Royal
Sawclose, Bath BA1 1ET
Tel: 01225 448815 Fax: 01225 444080
Contact: Ann Meddings, Operations Manager

Ceremony

For the theatrically minded, ceremonies can even take place on the stage at the Theatre Royal, to a capacity audience of 950! Four other rooms in the 1805 suite are also licensed. These rooms are designed by a leading theatre designer and each has its own entrance, kitchen and bar. Wheelchair access is limited to the auditorium. An unlimited number of weddings can take place here on any day of the year except Christmas Day.
Price guide: from £200

Reception

While no accommodation is available on the premises, the theatre has preferential rate agreements with local hotels and guest houses.
Catering: from £16pp

STOP PRESS
Royal Crescent Hotel, Bath
01225 739955

Barns Hotel
Cardington Road
Bedford, Beds MK44 3SA
Tel: 01234 270044 Fax: 01234 273102
Contact: Rachelle Ranson, Conference Manager/ Matthew Bryam, Operations Manager

Ceremony

This riverside hotel comprises a 13th Century tithe barn and a 16th Century manor house. Couples may arrive and depart by boat. Numerous rooms are licensed for ceremonies (limited wheelchair access), allowing for group sizes from 10 to 120. Ceremonies can take place on Saturdays and Sundays.
Price guide: from £195

Reception

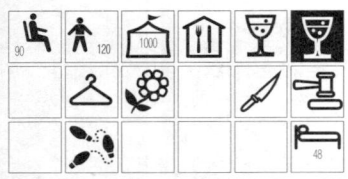

Catering: Buffets from £10.50pp Sit down from £16.50pp

Beadlow Manor
Golf & Country Club
Nr Shefford, Beds SG17 5PH
Tel: 01525 860800 Fax: 01525 861345
Contact: Simon Johnson, Sales & Marketing Manager

Ceremony

The Club is set in 300 acres of rural Bedfordshire and features two 18-hole golf courses and lakes. The original building dates from the mid-19th Century, but there have been modern additions over the years.
Two suites are available for ceremonies, the olde worlde style Bedfordshire Suite with a sitting capacity of up to 85, and the larger Manhattan Suite.
Wheelchair access is more difficult to the older parts of the building. Ceremonies cannot be held without a reception.
Price guide: £85

Reception

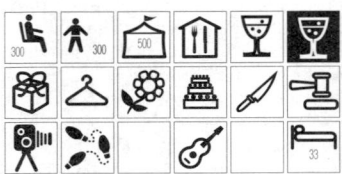

Italian food is a speciality. The wedding package includes a complimentary suite for the couple in their wedding night, and use of the Club's own cake stand and knife. In addition to the rooms on the premises, the Club has other accommodation nearby. In the past, the Club has hosted Medieval and Gothic style weddings (all in black), has organised fireworks and allowed helicopters to land in the grounds. Guests staying overnight have full complementary use of the health centre which includes sauna and Jacuzzi.
Price guide: Buffet from £7.35pp Sit down from £19.70pp

Flitwick Manor
Flitwick,
Beds MK45 1AE
Tel: 01525 712242 Fax: 01525 718753
Contact: General Manager

Ceremony

Flitwick Manor is set in its own grounds with a croquet lawn and tennis court. The listed building offers two rooms for wedding ceremonies, accommodating 24 and 40 people. In 1996 only one ceremony was allowed per day, on any day except Christmas Day and Good Friday.
As we go to press, the hotel is undergoing a change of ownership, so prices and facilities may yet change.
Price guide: £100

Reception

Flitwick boasts a celebrity chef, and can be available exclusively for your wedding for 24 hours. Otherwise, weddings will usually finish by 6pm.
Catering: £35 to £50pp

Moore Place Hotel
The Square,
Aspley Guise
Milton Keynes
Beds MK17 8DW
Tel: 01908 282000 Fax: 01908 281888
Contact: Brian Haddleton, Food & Beverage Manager

Ceremony

This Georgian mansion, originally built as a family home, is set in the village of Aspley Guise. Two rooms are licensed for ceremonies: the Greenhouse Restaurant (80 max) and the Buckingham Suite (15 max). The restaurant is set in a courtyard overlooking a water cascade and ornamental pond. Ceremonies can take place here any day of the week between 8am and 6pm, but must be accompanied by reception at the hotel.
Price guide: from £70

Reception

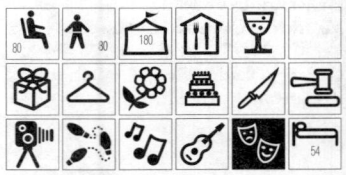

Food and drink packages pre-booked for Friday, Sunday or a Bank Holiday will be entitled to a 10% discount. Special accommodation rates are also offered for wedding guests.
Catering: £18.95pp

Woburn Abbey
Woburn
Beds MK43 0TP
Tel: 01525 290666 Fax: 01525 290271
Contact: Nigel Robinson, Catering Manager

Ceremony

Woburn Abbey is a stately home set in a 3,000 acre deer park. Guests must be seated at the ceremony, which can take place in one of two rooms, but there is ample capacity for most wedding parties. The smaller of the two marriage rooms (the Lantern Room) has the capacity for up to 70. Ceremonies can take place on any day except Christmas Day, Boxing Day and New Year's Day, but only for couples holding their reception at the Abbey.
Price guide: £500 + VAT

Reception

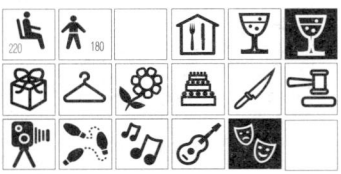

There is no accommodation on the premises, but preferential rates are available locally.
Catering: from £27.50pp.

Aurora Garden Hotel
14 Bolton Avenue
Windsor,
Berks
Tel: 01753 868686 Fax: 01753 831394
Contact: Josephine Currie, Managing Partner or Duty Manager

Ceremony

This country house hotel and restaurant is situated in a residential part of the town, and set in its own acre of gardens.
Up to three ceremonies per day are permitted in the Lavender Suite.
Price guide: £250

Reception

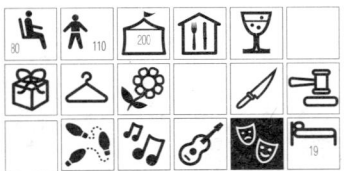

The in-house catering team can provide vegetarian or ethnic dishes if required.
Catering: Buffet from £16.95pp Sit down from £18.95pp

The Bear at Hungerford
Charnham Street
Hungerford, Berks
Tel: 01488 82512 Fax: 01488 684357
Contact: Joanne Clayton, Sales Manager

Ceremony

This English Heritage property allows ceremonies on any day, with a maximum of two ceremonies per day.
Price guide: from £200

Reception

A honeymoon suite is offered free of charge to the wedding couple as part of the package.
Catering: Buffet from £6.95 Sit down from £22pp (incl drinks)

Berystede Hotel
Bagshot Road, Sunninghill
Ascot, Berks
Tel: 01344 23311 Fax: 01344 873061
Contact: Debbie Guy, Sales Manager

Ceremony

Only one ceremony is permitted per day at this hotel which is set in nine acres of landscaped gardens. There is one ceremony room, which has limited wheelchair access.
Price guide: £175

Reception

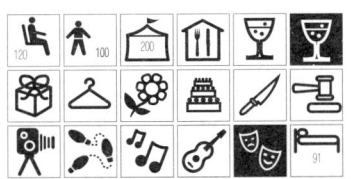

Despite the acreage around the hotel, there is unfortunately no suitable site for helicopters or balloons. However, the hotel is able to arrange all the facilities you are likely to require from music and entertainment to toast master and transport.
Catering: Buffets from £24.50pp Sit down package from £48.00

Boulters Lock Hotel
Boulters Island
Maidenhead, Berks SL6 8PE
Tel: 01628 21291 Fax: 01628 26048
Contact: Jean Dunstone,
Sales & Marketing Manager

Ceremony

The hotel (built in 1726 as a miller's house) is set on Boulters Island and has panoramic views of the River Thames. The hotel features in Jerome K Jerome's 'Three Men in a Boat'. Ceremonies are allowed on any day of the week, but confetti is not permitted.
Price guide: £250

Reception

The hotel has its own pontoon, so bride and groom could arrive or leave their wedding by boat. Accommodation is available at the hotel, and the hotel also has preferential arrangements with other local establishments.
Catering: from £25pp

Bull Inn
High Street,
Bisham, Berks
Tel: 01628 484734 Fax: 01628 898424
Contact: Andres Lopez, Owner

Ceremony

Up to two ceremonies a day can take place in the ceremony room at the Bull, a traditional public house and restaurant.
Price guide: £200

Reception

The Bull is happy to cater for children separately to the main wedding party.
Catering: Buffets from £12pp Sit down from £17.50pp

Calcot Hotel
98 Bath Road
Calcot, Reading, Berks
Tel: 01734 416423 Fax: 01734 451223
Contact: Claire Piercey, Banquet Co-ordinator

Ceremony

Up to two ceremonies are permitted on any day except Christmas Day and Boxing Day.
Price guide: £600

Reception

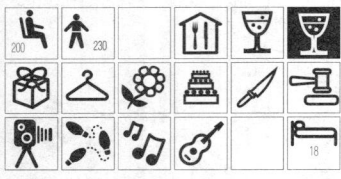

Catering: £18pp

Cantley House Hotel
Milton Road
Wokingham, Berks RG40 5QG
Tel: 01734 789912 Fax: 01734 774294
Contact: Maurice Monk, Proprietor or Charlotte Gallacher, Banqueting Manager

Ceremony

This Victorian country house, set in 59 acres, was formally the home of the Marquis of Ormonde. Up to two ceremonies are permitted on any day of the week.
Price guide: £250

Reception

Catering: from £25pp (including drinks)

Cliveden
Taplow
Maidenhead,
Berks SL6 0JF
Tel:01628 68561 Fax: 01628 661837
Contact: Kate Hewlett, Sales

Ceremony

Once the home of Lady Astor, Cliveden was built in 1851 and is set in 375 acres of landscaped grounds high above the Thames. Ceremonies, only one per day, can only take place here if the reception is also at Cliveden.
Price guide: £7,000 (see below)

Reception

Cliveden's wedding package for 56 guests includes use of various suites, accommodation on the eve and night of the wedding for bride and groom, and flowers. This package price does not include food and drink (one star Michelin). While entertainment and dancing are allowed, they must not interfere with the normal running of the hotel, or inconvenience other guests, which precludes loud bands or discos. This, of course, does not apply if you take over the whole hotel (190 guests with accommodation for up to 37 couples), plus a band and dinner, for £45,000.
Price guide: P.O.A.

The Copper Inn, Church Road
Pangbourne, Berks
Tel: 0118 984 2244 Fax: 0118 984 5542
Contact: Jenny Ellis, Conference & Events

Ceremony

This early 19th Century coaching inn is set in gardens within the village of Pangbourne. Only one ceremony can take place per day in the inn's Chiltern Suite.
Price guide: £500 (£125 with reception)

Reception

The Inn offers Mediterranean style food. While there is no room on the premises for evening dances, the Inn can arrange for the hire and licensing of the adjacent Pangbourne Hall, and can, of course, provide the catering.
Catering: £25pp

Courtyard by Marriott Reading
Bath Road, Padworth,
Reading, Berks RG7 5HT
Tel: 01734 714411 Fax: 01734 714442
Contact: Tim Cadman, General Manager

Ceremony

Part of the Whitbread Hotels Company, The Courtyard is a modern AA/RAC three-star hotel with a very traditional ambience. The hotel is available for wedding ceremonies on any day of the week except Sundays, with only one ceremony permitted per day.
Price guide: £600

Reception

Catering: from £19.50

Donnington Valley Hotel
Old Oxford Road
Donnington, Newbury, Berks
Tel: 01635 551199 Fax: 01635 551123
Contact: Barbara, PA to MD or Jo

Ceremony

This 58-bedroomed hotel and golf course, situated on the outskirts of Newbury, allows only one ceremony per day, but on any day of the week.
Price guide: £250

Reception

Catering: from £34.50pp

Easthampstead Park
Conference Centre
Wokingham, Berks RG40 3DF
Tel: 01734 780686 Fax: 01734 793870
Contact: Doug Wass, Manager

Ceremony

This is a Victorian country house (Grade II listed), set in 60 acres of parkland. Wedding ceremonies are allowed on all days except Bank Holidays. Only one ceremony allowed per day.
Price guide: £200

Reception

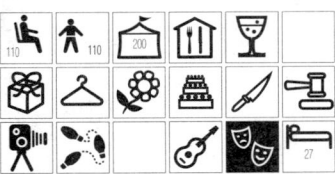

Catering: from £30pp (including drinks)

Foley Lodge Hotel
Stockcross
Newbury, Berks RG20 8JU
Tel: 01635 528770 Fax: 01635 528398
Contact: Kathy Kernutt, Conference & Banqueing Manager

Ceremony

This Victorian hunting lodge offers up to two ceremonies per day in its Wellingtonia Room.
Price guide: £600

Reception

Unusual weddings that have apparently taken place at Foley Lodge include Druid, Gypsy and Italian celebrations - so the hotel is clearly adaptable!
Catering: from £21.95pp

Harte & Garter Hotel
High Street
Windsor, Berks
Tel: 01753 863426 Fax: 01753 831394
Contact: Richard Varney, GM

Ceremony

The hotel is directly opposite the main entrance to Windsor Castle. The newly refurbished hotel boasts a regally decorated Victorian ballroom.
Two rooms are licensed and are available any day of the week with one ceremony per day. Ceremonies must be followed by a reception at the hotel.
Price guide: £200

Reception

Catering: Buffet from £17.50pp Sit down from £22pp

The Hideout
Easthampstead Park
Wokingham, Berks RG40 3BT
Tel: 01344 778686/750044
Contact: Mr or Mrs Bailey, Owners

Ceremony

This public house and Thai restaurant offers two wedding rooms, which have limted wheelchair access. The building is set in 80 acres of secluded grounds with 'no risk of disturbing the neighbours'.
Price guide: POA

Reception

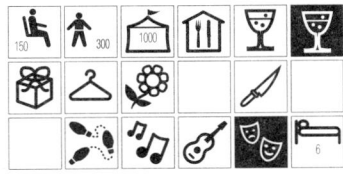

Naturally, Thai food is the catering speciality here. The restaurant obviously likes a good party and has a full unconditional entertainment licence until 2am. There is room on site for helicopters or hot air balloons.
Catering: Buffets from £7pp sit down from £15pp

Hollington House Hotel
Woolton Hill
Newbury, Berks RG20 9XA
Tel: 01635 255100 Fax: 01635 255075
Contact: Miss Christy Williams

Ceremony

This Edwardian country residence, set in 14 acres of woodland gardens, allows only one wedding ceremony per day, but on any day during the year. Confetti is not permitted.
Price guide: from £150

Reception

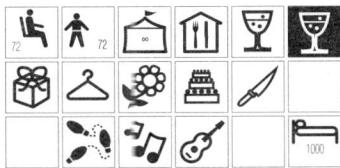

Catering at the House is traditional English with French influences. While several services are offered by the venue itself, others, namely the cake, photography, a disco, live music and a stage, can all be arranged on your behalf.
Catering: from £35

The Manor House
Church Road
Aldermaston,
Berks RG7 4HP
Tel: 01734 819333 Fax: 01734 819075
Contact: Fabrice Barlet, GM

Ceremony

This Grade II Victorian mansion, set in 137 acres, allows only one ceremony per day on any day except Bank Holidays. Leisure facilities at the hotel include tennis, putting, croquet and snooker, as well as fishing in the hotel's private lake.
The Manor House claims to be 'almost fully booked for 1997', and was rather unhelpful when we requested an update for this entry. We trust and hope they do not extend this level of customer service to couples getting married.
Price guide: P.O.A.

Reception

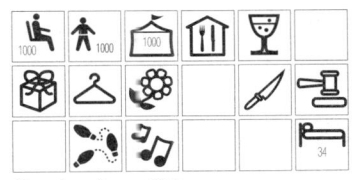

Catering: from £30pp

Mill House Hotel & Restaurant
Old Basingstoke Road
Swallowfield,
Reading, Berks RG7 1PY
Tel: 01734 883124 Fax: 01734 885550
Contact: Kim Pybuf, Partner

Ceremony

Built in 1823, The Mill House originally formed part of Stratfield Saye
estate, home to the 1st Duke of
Wellington. Its wedding packages
include an MC, four-poster bridal suite
for the couple, floral arrangements, silver cakestand and knife, red carpet on
arrival and colour co-ordinated linen.
Price guide: £185

Reception

Innovative and enticing drinks packages and
menus help couples plan their perfect day.
Catering: from £20pp

Monkey Island Hotel
Bray-on-Thames
Berks SL6 2EE
Tel: 01628 23400 Fax: 01628 784732
Contact: Sue Cook, Conference &
Banqueting

Ceremony

Set on an island in the Thames, this
Grade I listed building is a Regency-
style hunting lodge, once the residency
of the Duke of Marlborough. It can be
reached via a footbridge, boat or helicopter. The hotel now has three rooms
licensed for ceremonies.
Price guide: £500

Reception

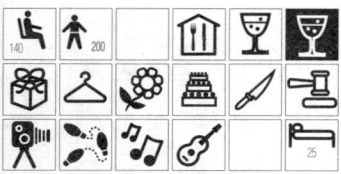

There are various rooms to choose
from, including one over the river.

While a marquee is available, this is not
recommended for full catering.
Limousine, executive coach, boat hire and
car hire are all available. The package
includes overnight room and champagne.
Catering: £75pp (package)

New Mill Restaurant
New Mill Road, Eversley,
Reading, Berks RG27 0RA
Tel: 01189 732105 Fax: 01734 328780
Contacts: Anthony Finn, General
Manager or Richard Haswell,
Restaurant Manager

Ceremony

This Grade II listed restored watermill
can be hired on any day of the year up to
a maximum of three ceremonies in a day.
Price guide: from £200

Reception

The New Mill is known for its award-
winning British cooking. Although
none is available on the premises, a list of
local accommodation can be provided.
Catering: from £20pp

Oakley Court Hotel
Windsor Road, Water Oakley
Windsor, Berks SL4 5UR
Tel: 01753 609988 Fax: 01628 776783
Contact: Conference & Banqueting
Department

Ceremony

This four star hotel is set in 35 acres of
landscaped gardens sweeping down to
the River Thames.
Price guide: £1000 (£500 in package option)

Reception

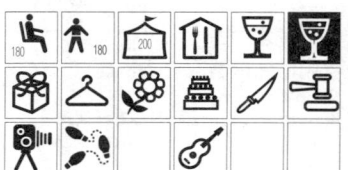

The hotel offers a comprehensive wedding package, from £75 per person,
which includes drinks (including champagne on arrival and for toasts), flowers,
evening disco or harpist playing
throughout the meal, toastmaster, and
overnight accommodation for bride
and groom. Special accommodation
rates are also available for guests. For
the reception, children under 5 are free,
and children between the ages of 5 and
12 are charged half price.
Catering: from £75pp (package)

The Old Mill
Station Road, Aldermaston
Berks RG7 4LD
Tel: 01734 712365 Fax: 01734 712371
Contact: Robin or Diane Arlott, Owners

Ceremony

This Grade II listed building is set in 20
acres alongside the river Kennet.
Ceremonies can take place on any day
of the week in the Stable Room.
Price guide: £50 – £200

Reception

The restaurant, which recently hosted a
reception for a Blind Date couple,
offers home cooked food. While no
accommodation is available on site, a
list of local establishments is available.
There is room for helicopters or hotel
air balloons to land on site, and couples
can arrive or depart by boat.
Catering: Buffets from £8pp Sit down £13pp

Royal Berkshire Hotel
London Road
Sunninghill
Ascot, Berks SL5 0PP
Tel: 01344 23322 Fax: 01344 27100
Contact: Conference Office

Ceremony

This old manor house, dating from
1705, was orginally built for the
Churchill family. It is now a Hilton
International hotel under the Country

Style brand. The hotel is set in 15 acres of landscaped garden, with a sunken garden as a special feature. Two ceremony rooms are available any day of the year.
Price guide: from £500

Reception

The hotel offers wedding packages starting at £60pp; this includes drinks, overnight accommodation for the bride and groom and preferential overnight rates for guests.
Catering: from £60pp

Taplow House Hotel
Berry Hill
Taplow, Maidenhead
Berks SL6 0DA
Tel: 01628 70056 Fax: 01628 773625
Contact: Rachel Shepherd,
Banqueting Co-ordinator

Ceremony

Taplow House stands in six acres of grounds featuring protected trees. The hotel offers a choice of two rooms for ceremonies, which can take place on any day except Christmas Day. Confetti is permitted outside only.
Price guide: £250

Reception

Special children's menus are offered at the Taplow House. As well as offering accommodation, the hotel has preferential rate agreements with several other local establishments.
Catering: from £25pp

STOP PRESS
Civil Service College, Ascot 01344 634250
Holiday Inn Maidenhead 01628 23444
Reading Town Hall 01189 399820
Waterside Inn, Bray 01628 20691

Cadbury House Country Club
Frost Hill, Congresbury
Bristol, BS19 5AD
Tel: 01934 834343 Fax: 01934 834390
Contact: Christine Pepler, Deputy Manager

Ceremony

This is an 18th Century house set in 14 acres of private park land. It is currently a restaurant and leisure club (with pool, golf, etc), but an 80 bedroom hotel is planned. Up to three ceremonies are allowed at Cadbury House Country Club per day on all days allowed by the registrar. Confetti is not permitted.
Price guide: £75

Reception

Catering for children under 14 will be quoted at a reduced rate, although the club would not normally provide separate catering for children.
Catering: from £16pp

Forte Crest Bristol
Filton Road, Hambrook
City of Bristol, BS16 1QX
Tel or Fax: 0117 956 4242
Contact: Chris Swire, Banqueting Manager

Ceremony

The hotel is set in its own extensive landscaped grounds which feature two ornamental ponds. It has two rooms with licences to hold weddings, the smaller of which can accommodate up to 25 guests. Up to two ceremonies are permitted per day on any day of the week.
Price guide: from £100

Reception

The wedding package is an all-inclusive price which includes drinks on arrival, with the meal and for toasts, plus flowers and complimentary overnight accommodation for bride and groom. The hotel recently hosted a show business wedding, complete with opera singer.
Catering: from £29.50pp

Goldney Hall
University of Bristol
Lower Clifton Hill Road
City of Bristol, BS8 1BH
Tel: 0117 926 5698 Fax: 0117 929 3414
Contact: Ann Longney, Hall Secretary

Ceremony

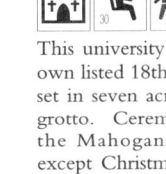

This university hall of residence has its own listed 18th Century formal gardens set in seven acres, featuring a folly and grotto. Ceremonies can take place in the Mahogany Parlour on any day except Christmas Day. Ceremonies on Saturday or Sunday must be followed by a reception at the hall. Confetti is not permitted.
Price guide: from £175

Reception

There are 30 self-contained flats within the hall, but these are only available during vacation time; July, August and September.

SS Great Britain
Great Western Dock
Gas Ferry Road
City of Bristol, BS1 6TY
Tel: 0117 9225737 Fax: 0117 9304358
Contact: Carol Wilkins, Purser

Ceremony

The historic SS Great Britain was built in Bristol in 1843 as a liner and cargo vessel. It is now undergoing restoration, with the first class dining saloon restored in 1992 to its original 1843 condition. Up to four ceremonies are

permitted per day, on all days except Bank Holidays. Confetti on the quay-side only.
Price guide: £295

Reception

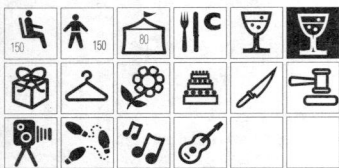

Accommodation is not available on board, but preferential rates have been agreed with local hotels and guest houses.
Catering: from £20pp

Swallow Royal Hotel
College Green
City of Bristol, BS1 5TA
Tel: 0117 9255100 Fax: 0117 9259951
Contact: Peta Robinson, Conference & Banqueting Sales Manager

Ceremony

The Swallow Royal is a listed Victorian building (1863), occupying a central position next to the cathedral. Only one ceremony is permitted per day. Three rooms are available with capacities ranging from 40 to 200. Days not available include Christmas Day, Good Friday and Easter Sunday. Confetti is not allowed.
Price guide: from £175

Reception

Catering: from £23pp

Bassetsbury Manor
Bassetsbury Lane
High Wycombe, Bucks HP11 1BB
Tel: 01494 421889 Fax: 01494 421808
Contact: Alan Stafford, Halls Manager or Russell Page on 01494 421883

Ceremony

This 17th Century manor house sits overlooking The Rye, next to a mill-stream. Three rooms are available for ceremonies; two of which can be made into one. Ceremonies can take place here from Thursday to Sunday, but not on Christmas Day or New Year's Day. Confetti is not encouraged.
Price guide: £50 (Mon-Sat) £75 (Sun)

Reception

While the Manor has appointed contract caterers, couples can use their own caterers, if preferred. From April to October, when the croquet lawns are in use, only a small marquee can be erected (capacity 140). The Manor recently hosted a Medieval themed wedding, with authentic music, food and costume.
Catering: from £8pp

Burnham Beeches Hotel
Grove Road
Burnham, Bucks SL1 8DP
Tel: 01628 429955 Fax: 01628 603994
Contact: Laura Gee, Events Co-ordinator

Ceremony

This Georgian manor is set in over ten acres of grounds on the edge of Burnham Beeches. Two rooms are available for ceremonies, the smaller and oldest of which has room for up to 40 guests. Up to three ceremonies per day are permitted at the hotel, on any day of the week.
Price guide: £200

Reception

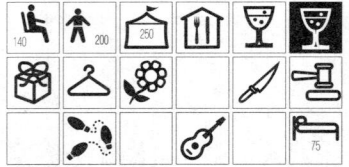

One of the main reception suites opens up on to lawns, making it ideal for Summer receptions. The hotel has arranged fireworks for weddings, and couples have arrived and left by helicopter.
Price guide: £45pp (package inc drinks)

Compleat Angler Hotel
Marlow Bridge
Marlow,
Bucks SL7 1RG
Tel: 01628 484444 Fax: 01628 486388
Contact: Ms Micky Dunsbier

Ceremony

This country house hotel sits on the banks of the river Thames within walking distance of the centre of Marlow, a short drive to Heathrow, and 30 miles from the centre of London. Two rooms are licensed for ceremonies, the smallest of which has a sitting capacity for 60.
Price guide: from £200 (if reception also booked) £500 for ceremony only.

Reception

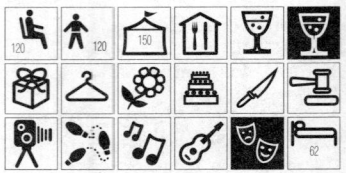

Catering: from £65pp (including drinks package)

Forte Posthouse Aylesbury
Aston Clinton Road
Aylesbury,
Bucks HP22 5AA
Tel: 01296 393388 Fax: 01296 392211
Contact: Wendy Marceta, Venue Guarantee

Ceremony

This modern hotel, which features a courtyard (decked in flowers in the summer), has two suites available for wedding ceremonies, (the smaller takes up to 40 guests). Ceremonies must be followed by reception here.
Price guide: £250

Reception

Catering: Buffets from £5.95 Sit down from £15.65pp

The Grovefield Hotel
Taplow Common
Burnham, Bucks SL1 8LP

Tel: 01628 603131 Fax: 01628 668078
Contact: Jacqui Bagnall, GM or Tracey
Lynch Conference Manager

Ceremony

A turn-of-the-century Edwardian
house set in eight acres, Grovefield
Hotel can accommodate up to two
wedding ceremonies per day on any
day of the week.
Price guide: £250

Reception

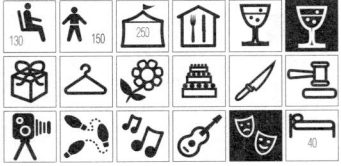

The hotel offers several wedding and
catering packages. Special touches
include ice carving, petits fours with
the bride and groom's names on and
bread rolls in the couple's initials.
Catering: £42.50 (package including
accommodation)

Hatton Court Hotel
Bullington End, Hanslope
Bucks MK19 7BQ

Tel: 01908 510044 Fax: 01908 510945
Contact: Catherine Banfield,
Conference & Events Sales Manager

Ceremony

This country house is set in six acres of
private gardens. It is described as 'typical mid-Victorian architecture with
Gothic mullioned windows and main
porchway'. The interior features
include an oriental lounge and a conservatory. The marriage room is only
available on Fridays and Saturday.
Price guide: P.O.A.

Reception

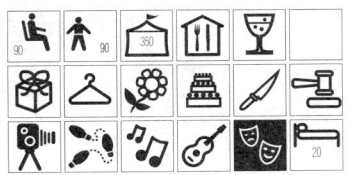

The sit down meal packages may start
at £29.50, but rise to £67.50 per head.
The latter includes delicacies such as
'Charentais melon filled with ragout of
lobster tail and king scallops with a
truffle and hazelnut vinaigrette' - and
that's just for starters! Local entertainment is provided by Towcester
Racecourse (7 miles) and Silverstone
(10 miles).
Catering: Buffets fr £7.50pp Sit down fr £29.50

Missenden Abbey
Management Centre
Great Missenden
Bucks HP16 0BD

Tel: 01494 866811 Fax: 01494 866737
Contact: Sue Newman,
Marketing Executive

Ceremony

This restored 12th Century abbey is a
management centre from Monday to
Friday, but is available for weddings at
the weekends (usually including
Fridays). Ceremonies are limited to
one per day. Two marriage rooms are
available.
Price guide: £300

Reception

As well as the Abbey Library, where
the stained glass windows are an attractive feature, Missenden offers a choice
of three adjoining dining rooms, available singly or together. The ceremony
price guide is reduced to £125 if the
reception is also held at the Abbey.
Hire of the Abbey for a reception is
£850.
Catering: £25pp

Pinewood Studios
Pinewood Road, Iver
Bucks SL0 0NH

Tel: 01753 656953 Fax: 01753 653616
Contact: Vivienne Harrison, Events
Co-ordinator

Ceremony

The Ballroom, the Green Room and
the Gatsby Room are all part of
Pinewood Studios and are licensed for
weddings. Wheelchair access is limited.
Price guide: POA

Reception

Catering: Buffets from £20pp Sit
Down from £32pp

Stowe School
Stowe
Buckingham,
Bucks MK18 5EH

Tel: 01280 813650 Fax 10280 822769
Contact: Ms Chris Shaw, Commercial
Director

Ceremony

Stowe School is an attractive period
building set in extensive grounds. It
offers couples a choice of three rooms
for their ceremony: The Music Room,
which holds up to 100; The Marble
Hall, which holds up to 200; and, for
the more intimate party, the Blue
Room, with a maximum capacity of
40. It is possible to hold your ceremony at Stowe without a reception.
The School is only available in the
Easter and Summer holidays. During
these periods, however, up to two ceremonies can be held per day, seven
days per week.
Price guide: £350 - £850

Reception

Price guide: from £12.50 (buffet) -
£28pp (waited)

Tythrop Park
Kingsey, Aylesbury
Bucks HP17 8LT

Tel: 01865 351203 Fax: 01865 351613
Contact: JR Parke, Events Manager

Ceremony

This Carolean house is set in 60 acres of mature grounds. Ceremonies are held in the galleried hall where there is a minimum capacity for 20 guests. Only one ceremony is permitted per day. Confetti is not permitted.
Price guide: £500

Reception

Catering: Buffets from £21pp Sit down from £27.50pp

Villiers Hotel
3 Castle Street
Buckingham, Bucks MK18 1BS
Tel: 01280 822444 Fax: 01280 822113
Contact: Jean Rush, House Manager

Ceremony

This Grade II listed old town hall features a ballroom that was refurbished in 1994. One ceremony per day on any day of the week.
Price guide: £300

Reception

The Villiers Hotel will tailor menus to each couple's requirements and also offers complimentary sampling of selected dishes. The wedding package includes preferential overnight rates for all guests, and a complimentary first anniversary dinner for the bride and groom.
Catering: £15 - £25pp

Waddesdon Manor (The Dairy)
Queen Street, Waddesdon
Aylesbury, Bucks HP18 0JW
Tel: 01296 651236 Fax: 01296 651142
Contact: Mrs Soames

Ceremony

Set in a private area of the grounds of Waddesdon Manor (National Trust), this converted model dairy features a central courtyard with a water garden. Two rooms have licences: the Wintergarden and the West Hall. Ceremonies can take place on any day at the management's discretion. Confetti is not permitted.
Price guide: £4000

Reception

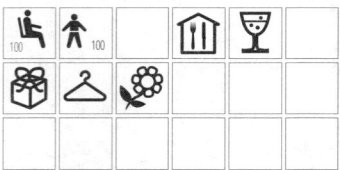

A late night drinking licence can be applied for if required. A list of local, preferential rate accommodation is available on request.
Catering: from £45pp

Wycombe Swan
St Mary Street,
High Wycombe,
Bucks HP11 2XE
Tel: 01494 514444 Fax: 01494 538080
Contact: Roger Keele, Asst GM

Ceremony

The main licensed area in this theatre is the Oak Room (capacity 130 seated), but the Swan Theatre is also licensed (capacity 1076 seated), as is the Town Hall (capacity 400 seated). Confetti is not permitted.
Price guide: £250 + VAT

Reception

Sit down meals start at £16 per person. Contract catering at the Swan is operated by Top Hat (Contact Frank Korntner - Tel: 01494 537777). A list of local accommodation is available on request.
Catering: from £4.50pp

STOP PRESS
Milton Keynes Civic Offices 01908 691691
Quality Friendly Hotel, Milton Keynes
01908 561666

Bell Inn
High Street
Stilton
Cambs PE7 3RA
Tel: 01733 241066 Fax: 01733 245173
Contact: Mrs Kate Robinson, Manager

Ceremony

This listed 15th Century coaching inn is the birthplace of Stilton cheese. The Inn's Marlbourough Suite is licensed for weddings which can take place here on Fridays and Sundays only. Ceremonies must be followed by reception at the Inn.
Price guide: £100

Reception

The Inn is Egon Ronay recommended.
Catering: Buffets from £8pp Sit down from £15pp

Brook House Motel
Brook Street,
Soham,
Ely, Cambs
Tel: 01353 720324 Fax: 01353 720324
Contact: Mrs W M Day

Ceremony

Ceremonies can take place at the motel on any day of the week, except Bank Holidays.
Price guide: £100 (Free with reception)

Reception

Catering: £5pp - £15pp

Chilford Halls
Linton, Cambs CB1 6LE
Tel: 01223 892641 Fax: 01223 894056
Contact: Rosemary Neilson

Ceremony

Chilford Halls is a small estate of 50 acres owned by the Alper family. The estate boasts the largest vineyard in Cambridgeshire, and has a 12 acre field for any outdoor activity. Three separate areas are available for ceremonies in the main building (which dates from the mid-18th Century); the smallest of which seats up to 65 (ceremonies for 30 would be the minimum number for a ceremony). Ceremonies can take place on any day of the year except Christmas Day, Boxing Day, New Year's Eve or New Year's Day.
Price guide: £250

Reception

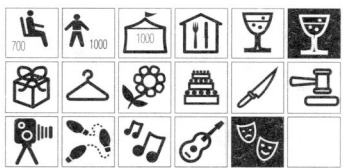

One of the most unusual features of the venue is that Chilford Halls can provide its own estate bottled wine for your reception. A variety of standard menus is available to simplify food selection. Special services include ribbon displays and balloon nets.
Catering: £8.75pp to £35pp

The Dolphin Hotel
Bridge Foot
London Road
St Ives,
Cambs
PE17 1EP
Tel: 01480 466966 Fax: 01480 495597
Contact: Stephanie Hubbard,
General Manager

Ceremony

The Dolphin is in the town centre and has river frontage and a large garden with patio area. Couples can arrive and depart by boat. The Meadow Suite is licensed and one ceremony can take place here per day on any day of the year. Confetti is not permitted.
Price guide: £200

Reception

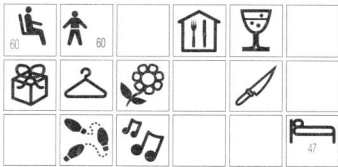

Catering: from £16pp

The Grange
Old North Road
Kneesworth
Nr Royston
Cambs SG8 5DS
Tel: 01763 248674 Fax: 01763 246641
Contact: Patsy Toulson or Jack Thompson

Ceremony

The Grange is a private Georgian farm house with Victorian conservatory and a barn. Weddings followed by reception here have exclusive use of the house.
Ceremonies can take place here on any day of the year except between Christmas and New Year.
Price guide: £47

Reception

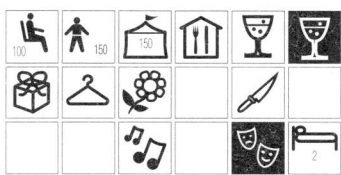

The 'up and coming' chef at The Grange apparently does particularly good Indian and Italian cuisine, as well as a 'rather good' Beef Wellington.
Catering: from £38pp

The Haycock Hotel
Wansford
Peterborough
Cambs PE86JA
Tel: 01780 782223 Fax: 01780 783508
Contact: Andrew Underwood,
General Manager

Ceremony

We are delighted to welcome a new GM to The Haycock, a 17th Century coaching inn set in award winning gardens in the village of Wansford. The hotel offers two licensed rooms where ceremonies can take place on any day of the week.
Price guide: £100 –£200

Reception

Three rooms are available where traditional cuisine is offered alongside modern and international dishes.
Catering: From £21.95pp

Hinchingbrooke House
Brampton Road
Huntingdon
Cambs
PE18 6BN
Tel: 01480 452119 Fax: 01480 432054
Contact: Mrs Pauline Steel,
Lettings Officer

Ceremony

This English Heritage property is the ancestral home of the Cromwells. Wedding ceremonies can currently only take place here on a Saturday. Confetti is not permitted. Ceremonies must be followed by a reception at the house. In addition to the ceremony fee, there is a fee of £650 for booking the whole of the ground floor of the house, which becomes yours for the day.
Price guide: from £80

Reception

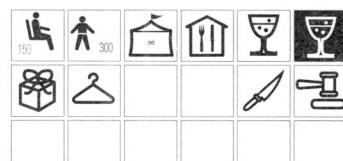

The Old Dining Room, with access to the York Stone Terrace, is one of the many rooms within Hinchingbrooke House available for receptions. The Hinchingbrooke Performing Arts Centre is also situated within the grounds of the house.
Catering: Buffets from £2.95pp Sit down from £15pp

Newnham College
Sidgwick Avenue
Cambridge
Cambs CB3 9DF
Tel: 01223 335801 Fax: 01223 357898
Contact: Mrs Heather Wynn

Ceremony

Founded in 1871, Newnham College is one of the only all-women colleges at Cambridge. Built from Victorian red brick in the Queen Anne revival style, it has four rooms for ceremonies, with capacities from 70 to 100. During the University term, ceremonies can only take place on a Saturday. Other days when weddings are not possible include Christmas Day and New Year's Day. Up to two ceremonies are allowed per day. Confetti is not permitted.
Price guide: £150

Reception

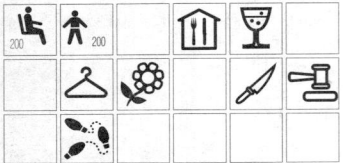

Catering: £28.50 - £40pp

Old Bridge Hotel
1 High Street
Huntingdon
Cambs
PE18 6TQ
Tel: 01480 52681 Fax: 01480 411017
Contact: Samantha Webb,
Sales & Reservations Manager

Ceremony

This Georgian, ivy covered, building sits on the banks of the River Ouse. Up to two ceremonies are permitted per day.
Price guide: £75

Reception

Catering: from £17.95

Oliver's Lodge Hotel
Neddingworth Road
St Ives,
Cambs PE17 4JP
Tel: 01480 463252 Fax: 01480 461150
Contact: Christopher Langley,
Managing Director

Ceremony

This Victorian hotel (with recent extensions) has three rooms licensed for civil ceremonies.
Price guide: £200

Reception

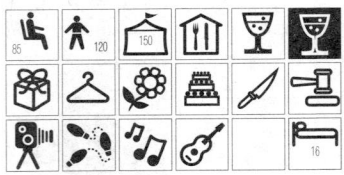

Catering specialities at Oliver's include individual Beef Wellingtons, Chicken and Asparagus En Croute, and whole sirloin or fillet of beef carved in front of your guests. A room can be made available for the bride and groom during their wedding day at no extra charge.
Catering: £7 - £21pp

The Pink Geranium
Station Road, Melbourn
Cambs SG8 6DX
Tel: 01763 260215 Fax: 01763 262110
Contact: Charles Ockenden, Manager
or Sally Saunders, Proprietor

Ceremony

This 15th Century thatched, pink, cottage has a conservatory and enclosed south facing garden. The conservatory and Garden Room hold the wedding licence. These rooms have limited wheelchair access. Ceremonies must be followed by reception at the Pink Geranium.
Price guide: FOC

Reception

The Pink Geranium boasts a celebrity chef proprietor, Steven Saunders, who produces English/French style cuisine.
Catering: Buffets from £20pp Sit down from £25pp

Robinson College
Cambridge CB3 9AN
Tel/Fax: 01223 339140
Contact: Roger Greeves, College Chaplin

Ceremony
Ceremony and wedding facilities at the College are only available to members of the College.

Slepe Hall Hotel
Ramsey Road
St Ives, Cambs PE17 4RB
Tel: 01480 463122 Fax: 01480 300706
Contact: Mr T O'Connell, Partner

Ceremony

This Grade II listed building was formerly a girls' school. Up to three ceremonies can take place on any day of the week. There is no charge for the ceremony room if the reception is also at the hotel.
Price guide: from £50

Reception

Catering: Buffets from £6.75pp Sit down from £12.50pp

Swallow Hotel
Lynch Wood
Peterborough
Cambs PE2 6GB
Tel: 01733 371111 Fax: 01733 236725
Contact: Mrs Wendy Bannister, Sales Office Manager

Ceremony

This modern hotel is set in 11 acres, including an ornamental lake. It also features its own leisure club. Two licensed rooms available.
Price guide: £80

Reception

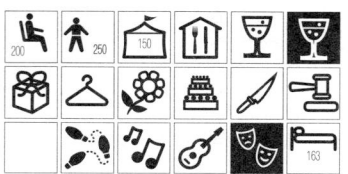

Catering: Buffet from £9pp Sit down from £20pp

STOP PRESS

The George Coaching Inn
01480 810307
Greshams   01223 354012
Heydon Grange Golf & Country Club
01763 208988
The Moller Centre   01223 465500

Alderley Edge Hotel
Macclesfield Road
Alderley Edge
Cheshire SK9 7BJ
Tel: 01625 583033 Fax: 01625 586343
Contact: Denise Buck, Conference Manager

Ceremony

Originally a mill owner's private residence (1850), this country house hotel is set in its own grounds with views over the surrounding countryside. Ceremonies can take place on any day of the week (except Christmas Day and New Year's Eve), in one of two rooms, and are restricted to one per day.
Price guide: £100

Reception

The hotel's Head Chef won Wedgwood Chef of the Year 1996 and was 1995 Northern Chef of the Year. The hotel has its own bakery, and all breads, cakes and desserts are made in-house. Wedding packages start at £30pp, and include complimentary four-poster honeymoon suite, use of a changing room all day, and special rates for wedding guests. The reception suite is self-contained with its own bar and cloakrooms.
Catering: Buffets fr £8.95pp sit down fr £16.50

Arley Hall
Arley, Nr Northwich, Cheshire
Tel: 01565 777353 Fax: 01565 777465
Contact: Mr Eric Ransome, Estate Manager

Ceremony

Arley Hall is the ancestral home and estate (over 2000 acres) of Viscount Ashbrook. It is a mock Jacobean house, built in the 1840s, and features a Grade II listed hall, distinctive ceilings and wood panelling and famous gardens. Ceremonies are limited to one per day, on any day except Christmas. Confetti is not permitted.
Price guide: P.O.A.

Reception

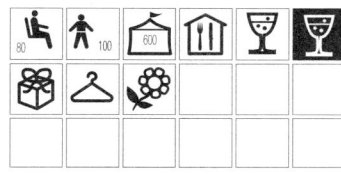

The Hall's caterer will 'provide whatever your require', although children cannot be catered for separately. While accommodation is not available on the premises, a list of local accommodation, with which the Hall has preferential rates, can be provided. Suppliers of services not offered by the Hall itself can be recommended.
Catering: P.O.A.

Astbury Water Park
Newcastle Road, Congleton
Cheshire, CW12 4HL
Tel: 01260 299771 Fax: 01260 298960
Contact: Restaurant Manager

Ceremony

This outdoor pursuits centre has its own restaurant overlooking the 43 acre lake. Weddings can take place here on any day except Sundays and Bank Holidays.
Price guide: P.O.A.

Reception

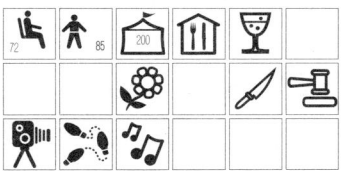

The Park can arrange cars, horses and carriages, and balloons.
Catering: £4.95 – £18.95pp + VAT

The Belfry Hotel
Stanley Road,
Handforth,
Cheshire SK9 3LD
Tel: 0161 437 0511 Fax: 0161 499 0597
Contact: Juanita Brown, Conference & Banqueting or Dawn Holding, Sales Manager

Ceremony

This modern, family-run hotel, situated near the airport, is available for ceremonies on any day except Christmas Day, Boxing Day and New Year's Day. Ceremonies are restricted to one per day.
Price guide: £100

Reception

Overnight accommodation for the bride and groom is offered as part of the wedding package. In addition, wedding guests can stay at the hotel (b&b) on Friday, Saturday or Sunday nights for £30 per person.
Catering: £16.50pp

Brereton Hall
Sandbach
Cheshire CW11 9RZ
Tel: 01477 535516 Fax: 01477 533093
Contact: Mary Creigh, Owner (1996)

Ceremony

As we go to press, the Hall is being sold, so no bookings are being taken for 1997. Couples should contact the Hall for an update. Below is the 1996 entry. This Grade I listed private home, completed in 1585, is claimed to be the first brick built mansion in Cheshire. Up to two weddings per day can be held on any day of the year. Confetti is permitted.
Price guide: £300

Reception

Brereton Hall has its own regular contract caterer, but couples are free to use a contract caterer of their choice for a small extra charge. The regular caterers are able to cater separately for children, if required. The site is suitable for a marquee with a capacity to accommodate between 180 and 200 guests.
Catering: £12 - £20pp

The Bridge Hotel
Prestbury,
Macclesfield
Cheshire SK10 4DQ
Tel: 01625 829326 Fax: 01625 827557
Contact: Mrs Elaine Grange, Director

Ceremony

Once a row of timbered cottages (dating from 1626), The Bridge Hotel stands by the River Bollin in the village of Prestbury. The hotel has two marriage rooms, both of which have patios and views over the gardens. Ceremonies are restricted to one per day on any day except Sunday.
Price guide: £750

Reception

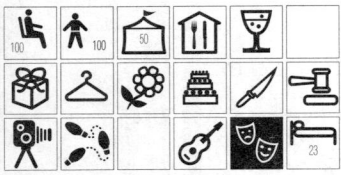

The hotel offers a broad selection of dishes from which couples can compile their own menus. Children cannot be catered for separately. The wedding package includes an overnight stay for the newly weds.
Catering: from £9.55pp (three course)

The Bull's Head Hotel
Mill Street,
Congleton
Cheshire CW12 1AB
Tel: 01260 273388 Fax: 01260 298049
Contact: Mr Foster, Restaurant Manager

Ceremony

This renowned coaching house dates from 1641. Only one ceremony is permitted here per day, on any day of the year. The Bull's Head will allow couples to get married on the premises without also holding their reception at the venue.
Price guide: £75

Reception

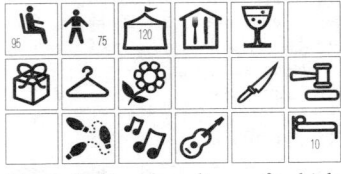

The Bull's Head has a licence for drinks with supper only. The site is suitable for a marquee with a capacity of up to 120 guests. Children can be catered for separately, if required.
Catering: from £18.50pp

The Chester Grosvenor
Eastgate, Chester, Cheshire
Tel: 01244 324024 Fax: 01244 313068
Contact: Alison Prenderleith

Ceremony

This well-known 130 year old city centre hotel has four marriage rooms available for ceremonies on any day of the year.
Price guide: from £125

Reception

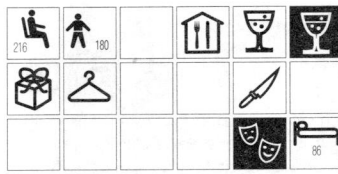

In addition to the above services, the hotel can also provide a red carpet, silver for the tables, personalised menus, and special accommodation rates for guests.
Catering: from £22.50pp

Chester Town Hall
Northgate Street, Chester
Cheshire
Tel: 01244 324324 Fax: 01244 341965
Contact: Linda Clements, Marketing

Ceremony

The Town Hall allows up to three ceremonies per day on any day except Sundays and Bank Holidays. Confetti is not permitted.
Price guide: £150

Reception

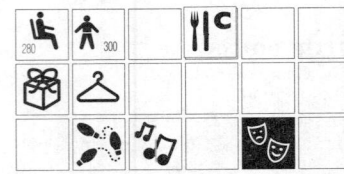

You can bring in your own caterer for the wedding reception, therefore we cannot offer any price guide.
Price guide: P.O.A.

The Chimney House Hotel
Congleton Road,
Sandbach
Cheshire CW11 0ST
Tel: 01270 764141 Fax: 01270 768916
Contact: Jill Galley, Conference & Banqueting Co-ordinator

Ceremony

The Chimney House, which belongs to the Country Club Hotel Group, is a tudor style half timbered building set in eight acres of woodland. Up to two ceremonies per day can take place in the Patio Restaurant on any day of the year. Helicopters and hot air balloons can use the grounds.
Price guide: £100

Reception

Catering: Buffets from £7pp Sit down from £16pp

Cottons Hotel
Manchester Road,
Knutsford
Cheshire WA16 0SU
Tel: 01565 650333 Fax: 01565 755351
Contact: Sandy Taylor, Banqueting Manager

Ceremony

This purpose-built modern hotel has a French New Orleans theme, and is part of the Shire Inns group. Up to three ceremonies can take place here each day on any day of the week. It is not possible to hold ceremonies here without also booking the reception at the hotel.
Price guide: F.O.C.

Reception

In keeping with the theme of the hotel, the restaurant offers cajun and creole dishes. The hotel also has its own leisure centre offering an indoor swimming pool, whirlpool, sauna, solarium and gym.
Catering: from £17pp

Crabwall Manor
Parkgate Road, Mollington
Chester, Cheshire CH1 6NE
Tel: 01244 851666 Fax: 01244 851400
Contact: Keith Raxter, Deputy Manager

Ceremony

This Grade II listed building (dating from 1077) became a hotel in 1987, and is now a member of the Small Luxury Hotels of the World. The hotel is set in 11 acres of wooded parkland, with landscaped gardens. A maximum of two weddings can be held here at any one time, in any of the three marriage rooms.
Price guide: £200

Reception

Head Chef at the Manor is Michael Truelove (formerly of the two Michelin starred Box Tree Restaurant in Ilkley). The Manor itself has now

gained three AA Rosettes for its food. The Manor's approach is very flexible and, while there are some services it cannot offer itself, it has contacts with many nationally acclaimed professionals. As part of the wedding package, wedding guests are offered special overnight rates. The hotel has its own helipad.
Catering: from £23pp

Craxton Wood Hotel
Parkgate Road
Puddington, Cheshire
Tel: 0151 339 4717 Fax: 0151 339 1740
Contact: Mrs Petranca

Ceremony

Craxton Wood allows only one ceremony per day on any day except Sundays and Bank Holidays. The ceremony must be followed by reception at the hotel.
Price guide: FOC

Reception

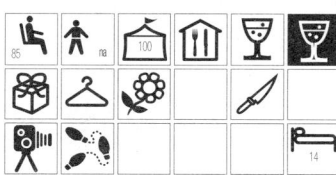

Catering: from £21.85pp

Crewe Municipal Buildings
Earle Street, Crewe,
Cheshire CW1 2BJ
Tel: 01270 537569 Fax: 01270 537605
Contact: David Owen

Ceremony

The Civic Suite comprises two rooms which can be used for weddings. Up to four weddings per day are permitted here, on any day except Bank Holidays. Confetti is not allowed.
Price guide: from £120

Reception

Couples may choose their own caterers, therefore we are unable to give a price guide. Catering for the reception could be provided by the venue if requested, however. A piano is available if required.

The Crown Hotel
High Street, Nantwich
Cheshire CW5 5AS
Tel: 01270 625283 Fax: 01270 628047
Contact: Philip J Martin, General Manager

Ceremony

This Grade I listed building, built in 1583, is situated in the town centre. The Minstrels' Gallery and Royal Cavalier Room hold licences for ceremonies on any day of the year except Christmas Day. Ceremonies must be followed by reception at the hotel.
Price guide: £50

Reception

Catering: POA

De Vere Lord Daresbury Hotel
Chester Road, Daresbury
Warrington, Cheshire
Tel: 01925 267331 Fax: 01925 601666
Contact: Miss Mary Clark

Ceremony

This four star hotel and leisure club, near the home village of Lewis Carroll, gives priority to ceremonies with receptions booked at the hotel. If this is the case, there is no room hire charge for the ceremony.
Price guide FOC (with reception)

Reception

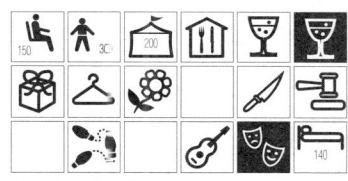

The hotel offers a 20% reduction on

the food costs if the wedding is held on a Sunday. Also included in the wedding package is a complimentary bridal suite , typed menus, and candelabra. The hotel also has a resident pianist.
Catering: Buffets from £8.50pp Sit down from £16pp

Everglades Park Hotel
Derby Road, Widnes
Cheshire WA8 0UJ
Tel: 0151 495 2040 Fax: 0151 424 6536
Contact: Bill Heslop, General Manager

Ceremony

This purpose-built modern hotel, which has gardens to the rear and a swimming pool, allows up to three ceremonies per day on any day of the year. Receptions must be booked with the ceremony.
Price guide: from £50

Reception

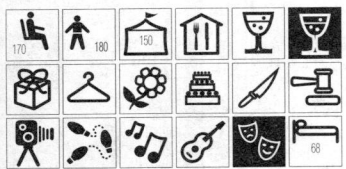

Catering: £15pp (three courses)

Finney Green Cottage
134 Manchester Road
Wilmslow, Cheshire SK9 2JW
Tel: 01625 533343 Fax: 01625 548579
Contact: Kay or Pat Johnson

Ceremony

This historic listed guest house dates from the 16th Century. Weddings may take place in the dining room, which will take 30 people standing, although the room has been approved for up to 50.
Price guide: £100

Reception

Reception facilities cannot be provided at the cottage. The three bedrooms are priced from £40 per night.

Fir Grove Hotel
Knutsford Old Road, Warrington
Cheshire WA4 2LD
Tel: 01925 267471 Fax: 01925 601092
Contact: Liz Hesketh, Banqueting

Ceremony

This hotel, restaurant and public house offers two ceremony rooms; the Grappenhall Suite (up to 200) and the Appleton (up to 110). Up to three ceremonies are permitted per day, on any day except Christmas Day. Confetti is not permitted.
Price guide: £100

Reception

Catering: from £12pp

Forte Posthouse Runcorn
Wood Lane
Beechwood, Runcorn
Cheshire WA7 3HA
Tel: 01928 714000 Fax: 01928 712681
Contact: Barbara Gerring

Ceremony

There are no restrictions on the number of weddings that can be held per day at the Posthouse. Ceremonies can also be held on any day of the year.
Price guide: POA

Reception

Catering: from £17pp

Hartford Hall
81 School Lane
Hartford, Northwich
Cheshire CW8 1PW
Tel: 01606 75711 Fax: 01606 782285
Contact: Margaret Livingstone-Evans, Manager

Ceremony

This former nunnery and manor house, which dates from the 16th Century, still retains many period features, and is set in its own grounds. Ceremonies can take place in the Nun's Room (home of the resident ghost) on any day except Sundays and Christmas Day. Only one ceremony can take place per day.
Price guide: from £75 (£20 with reception)

Reception

In addition to more formal receptions, the venue offers informal midweek champagne specials (from £9.95pp) which are held in the garden, weather permitting.
The Hall can provide a complimentary room for the bride and groom. Should their own accommodation be booked up, other establishments will be recommended.
Catering: Buffets from £15pp Sit down from £20pp

The Hunting Lodge
Adlington Hall
Adlington, Macclesfield
Cheshire SK10 4LF
Tel: 01625 827595 Fax: 01625 820797
Contact: Julie Williams/Helen Broadhead

Ceremony

The Hunting Lodge is a converted Georgian mews in the grounds of Adlington Hall. The Lodge is a banqueting suite, and holds a wedding licence for the entire suite which can be sectioned off as required. The Lodge is hired out on an a exclusive use basis. Helicopters and balloons can take off from the grounds with special permission from the Hall.
Price guide: from £100

Reception

Catering: Buffets from £8.60pp Sit down from £17.85pp

Jarvis Abbots Well Hotel
**Whitchurch Road
Christleton, Chester CH3 6PQ**
Tel: 01244 332121 Fax: 01244 335287
Contact: Karen Freeman, Sales

Ceremony

The Abbots Well allows for up to three ceremonies per day on any day of the year, including Bank Holidays. Confetti is not permitted. The price of the ceremony varies between £100 and £250 depending on the size of the wedding party.
Price guide: from £100

Reception

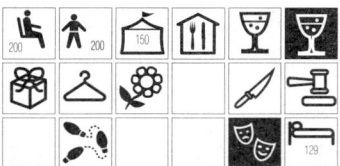

Flowers are usually included in the wedding package at the hotel, which can also supply fun packs for children, menu cards and one month's free use of the health club. The hotel also offers to send out your wedding invitations at their expense.
Catering: Buffets from £7.50 Sit down from £16.50

Lion & Swan Hotel
**Swan Bank, Congleton
Cheshire CW12 1JR**
Tel: 01260 273115 Fax: 01260 299270
Contact: Mr Simms/Julie Bratt

Ceremony

This three star hotel and restaurant was formerly a 15th Century coaching inn, and is based in the town centre. Weddings can take place in one of two ceremony rooms on any day of the year.
Price guide: £25

Reception

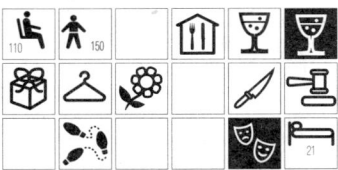

If you book a full day at the hotel, the bride and groom will be offered the bridal suite, free of charge for their wedding night. Wedding guests are also offered a discount on accommodation.
Catering: Buffets £6.25pp Sit down £11.50pp

Mere Golf & Country Club
Chester Road, Mere, Knutsford, Cheshire WA16 6LJ
Tel: 01565 830155 Fax: 01565 830713
Contact: Yvette Roule, Conference & Banqueting Co-ordinator

Ceremony

Mere is a private golf and country club. Several rooms are licensed for weddings which can take place here any day of the year except Christmas Day.
Price guide: POA

Reception

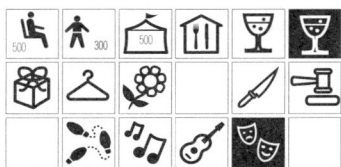

Helicopters may use the club grounds.
Catering: from £25pp

Mollington Banastre Hotel
Parkgate Road, Chester
Tel: 01244 851471 Fax: 01244 851165
Contact: Banqueting Manager

Ceremony

This country house dating from 1857 is set in over eight acres, which includes formal gardens, croquet lawns and tennis. Ceremonies can take place here on any day of the year.
Price guide: from £150

Reception

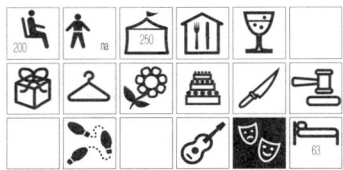

Specialities of the house include a pig roast barbecue. A late night drinking licence can be applied for if required. In the past, the hotel has also arranged fireworks for wedding parties, and has its own helipad.
Catering: from £19.50pp

Mottram Hall Hotel
**Wilmslow Road
Mottram St Andrew
Prestbury, Cheshire SK10 4QT**
Tel: 01625 828135 Fax: 01625 828950
Contact: Helen Russell

Ceremony

This Georgian hotel permits up to three ceremonies per day, on any day of the year except Sunday. Confetti is not permitted.
Price guide: £150

Reception

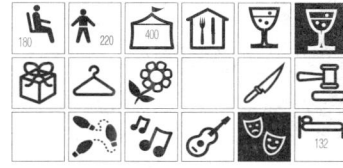

Catering: from £21.00pp

Neston Civic Hall
**Hinderton Road, Neston
South Wirral, Cheshire**
Tel: 0151 336 3991 Fax: 0151 353 0064
Contact: Anne Tudor, Information Officer

Ceremony

This Victorian building is close to the town centre, and has a large grassed area to the rear. It has recently been refurbished and modernised and now offers two ceremony rooms. Ceremonies can take place here any day but Christmas Day or Good Friday.
Price guide: POA

Reception

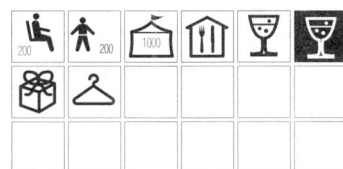

While there is catering available on site, you may also bring in your own caterers to this venue. The venue can recommend florists, photographers and entertainment.
Price guide: POA

Nunsmere Hall Hotel
Tarporley Road, Oakmere
Northwich, Cheshire CW8 2ES
Tel: 01606 889100 Fax: 01616 889055
Contact: Malcolm McHardy, Director

Ceremony

This historic hall is surrounded on three sides by a 60 acre lake. Helicopters and balloons can also land on site. Only one ceremony is permitted here per day, and this may take place in one of three licensed rooms on any day of the week. The room hire fee includes flowers and harpist.
Price guide: £500

Reception

Catering: Sit down from £26.50

The Oakland Hotel
Millington Lane
Gorstage
Weaverham
Northwich CW8 4SU
Tel: 01606 853249 Fax: 01606 852419
Contact: Chris Kay

Ceremony

Up to two ceremonies per day can take place in the Restaurant.
Price guide: £25

Reception

Catering: Buffets from £4.50pp
Sit down from £15.50pp

Park Royal International Hotel
Stretton Road
Stretton
Warrington
Cheshire
WA4 4NS

Tel: 01925 730706 Fax: 01925 730740
Contact: Mrs Mfanwy Quine,
Sales & Marketing Manager

Ceremony

The modern Park Royal allows up to four ceremonies per day on any day of the year.
Price guide: POA

Reception

As part of the wedding package, the hotel offers complimentary overnight accommodation, champagne and flowers for bride and groom on their wedding night. An extension adding about 30 more bedrooms to the hotel should be completed this year.
Catering: POA

The Parkgate Hotel
Boathouse Lane
Parkgate
Cheshire
L64 6RD
Tel: 0151 336 5001 Fax: 0151 336 5084
Contact: Mrs J Campbell, Proprietor

Ceremony

The hotel is located on the Dee estuary, 10 miles from Chester. It has several function rooms ranging in capacity from 35 guests to 250.
Price guide: £100

Reception

In addition to accommodation on the premises, the hotel can recommend other local establishments with which it has preferential rate agreements.
Catering: from £6pp

Peckforton Castle
Stone House Lane, Peckforton
Cheshire CW6 9TN
Tel: 01829 260930 Fax: 01829 261230
Contact: Mrs E Graybill, Director

Ceremony

Peckforton claims to be the only intact Medieval style castle in Britain – it was actually built during the Victorian era and is now Grade I listed. It was recently used for the filming of Robin Hood. Three rooms are available for ceremonies; the Library (for 60), the Octagonal Stone Dining Room (for 120) and The Great Hall (for 200). Ceremonies can take place here any day except Sundays, between 11am and 4pm. Blessings can also take place here in the castle's own chapel.
Price guide: from £100

Reception

The castle is able to offer a medieval banquet, in keeping with the building, complete with open fire, and ceremonial sword for cutting the cake. Children (2-12 years) are catered for at a discount rate. The Castle can also arrange a barn dance or a concert harpist, as well as a professional disco. It can even organise a horse and carriage if required. A peal of wedding bells can also be arranged.
Catering: from £17.50

Portal Golf & Country Club
Oaklands Course
Forest Road, Tarporley
Tel: 01829 733884 Fax: 01829 733666
Contact: Anne Hill or Sue Harrison

Ceremony

Just to confuse you, there are two golf courses at the Portal Club; the Championship course and the Premier course, each with club houses attached. The one with the wedding licence is the Premier course, which offers ceremonies any day of the year, and limits these to one per day.

Reception

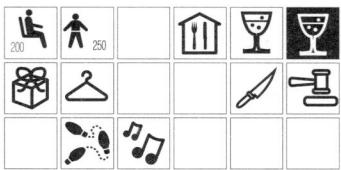

Catering: POA

The Queen Hotel
City Road
Chester
Cheshire CH1 3AH

Tel: 01244 350100 Fax: 01244 318483
Contact: Stephen Lee,
General Manager

Ceremony

This Victorian building, built in 1860, is Grade II listed and located just outside the city centre. Only one ceremony is permitted per day, on any day of the year.
Price guide: £125

Reception

Catering: from £22pp

The Racecourse
Chester
Cheshire CH1 2LY

Tel: 01244 323170 Fax: 01244 344971
Contact: Ray Walls, Racecourse Manager

Ceremony

Chester is the oldest racecourse in the country and can permit ceremonies on any day but is dependent on the racing calendar. Ceremonies can take place in the Long Room, and the Board Rom on the County Stand and the Leverhulme Suite.
Price guide: POA

Reception

While there is no accommodation at the racecourse, a list of local establishments with which the course has preferential rate agreements is available on request.
Catering: from £15pp

Rake Hall Hotel
Rake Lane
Little Stanney
Chester CH2 4HS

Tel: 0151 355 9433 Fax: 0151 355 0526
Contact: Ken Hughes,
General Manager

Ceremony

The Rake Suite and the Garden Suite both hold licences. Ceremonies may take place here on any day of the year. Helicopters and hot air balloons may use the grounds of the Hall.
Price guide: FOC

Reception

Catering: Buffets from £5.95pp Sit down from £10.95pp

Rheingold Riverside Inn
Warrington Road
Acton Bridge
Northwich, Cheshire

Tel: 01606 852310 Fax: 01606 851313
Contact: Simon Long

Ceremony

The Inn sits on the banks of the river Weaver. Bride and groom can arrive and depart by boat as the Inn has a jetty and its own boat. 1996 saw a change of ownership for the Inn, and the new owner is undertaking major refurbishment of the premises. Consequently they are unwilling to commit to bookings for weddings in 1997. Couples should phone for an update.
Price guide: £50 (1996 rate)

Rookery Hall Hotel
Worleston
Nantwich
Cheshire
CW5 6DQ

Tel: 01270 610016
Fax: 01270 626027
Contact: Belinda Ryan,
Sales Manager

Ceremony

Ceremonies can take place here any day except Sunday, but must be followed by a reception at the hotel. Only one ceremony is permitted per day.
Price guide: P.O.A.

Reception

Catering: from £32.50pp

Rowton Hall Hotel
Whitchurch Road
Rowton
Chester

Tel: 01244 335262 Fax: 01244 335464
Contact: Mr D Begbie,
Hotel Director

Ceremony

This country manor house, built in 1779, stands in eight acres of award winning gardens. Four rooms are licensed taking from 10 to 200 guests on any day except Sunday and Bank Holidays. Helicopters and hot air balloons can make use of the grounds.
Price guide: £100

Reception

Catering: Buffets from £13.35pp Sit down from £19.70pp

**Sandhole Farm
Hulme Walfield
Congleton
Cheshire
CW12 2JH**
Tel: 01260 224419 Fax: 01260 224766
Contact: Veronica Worth, Proprietor

Ceremony

This is a privately owned farmhouse, with a former stable block converted into 15 en-suite bedrooms. Weddings can take place here on any day except Sundays.
Price guide: £100

Reception

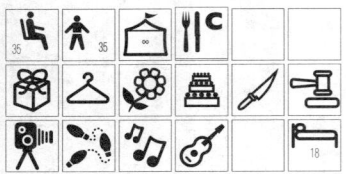

You can bring in your own caterer to Sandhole Farm, so we are unable to provide a price guide. A drinking licence can be applied for as required.
Catering: P.O.A.

**Stanneylands Hotel
Stanneylands Road
Wilmslow, Cheshire SK9 4EY**
Tel: 01625 525225 Fax: 01625 537282
Contact: Ms Tracy Lavin, Conference & Banqueting Manager

Ceremony

The Stanneylands Hotel claims extensive and unusual gardens. It will permit one ceremony per day on any day except Christmas Day, Boxing Day, New Year's Eve and New Year's Day.
Price guide: £100

Reception

The cuisine at the hotel holds two AA Rosettes.
Catering: from £17.75pp

**Statham Lodge Hotel
Warrington Road
Statham
Lymm
Cheshire WA13 9BP**
Tel: 01925 752204   Fax: 01925 757406
Contact: Reception

Ceremony

This Georgian manor house is set in its own landscaped grounds featuring an 8-hole pitch and putt course.
Four rooms are licensed for ceremonies, two of which are on the ground floor and have good wheelchair access. Ceremonies can take place on any day except Christmas Day, Boxing Day, New Year's Eve and New Year's Day.
Price guide: from £75

Reception

In the past the hotel has hosted medieval banquets, Caribbean weddings and Indian weddings. A discount is offered to wedding guests who wish to stay overnight at the hotel.
Catering: Buffets from £5.50pp Sit down from £17pp

**Tabley House
Knutsford
Cheshire WA16 0HB**
Tel: 01565 750151 Fax: 01565 653230
Contact: Peter Startup, Administrator, or Brenda Fold, Assistant

Ceremony

This Grade I listed Palladian mansion belongs to The Victoria University of Manchester. It has two rooms licensed for ceremonies; The Gallery (100) and The Portico (50). The house is technically available on any day of the year, but it is recommended to avoid 2-4.30pm Thursday to Sunday, as the house is then open to the public. Real rose petals are preferred to paper confetti, and are traditional at Tabley.

Price guide: £75 + £1pp over 10 people

Reception

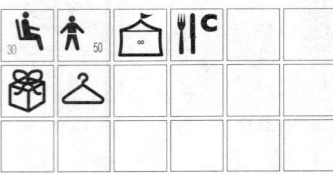

Tabley allows couples to arrange wedding receptions at the house in their own style, with their own suppliers: but is happy to offer plenty of ideas.
Price guide: P.O.A.

**Tatton Park
Knutsford
Cheshire WA16 6QN**
Tel: 01565 632914 Fax: 01565 650179
Contact: Karen Hay, Events & Function Manager

Ceremony

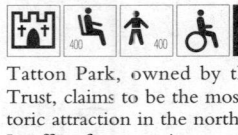

Tatton Park, owned by the National Trust, claims to be the most visited historic attraction in the north of England. It offers four marriage rooms, ranging in capacity from 40 to 400. These include Lord Egerton's Apartment (for 43) which features a covered balcony that overlooks the Italian garden, deer park and lakes. Confetti is not permitted.
Price guide: from £300

Reception

In addition to the above services Tatton Park can provide a PA system, and stage lighting.
Catering: from £15pp

**Walmoor House
Dee Banks, Chester**
Tel: 01244 322633

Walmoor House, the headquarters of the Cheshire Fire Brigade in 1996, was in the process of being sold as Noble's went to press. It is unlikely that weddings will continue here.

Walton Hall
Walton Lea Road, Higher Walton
Warrington, Cheshire
Tel: 01925 263797 Fax: 01925 861868
Contact: Nick Iddon, Hall Manager

Ceremony

Wedding ceremonies at this listed building are permitted on any day except Sundays and Bank Holidays. Up to four ceremonies per day.
Price guide: £150

Reception

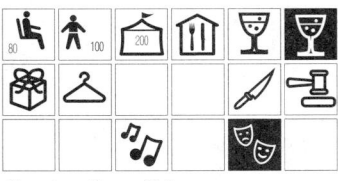

Catering: from £15pp

Warmington Grange
School Lane, Warmington
Sandbach, Cheshire CW11 3QN
Tel: 01270 526276/257/412
Fax: 01270 526413
Contact: Christopher Wright, Owner

Ceremony

Lord Crewe's former shooting and hunting lodge, set in landscaped gardens with 'water features', is 200 years old and Grade II listed. Ceremonies can take place in Lancelot's Garden Suite or in the Drawing Room. Wheelchair access is limited.
Price guide: £100

Reception

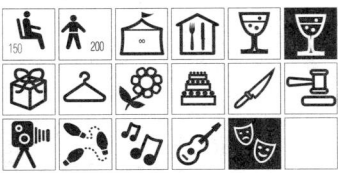

While no accommodation is available on the premises, the Grange has preferential rate agreements with local establishments. There is plenty of room in the gardens for helicopters and balloons to land on site.
Catering: Buffets from £3.50pp Sit down from £12.50pp

The White Lion Inn
Main Road, Weston
Crewe, Cheshire CW2 5NA
Tel: 01270 500303 Fax: 01270 500303
Contact: Mrs AJ Davies, Proprietor

Ceremony

Originally a Tudor farmhouse, the Inn has now been extended to offer a hotel, restaurant and bars; the heavily beamed lounge bar is in the original part of the building. Outside there are gardens and a bowling green. The ceremony room is in the more modern conference room, and weddings can take place here on any day except Bank Holidays. Preference is given to those holding their reception at the inn. Wheelchair access is limited.
Price guide: £95

Reception:

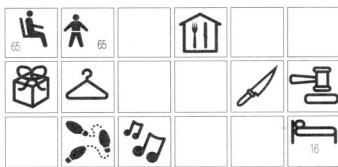

Catering: From £17pp

Wildboar Hotel & Restaurant
Whitchurch Road, Nr Beeston
Tarporley, Cheshire CW6 9NW
Tel: 01829 260309 Fax: 01829 261081
Contact: Jane Slaney/Sue Duxbury

Ceremony

This black and white 17th Century hunting lodge is a typical building of the area. Ceremonies can take place in The Gallery and the Penthouse Suite.
Price guide: £150

Reception

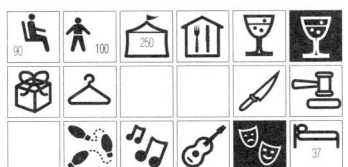

This venue holds an AA Rosette for its cuisine. A four-poster honeymoon suite is available for bride and groom, and is offered free if the reception is also booked here. Discounted accommoda-

tion is also offered for wedding guests. If a marquee is required, a fountain can be set up as an unusual centrepiece. There is room on site for helicopers and balloons.
Catering: Buffet fr £9.85pp sit down fr £16pp

Willington Hall Hotel
Willington
Tarporley, Cheshire CW6 0NV
Tel: 01829 752321 Fax: 01829 752596
Contact: Mr R Pigot, Owner

Ceremony

This neo-Elizabethan manor house was actually built in 1825, and was converted to a hotel by the owning family nearly 20 years ago. The house is set in its own park with a lake.
Two rooms have licenses for ceremonies. These are available on any day except Sundays and Bank Holidays.
Price guide: £2

Reception

Wedding parties have exclusive use of the house, although sadly evening parties are not possible. It is possible for helicopters and hot air balloons to land on site.
Catering: £18pp

Wilmslow Moat House Hotel
Altrincham Road
Wilmslow, Cheshire SK9 4LR
Tel: 01625 889988 Fax: 01625 539357
Contact: Conference Office

Ceremony

This modern hotel is three miles from the airport. It is currently designed in a Swiss chalet style, but a £1.5m refurbishment will soon add a conservatory (extending the restaurant): plus improve facilities for the disabled. The hotel has a garden to the side which runs alongside the River Bollin. The reception must also be at the hotel.
Price guide: F.O.C. (with reception)

Reception

The hotel is very popular for Indian weddings, for which the hotel welcomes specialist caterers to its kitchens. The hotel offers several reception packages, including drinking packages starting at £6.75pp.

Catering: Sit down fr £15.50pp Buffet fr £6.20pp

Wincham Hall Hotel
Hall Lane, Wincham
Cheshire CW9 6DG

Tel: 01606 43453 Fax: 01606 40128
Contact: Sarah, Hotel Manager
or Jackie Myers, Marketing Manager

Ceremony

This period country residence (part is listed) is set in five acres of landscaped grounds with a walled garden and lily pond. The hotel has a licence for three rooms ranging in capacity from 15 to 100. The smaller room on the first floor has no wheelchair access. Ceremonies can take place here on any day except Sundays and Christmas Day, and are restricted to one per day. It is not possible to hold wedding ceremonies here without also booking reception facilities. Confetti is allowed at the Wincham Hall Hotel. The hotel says it can offer a number of unusual services to weddings parties.

Price guide: from £50

Reception

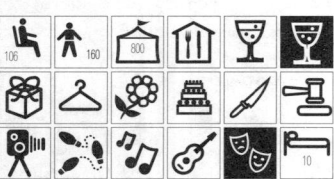

The hotel offers a comprehensive midweek reception package which includes the 'eight essential services' (everything but the stress!) such as hire of two suits, video and vintage car, for 40 wedding guests at £2290. Guest numbers over the 40 are charged at £17.50 per head. A complimentary bridal suite is offered to the couple if there are over 50 wedding guests. The grounds are suitable for

use by hot air balloons and helicopters.
Catering: Buffet fr £7.95pp Sit down fr £15.50pp

Winnington Hall
Winnington Lane
Northwich
Cheshire CW8 4DU

Tel 01606 784177 Fax: 01606 741873
Contact: Shirley Jones, Manager

Ceremony

This listed building is both a restaurant and conference centre. It can host up to two ceremonies per day, every day of the year except Sundays, Christmas Day and Boxing Day. If required, ceremonies can be held without booking the venue's reception facilities. Confetti is not allowed.

Price guide: £100

Reception

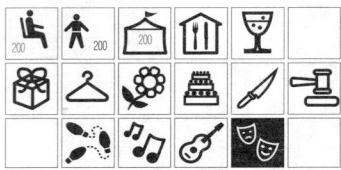

The Winnington Hall claims to specialise in first rate food, and can provide balloons for wedding parties.

Price guide: £20pp

STOP PRESS

The Big Lock, Middlewich
01606 833489
Chester Moat House
01244 899988
Ellesmere Port Civic Hall
0151 356 6890
Grosvenor Arms Hotel, Chester
01244 570560
Hoole Hall, Chester 01244 350011
Hooton Golf & Squash Centre, Little Sutton 0151 356 6780
Inglewood, Ledsham 0151 339 5105
The Lymm Hotel, Lymm
01925 752233
Manchester Airport Moat House
01625 889988
The Manor House, Alsager
01270 884000
Old Hall Hotel, Sandbach
01270 761221
The Patten Arms, Warrington
01925 636602
The Pinewood Hotel, Handforth
01625 529211

Sutton Hall Hotel, Sutton
01260 253211
The Woodhey Hotel, Little Sutton
0151 339 5121

Alverton Manor
Tregolls Road
Truro, Cornwall TR1 1XQ

Tel: 01872 76633 Fax: 01872 222989
Contact: Barbara Wren, Admin Manager

Ceremony

The Manor is a Grade II listed former convent set in six acres. It has two marriage rooms; the Old Chapel/Great Hall and the Library. There is no room hire charge if the reception is in the same room. Ceremonies are not allowed without a reception.

Price guide: £150 (for Saturday)

Reception

A complimentary bridal suite is provided to the couple on their wedding night.
Catering: from £12.95pp

Atlantic Hotel
Dane Road, Newquay, Cornwall

Tel: 01637 872244 Fax: 01637 874108
Contact: Mrs Stones, Manager

Ceremony

The hotel is available to hold ceremonies seven days a week with a maximum of one permitted per day. Confetti is allowed.

Price guide: £150

Reception

The hotel has 90 bedrooms but also operates preferential rate agreements with local hotels and guest houses. In

addition to the services indicated, the hotel offers a red carpet, and champagne breakfast. The Atlantic Hotel is suitable for larger parties because, in addition to waited service for 400 or buffets for 550, the hotel's grounds can house large capacity marquees.
Price guide: £9.50pp

Barrowfield Hotel
Hilgrove Road
Newquay, Cornwall TR7 2QY
Tel: 01637 878878 Fax: 01637 879490
Contact: Mrs Fran Bradshaw

Ceremony

Price guide: £50

Reception

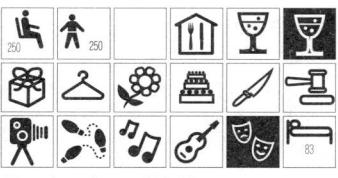

Catering: from £10.00pp

Budock Vean Hotel
Mawnan Smith, Falmouth
Cornwall TR11 4QJ
Tel: 01326 250288 Fax: 01326 250892
Contact: Judy Carter, Assistant Manager

Ceremony

This golf and country house hotel is set in 65 acres of gardens and woodlands with its own foreshore to the Helford River. Couples can arrive and depart by boat, dependant upon the tide. Helicopters and hot air balloons can also land on site. Only one ceremony is allowed per day, and three ceremony rooms are offered.
Price guide: from £100

Reception

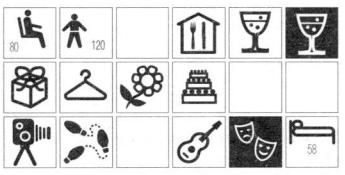

Free accommodation is offered to the couple on their wedding nights, and guests are offered discount rates.
Catering: Sit down from £12pp

The Bullers Arms Hotel
Marhamchurch
Bude, Cornwall EX23 0HB
Tel: 01288 361277 Fax: 01288 361541
Contact: Tony Perry, GM

Ceremony

Price guide: Min £400 on reception

Reception

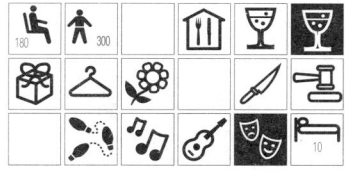

Catering: Sit down from £10.50pp

Carlyon Bay Hotel
St Austell, , Cornwall PL25 3RD
Tel: 01726 812304 Fax: 01726 814938
Contact: Mr P J Brennan, Manager

Ceremony

Dramatically located on craggy cliffs above the Bay, this venue enjoys spectacular sea views. In addition, the hotel is set in 250 acres of grounds, including championship golf course and pool.
Price guide: from £100

Reception

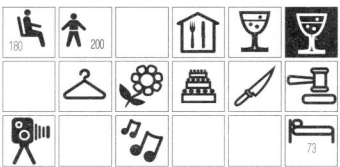

The hotel features 73 en-suite bedrooms.
Catering: from £14pp

Castle, The
Bude, Cornwall EX23 8LG
Tel: 01288 353576 Fax: 01288 353576
Contact: Peter Judson, Town Clerk

Ceremony

The Castle, which houses the local town council, was built in the early 19th Centruy by Sir Goldsworthy Gurney, and is set on the sands of the Atlantic coast. Ceremonies are held in the The Council Chamber Monday to Saturday excluding all Bank Holidays.
Price guide: £100

Reception

No reception facilities are provided.

Green Lawns Hotel
Western Terrace
Falmouth, Cornwall TR11 4QJ
Tel: 01326 312734 Fax: 01326 211427
Contact: Mrs Symons, Manageress

Ceremony

Price guide: F.O.C (with reception)

Reception

Catering: from £7.50pp

Hannafore Point Hotel
West Looe, Cornwall PL13 2DG
Tel: 01503 263273 Fax: 01503 263272
Contact: Briar Payne, GM

Ceremony

The hotel overlooks Looe Bay and offers ceremonies seven days a week excluding Christmas Day and Boxing Day. Ceremony prices range from £150 to £200 depending on the time of year.
Price guide: from £150

Reception

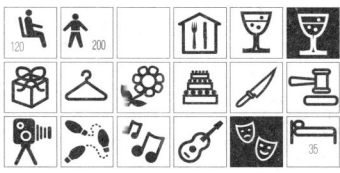

Catering is in-house with a capacity of 200 in a buffet format. Catering costs vary between £10 and £20pp.
Catering: from £10pp

Headland Hotel
Newquay
Cornwall TR7 1EW
Tel: 01637 872211 Fax: 01637 872212
Contact: Mrs Carolyn Armstrong,
Proprietor & Director

Ceremony

This Grade II listed building is set on a
Cornish headland surrounded by sea,
just yards from Newquay's Fistral
Beach. Ceremonies are free of charge
with receptions. A fee of £10 per person is made for ceremonies only.
Price guide: F.O.C. or POA

Reception

Although the hotel offers catering
facilities for as many as 600, they
are equally happy to cater for intimate groups. The hotel prides
itself on the provision of fresh local
produce, with seafood being a speciality. A complimentary
overnight stay at the hotel is
offered to couples with reduced
rates for friends and relatives. In
addition to the services indicated,
the hotel has its own hot air balloon giving couples the opportunity to fly away from their wedding
in true style.
Catering: POA

Hotel California
Pentire Crescent
Newquay
Cornwall TR7 1PU
Tel: 01637 879292 Fax: 01637 875611
Contact : Manager

Ceremony

The hotel has four rooms licensed to
hold ceremonies; the largest with a
standing capacity of 500. Ceremonies
are available seven days a week excluding Christmas Day, Boxing Day and
New Year's Eve. Ceremonies are free
of charge if held in conjunction with
receptions.
Price guide: from £40

Reception

Catering: £12.50pp

Land's End Hotel
Land's End, Sennen
Penzance, Cornwall TR19 7AA
Tel: 01736 871844 Fax: 01736 971599
Contact: Mr Richrd Smith, Hotel
Manager

Ceremony

Set on a cliff-top overlooking Land's
End Point, the hotel has two marriage
rooms, The Atlantic Restaurant (overlooking the sea) and the Ocean
Conservatory. Up to three ceremonies
per day: on any day of the year.
Price guide: from £75

Reception

Catering: from £12.75pp

Polhawn Fort
Military Road, Rame
Torpoint, Cornwall PL10 1LL
Tel: 01752 822864 Fax: 01752 822341
Contact: John Wicksteed, Proprietor

Ceremony

This Grade II listed Napoleonic
coastal fort, situated on the Rame
Peninsular, is available for private
and exclusive use only, and is generally hired for a full weekend
period. Because the Fort is hired
on an exclusive basis ceremonies
may be held any day of the week
with no restrictions on Bank
Holidays. Prices for the hire of the
Fort (from £1,790) include the
cost of the ceremony, and use of all
facilities (including tennis court).

Reception

Catering is on a contract basis and,
although the Fort has a list of recommended caterers available, couples may
provide their own. The Fort features
two grand master bedrooms, four double bedrooms and two single bedrooms,
sleeping up to 20 guests in total, however a list of further local accommodation is available. All the services indicated are available by arrangement.
The Fort is complete with all modern
conveniences.
Catering: P.O.A.

The Queens Hotel
The Promenade
Penzance
Cornwall TR18 4HG
Tel: 01736 62371 Fax: 01736 50033
Contact: Vyvyan Jenkin, General
Manager

Ceremony

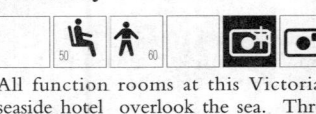

All function rooms at this Victorian
seaside hotel overlook the sea. Three
rooms are used for wedding ceremonies.
Price guide: from £100

Reception

Couples holding ceremony and reception at the hotel are offered a complimentary room for the night while their
guests are offered a discount on accommodation. Unusual weddings here
have included a medieval banquet
including roast pig.
Catering: Buffets from £5.20pp Sit
down from £10.20pp

Rose-in-Vale Country
House Hotel
Mithian, St Agnes
Cornwall TR5 0QD

Tel: 01872 552202 Fax: 01872 552700
Contact: Mrs V M Arthur, Proprietor

Ceremony

This Grade II listed country house dates back to the 1760s and is set in 11 acres of woods, pasture and gardens. Ceremonies are available seven days a week with a maximum of two permitted per day.
Price guide: from £75

Reception

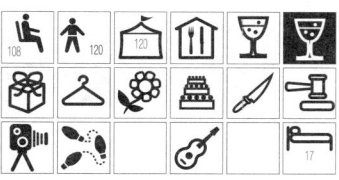

The hotel has its own marquee sited in the grounds. This features a bar and a dancefloor. In addition, a classical pianist is available to take advantage of the hotel's own baby grand piano. On application, a room will be made available for the bride and groom to change in. Amongst other plaudits, the hotel boasts an RAC Merit Award and has been graded as an AA three star hotel.
Catering: from £12pp

Royal Duchy Hotel
Cliff Road
Falmouth
Cornwall TR11 4NX
Tel: 01326 313042 Fax: 01326 319420
Contact: Mr Darryl Reburn, Hotel Manager

Ceremony

Ceremonies are available Monday to Saturday excluding Good Friday and Christmas Day. Ceremonies without receptions are permitted. Prices vary with the time of year.
Price guide: F.O.C. (with reception)

Reception

Catering is in-house and the hotel

holds an AA Rosette for its cuisine. A wide selection of sample menus is available.
Catering: from £16pp

Trevigue
Crackington Haven
Bude
Cornwall EX23 0LQ
Tel: 01840 230418 Fax: 01840 230418
Contact: Gayle Crocker, Wedding Co-ordinator

Ceremony

This National Trust owned farmhouse is built around a cobbled courtyard and offers ceremonies seven days a week with only one permitted per day.
Price guide: POA

Reception

Catering is in-house and, although the farmhouse holds a liquor licence, this does not extend to a late night licence. Trevigue prides itself on the use of top quality produce enhanced by the subtle use of sauces, herbs and seasonings. The venue has hosted live music in the past, such as classical string quartets. In addition to the three bedrooms situated in the farmhouse, a further two rooms are located in the Mediterranean-style annexe a few hundred yards from the main building.
Catering: from £12pp

STOP PRESS
Mullion Cove Hotel, Mullion
01326 240328
The Porthminster Hotel, St Ives
01736 795221
Sconner House Inn, Nr Torpoint
01503 230297

Abbey House Hotel
Abbey Road
Barrow in Furness
Cumbria LA13 0PA
Tel: 01229 838282 Tel: 01229 820403
Contact: Heather Holding, Sales Manager

Ceremony

This Lutyens building was built in 1914 and is set in 14 acres in front of Furness Abbey. Five rooms are licensed and are available any day of the week. Helicopters and hot air balloons can use the grounds.
Price guide: from £75

Reception

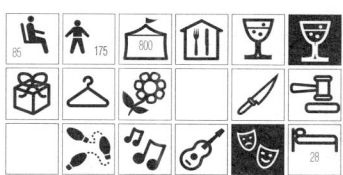

Catering: Buffets from £5.50 Sit down from £12pp

Armathwaithe Hall Hotel
Bassenthwaithe Lake
Keswick
Cumbria
CA12 4RE
Tel: 017687 76551
Fax: 017687 76220
Contact: Joan Tomkinson, Sales Manager

Ceremony

This 17th Century former stately home is now a family owned and run hotel, set in 400 acres of lakeside grounds. Special features include wood panelled public rooms and log fires. Three rooms are available for ceremonies, which can only be conducted here if the reception is also held on the premises.
Price guide: from £75

Reception

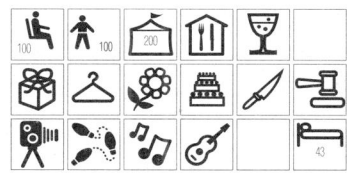

In addition to the services above, both wedding cars, and horses and carriages, can be arranged by the hotel.
Catering: from £18.95pp

Broad Oaks
Bridge Lane
Troutbeck, Nr Windermere
Cumbria LA23 1LA
Tel: 01539 445560 Fax: 01539 488766
Contact: T Pavolyn, Owner

Ceremony

Weddings at this country house can only be arranged if accommodation is also taken.
Price guide: from £150

Reception

Catering: from £19pp

Broughton Craggs Hotel
Great Broughton
Cockermouth
Cumbria CA13 0XW
Tel: 01900 824400 Fax: 01900 825350
Contact: Sandra Taylor

Ceremony

This hotel and restaurant is willing to conduct up to two ceremonies per day, seven days a week, even if the reception is not held at the venue. Two rooms (The Craggs Lounge and The Main Dining Room) are licensed and confetti is allowed.
Price guide: F.O.C. (with reception)

Reception

Price guide: P.O.A.

The Burnside Hotel
Kendal Road
Bowness on Windermere
Cumbria LA23 3EP
Tel: 015394 42211 Fax: 01394 43824
Contact: Mrs Brenda Watson

Ceremony

Set in its own gardens overlooking Lake Windermere, The Burnside has four rooms that are licensed for weddings. Ceremonies can be held daily throughout the year.
Price guide: £100

Reception

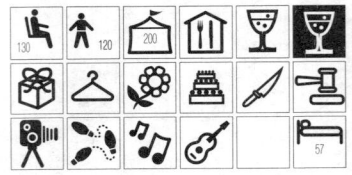

Again, the hotel offers several rooms, according to requirements. A wide range of services is offered, including reduced accommodation rates for guests.
Caatering: from £16pp

Castle Inn Hotel
Bassenthwaithe
Nr Keswick
Cumbria CA12 4RG
Tel: 017687 76401 Fax: 017687 76604
Contact: Liz Arnell
Sales Manager

Ceremony

The Castle Inn enjoys views of Bassenthwaite Lake and the highest mountains in England. Five rooms hold wedding licences, ranging in capacity from 2 to 175.
Price guide: from £50

Reception

Catering: Buffets from. £6.95pp Sit down from £15pp

Cragwood Country House Hotel
Ecclerigg
Windermere
Cumbria LA23 1LQ
Tel: 015394 88177 Fax: 015394 42145
Contact: Phil Hornby, Manager

Ceremony

Cragwood is a traditional country house hotel, set in 20 acres of gardens and woodland, and is the sister venue to Merewood. The ceremony room here can seat up to 50 people, and is available daily throughout the year.
Price guide: £100

Reception

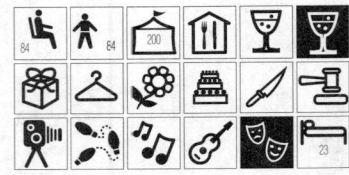

Catering: from £22pp

Crown Hotel
Wetheral
Carlisle, Cumbria CA4 8ES
Tel: 01228 561888 Fax: 01228 561637
Contact: Lynn Parratt, Banq Manager

Ceremony

Ceremonies are offered daily throughout the year. Three rooms are available, seating from 15 up to 150 people. Room hire includes a floral arrangement.
Price guide: from £75

Reception

Extra services include red carpet on arrival, and reduced accommodation rates for guests.
Catering: from £13.95pp

Eccle Riggs Manor Hotel
Foxfield Road
Broughton in Furness
Cumbria LA20 6BN
Tel: 01229 716398 Fax: 01229 716958
Contact: Ms Vanessa Hayes, GM

Ceremony

A maximum of two ceremonies can be held daily except Christmas Day.
Price guide: from £85

Reception

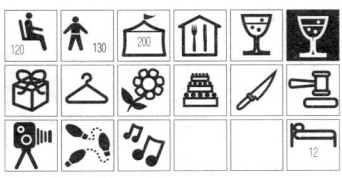

Catering: from £5pp

Ennerdales Country House Hotel
Cleator
Cumbria CA23 3DT
Tel: 01946 813907 Fax: 01946 815260
Contact: James Lamb, GM

Ceremony

This Grade II listed building is set in landscaped gardens with fountain. The Fountain Room and Muncaster Rooms are licensed for ceremonies, which here must be followed by reception. Helicopters and hot air balloons may use the grounds.
Price guide: £100

Reception

Catering: Buffets from £8pp Sit down from £13pp

Greenhill Hotel
Red Dial
Wigton
Cumbria CA7 8LS
Tel: 016973 43304 Fax: 016973 45168
Contact: Marianne Phillips

Ceremony

The Library, Conservatory, Dining Room and Function Suite are all licensed, capable of accommodating parties from 20 to 250.
Price guide: from £50

Reception

Catering: Buffets from £7pp Sit down from £15pp

Gretna Chase Hotel
Sark Bridge
Gretna, Cumbria DG1 5JB
Tel: 01461 337517 Fax: 01461 337766
Contact: Margaret or Patricia, Banqueting Manageresses

Ceremony

Two ceremony rooms are licensed at the Gretna Chase, with capacities of 30 to 50 guests. Weddings can be held Sunday to Thursday. Confetti is not permitted.
Price guide: from £85

Reception

Although this hotel has a Dumfriesshire postcode, it is actually on the English side of the border. Built in 1856 for runaway couples, the hotel offers the romance of getting married in Gretna, while remaining under English law. It is set in award-winning gardens.
Catering: £12.50 - £19.50pp

Holbeck Ghyll Country House Hotel
Holbeck Lane
Windermere
Cumbria LA223 1LU
Tel: 015394 32375 Fax: 015394 34743
Contact: David or Patricia Nicholson, Proprietors

Ceremony

This upmarket 19th Century hunting lodge features views over Lake Windermere. Three of its rooms are licensed for wedding ceremonies, The Lounge, The Lonsdale Room and the Terrace Restaurant, allowing for a minimum of two and maximum of 40 guests. Lawns, lakes and the Langdale mountains offer an appealing backdrop to photographs. There is no suitable site for helicopters to land.
Price guide: £50

Reception

This venue has two AA Rosettes for its cuisine.
Catering: Buffets from £20pp Sit down from £25pp

Lakeside Hotel
Newby Bridge
Cumbria LA12 8AT
Tel: 015395 31207 Fax: 015395 31699
Contact: Jonathon Robb or Kate Willock

Ceremony

This traditional lakeland coaching inn is set on the south shore of Lake Windermere, with its own jetties and boats. Three separate areas of the hotel have been granted a licence, but only one ceremony is permitted per day.
Price guide: from £195

Reception

The hotel has an AA Rosette and an RAC award for its food and restaurant. The price below is based on the hotel's wedding packages, which include drinks. The hotel can arrange hour long 'cocktail' cruises on the lake for up to 200 people: appropriate between day and evening receptions. Hot air balloons can also take off from behind the hotel.
Catering: from £29.50

The Langdale Chase Hotel
Windermere
Cumbria CA23 1LW
Tel: 015394 32201 Fax: 015394 32604
Contact: Mr Thomas Noblett, GM

Ceremony

This lakeside hotel features large gardens and views across the lake to the mountains. Five rooms are licensed. Couples can arrive or depart by boat here or make a grand entrance or exit by helicopter or balloon.
Price guide: £50

Reception

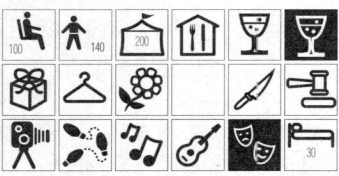

Catering: Buffets from £9pp Sit down from £14pp

Leeming House Hotel
Watermillock, Ullswater
Nr Penrith, Cumbria CA11 0JJ
Tel: 017684 86622 Fax: 017684 86443
Contact: General Manager

Ceremony

This Forte hotel is set in 27 acres on the shores of Ullswater. There are three marriage rooms which are offered any day except Christmas Day and New Year's Day. There is no room hire charge if the reception is also at the hotel. For ceremonies only, price depends on time of year and day.
Price guide: F.O.C. (with reception) or P.O.A.

Reception

This busy hotel (two AA Rosettes) is not really able to cater for evening functions unless the whole hotel is taken on an exclusive use basis. However, between March and

October, a steam boat (for up to 200) operates on the lake. This can be hired for dinner/dances, etc. The hotel also has a helipad and space for hot air balloons. Cake makers and photographers can both be recommended.
Catering: from £27.50pp (3-course meal)

Linthwaite House Hotel
Crook Road
Windermere
Cumbria LA23 3JA
Tel: 015394 88600 Fax: 015394 88601
Contact: Tina Slingo, Anne Marie Lennon

Ceremony

This hotel is set in 14 acres of grounds with views of Lake Windermere. The three licensed rooms range in capacity from 24 to 64 and are available any day except Sundays, and the Christmas and New Year Bank Holidays. Ceremonies must be followed by reception here. Couples may arrive or depart by boat and may leave by hot air balloon.
Price guide: from £150

Reception

The hotel prides itself on its use of local produce in its modern British cuisine. Exclusive use of the entire hotel is possible - in fact recently a couple flew their entire family over from Hong Kong for their wedding here.
Catering: Buffet from £19pp Sit down from £26pp

Low Wood Hotel
Windermere
Cumbria LA23 1LP
Tel: 015394 33338 Fax: 015394 34072
Contact: Teresa Whiteside, Sales Manager

Ceremony

The Low Wood is situated on the shores of Lake Windermere with views across the lake to the Langdale Pikes.

Numerous rooms are licensed for weddings which can take place here any day of the year except Christmas Day. Ceremonies must be followed by reception at the hotel.
Price guide: £200

Reception

Helicopters and hot air balloons may use the hotel grounds, and couples can arrive and/or depart from their wedding by boat.
Catering: from £13.95pp

Merewood Country House Hotel
Ecclerigg, Windermere
Cumbria LA23 1LH
Tel: 015394 46484 Fax: 015394 42128
Contact: Christopher Dalzell, Manager

Ceremony

Merewood is the sister hotel of Cragwood. Weddings are possible for parties of up to 70 people, throughout the year, with one allowed per day. An administration cost of £50 is charged.
Price guide: £50

Reception

Catering: from £20pp

Michael's Nook
Country House Hotel
Grasmere, Cumbria LA22 9RP
Tel: 015394 35496 Fax: 015394 35645
Contact: Janette, Executive Assistant

Ceremony

This hotel has three licensed rooms: the Dining Room, the Drawing Room and the Oak Room. One ceremony per day can be held seven days per week

but Saturday availability is limited in season. Restricted wheelchair access.
Price guide: from £75

Reception

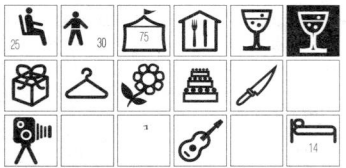

Wedding cake, photography and live music can all be provided on arrangement. Children cannot be catered for separately. Michael's Nook does not operate preferential rate agreements with any local hotels.
Catering: £27.50 to £38pp

Mirage at Milton Hall
Brampton, Cumbria CA8 1JA
Tel: 016977 41774 Fax: 016977 2800
Contact: June Aston, Administrator

Ceremony

Mirage is the recently refurbished function suite at Milton Hall and is in a country setting with extensive views. Only one ceremony per day can be held at Mirage, but this must be followed by reception at the venue.
Price guide: No charge

Reception

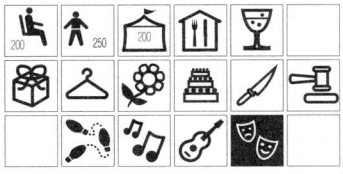

Helicopters and balloons can land and take off in the grounds of Mirage. While there is no accommodation on site, the venue can provide a list of local establishments.
Catering: Buffets from £6pp Sit down from £15pp

Naworth Castle
Brampton, Cumbria CA8 2HF
Tel: 016977 3229 Fax: 016977 3679
Contact: Colleen Hall, Events Manager

Ceremony

Wedding ceremonies at Naworth Castle (which dates from 1335) are held in the Old Library, (100 seated - 150 standing).
Price guide: £300 plus vat

Reception

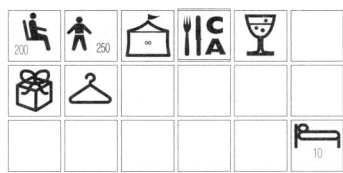

Wedding breakfasts are held in the Great Hall (200 seated), with additional rooms available on request. All weddings exclusive use only. The smallest wedding held here so far was for two people! Horse riding, clay pigeon shooting and fishing are also all available here.
Catering: from £18pp, plus vat

North Lakes Hotel
Ullswater Road
Penrith
Cumbria CA11 8QT
Tel: 01768 868111 Fax: 01768 868291
Contact: Hilary Carruthers, Banqueting Manager

Ceremony

The North Lakes has four rooms available for weddings, for groups of 2 to 200 people. Ceremonies are possible daily, all year round, except for Easter Sunday and Christmas Day. Confetti is not allowed.
Price guide: from £50

Reception

The hotel can arrange a wide range of additional services.
Catering: from £19.95pp

Old England Hotel
Church Street
Bowness on Windermere
Cumbria LA23 3DF
Tel: 015394 42444 Fax: 015394 43432
Contact: Valerie Lockley, Banqueting Manager

Ceremony

Four rooms hold a licence (Belle Isle, Lake, Garden & Bury), with one or two ceremonies per day available 365 days of the year. The hotel has its own jetties and gardens.
Price guide: £80 - £150

Reception

Catering: £18pp

Samling at Dovenest
Ambleside Road
Windermere
Cumbria LA23 1LR
Tel:015394 31922 Fax: 015394 30400
Contact: Brigette Beser, Sales Manager

Ceremony

Samling is apparently the Cumbrian word for 'gathering', for those of you wondering. Those gathering here would enjoy an 18th Century building, now a sophisticated private hotel available for exclusive use. The house is set in 67 acres of landscaped gardens with a pond. Ceremonies here must be followed by reception. The Samling offers an inclusive package for 20 which includes 24 hour use of the house and grounds, with dinner, bed and breakfast and lunch, plus drinks, all for £350 per couple, or £250 per person. The Samling is a three minute walk from Lake Windermere. Helicopters and hot air balloons may use the grounds.
Price guide: £250pp (for inclusive 24 hr package)

Reception

The overnight accommodation is in 10 suites (ie with sitting room each). The

chef, who uses local produce where possible, is a former chef for David Bowie.
Catering: This is an all-in package - see above.

Skiddaw Hotel
Main Street
Keswick, Cumbria CA12 5BN
Tel: 017687 72071 Fax: 017687 74850
Contact: Maria, Sales Manager

Ceremony

This town centre hotel offers four ceremony rooms accommodating a minimum of four guests. Up to four ceremonies are permitted per day. Confetti is not permitted.
Price guide: from £45

Reception

Catering: Buffets from £15pp Sit down from £13pp

Stakis Keswick Lodore
Swiss Hotel
Borrowdale
Keswick, Cumbria CA12 5UX
Tel: 017687 77285 Fax: 017687 77343
Contact: Valerie Ayre, Deputy Manager

Ceremony

The hotel has two rooms licensed to hold weddings: the main lounge and the garden lounge. Preferential rates have been arranged with local establishments for wedding guests. One or two small weddings per day.
Price guide: from £125

Reception

Catering: £15 - £25pp

Swan Hotel
Newby Bridge
Cumbria LA12 8NB
Tel: 015395 31681 Fax: 015395 31917
Contact: Wendy Eden

Ceremony

The Swan is situated at the southern tip of Lake Windermere. Ceremonies are restricted to one per day, but the hotel is not available over the Easter holiday weekends, Spring Bank Holiday or the late Summer Bank Holiday.
Price guide: £125

Reception

Local specialities include venison, Morecambe Bay Shrimps and Cumberland Farmhouse Cheese.
Catering: £25pp

Tufton Arms Hotel
Market Square
Appleby in Westmoreland
Cumbria CA16 6XA
Tel: 017683 51593 Fax: 017683 52761
Contact: Teresa Burton

Ceremony

This 16th Century old coaching inn, with Victorian additions, it located in the centre of Appleby. Four rooms are licensed, two on the ground floor and with good wheelchair access. The venue is closed over the Christmas period.
Price guide: £90 (FOC if reception costs over £500)

Reception

The Tufton Arms holds an AA Rosette for its cuisine and is AA, RAC, Egon Ronay and Johanssen recommended.
Catering: from £12.50pp

Tullie House
Museum & Art Gallery
Castle Street
Carlisle
Cumbria
CA3 8TP
Tel: 01228 34781 Fax: 01228 810249
Contact: Barbara Lamont, Bookings Co-ordinator

Ceremony

This award-winning Museum offers ceremonies in the Victorian Function Room: the original lecture theatre. The Grade I listed building provides an excellent backdrop for photography, both indoors and in the gardens. Room hire is charged at £130 if the reception is held at Tullie House, and at £230 otherwise.
Price guide: from £130

Reception

The Garden restaurant offers classical menus. Vegetarian options are included. Although no overnight accommodation is available, preferential rates have been arranged with local hotels/guest houses.
Catering: from £13.50pp

Ullswater Hotel
Glenridding
Penrith,
Cumbria
CA11 0JJ
Tel: 017684 Fax: 017684 82303
Contact: David Mohum

Ceremony

The Ullswater Hotel is set in 40 acres of private grounds on the shores of Lake Ullswater with three landing jetties, a helipad, separate children's play area and a scenic location among the fells. The hotel is also situated 200 yards from the Ullswater Steamer, which is available for private hire for trips on the lake.
Price guide: P.O.A.

Reception

Catering: £13.50 - £25pp

Wordsworth Hotel
Grasmere
Cumbria LA22 9SW
Tel: 015394 35592 Fax: 0153 94765
Contact: Robin Lees, General Manager

Ceremony

The Wordsworth offers a maximum of two ceremonies per day, excluding Christmas and New Year. Up to 120 people can be accommodated in the ceremony room.
Price guide: from £100

Reception

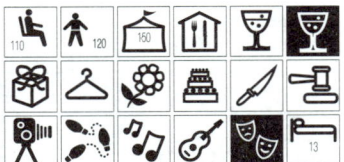

The reception facilities are suitable for up to 110 people for waited service, or for 120 for a buffet. A marquee could be used, for up to 150. The hotel has its own overnight accommodation, or can arrange preferential rates with local establishments.
Catering: from £11.50pp

STOP PRESS
Bankfield, Kirkstanton 01229 772276
Dalston Hall Hotel, Dalston 01228 710271
Ladstock Country House Hotel, Keswick 017687 78210
Netherwood Hotel, Grange over Sands 015395 32552
The Washington Central Hotel, Workington 01900 65772

Breadsall Priory Hotel X
Moor Road
Morely, Nr Derby
Derbyshire DE7 6DL
Tel: 01332 832235 Fax: 01332 833509
Contact: The Manager

Ceremony

This listed building used to belong to the Darwin family. Set in 400 acres of mature parkland, it offers ceremonies seven days a week with no restrictions on the time of year.
Price guide: £200

Reception

Parking is available for up to 300 cars.
Catering: £19.95 - £35pp

Brookfield Hall on Long Hill
Long Hil
Buxton
Derbyshire
SK17 6SU
Tel: 01298 24151 Fax: 01298 24151
Contact: Roger Handley, Proprietor

Ceremony

This Victorian manor house is set in 10 acres of grounds and has been restored to its original state. Two rooms are licensed; the reception hall and the drawing room, with capacities varying from 10 to 60. Ceremonies are available without receptions but are more expensive.
Price guide: £58.75 - £117.50

Reception

The Hall offers a complimentary overnight suite for the couple, while reduced accommodation rates in the hotel's seven remaining bedrooms can be arranged for wedding guests. Children can be catered for separately, if required.
Catering: from £18.50pp

Dales & Peaks Hotel
Old Road, Darley Dale
Matlock DE4 2ER
Tel: 01629 733775
Contact: Mr Banks, Owner

Ceremony

The hotel is housed in a Victorian building with a 3/4 acre walled garden. The Red House Stables, adjacent to the hotel, house a vintage car and carriage museum, the exhibits of which were recently used in the film of Jane Eyre. These vehicles can also be used for weddings. Two rooms in the hotel are licensed for cermeonies. Ceremonies on a Saurday must be follwed by reception at the hotel.
Price guide: £50

Reception

Evening functions are not posible at the hotel.
Catering: from £16.95 (inc drinks)

Darwin Forest Country Park
Darley Moor
Darley Two Dales, Matlock
DE4 5LN
Tel: 01629 732428 Fax: 01629 735015
Contact: Quentin Gregory

Ceremony

This £5million holiday complex is set in 50 acres and has over 80 self-catering log cabins. For this reason, ceremonies here should be booked alongside catering and accommodation. Helicopters and hot air balloons can use the site.
Price guide: from £100

Reception

Catering: POA

East Lodge Country House Hotel
Rowsley, Matlock DE4 2EF
Tel: 01629 734474 Fax: 01629 733949
Contact: Mrs Mills Proprietor

Ceremony

The hotel was once the East Lodge to Haddon Hall and is set in 10 acres of grounds. It is set on the outskirts of the Derbyshire Peak District and has two rooms licensed to hold ceremonies with capacities of 20 and 70. One ceremony per day is permitted, and only if held in conjunction with reception.
Price guide: £150

Reception

Catering: from £18.95pp

Hardwick Hall
Doe Lea, Chesterfield
Derbyshire
Tel: 01246 850430
Contact: Mr Priddle

While it is still officially authorised to hold wedding ceremonies, Hardwick Hall has ceased holding ceremonies .

Hassop Hall
Hassop, Nr Bakewell
Derbyshire
Tel: 01629 640488 Fax: 01629 640577
Contact: Mr Chapman, Owner

Ceremony

Ceremonies are available from Monday to Saturday, but must be followed by reception here. Confetti isnot permitted.
Price guide: POA

Reception

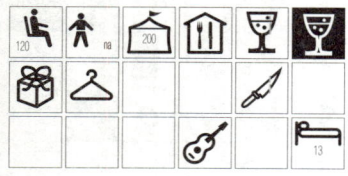

A late night drinking licence is held for the restaurant and residential guests only. the hotels offers its own pianist for receptions.
Price guide: POA

Heanor & Loscoe Town Hall
Market Place
Heanor, Derbyshire DE75 7AA
Tel: 01773 533050
Contact: DR Bostock, Town Clerk

Ceremony

This town centre, Grade II listed building (recently rescued from dereliction) provides three cermony rooms with capcities ranging from 15 to 210. Weddings can take place here on any day of the year.
Price guide: £25

Reception

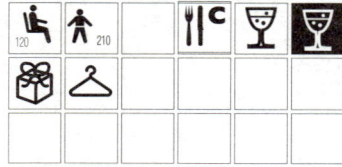

Outside caterers or self catering is permitted at the Town Hall, and drinks licences can be obtained if required. A list of local accommodation can also be provided.

Kedleston Hall, Derby DE22 5JH
Tel: 01332 842191 Fax: 01332 841972
Contact: Property Manager

Ceremony

This National Trust Property offers three ceremony rooms with capacities ranging from 30 to 100. Ceremonies can take place on Thursdays and Fridays only from April to October. At other times, only by arrangement with the Property Manager.
Price guide: from £200

Reception

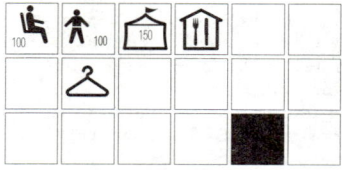

Catering: from £21pp

Lion Hotel & Restaurant
Belper
Derbyshire DE56 1AX
Tel: 01773 824033 Fax: 01773 828393
Contact: Ian Miller

Ceremony

This olde worlde hotel, dating from the 18th Century, is sited in the centre of Belper. Three rooms are licensed.
Price guide: £100

Reception

The wedding package at the hotel includes complimentary overnight accommodation for bride and groom, complimentary floral arrangements, menu cards, toastmaster, discounts for children and accommodation discounts for guests. Drinks packages start at £5.95pp.
Catering: from £11.95

Locko Park
Sponden
Derby DE21 7BW
Tel: 01332 662785 Fax: 01332 281942
Contact: Miss GL Phillipson, Assistant Agent

Ceremony

This listed private house is set in formal gardens and surrounded by parkland. The Picture Gallery, Dining Room and Billiard Room are all licensed for ceremonies and are available on Wednesdays, Fridays and Saturdays from 1st October to 30th April inclusive.
Price guide: from £250

Reception

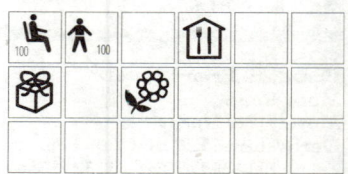

All catering is managed in-house, and is

arranged on an individul basis, hence no price guides. While discos and modern music are not permitted, classical music is welcomed.

Mackworth Hotel
Ashbourne Road,
Derby DE22 4LY

Tel: 01332 824324 Fax: 01332 824692
Contact: Banqueting Manager

Ceremony

This listed building also features a permanent marquee and offers ceremonies on all days except Sunday.
Price guide: £150

Reception

Catering: from £15.95pp

Makeney Hall
Makeney, Milford
Derbyshre DE56 0RS

Tel: 01332 842999 Fax: 01332 842777
Contact: Janet Gould, Operations Manager

Ceremony

A Victorian country house hotel, Makeney Hall is set in six acres of gardens on the edge of the Derwent Valley. Helicopters can land on site. Five rooms are licensed for ceremonies and are available on any day except Sundays and Bank Holidays. Receptions must also be booked at this venue.
Price guide: £100

Reception

Catering: Buffets from £7.50pp Sit down from £23pp

Mickleover Court Hotel
Mickleover
Derby DE3 5XX

Tel: 01332 521234 Fax: 01332 521238
Contact: Isobel Spray

Ceremony

This modern hotel was originally designed with the disabled in mind and features customised bedrooms. Ceremony capacities range from 40 to 300.
Price guide: from £80

Reception

The hotel prides itself on its catering specialities including Italian and traditional cooking. The hotel can provide red carpet, wedding car and table plans.
Catering from £8.95pp

Midland Hotel
Midland Road
Derby DE1 2SQ

Tel: 01332 345894 Fax: 01332 293522
Contact: Jane Cryer, Deputy GM

Ceremony

This traditional style building dates back to the middle of the 19th Century and features a tree lined garden. Ceremonies are available without receptions at a cost of £500, and are not available on Sundays or Bank Holidays.
Price guide: £150 (with reception)

Reception

Wedding guests are offered reduced overnight accommodation rates.
Catering: from £21.15 (including drinks)

Morley Hayes
Main Road
Morley
Derby DE7 6DG

Tel: 01332 780480 Fax: 01332 781094
Contact: Functions Manager

Ceremony

The Morley Hayes is a family owned and run 18 hole golf course, function suite, bar and restaurant. Three rooms are licensed for weddings. Helicopters and hot air balloons can use the grounds.
Price guide: £350

Reception

Catering: Buffets from £7.45pp   Sit down from £17pp

New Bath Hotel
New Bath Road
Matlock Bath
Derbyshire DE4 3PX

Tel: 01629 583275 Fax: 01629 580268
Contact: Celina Tann

Ceremony

The hotel offers ceremonies Monday to Saturday. These are only available if followed by reception here.
Price guide: £75

Reception

Catering: £18.95pp

Oaklands Manor
Long Hill
Buxton
Derbyshire SK17 6ST

Tel: 01298 72565 Fax: 01298 73053
Contact: Keith Highet, Manager

Ceremony

This banqueting and business centre is set in a Victorian manor house overlooking the Wye Valley. Two rooms are available for ceremonies.
Price guide: £50

Reception

Catering: Buffets from £7.75pp Sit down from £13.75pp

Ringwood Hall Hotel
Brimington, Chesterfield,
Derbyshire S43 1DQ
Tel: 01246 280077 Fax: 01246 472241
Contact: Sarash McGowan, Group Co-ordinator

Ceremony

Set in 28 acres of gardens, Ringwood Hall offers three rooms for ceremonies. Up to six ceremonies are permitted per day on any day of the year.
Price guide: POA

Reception

Helicopters and hot air balloons can use the Hall grounds, which have also been host to firework displays.
Catering: Buffets from £5.95 Sit down from £15.50

Risley Hall Hotel
Derby Road, Risley
Derbyshgire DE72 3SS
Tel: 0115 939 9000 Fax: 0115 939 7766
Contact: Sales & Marketing Manager

Ceremony

This 16th Century Grade II listed building is set in five acres of gardens. The Baronial Hall, where ceremonies take place, was once the Prince of Wales' hunting lodge.
Price guide: £150

Reception

Flower arrangements are included in the standard wedding package.
Catering: from £23.50pp

Royal Regency Banqueting Suites
Wharncliffe Road
Ilkeston, Derby DE7 5HF
Tel: 0115 932 7777 Fax: 0115 944 1809
Contact: Assistant Manager

Ceremony

This venue is a member of the Ilkston Co-op Group. One room is licensed to hold ceremonies with one ceremony permitted per day on any day of the week.
Price guide: £75

Reception

Five rooms are available for receptions with varying capacities of 50 to 350, although there is no accommodation on site, a list of local establishments with preferential rate agreements is provided on request.
Catering: from £13.95pp

Yew Lodge Hotel
Packington Hill
Kegworth, Derby DE74 2DF
Tel: 01509 672518 Fax: 01509 674730
Contact: Carol Patrick/Katrina Andries Conference & Banqueting.

Ceremony

This hotel, restaurant and conference centre offers two ceremony rooms which are available any day of the year. The hotel features gardens and a lounge with an open fire.
Price guide: £350

Reception

The hotel can arrange most wedding requirements, including fireworks, and has even hosted a double wedding for twins.
Catering: Buffet from £7.50pp Sit down from £12.50pp

STOP PRESS
Derbyshire County Office, Matlock
01629 580000
International Hotel, Derby
01332 369321
Jarvis Newton Park Hotel, Newton Solney 01283 703568
Old Vicarage Country House Restaurant, Rideway Village
0114 247 5814
Riber Hall, Matlock 01629 582795
Sitwell Arms Hotel, Renishaw
01246 435226
Swallow Hotel, South Normanton
01773 812000

Bitton House
Bitton Park Road
Teignmouth, Devon TQ14 9DF
Tel: 01626 775030
Contact: Mr Lambert, Town Clerk

Ceremony

Bitton House is set in its own grounds and has a gun deck with cannons and balustrading, suitable for wedding photographs (it takes about 30 people).
Price guide: from £45

Reception

Couples my bring their own caterers to this venue, although several can be recommended by Bitton House.
Catering: from £3.50 (buffet) £7.50 (waited)

Boringdon Hall Hotel
Colebrook
Devon PL7 4DP
Tel: 01752 344455 Fax: 01752 346578
Contact: Melanie Winter/Elaine Whitehead

Ceremony

This Grade I listed mansion sits in its own grounds on the edge of Dartmoor. Interior features include a Great Hall with minstrel's gallery.
Price guide: £150

Reception

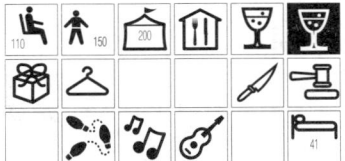

Boringdon Hall's wedding package includes a 50% discount for all children under 11. Infants are catered for free. Other facilities at the hotel include indoor pool, sauna, tennis and a nine-hole pitch and putt golf course.
Catering: £20pp

Buckland-Tout-Saints Hotel
Goveton, Kingsbridge
Devon TQ7 2DS
Tel: 01548 853055 Fax: 01548 856261
Contact: Mr Taylor or Julie

Ceremony

This Queen Anne mansion is set in extensive grounds featuring a terrace. Three rooms are licensed for ceremonies. Helicopters and hot air balloons can use the grounds.
Price guide: from £100

Reception

Discos and dances can take place in the marquee, as the house is not suitable. Past weddings have featured a jazz band playing on the terrace.
Catering: Buffets from £11pp
Sit down from £25pp

Burgh Island Hotel
Burgh Island, Bigbury on Sea
Devon TQ7 4BG
Tel: 01548 810514 Fax: 01548 810243
Contact: Tony Porter, Proprietor

Ceremony

Burgh Island Hotel is an Art Deco building, built in 1929, set on its own 26 acre tidal island. It can be reached across the sands when the tide is out (6 hours a day), or via the hotel's own sea tractor when the tide is in. The hotel also has its own smugglers pub on the island (built 1336), as well as a helipad. The nature of the hotel means that it is most suitable for smaller wedding groups, or larger groups if it is taken on an exclusive use basis. (An exclusive-use 2-day package for 36 people, including meals is £7822). One of its claims to fame is that Edward and Mrs Simpson apparently retreated to the hotel to escape the press. It is not possible to hold ceremonies here without also holding the reception at the hotel. Confetti is not permitted. A changing room can be provided for bride and groom on the wedding day, subject to availability.
Price guide: from £150 + vat

Reception

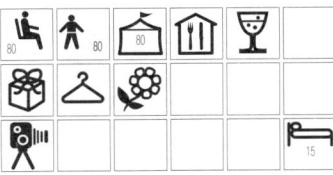

Fish and seafood are a speciality of the hotel which has its own lobster fisherman in season (May to September). The hotel can recommend cake makers. Dances and other live entertainment can only be permitted if the hotel is taken on an exclusive use basis. Overnight accommodation is offered in suites, with their own lounges.
Catering: from £32pp (sit down including canapes and coffee with petits fours)

Deer Park Hotel
Weston
Honiton
Devon EX14 0PG
Tel: 01404 41266 Fax: 01404 46598
Contact: Janet Gwynn, Hospitality

Ceremony

This Georgian mansion (built 1720) is set in 35 acres of parkland. Ceremonies can take place on any day except Christmas Day and New Year's Eve, but must be followed by reception at the hotel. Helicopters and hot air balloons can use the grounds.
Price guide; £150 + vat

Reception

Catering: from £16pp + vat

The Devon Hotel
Matford, Exeter EX2 8XU
Tel: 01392 59268 Fax: 01392 413142
Contact: Mr Parkhouse

Ceremony

The Devon Hotel is 10 minurtes from the centre of Exeter, and has three rooms licensed for ceremonies. Ceremonies must be followed by reception at the hotel.
Price guide: £200

Reception

Catering: Buffets from £5.50pp Sit down from £13pp

The Duke of Cornwall
Millbay Road, Plymouth
Devon PL1 3LG
Tel: 01752 266256 Fax: 01752 600062
Contact: Tracey Smith, Conf. Manager

Ceremony

This Grade II listed building was apparently once described by Sir John Betjeman as the finest example of Victorian architecture in Plymouth. It is now a Best Western hotel, with three AA and RAC stars. Inside it retains many original features including a sweeping staircase. Up to three weddings per day are allowed.
Price guide: £200

Reception

The hotel holds an AA rosette award for fine food. Children can be catered for separately.
Catering: from £5.50pp

Durrant House Hotel
Heywood Road, Northam
Devon EX39 3QB
Tel: 01237 472361 Fax: 01237 421709
Contact: Maria Borg, Owner

Ceremony

This old Georgian mansion set in three acres, has its own swimming pool, sauna and solarium, and is planning a leisure complex for 1997. Ceremonies can take place in one of three rooms; the Venetian Banqueting Suite, the Regency Room and the Garden Room. Ceremonies can take place here on any day except Bank Holidays.
Price guide: £50

Reception

The venue can arrange horse and carriage for you. Helicopters would have to land nearby, however, as there are overhead cables close to the site.
Catering: from £11.50 (buffet) – £14pp (waited)

East Devon Council Offices
The Knowle, Sidmouth
Devon EX10 8HL
Tel: 01395 516551 Fax: 01395 577853
Contact: Diana Vernon, Admin Officer or Jeff Bailey, Technical Services Manager

Ceremony

Three rooms have been granted a licence for civil wedding ceremonies at Knowle; The Council Chamber (max 170), the Committee Room (max 85) and the Members' Area (max 160). The building is set in 16 acres of parkland overlooking Lyme Bay. Ceremonies can only take place here on a Saturday.
Price guide: from £63.50

Reception

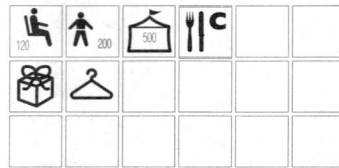

Couples can provide their own caterer for receptions at this venue, therefore a price guide cannot be given. A list of local accommodation can be provided on request.

Escot House & Gardens
Escot, Ottery St Mary
Devon EX11 1LU
Tel: 01404 822188 Fax: 01404 822903
Contact: Mrs Lucy Kennaway, Owner

Ceremony

Escot is a Georgian manor house set in parkland and gardens with lake views. Five rooms are licensed for ceremonies for a minimum of 20 guests. Helicopters and hot air balloons may use the grounds, and boating is possible on the lake.
Price guide: £150

Reception

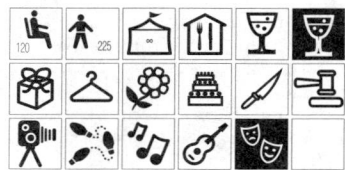

A speciality of the kitchens is wild boar farmed on the estate. Past weddings have included bride and groom arriving on horseback, and a humanist wedding ceremony.
Catering: Buffets from £5pp Sit down from £10pp

Huntsham Court
Huntsham, Tiverton
Devon EX16 7NA
Tel: 01398 361365 Fax: 01398 361456
Contact: Andrea Bolwig, Owner

Ceremony

Ceremonies at this Grade II listed Victorian gothic country house can take place on any day of the year, with only one permitted per day.
Price guide: £250

Reception

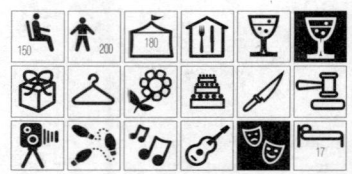

The Court provides British and continental style cuisine.
Catering: P.O.A.

Imperial Hotel
Park Hill Road, Torquay
Devon TQ1 2D
Tel: 01803 294301 Fax: 01803 298293
Contact: Food & Beverage Manager

Ceremony

This well-known resort hotel can hold ceremonies on any day except Sunday.
Price guide: £200

Reception

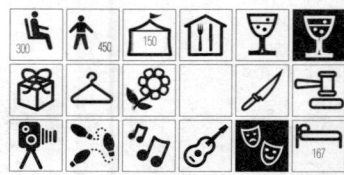

In addition to the above services, the hotel can also print menus and place cards for you.
Catering: P.O.A.

Langstone Cliff Hotel
Dawlish Warren
Dawlish, Devon EX7 0NA

Tel: 01626 865155 Fax: 01626 867166
Contact: Geoffrey or Mark Rogers,
Partners

Ceremony

Langstone Cliff is a Grade II listed
building set in its own grounds of 19
acres, on Devon's south coast. It has an
outdoor pool and a hard tennis court.
Price guide: £200

Reception

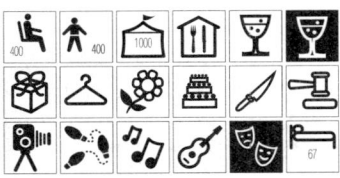

Transport, balloons and a cabaret can all
be organised by the hotel, which can
also offer barbecues, supper dances and
children's parties and teas.
Catering: from £9pp

Lewtrenchard Manor
Lewdown
Okehampton
Devon EX20 4PN

Tel: 01566 783256 Fax: 01566 783332
Contact: Mrs S Murray, Owner

Ceremony

The Manor was built in about 1600
and was once the home of the com-
poser of 'Onward Christian Soldiers'.
Internally, the house features ornate
ceilings and oak panelling, carvings and
open fireplaces. It is now the home of
the Murray family. Four rooms are
licensed for ceremonies. The grounds
can be used by hot air balloons and
helicopters.
Price guide: £200

Reception

Catering: from £22.50pp

Moorlands Link Hotel
Yelverton
Devon PL20 6DA

Tel: 01822 852245 Fax: 01822 855004
Contact: Irene, Functions Co-ordinator

Ceremony

Up to two ceremonies per day can
take place at Moorlands Link, but
ceremonies must be followed by
reception at the hotel. Weddings
can take place any day except
Christmas Day. Confetti is not
permitted. Wheelchair access is
limited to the Ballroom.
Price guide: from £150

Reception

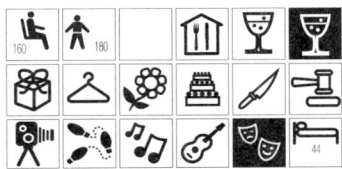

Overnight accommodation can be
offered at a special rate to your wedding guests.
Catering: P.O.A.

Northcote Manor
Burrington
Nr Exmoor
Devon EX37 9LZ

Tel: 01769 560501 Fax: 01769 560770
Contact: Norbert Spichtinger,
Proprietor

Ceremony

The Manor is a Grade II listed building
and the former estate of the Earls of
Bedford and Portsmouth. It is set in 20
acres of lawns, landscaped gardens and
woodland, and features a tennis court
and golf practice area. There are also
horses available for riding. One ceremony can take place here on any day of
the year.
The Manor offers a wedding package which includes marriage ceremony in the Oak Room (not registrar's fees), use of the Northcote
Room for reception, overnight stay
in the honeymoon suite, use of a
vintage Rolls Royce and a free
night in a double room on the couple's first anniversary, all for £395.
Price guide: P.O.A.

Reception

"Sophisticated Continental" cuisine.
Catering: £20pp - £40pp

Park Hotel
Taw Vale, Barnstaple, Devon

Tel: 01271 72166 Fax: 01271 23157
Contact: Michael Woodford, Manager

Ceremony

The Park Hotel is five minutres from
the town centre in a park and riverside
location. Two rooms are licensed for
ceremonies.
Price guide: £200

Reception

Catering: Buffets from £4.95 Sit down
from £12.50pp

Powderham Castle
Kenton, Exeter
Devon EX6 8JQ

Tel: 01626 890243 Fax: 01626 890729
Contact: Tim Faulkner, General
Manager

Ceremony

Powderham Castle dates from Medieval
times and has been the historic family
home of the Earl of Devon for over
600 years. It is set within an extensive
landscaped deer park alongside the
River Exe. The castle was also used as
the location for the film, The Remains
of the Day staring Anthony Hopkins
and Emma Thompson. The castle is
usually only available for ceremonies on
Saturday, but ceremonies can be held
on other days by arrangement. Confetti
is not allowed.
Price guide: £500

Reception

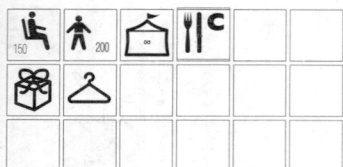

Catering at the castle is through a contract caterer which can be of your choice, hence it is not possible to give a price guide. While there is no accommodation available on the premises, a list of local accommodation with which the castle has preferential rate agreements, is available.

The Royal Hotel
Barnstaple Street
Bideford
Devon EX39 4AZ
Tel: 01237 472005 Fax: 01237 478957
Contact: Mr Nigel Maun

Ceremony

The Royal was originally built by a merchant in the 18th Century and is sited by the River Torridge. Couples can arrive and depart by boat. Three rooms are licensed for ceremonies.
Price guide: from £45 + vat

Reception

Traditional English carvery is one of the specialities of the house. Complimentary overnight accommodation is offered to bride and groom if the reception is booked here.
Catering: Packages including drink from £15.90pp

Tavistock Town Hall
Tavistock
Devon PL19 0AU
Tel: 01822 617232
Contact: Mr Cridland, Town Hall Supervisor

Ceremony

Two ceremony rooms are available in this 1860 building in the main square in the centre of Tavistock. These are available on any day except Bank Holidays.
Price guide: £65 (local residents) £85 (to those living outside the area)

Reception

Couples may appoint their own caterers for receptions at the Town Hall. The bar is licensed until 2am on all days except Saturday when it is licensed until midnight.

Tiverton Castle
Tiverton
Devon EX16 6RP
Tel: 01884 253200 Fax: 254200
Contact: Mr & Mrs AK Gordon, Owners

Ceremony

This Grade I listed medieval castle is easily accessed from the M5 and Tiverton Parkway station. Four rooms are licensed for ceremonies, which can take place on any day except at Christmas. Access is also limited when the castle is open to the public. Wheelchair access is limited.
Price guide: £300 (£250 if less that 30 guests)

Reception

The accommodation on offer is self-catering (with 4-keys rating).
Catering: POA

STOP PRESS
Bishops Court Hotel, Torquay
Tel: 01803 294649
Elfordleigh Hotel & Country Club, Plympton
Tel: 01752 336428

Haldon Belvedere, Dunchideock
01392 59268
Kitley, Plymouth 01752 881555
Old Forte House, Newton Abbot
01626 61101
Overmead Hotel, Torquay
Tel: 01803 295666
Saunton Sands Hotel, 01271 890212
Yarner, Bovey Tracey 01364 661354

Bridge House Hotel
2 Ringwood Road
Longham
Nr Ferndown
Dorset BH22 9AN
Tel: 01202 578828 Fax: 01202 572620
Contract: Simon Ball, Manager

Ceremony

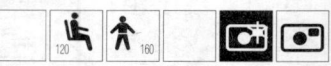

The hotel is set on the banks of the River Stour, and has an island garden. Three suites are licensed and are available on any day except Christmas Day.
Price guide: from £70

Reception

Themed weddings held here have included a 1960s' and Teddy Boys wedding!
Catering: Buffets from £3.95pp Sit down from £10.95pp

Carlton Hotel
East Overcliff, Bournemouth
Dorset BH1 3DN
Tel: 01202 552011 Fax: 01202 299573
Contact: General Manager

Ceremony

This hotel was in the process of being sold as we went to press, so couples would be advised to call the hotel for an update on prices. Below is the 1996 entry.
The Carlton Hotel sits overlooking Bournemouth Bay with views to the Needles on the Isle of Wight, Studland Point and the Purbecks. One ceremony is permitted here per day on any day of the year. It is not possible to

book a ceremony here without also booking reception facilities, however.
Price guide: £150

Reception

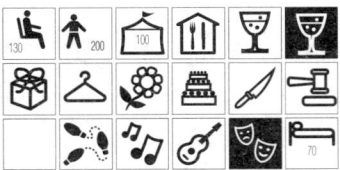

In addition to the services above, the hotel can provide linen to your colour choice and candelabra. The wedding package also includes complimentary overnight accommodation for bride and groom. Helicopters can land by arrangement. Chauffeur driven cars available.
Catering: from £23.50pp

Coppleridge Inn
Motcombe, Shaftesbury
Dorset SP7 9HW
Tel: 01747 851980 Fax: 01747 851858
Contact: David Dawson, Manager

Ceremony

The Inn is a converted 17th Century farm set in 15 acres of meadow and woodland. The Inn's function room is an oak timbered former barn. Ceremonies can take place here on any day of the year.
Price guide: £100

Reception

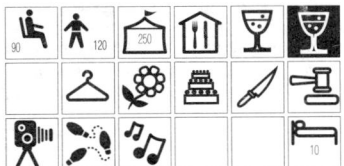

The Inn offers dishes using its own free range chickens.
Catering: £5pp - £20pp

Dorchester Municipal Buildings
High East Street
Dorchester, Dorset
Tel: 01305 265840 Fax: 01305 266085
Contact: Mrs Mary Gillett, Administrator

Ceremony

The Municipal Buildings are Grade II listed and date from the mid 19th Century. The Buildings comprise a suite of rooms ranging in capacity from 40 to 120. Up to two ceremonies a day can take place here on any day except Sunday, Christmas Day and Boxing Day. Confetti is not permitted.
Price guide: £50

Reception

Couples may choose their own caterers for this venue: kitchens will be made available.
Catering: P.O.A.

Hotel Rembrandt
12-16 Dorchester Road
Weymouth
Dorset DT4 7JU
Tel: 01305 764000 Fax: 01305 764022
Contact: Rebecca Buckland, Hotel Administrator

Ceremony

The Rembrandt offers two marriage rooms, the Garden Room (max 100) and the Aylesbury Room (max 70). These are available on any day except Christmas Day, New Year's Eve and New Year's Day. Unfortunately there is no area suitable for outdoor photography.
Price guide: £150

Reception

In addition to the range of services listed above, the hotel can provide a choice of coloured linen, special archway ribbons for use in the reception decorations, complimentary bridal suite for the couple on the wedding night, 1st anniversary meal and special accommodation rates for wedding guests.
Catering: from £5.75pp (buffet) - £15pp (waited)

Langtry Manor Hotel
Derby Road, East Cliff
Bournemouth, Dorset BH1 3QB
Tel: 01202 553887 Fax: 01202 290115
Contact: Tara Howard, GM

Ceremony

This listed building was built by Edward VII for his mistress Lillie Langtry. The marriage room is the Dining Room which features an inglenook fireplace, minstrel's gallery, huge stained glass windows, chandeliers and 16th Century tapestries. Ceremonies can take place here on any day except Christmas Day and Boxing Day. Confetti is not permitted.
Price guide: £200

Reception

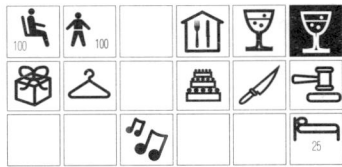

For the reception waiters and waitresses will be dressed in mob caps and frilly aprons in true Edwardian style. The reception can take place in the Dining Room or in the Royal Suite in the Langtry Lodge. The latter room is also available for your evening party. The Manor also offers several honeymoon suites with four poster beds or spa baths. Lillie's room, for instance, features a four poster bed and heart shaped corner bath. Edward VII's own personal bedroom is also available.
Catering: £14.95pp - £27pp

Lyme Regis Guildhall
Bridge Street, Lyme Regis
Dorset DT7 3QA
Tel: 01297 445175 Fax: 01297 443773
Contact: Mrs JM Amesbury, Town Clerk

Ceremony

This ancient building's history dates back to the Stuart period. The Main Chamber, with its curved ceiling and coat of arms featuring the Fleur de Lys, was once the local court. Ceremonies can take place in the Main Council Chamber of any day except Sunday and Bank Holidays.
Price guide: £75

Reception

The nearesrt venue for receptions is the Marine Theatre. Contact the Manager Mr Peter Hammond for details (01297 442394)

The Manor Hotel
West Bexington
Dorchester DT2 9DF
Tel: 01308 897616 Fax: 01308 897035
Contact: Richard Childs, Proprietor

Ceremony

Mentioned in the Doomsday Book, The Manor is an ancient stone building set within 500 yards of Chesil Beach. Three rooms have wedding licences, but these have limited wheelchair access.
Price guide: from £100

Reception

Helicopters and hot air balloons can land on site here, but despite its proximity to the sea, couples could not realistically arrive or depart by boat.
Catering: Buffet from £12pp Sit down from £15pp

The Mansion House Hotel
Thames Street, Poole, BH15 1JN
Tel: 01202 685666 Fax: 01202 665709
Contact: Jackie Godden, MD

Ceremony

This Georgian house is set in a town mews just off Poole's busy quay. It is a Grade II listed building with an elegant feature staircase. Ceremonies can take place here on any day of the year.
Price guide: £125

Reception

The hotel offers modern English cuisine. As part of the wedding package, the hotel offers a complimentary bridal suite and special rates.
Catering: P.O.A.

Salterns Hotel
38 Salterns Way
Lilliput, Poole
Dorset BH14 8JR
Tel: 01202 707321 Fax: 01202 707488
Contact: Linda Hioco, Marketing & Events Manager

Ceremony

Salterns Hotel enjoys a waterside location and boasts views over Poole Harbour from the two wedding rooms. Wheelchair access is very limited.
Price guide: £125

Reception

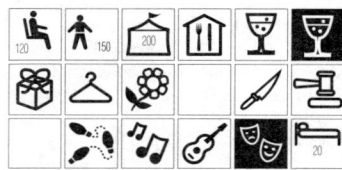

The hotel has an AA two rosette credited restaurant. Helicopters can land on site, and the hotel can arrange arrival or departure by boat if requested.
Catering: Buffets from £7.75pp Sit down from £19.50pp

Stafford House
West Stafford
Dorchester
Dorset DT2 8AA
Tel: 01305 263668 Fax: 01305 266903
Contact: Mrs Kay Pavitt, Owner

Ceremony

Jane Austen's Emma was recently filmed in the grounds at Stafford House (Emma was proposed to under the oak!). If that's not enough romance or glamour, Hardy apparently also wrote The Waiting Supper about the house. This is a Grade I listed private house with private riverside walks. The Library and the Drawing Room are licensed for weddings which can take place on any day of the year.
Price guide: from £250

Reception

A choice of contract caterers is offered for those wishing to hold their reception at the house, so prices vary depending on what is required.
Catering: POA

Swallow Highcliff Hotel
105 St Michael's Road
West Cliff, Bournemouth
Dorset BH2 5DU
Tel: 01202 557702 Fax: 01202 292734
Contact: Barbara Crabb, Conference and Banqueting Sales Manager

Ceremony

This Victorian cliff-top hotel overlooks Bournemouth beach. Two suites are available for ceremonies; the Shaftesbury Suite and the Purbeck Suite. Weddings may take place here on any day of the year.
Price guide: £250

Reception

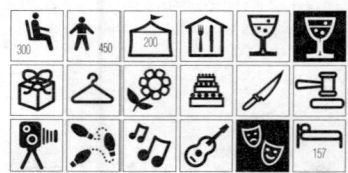

Additional services to those mentioned above include a red carpet, and champagne for the bride and groom on arrival.
Catering: from £14pp

Winter Gardens Hotel
Tregonwell Road
Bournemouth, Dorset BH2 5NU
Tel: 01202 555769 Fax: 01202 551330
Contact: Lorraine Ayrton, Front of House Manager

Ceremony

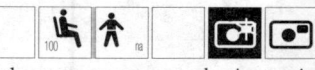

Only one ceremony per day is permitted at the Winter Gardens Hotel. This can be held on any day of the week,

except Sunday. There is no wheelchair access to the hotel. The price guide below refers to room hire only, and does not include the registrar's fee. The hotel permits confetti.
Price guide: from £50

Reception

The hotel can offer themed weddings or cater for special dietary requirements.
Catering: from £6pp

Yenton Hotel
5 Gervis Road
East Cliff
Bournemouth
Dorset BH1 3ED
Tel: 01202 556334 Fax: 01202 298835
Contact: Mr M C McIntosh, Proprietor

Ceremony

The Yenton is set in an acre of gardens on a tree lined avenue. The Tudor Restaurant and Brodies Restaurant are both licensed for civil ceremonies, which can take place here on any day of the year except Christmas Day.
Price guide: P.O.A.

Reception

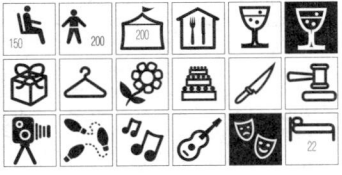

The chef at the hotel was head chef at a five star hotel before joining the Yenton. The hotel specialises in barbecues and garden parties and can arrange all kinds of entertainment including discos, bands and cabaret artists.
Catering: £5pp - £25pp

STOP PRESS
The Royal Chase Hotel, Shaftesbury
Tel: 01747 853355

Bishop Auckland Town Hall
Market Place
Bishop Auckland
Durham DL 14 7NP
Tel: 01388 602610 Fax: 01388 604960
Contact: Gillian Wales, Centre Manager

Ceremony

This Grade II listed civic building is located in the town centre and offers four ceremony rooms. These are available on any day except Bank Holidays.
Price guide: £22

Reception

Catering: Buffets from £1.50pp Sit down from £9.95pp

The Bowes Museum
Newgate
Barnard Castle
Co Durham DL12 8NP
Tel: 01833 690606 Fax: 01833 637163
Contact: Mrs G Conran, Curator

Ceremony

 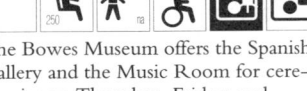

The Bowes Museum offers the Spanish Gallery and the Music Room for ceremonies on Thursdays, Fridays and Saturdays. It is closed on Christmas Day, Boxing Day and New Year's Day. Confetti is not permitted.
Price guide: from £350

Reception
There are no reception facilities at this venue.

The George Hotel
Piercebridge, Darlington
Co. Durham DL2 3SW
Tel: 01325 374576 Fax: 01325 374577
Contact: Mrs Jennifer Wain, Owner

Ceremony

This old coaching inn, with a landscaped riverside setting, offers cere-

monies seven days a week although only one is permitted per day.
Price guide: £45

Reception

The George Hotel prides itself on its family-owned personal touch. As part of its wedding package, the hotel offers free overnight accommodation in the bridal suite for the bride and groom. The hotel also gives a 10% discount off the normal accommodation rates for wedding guests. The reception price guide quoted below includes drinks.
Catering: £22pp

Headlam Hall Hotel
Nr Gainford, Darlington
Co Durham DL2 3HA
Tel: 01325 730238 Fax: 01325 730790
Contact: David Jackson, Manager

Ceremony

This listed building is set in large formal gardens in a secluded rural location. Two ceremony rooms are available on any day of the week except Saturday, with only one ceremony permitted per day. There is room in the grounds for helicopters and hot air balloons to take off.
Price guide: £150

Reception

Catering: Buffets from £15.50pp Sit down from £17.50pp

Lord Crewe Arms Hotel
Blanchland, Co. Durham DH8 9SP
Tel: 01434 675251 Fax: 01434 675337
Contact: Wendy Hart, Receptionist

Ceremony

This scheduled ancient monument offers ceremonies seven days a week with one permitted per day. Ceremonies are only accepted in conjunction with receptions. Confetti is allowed.
Price guide: POA

Reception

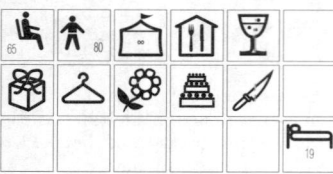

The hotel site is suitable for a marquee with unlimited capacity, while the hotel's restaurant holds an AA rosette.
Catering: from £16.75pp

The Morritt Arms Hotel
Greta Bridge
Rokeby
Nr Barnard Castle
Co. Durham
DL12 9SE
Tel: 01833 627232 Fax: 01833 627392
Contact: Barbara-Anne Johnson, Owner.

Ceremony

The Morritt Arms Hotel is a 17th Century listed building built on the site of a Roman settlement which is still visible today. Its Dickens bar features murals by John Gilroy. Ceremonies are available seven days a week with a maximum of two permitted per day. Ceremony prices vary according to number of guests, from £150 for 25 people, £200 for 25-75 people and £250 for 75-150 people.
Price guide: from £150.

Reception

The hotel has 17 individual, en-suite rooms, some featuring four poster or traditional brass beds - a bridal suite is also available. The site is suitable for a marquee to a capacity of 500.
Catering: from £10pp

Shotton Hall
Peterlee, Co. Durham SR8 2PH
Tel: 0191 5862491 Fax: 0191 5860370
Contacts: Kay Colborn, Deputy Town Clerk and Billy Davies, Banqueting

Ceremony

Shotton Hall, built in 1760 and set in 17.5 acres of grounds, is available to hold ceremonies seven days a week, excluding Christmas Day, New Year's Day, Good Friday and Boxing Day. A maximum of four ceremonies per day are permitted. The price guide to hold ceremonies varies according to the time of week; £20 for weekdays and £30 at weekends and Bank Holidays. The master staircase provides a good setting for indoor photography.
Price guide: from £20

Reception

Reception facilities include a waited service with a capacity of 180 and buffet service for 280. Although Shotton Hall does not have accommodation facilities, a list of accommodation is available.
Catering: from £3.50pp

Walworth Castle Hotel
Walworth, Darlington DL2 2LY
Tel: 01325 485470 Fax: 01325 462257
Contact: Mrs RA Culley

Ceremony

This 12th Century castle is set in 18 acres of gardens and woodland and offers six ceremony rooms.
Price guide: from £50

Reception

Catering: Buffets from £5.50pp Sit down from £14.95pp

STOP PRESS
Hallgarth Golf & Country Club, Darlington 01325 300400
Hardwicke Hall Manor Hotel, Hesleden 01429 836326

Country Park Inn, Cliff Road
Hessleforeshore
Hessle, HU13 0HB
Tel: 01482 644336 Fax: 01482 644336
Contact: Mrs Cross, Conference & Banqueting Co-ordinator

Ceremony

The original part of the building dates back to the 1800s while the Function Suite is a modern addition. The Function Suite is actually set on the banks of the Humber and is only a matter of inches away at high tide. One room is licensed to hold ceremonies at the conference centre, seven days a week, with no restrictions on the number held per day. It is possible to hold ceremonies without reception facilities and confetti is permitted.
Price guide: £200

Reception

Catering prices start from £8.50 a head for a buffet style reception, increasing to £12.50 a head, for a banquet style format. The Conference Centre would like to point out that any catering provisions, including religious dietary requirements, will be considered. Although no accommodation is available on the premises, the centre operates preferential rate agreements with several local hotels and guest houses.
Catering: from £8.50pp

Grange Park Hotel
Main Street
Willerby, HU10 6EA
Tel: 01482 656488 Fax: 01482 655848
Contact: Karen Amann, Conference/Banqueting Co-ordinator

Ceremony

The hotel has two rooms licensed to hold ceremonies, the Mulberry Suite and the Birch Suite, these have recently been refurbished to a high standard to complement ceremonies. Room hire charges for ceremonies are £200 at weekends and £150 for week days. A pedestal of flowers will also be provided for the ceremony room itself. The hotel also features extensive car parking facilities, a helipad and 11 acres of landscaped gardens. Ceremonies are available Monday-Saturday, with no restrictions on Bank Holidays and are only available when held in conjunction with reception facilities.
Price guide: £150-200

Reception

A complimentary overnight stay is available for the bride and groom although a honeymoon suite is available if preferred at a 50% reduction. Special accommodation rates are also available for wedding guests and, when full, the hotel operates preferential rate agreements with other local guest houses. The hotel boasts English cooking in a modern style, and has an adjoining pub and restaurant which specialises in Italian cuisine. The guide indicated below is the starting price, per person, for a sit-down reception which rises to £18pp for buffet style catering.
Catering: from £16.50

Rowley Manor Hotel
Little Weighton
East Riding of Yorkshire
HU20 3XR
Tel: 01482 848248 Fax: 01482 849900
Contact: Mario F Ando, Proprietor

Ceremony

This listed Georgian country house is set in 34 acres of lawns, rose gardens and parklands and was once the rectory to St Peter's church which is also found within the grounds. The rectory is said to have been built in 1621 and in 1928 the house was purchased by a shipping magnate who commissioned the famous Pine panelling by Grinling Gibbons which now forms a central

feature in the study where ceremonies take place. Ceremonies are available throughout the week, excluding Saturdays, with a maximum of one ceremony held per day.
Price guide: from £100+VAT

Reception

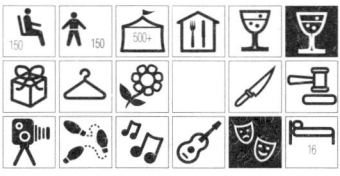

The manor boasts a selection of buffet, finger buffet and sit-down reception menus, including menus which allow the guests to carve meats at their own table. The manor specialises in fresh produce and fresh fish, and it is possible for bridal parties to devise their own menu or interchange dishes from one menu to another. A typical drinks package starts at £8.75 per head.
Catering: £19.95pp

STOP PRESS
Tickton Grange Hotel, Beverley
01964 543666

The Anchor Inn
Anchor Lane
Barcombe
Nr Lewes
East Sussex BN8 5BS
Tel: 01273 400414 Fax: 01273 401029
Contact: Mrs Jaci Bovet-White, Proprietor

Ceremony

This rural 18th Century riverside smuggling inn offers its oriental style Pagoda Room for wedding ceremonies on any day except Bank Holidays.
Price guide: £175 (£100 with reception)

Reception

The Inn tailors each menu to suit. If your reception is for over 20, the honeymoon suite is offer free for the bride and groom to use on their wedding

night. Couples can arrive here by helicopter or balloon (which the Inn can arrange). In addition, the Inn has 30 of its own flat bottomed six seater hand propelled boats. The Inn also has its own white Rolls Royce and access to other classic cars.
Catering: Buffets from £7.50pp Sit down from £12.50pp

Anne of Cleves House
52 Southover High Street
Lewes
East Sussex BN7 1JA
Tel: 01273 474610 Fax: 01273 486990
Contact: Stephen Watts, Senior Custodian

Ceremony

Although it bears her name, this Tudor property was part of Anne of Cleves' estate from which she received rent. It is now a local history museum owned by the Sussex Archaelogical Society. Ceremonies can take place in the East Room on Fridays, Saturdays and Sundays.
Price guide: £200

Reception

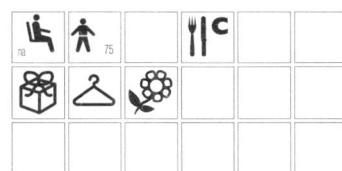

Outside caterers would have to be appointed for a reception at the House. Tudor weddings have, not surprisingly, proved popular here.

Barnsgate Manor Vineyard
Heron's Ghyll
Nr Uckfield
E Sussex
TN22 4DB
Tel: 01825 713366 Fax: 01825 713543
Contact: Keith Johnson, Proprietor

Ceremony

An old stone flagged barn is the marriage room on this 55 acre estate, which is also home to 60 llamas and alpacas. Ceremonies can take place here on any day of the year.
Price guide: £200

Reception

Receptions can be held in the Manor House Restaurant or the Ashdown Restaurant and Disco Cellar, both of which have patios and views over the Ashdown Forest. The vineyard's own wine is, naturally, available for receptions, and includes white and rose wines, as well as an apple wine.
Catering: POA

Beauport Park Hotel
Battle Road
Hastings
E Sussex
TN38 8EA

Tel: 01424 851222 Fax: 01424 852465
Contact: Stephen Bayes, General Manager

Ceremony

Beauport Park is a Georgian country house (1719) set in 35 acres of woodland and gardens, and situated just three miles from Hastings and Battle. Ceremonies can take place here on any day except over the Christmas Holiday.
Price guide: £175 (£125 with reception)

Reception

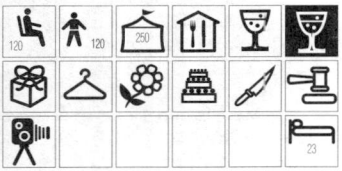

Your reception at Beauport Park can take place in an air conditioned suite. Both the hotel's restaurant and its cocktail bar overlook the formal Italian and sunken gardens. Children under 12 years old are charged at two thirds full price, while children under 3 years old are catered for free. Special weekend rates can be offered to your wedding guests. In addition to the above services, the hotel can also provide a PA system if required.
Catering: £16.50pp

Bentley Wildfowl
& Motor Museum
Halland, Nr Lewes
E Sussex BN8 5AF
Tel & Fax: 01825 840573 or 01825 841322
Contact: Barry Sutherland, Manager

Ceremony

The Motor Museum and Wildfowl Collection are set in the grounds of The Bentley Estate, which covers some 100 acres and includes Bentley House, a Tudor farmhouse that has been converted into a Palladian style mansion. The Museum prefers that weddings do not take place on Bank Holiday weekends. While confetti is not permitted, rice is.
Price guide: £150

Reception

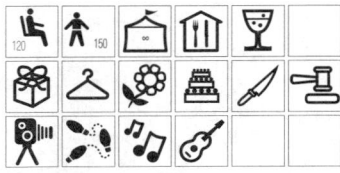

While there is in-house catering, you can also appoint a contract caterer from an approved list. A late night drinking licence can be applied for if required. In addition to the services offered above, the Museum can also provide a veteran, vintage or classic car from its collection. A list of local accommodation is available.
Catering: £10 - £50pp

Buxted Park
Country House Hotel
Buxted Park
Uckfield
E Sussex TN22 4AY
Tel: 01825 732711 Fax: 01825 732770
Contact: Lisa Collins, Conference & Banqueting Co-ordinator

Ceremony

Buxted Park and Country House Hotel is a Georgian mansion, dating from 1725. The hotel is set in 312 acres of parkland featuring exotic plants and lakes. The Library is the licensed marriage room which is available on any day of the year.
Price guide: £150

Reception

Receptions can take place in the hotel's restaurant (for 45) or in its newly renovated Orangery (for 50). Larger parties can be catered for in the Ballroom and Coat of Arms Lounge.
Catering: £47.50pp

Cinque Ports Hotel
Bohemia Road
Hastings
East Sussex TN34 1ET
Tel: 01424 439222 Fax: 01424 437277
Contact: Colin Wilson, General Manager

Ceremony

Cinque Ports allows wedding ceremonies in its Library on any day of the year.
Price guide: £65

Reception

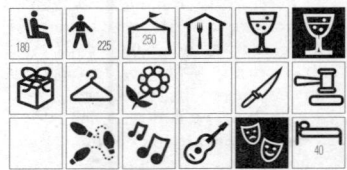

Catering: Buffets from £6.50 Sit down from £12.75

De La Warr Pavilion
Marina, Bexhill-on-Sea
East Sussex TN40 1DP
Tel: 01424 212023 Fax:01424 787940
Contact: Nick Crane

Ceremony

This 1930's Grade I listed civic building is a popular film set (Poirrot was filmed here) and is situated on the seafront with views across the Channel. This Art Deco building has one ceremony room which is available on any day except Christmas Day. Confetti is not permitted.
Price guide: £100

Reception

Two rooms are available for receptions. You may chose your own caterer for this venue.

The Dower House
Bayham Abbey
East Sussex
TN8 8DE
Tel: 01732 778024
Contact: Abigail Penney
Manager

Ceremony

The Dower house (built c1750) was once the home of Lord Camden (of Camden Town fame), and was built in the grounds of what was once an abbey (founded 1208). The ruins of the abbey remain in the grounds, very near to the house, and can be seen from the ceremony room windows. The house (Georgian Gothic in style) and abbey are now under the management of English Heritage.
There is no electric light in the ceremony room itself, and weddings have been held here in candlelight. Confetti here should be flower petals only. Hot air balloons may use the grounds, and horses and carriage may drive anywhere around the abbey grounds.
Price guide: £250

Reception

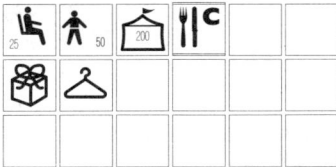

A marquee is set up in the grounds for larger wedding parties, but you can chose your own caterer. Receptions in the house carry restrictions of no smoking and no beer. Wedding parties have exclusive use of the grounds in the evening (the abbey is often open to the public).

The Grand Hotel
King's Road
Brighton
East Sussex BN1 2FW
Tel: 01273 321188 Fax: 01273 202694
Contact: Conference Manager

Ceremony

This famous hotel, built in 1865 and a listed building, is situated on Brighton's seafront. The Emporess Suite is licensed for wedding ceremonies. This breaks down into four separate rooms, the smallest of which will seat 40. Ceremonies must be followed by a reception at the hotel.
Price guide: from £250

Reception

Catering: Packages, including drinks from £39pp

Herstmonceux Castle
Hailsham
E Sussex N27 1RP
Tel: 01323 834479 Fax: 01323 834499
Contact: Banqueting co-ordinator

Ceremony

Herstmonceux is a 15th Century brick built moated castle. It has five rooms licensed for weddings including the ornate Ballroom, which features wood panelling, fireplace and a painted Palladian plaster ceiling. It overlooks an Elizabethan walled garden and courtyard.
Price guide: £250

Reception

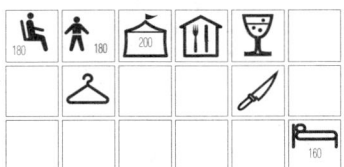

Overnight accommodation is available at Bader Hall on the castle estate.
Catering: £18.55 - £29.95pp

Horsted Place
Little Horsted, Uckfield
Tel: 01825 750581 Fax: 01825 750240
Contact: Sally Chettle, Conference & Banqueting Co-ordinator

Ceremony

This Victorian Gothic mansion permits only one ceremony per day, for a minimum of 20 guests. Confetti is only allowed outside.
Price guide: from £200

Reception

Horsted Place can also arrange car hire if required. A bedroom is usually available on site.
Price guide: P.O.A.

The Manor Barn
c/o Bexhill Old Town Preservation Society
8 High Street, Bexhill TN40 2HA
Tel: 01424 220231
Contact: Miss Madeley, Secretarial Services Manager

Ceremony

This was once the ball room of the late Earl De La Warr and is set amongst the ruins of the Earl's old manor house in a parkland setting. The ceremony licence is held for the hall only.
Price guide: £54

Reception

Couples wishing to hold their reception at the Manor Barn would have to arrange their own catering.

Netherfield Place
Battle, East Sussex TN33 9PP
Tel: 01424 774455 Fax: 01424 774024
Contact: Michael Collier, Proprietor or Nicky Keeling Assistant Manager

Ceremony

This country house hotel set in 30 acres has a licence for its Bayeux room which has limited wheelchair access and is available on all days except Bank Holidays.
Price guide: POA

Reception

Helicopters and hot air balloons may use the grounds.
Catering: Buffets from £7.50pp Sit down from £18pp

Newick Park
Newick
East Susex BN8 4SB
Tel: 01825 723633 Fax: 01825 723969
Contact: Virginia Childs, GM

Ceremony

This Grade II listed Georgian building features Victorian gardens with views over the lake to the South Downs. The Library is the ceremony room and is available all year.
Price guide: from £100 (with reception)

Reception

Newick boasts an award winning chef.
Catering: from £20pp

The Old Ship Hotel
King's Road, Brighton
East Sussex BN1 1NR
Tel: 01273 329001 Fax: 01273 820718
Contact: Alison Tanner

Ceremony

The Old Ship is housed in a Regency building (Grade I listed) and claims to be Brighton's oldest hotel. It is situated on Brighton's seafront, opening up

interesting opportunities for outdoor photography. Ceremonies can take place here on any day of the year, but must be followed by a reception at the hotel.
Price guide: POA

Reception

Receptions can take place in the Paganini Ballroom or the Regency Suite, or both rooms can be used together. Four smaller rooms are also available for receptions of between 20 and 75 guests.
Price guide: from £20pp

The Palace Pier
Madiera Drive
Brighton BN2 1TW
Tel: 01273 609361 Fax: 01273 684289
Contact: RG Strevens, Deputy GM

Ceremony

This famous pier features the Victorias Bar and Palm Court Restaurant which are available for ceremonies from Monday to Friday, but not during Bank Holidays. Ceremonies must be followed by reception here.
Price guide: POA

Reception

Catering: from £6pp

The Powdermills Hotel
Powdermill Lane
Battle, E Sussex TN33 0SP
Tel: 01424 775511 Fax: 01424 774540
Contact: Nick Walker, Manager

Ceremony

The Powdermills Hotel is housed in a

listed building (built 1720), that was originally a famous gunpowder mill. The hotel is set in 150 acres. Only one ceremony is permitted per day on any day of the year. Confetti is not permitted.
Price guide: £175

Reception

The Powdermills Hotel claims a famous chef, and has won many awards for its fine classical cuisine.
Catering: £20pp - £25pp

Queens Hotel
1-5 King's Road
Brighton
E Sussex BN1 1NS
Tel: 01273 321222 Fax: 01273 203059
Contact: Sally Dossetter, Conference & Event Co-ordinator or Nichola Humphrey

Ceremony

Ceremonies can take place on any day of the year at this seafront hotel. Wheelchair access is limited. Outdoor photography can take place in gardens near to the hotel.
Price guide: £175

Reception

Price guide: £16.50pp

The Royal Pavilion
Brighton
E Sussex BN1 1EE
Tel: 01273 603005 Fax: 01273 779108
Contact: Debbie Steel, Functions Co-ordinator

Ceremony

The Royal Pavilion is the famous sea-side palace of King George IV. The Red Drawing Room is available for wedding ceremonies on Fridays and Saturdays, but not Christmas Day or Boxing Day. Confetti is not permitted in the building although biodegradable confetti is allowed in the gardens. The wedding couple may have their photographs taken in either of the two main state rooms.
Price guide: from £275

Reception

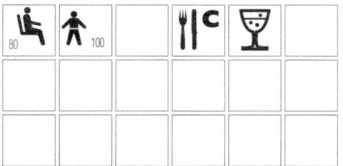

Catering for receptions must be arranged by the couple. A list of local accommodation is available.
Catering: P.O.A

Uckfield Civic Centre
Bell Farm Lane
Uckfield E Sussex TN22 1AE
Tel: 01825 761659 Fax: 01825 765757
Contact: Catering Manager

Ceremony

This conference centre and restaurant offers especially good facilities for the disabled, including lifts and ramps. There is no restriction on the number of ceremonies that can take place here per day. Ceremonies may also be held on any day of the week, except Sunday. The seated capacity for the ceremony can be increased to 350 from 160 if the wedding guests are seated theatre-style. Confetti is allowed at the civic centre, but the site is not suitable for the erection of a marquee.
Price guide: £200

Reception

One of the catering specialities of the Centre's Luxford Lounge Restaurant is home-made Baked Alaska.
Catering: £13 - £30pp

STOP PRESS
Ashdown Park Hotel, Forest Row
01342 824988
Boship Farm Hotel, nr Hailsham
01323 844826
Broomhill Lodge Hotel, Rye
01797 280421
Deans Place Hotel, Polegate
01323 870248
Hydro Hotel, Eastbourne
01323 720643

Chigwell Manor Hall
144 Manor Road
Chigwell, Essex IG7 5PX
Tel: 0181 500 2432 Fax: 0181 500 9926
Contact: Francis Rogers, Director

Ceremony

The banqueting halls have one room licensed to hold ceremonies with a minimum capacity of 30 and maximum of 100. Ceremonies are available seven days a week with no restrictions on the number held per day. It is possible to hold a ceremony without also booking reception facilities, Sunday - Thursday only. Wheelchair access will be available from 1997.
Price guide: P.O.A.

Reception

Catering is in-house with a capacity of 180. The site is not suitable for a marquee. Children can be catered for separately if required. Although Chigwell Manor does not have accommodation available on the premises, a list of accommodation offering preferential rate agreements is available.
Catering: from £15pp

Colchester Town Hall
High Street
Colchester, Essex CO1 1FR
Tel: 01206 282249 Fax: 01206 282228
Contact: Richard Buckle, Town Sargeant

Ceremony

This listed Victorian building has three

rooms licensed to hold ceremonies including the Council Chamber (80), the Grand Jury Room (100) and the Moot Hall (400). Ceremonies are held on Saturdays and Sundays.
Price guide: from £100

Reception

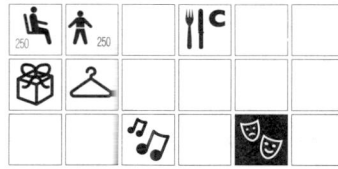

The Town Hall offer various ceremony and reception packages including a ceremony wedding breakfast and an evening reception deal. Catering is entirely on a contract basis to be supplied by the individual. The civic gardens approximately five minutes walk away, are recommended for outdoor photography. Piped music is available in the Moot Hall only.
Catering: POA

Cumberland Banqueting Suite
Pembury Road
Westcliff-on-Sea SS0 8DX
Tel: 01702 346656 Fax: 01702 344662
Contact: Mr M Nelkin, MD

Ceremony

The banqueting suite has two rooms licensed to hold ceremonies, the ballroom and the Princess suite, with capacities from 100 - 200. Ceremonies are available seven days a week with an unlimited amount permitted each day. Ceremonies are free of charge if held in conjunction with receptions.

Reception

Reception capacities vary from 100 to 300 depending on the chosen room and the format of catering. Although the banqueting suite does not provide accommodation on the premises, a list of local accommodation is available and preferential rate agreements have been organised with local hostelries.
Catering: from £15.00pp

Fennes
Fennes Road
Bocking
Braintree
Essex CM7 5PL
Tel: 01376 324555 Fax: 01376 551209
Contact: Edward James Tabor, Proprietor or Ann Drew, GM

Ceremony

The Fennes private house is a Grade II listed building set in a mature, partly moated garden and parkland. It is available to hold ceremonies seven days a week with no restriction on the number permitted a day. The ceremony, which takes place in the Drawing Room, overlooking the water fountain, is free of charge if held in conjunction with a reception.

Reception

Reception catering facilities may take place in the Dining Room, however for parties of over 30, receptions transfer to the house's solid floor, centrally heated marquee which has a capacity of approximately 200. Catering for up to 150 guests may be provided in-house although contract caterers are brought in for any number over this amount. Couples do not have to choose a contract caterer from an approved list. Although accommodation is not available on the premises, preferential rate agreements with local hotels and guest houses can be arranged, and Fennes can provide transport.
Catering: from £18pp.+ VAT drinks package from £6.25 + VAT

Forte Posthouse
Cranes Farm Road
Basildon
Essex SS14 3DG
Tel: 01268 533955 Fax: 01268 530119
Contact: Sarah Lane,

Ceremony

This modern hotel is situated beside a lake in its own landscaped gardens.

Ceremonies are available seven days a week with three ceremonies permitted a day. The price guide to ceremonies starts at £45 and rises to a maximum of £570, depending on your choice of four rooms and time of day.
Price guide: from £90

Reception

In addition to the services indicated here, the hotel offers free car parking and for weddings of 20 adults and over, the bride and groom are given complimentary wedding night accommodation, full English breakfast, champagne and flowers – a first anniversary celebration meal is also provided.
Catering: from £7.95pp.

Friern Manor Country House Hotel
Lower Dunton Road
Dunton
Brentwood
Essex CM3 3SL
Tel: 01268 543222 Fax: 01268 419739
Contact: Mark Ansell, General Manager

Ceremony

This Grade II listed Georgian manor has three areas licensed to hold ceremonies with varying capacities from 15 to 150. Ceremonies are available seven days a week excluding Boxing Day, with a maximum of two permitted a day. Confetti is allowed.
Price guide: £150

Reception

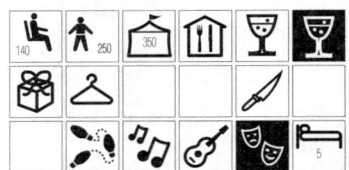

The manor has five bedrooms but also operates preferential rate agreements with other local hotels and guest houses. The venue boasts three baby grand pianos and a marquee with a capacity of up to 350. Ethnic cuisine is also available.
Catering: from £19.50pp.

The Heybridge Hotel
Roman Road
Ingatestone
Essex CM4 9AB
Tel: 01277 355355 Fax: 01277 353288
Contact: Cypriella Kyprianau or Beverley Ashcroft

Ceremony

This Tudor building dates back to 1494. The hotel specialises in conferences and banqueting and offers three ceremony rooms for a minimum of four guests. Wheelchair access is limited. Ceremonies here must be followed by reception at the hotel.
Price guide: POA

Reception

Catering: from £18pp

The Lawn
Hall Road
Rochford, Essex SS4 1PJ
Tel: 01702 203701 Fax: 01702 204752
Contact: Mrs Keddie, Owner

Ceremony

This Grade II listed Georgian mansion is set in three acres of grounds featuring rose gardens. The Blue Drawing Room is licensed to hold ceremonies with a maximum capacity of 80. Ceremonies are permitted seven days a week and are free of charge if held in conjunction with receptions.
Price guide: £295

Reception

An approved list of three caterers is available. A marquee with a capacity of of 400 can be linked to the house for convenience. The large 'brides' bed-

room, although not available for overnight accommodation, provides changing facilities for the bride and groom. The house has preferential rate agreements with local hotels and guest houses.
Catering: from £13pp

Layer Marney Tower
Nr Colchester
Essex CO5 9US
Tel/Fax: 01206 330784
Contact: Sheila Charrington, Owner

Ceremony

This Tudor gatehouse dates back to 1520. It has three licensed rooms with capacities from 10 to 200. There is wheelchair access to two of the rooms. Ceremonies are available seven days a week with restrictions on Christmas Day and New Year. One ceremony only Sat pm.
Price guide: £150

Reception

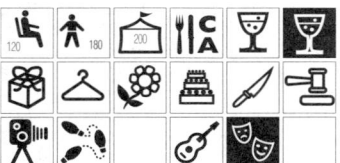

A list of local accommodation is available.
Catering: POA

Leez Priory
Hartford End
Chelmsford
Essex CM3 1JP
Tel: 01245 362555 Fax: 01245 361079
Contact: Sue Morhall, General Manager

Ceremony

This Grade I listed Tudor country house also features an ancient monument and has six rooms licensed to hold ceremonies. The rooms have varying capacities from 40 to 130, only some of which have wheelchair access. Ceremonies are available seven days a week with only one permitted per day on an 'exclusive use guaranteed' basis. The priory does not allow ceremonies to be performed without receptions, however ceremonies are free of charge when in conjunction with a reception.

Reception

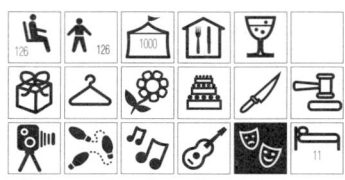

The priory has three double bedrooms, all en-suite, and features a lakeside lodge which sleeps four. In addition to this, a converted granary is planned for the early part of 1997 which may act as a bridal suite or for a family if preferred, again this will sleep four. A list of local accommodation is also available.
Price guide: from £25pp.

Maison Talbooth
Stratford Road
Dedham
Colchester
Essex CO7 6HN
Tel: 01206 322367 Fax: 01206 322752
Contact: Marian Barwell, Manager

Ceremony

Maison Talbooth is a Victorian country house set in the heart of Constable country. The hotel lounge is available for ceremonies any day of the week except Christmas Day. Ceremonies must be followed by reception at the hotel.
Price guide: £175

Reception

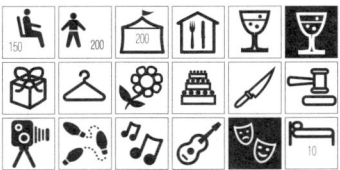

Receptions take place at The Talbooth Restaurant. Couples can arrive and depart by boat, and helicopters and hot air balloons can also use the grounds.
Catering: Buffets from £35pp Sit down from £48pp

The New Oysterfleet
Knightswick Road
Canvey Island
Essex SS8 7UX
Tel: 01268 510111 Fax: 01268 511420
Contact: Julio Moscoso,
General Manager

Ceremony

This conference centre enjoys a town centre location, overlooking a lake. Ceremonies may take place in the Lakeside Room on any day of the year. Confetti is not permitted.
Price guide: POA

Reception

Catering: POA

Orsett Hall Hotel
Prince Charles Avenue
Orsett
Grays
Essex
RM16 3HS
Tel: 01375 891402 Fax: 01375 891135
Contact: Stephen Haynes, Managing Director

Ceremony

This 17th Century listed building is set in 12 acres of grounds and has ceremonies available seven days a week excluding Saturdays during the months May to September. One ceremony is allowed per day. Confetti is permitted.
Price guide: £175

Reception

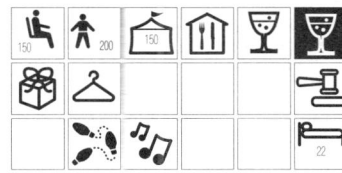

Three rooms are available to hold receptions, with varying capacities of 30 to 150, a marquee is also available with a capacity of 150. The hotel has 22 bedrooms but also operates preferential rate agreements with local hotels and guest houses. The provision of the toast-master is included in the price of the reception.
Price guide: from £20pp.

Packfords Hotel
16 Snakes Lane West
Woodford Green
Essex IG8 0BS
Tel: 0181 504 2642 Fax: 0181 505 5778
Contact: Mr Simon Packford, Owner

Ceremony

The hotel offers ceremonies six days a week, with Sundays being unavailable, with a maximum of one wedding per day. Confetti is permitted.
Price guide: £100

Reception

Buffet reception facilities are to a capacity of 130, with a capacity of 80 for a waited service. The hotel has 10 double bedrooms and one single and also operates preferential rate agreements with local hotels and guest houses.
Catering: from £18pp.

Parsonage Farm Guest House
Parsonage Farm
Abridge Road
Theydon Bois
Near Epping CM16 7NN
Tel: 01992 814242 Fax: 01992 814242
Contact: Mr Steve Dale or Mrs Marion Dale, Events Managers

Ceremony

This listed farmhouse is set in its own gardens, and features oak timber throughout. Ceremonies are available seven days a week with a maximum of five per day. Confetti is permitted outside only.
Price guide: £150

Reception

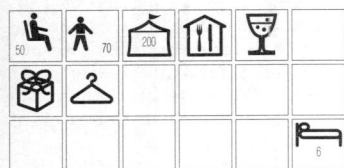

The guest house site is suitable for a marquee with a capacity of 200 and features six bedrooms, all en-suite. The guest house prides itself on its Provence style à la carte French menus, but regrets children cannot be catered for separately.
Price guide: from £25pp.

Pontlands Park Hotel
West Hanningfield Road
Great Baddow
Chelmsford
Essex CM2 8HR
Tel: 01245 476444 Fax: 01245 478393
Contact: Miss Angela Webb, General Manager

Ceremony

Pontlands Park is a Victorian mansion, originally built in 1897 and set in its own grounds. Ceremonies are available seven days a week with no restrictions on the number permitted a day. Confetti is allowed.
Price guide: £150

Reception

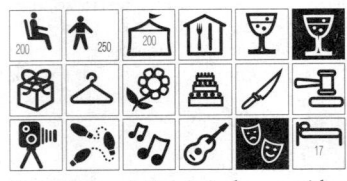

Reception catering is in-house with a maximum waited service capacity of 200 and buffet capacity of 250. A marquee is also available to a capacity of 200.
Catering: £30pp.

Prince Regent Hotel
Manor Road
Woodford Bridge
Essex IG8 8AE
Tel: 0181 5059966 Fax: 0181 506 0807
Contact: John Parket, Banqueting Manager

Ceremony

This Grade II listed building is available to hold ceremonies seven days a week with a maximum of three per day. Confetti is allowed. The price guide varies from £75 to £250.
Price guide: from £75

Reception

Catering facilities are provided in-house, although contract caterers are permitted on days other than Saturdays. Contract catering is necessary for Kosher and Asian weddings. A marquee is also available with a capacity of 150 and chauffeured cars are offered in addition to the services indicated.
Catering: £25pp.

The Roebuck
North End
Buckhurst Hill
Essex IG9 5QY
Tel: 0181 505 4636 Fax: 0181 504 7826
Contact: Ann Bush, Banqueting Co-ordinator

Ceremony

The hotel was originally an 18th Century coaching inn and has three rooms licensed for ceremonies with capacities varying from 25 to 150. However, there is only wheelchair access to two of the rooms. Ceremonies are available seven days a week and confetti is permitted outside only.
Price guide: £125

Reception

Indoor photography is recommended on the hotel's feature staircase, whilst the green in front of the hotel is recommended for outside photographs.
Catering: £20pp

Rose & Crown Hotel
East Gates
Colchester
Essex CO1 2TZ
Tel: 01206 866677 Fax: 01206 866616
Contact: Diana Warren, Front of House Manager

Ceremony

This 15th Century Tudor inn is now a listed building, and has recently undergone refurbishment. Three ceremony rooms are offered, suitable for 4 to 100 guests.
Price guide: POA

Reception

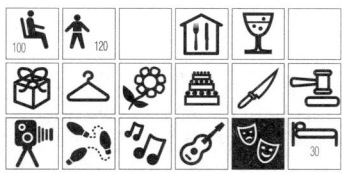

Catering: Buffet from £7.95pp Sit down from £23.50pp

South Lodge Hotel
196 New London Road
Chelmsford
Essex CM2 0AR
Tel: 01245 264564 01245 492827
Contact: Wedding Co-ordinator

Ceremony

This original Georgian house has a ceremony capacity of 40 and offers ceremonies seven days a week with no restrictions on the number permitted a day. Confetti is allowed.
Price guide: £100

Reception

Catering facilities are in-house and to a maximum of 100. The hotel has 42 bedrooms but also operates preferential rate agreements with local hotels and guest houses.
Catering: from £12pp.

Three Rivers Golf & Country Club
Stow Road
Cold Norton
Nr Purleigh
Essex CM3 6RR
Tel: 01621 828631 Fax: 01621 828060

Contact: Andrew Rimmington, Banqueting Manager

Ceremony

The ceremony room, the Lake Suite, is available any day of the week, with only one ceremony permitted per day. Helicopters and hot air balloons can land on site.
Price guide: from £250

Reception

Catering: Buffets from £8pp Sit down from £14pp

Tower Hotel
Main Road
Dovercourt
Nr Harwich
Essex CO12 3PJ
Tel/Fax: 01255 504952
Contact: Mrs Lynn Sherwood, GM

Ceremony

This listed period building overlooks the river. It offers one ceremony room, The River Room which is available on any day of the week. Confetti is permitted outside only.
Price guide: £100

Reception

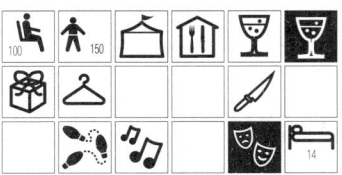

The hotel offers a choice of two honeymoon suites.
Catering: Buffets from £8pp Sit down from £12pp

The Westcliff Hotel
Westcliff Parade
Westcliff-on-Sea
Essex SS0 7QW
Tel: 01702 345247 Fax: 01702 431814

Contact: Mrs Sarah Davidson, Conference and Banqueting Manager

Ceremony

The hotel has one room licensed to hold ceremonies with a maximum capacity of 100. Ceremonies are available seven days a week with no restriction on the number held per day. Confetti is allowed.
Price guide: £250

Reception

The catering price guide ranges from under £10 to a maximum of £22. The hotel has 55 bedrooms in total with reduced rates offered to wedding guests, and a wide range of bridal suites available. In addition to the services indicated here, the hotel can also recommend car hire facilities.
Catering: from £7.75pp.

Whitehall Hotel
Church End
Broxted, Essex CM6 2BZ
Tel: 01279 850603 Fax: 01279 850385
Contact: Jonathon Beck, Assistant Manager

Ceremony

The family owned Whitehall Hotel is an Elizabethan manor house set in a walled garden. The hotel is conveniently situated for Stansted Airport. Three rooms are licensed, The Butlers Suite, the Audley Suite and the Restaurant, and these are available on Fridays, Saturdays and Sundays. Confetti is not permitted.
Price guide: £350

Reception

The hotel offers several wedding and party packages which include drinks, with discounts offered for Friday or Sunday weddings.
Catering: from £20pp

STOP PRESS

The Coach House, Braintree
01371 850228
Five Lakes Hotel & Country Club, Maldon 01621 868888
Kingsford Park Hotel, Kingsford
01206 734301
Marygreen Manor Hotel, Brentwood
01277 225252
Thurrock Masonic Hall, Grays
01375 375695
Warren Golf Club, Maldon
01245 223258

Bear of Rodborough Hotel
Rodborough
Stroud
Glos GL5 5DE
Tel: 01453 878522 Fax: 01453 872523
Contact: Mr Hutton, General Manager

Ceremony

This 17th Century building is surrounded by 500 acres of National Trust land. The Garden Room is available for wedding ceremonies every day except Christmas Day.
Price guide: from £50

Reception

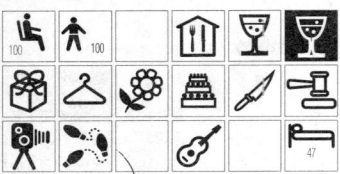

The restaurant serves traditional English cuisine. If the hotel is full, other local establishments can be recommended for your guests.
Catering: from £14pp

Bell's Hotel
Lord's Hill
Coleford
Glos GL16 8BD
Tel: 01594 832583 Fax: 01594 832584
Contact: Charlotte Clifford-Weston, GM

Ceremony

This hotel and golf club offers one ceremony per day, seven days a week: but only in conjunction with receptions. There is no room charge for the ceremony. Confetti is not permitted.
Price guide: FOC (with reception)

Reception

The Bell's Hotel, is attached to the Forest of Dean Golf Club, which is open to non-members.
Catering: from £12pp

Calcot Manor Hotel
Calcot, Glos GL8 8YJ
Tel: 01666 890391 Fax: 01666 890394
Contact: Paul Sadler, Manager

Ceremony

Calcot Manor is one of the oldest tithe barns in the country, and is available for ceremonies Monday to Saturday.
Price guide: £150

Reception

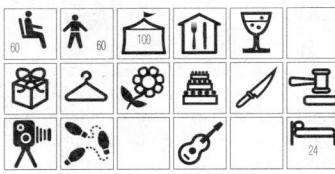

Only one large event is possible per day.
Catering: from £17pp

Charingworth Manor
Charingworth
Chipping Camden,
Glos GL55 6NS
Tel: 01386 593555 Fax: 01386 593353
Contact: Pamela Jackson, Sales Manager

Ceremony

This historic country house is set on a private estate in the rolling Cotswold countryside. The Conservatory and The Long Room hold wedding licences and are available any day of the year.
Price guide: £500

Reception

Helicopters and hot air balloons may use the grounds.
Catering: Buffets from £30pp Sit down from £35pp

Cheltenham Racecourse
Prestbury
Cheltenham
Glos GL50 4SH
Tel: 01242 570150 Fax: 01242 579356
Contact Sheila Day, Manager

Ceremony

The ceremony room is available daily throughout the year, although it would be wise to avoid Gold Cup Day. Two ceremonies are possible per day.
Price guide: £50 (with reception)

Reception

As one might expect from a venue used to dealing with large crowds, Cheltenham Racecourse emphasises the flexibility of its catering services. It is excellently equipped to deal with groups from as small as 10 up to larger parties of up to 350. Please note that the venue's in-house team is also available for outside catering assignments.
Catering: from £18pp

Clearwell Castle
Church Road
Clearwell, Coleford
Glos GL16 8LG
Tel: 01594 832320 Fax: 01594 835523
Contact: Dominic Haffner, Estate Manager

Ceremony

This Grade II listed stately home offers

ceremonies Friday to Saturday, with four possible daily.
Price guide: £150-£300

Reception

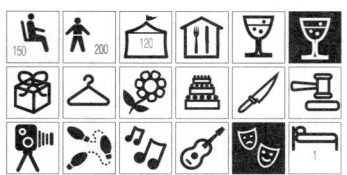

Indian cuisine is available.
Catering: from £25pp

The Close Hotel
Tetbury, Glos GL8 8AQ
Tel: 01666 502272 Fax: 01666 504401
Contact: Sophia McLeod or Jonathon Dawson

Ceremony

Part of the Virgin Collection, The Close Hotel, a small country house hotel, offers up to two ceremonies daily, excluding Bank Holidays.
Price guide: £199

Reception

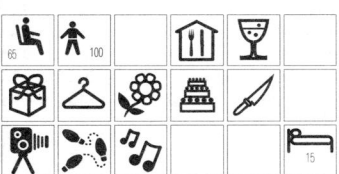

The hotel can be hired on an exclusive use basis, from £2,500.
Catering: Buffets from £8.95pp

The Fleet Inn and Restaurant
Twyning
Tewkesbury, Glos GL20 6DG
Tel: 01684 274310
Contact: Roy Probin, Catering Manager

Ceremony

The Fleet enjoys a riverside setting, where couples can arrive and depart by boat. The Avon Conservatory is the licensed wedding room and is available on any day of the year. Ceremonies must be followed by reception at the Inn.
Price guide: FOC (with reception)

Reception

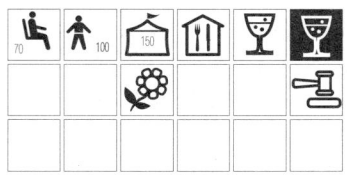

Catering: Buffets from £4.25pp Sit down from £14.95pp

Frogmill Inn
Shipton Oliffe
Cheltenham, Glos GL54 4HT
Tel: 01242 852237 Fax: 01242 820237
Contact: John Griffith, Proprietor

Ceremony

Frogmill Inn dates from the Domesday Book and is set in five acres.
Price guide: £50

Reception

Two dining areas, one for up to 60, one for up to 200. Can cater for special diets.
Catering: from £15pp

Grapevine Hotel
Sheep Street, Stow-on-the-Wold
Glos GL54 1AU
Tel: 01451 830344 Fax: 01451 832278
Web site: http://www.vines.co.uk/
Contact: Davids Nott, GM

Ceremony

This 17th Century hotel offers a maximum of two ceremonies per day, seven days a week, in its Georgian Room or Restaurant.

Reception

A conservatory restaurant, canopied by a grapevine, seats 80 for waited service. The two AA rosetted restaurant offers modern English cuisine with Continental influences.
Catering £15pp

Greenway
Shurdington
Cheltenham
Glos GL51 5UG
Tel: 01242 862352 Fax: 01242 862780
Contact: David A White, Proprietor

Ceremony

The Greenway is a 16th Century manor house set in seven acres. Ceremony facilities are available daily except Sundays, subject to a maximum of one event per day, in conjunction with reception bookings. No confetti.
Price guide: £350

Reception

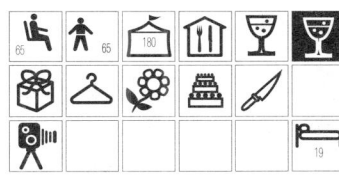

The restaurant holds three rosettes. The hotel offers various packages that can be tailored to your individual needs. A typical example, including wines/champagne costs £55pp. The management is happy to arrange additional services, such as car hire and hairdressing.
Catering: from £22pp

Hare & Hounds Hotel
Westonbirt
Tetbury
Glos GL8 8QL
Tel: 01666 880233 Fax: 01666 880241
Contact: Jeremy Price or Martin Price, Proprietors

Ceremony

The hotel offers ceremonies every day of the year, subject to a maximum of two daily. The Cotswold stone building is set in its own large gardens.
Price guide: from £150

Reception

Catering: from £18pp

Hatherly Manor Hotel
Down Hatherly Lane
Down Hatherly, Glos GL2 9QA
Tel: 01452 730217 Fax: 01452 731032
Contact: Maria Bone, Conf and Banq
Manager

Ceremony

This 17th Century manor house, set in
37 acres, is available for ceremonies on
any day except Saturdays, Christmas
Eve, Christmas Day, Boxing Day, New
Year's Eve and New Year's Day. Up to
two ceremonies are permitted per day.
Price guide: £75

Reception

The Manor House has an AA Rosette
for its food.
Catering: from £17pp

Hatton Court Hotel
Upton Hill
Upton St Leonards
Glos GL4 8DE
Tel: 01452 612412 Fax: 01452 612945
Contact: Jacqui Peachey, Conf & Banq
Manager

Ceremony

Hatton Court is a 17th Century
Cotswold manor house, set in seven
acres of gardens and 30 acres of pasture.
Its position at 600 ft above sea level
provides excellent views over the
Severn Valley. One ceremony is possible per day, excluding the Christmas
and New Year holiday period.
Price guide: £95

Reception

Hatton Court offers various inclusive
reception packages, which can be tailored to suit your needs.
Catering from £24.95pp

Lords of the Manor
Upper Slaughter
Cheltenham
Glos GL54 2JD
Tel: 01451 820243 Fax: 01451 820696
Contact: Richard Young, General
Manager

Ceremony

This former rectory dates from the 17th
Century, and is set in eight acres of
grounds including a trout lake and
parkland. It offers facilities for one ceremony daily from Monday to Saturday
throughout the year.
Price guide: from £200

Reception

The award-winning restaurant offers
reception facilities for a maximum of
120, but up to 400 could be accommodated in a marquee. Accolades include
a Michelin star and three AA rosettes.
Catering: from £26pp

Manor House Hotel
High Street
Moreton-in-Marsh
Gloucestershire GL56 0LJ
Tel: 01608 650501 Fax: 01608 651481
Contact: Miss Meriel Neighbour, GM

Ceremony

This listed building dates back to 1545.
It has links with the Creswyke family
and has its own resident ghost, and a

priest hole. The four Shires Suite is
licensed and will take from 50 to 108
guests.
Price guide: £150

Reception

The AA Rosetted restaurant can pre-
pare vegan and vegetarian dishes on
request.
Catering: Buffets from £16.50pp Sit
down from £20pp

Painswick Hotel
Painswick
Stroud
Glos GL6 6UF
Tel: 01452 812160 Fax: 01452 814059
Contact: Julia Robb, Manager

Ceremony

This Grade II listed Palladian style stone
building was formerly a rectory. It is
set in its own gardens featuring a croquet lawn. Ceremonies are possible
from Monday to Friday, with only one
per day. Confetti is not permitted.
Ceremonies can only be held with a
reception.
Price guide: £60

Reception

Catering: £18pp

Painswick House
Painswick
Glos GL6 6TH
Tel: 01452 813646 Fax: 01452 813204
Contact: Lady Dickinson, Owner

Ceremony

Painswick House is a privately owned
Georgian stately home, and permits one

ceremony per day throughout the year.
Price guide: POA

Reception

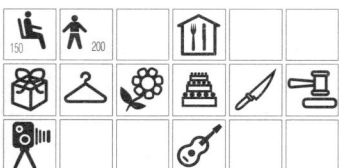

In-house catering is available, although alternative arrangements can be made for larger parties.
Catering: POA

Pittville Pump Room
Pittville Park
Cheltenham
Glos GL52 3JE
Tel: 01242 523852 Fax: 01242 526563
Contact: Mr Chris Aldred, Manager

Ceremony

This neo-classical Grade I listed building is managed by Cheltenham Borough Council and houses the Cheltenham Spa waters. Ceremonies can be held daily, excluding Christmas Day, subject to a maximum of four per day. There are several rooms available.
Price guide: £100 per hour

Reception

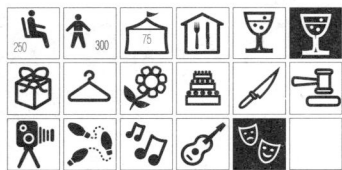

The Pump Room offers flexible menus – allowing guests to choose between courses on the day. A list of local accommodation options is available.
Catering: from £15pp

Prestbury House Hotel & Restaurant
The Burgage, Prestbury
Cheltenham Glos GL52 3DN
Tel: 01242 529533 Fax: 01242 227076
Contact: Jacqueline Whitbourn, Proprietor

Ceremony

This 300 year old country manor house is Grade II listed and set it four acres of grounds. The Georgian and Oak rooms hold the wedding licence and are available any day of the year, with one ceremony only per day. Helicopters and hot air balloons can land/take off on site.
Price guide: POA

Reception

Catering: POA

Puckrup Hall Hotel & Golf Club
Puckrup
Tewkesbury
Glos GL20 6EL
Tel: 01684 296200 Fax: 01684 850788
Contact: Maureen Harding, Conf & Banq Manager

Ceremony

This Regency mansion is set in over 140 acres of parkland, and has its own 18 hole golf course. The hotel's Gloucester Suite has the wedding licence. This room can be divided into four, with a minimum capacity for 20. Ceremonies are restricted to one per day.
Price guide: £150

Reception

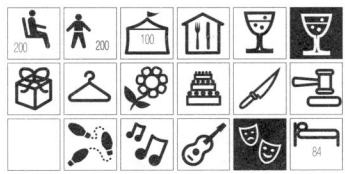

Two rooms are available for receptions; the Gloucester Suite and the Ballroom. The hotel has its own helipad and an area for hot air balloons. Drinks packages start at £9.25pp.
Catering: from £20pp

The Queens Hotel
Promenade
Cheltenham, Glos GL50 1NN
Tel: 01242 514724 Fax: 01242 262538
Contact: Vicky Hickson, Wedding Co-ordinator

Ceremony

Up to five ceremonies per day are permitted in The Gold Cup Room. Confetti is not permitted indoors or out.
Price guide: £150

Reception

Catering: Buffets from £7.50 Sit down from £18.75

Stonehouse Court Hotel
Stonehouse, Glos GL10 3RA
Tel: 01453 825155 Fax: 01453 824611
Contact: Rebekah Murphy, Business Co-ordinator

Ceremony

This Grade II listed manor house (1601), is built in typical Cotswold stone and is set in six acres of secluded gardens. Three rooms are available for wedding ceremonies and range in capacity from 20 to 80. Only the larger room is suitable for wheelchair access. Helicopters and hot air balloons may use the grounds.
Price guide: £150

Reception

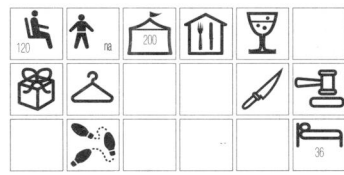

Catering: from £18pp

Stratton House Hotel
Gloucester Road
Cirencester, Glos GL7 2LE
Tel: 01285 651761
Contact: Claire Mallen

Ceremony

This country house hotel is set in its own grounds, 1/2 mile from Cirencester.
Price guide: POA

Reception

Catering: POA

The Swan Hotel
Bibury
Glos GL7 5NW
Tel: 01285 740695 Fax: 01285 740473
Contact: John Stevens, GM

Ceremony

The Swan offers facilities for daily ceremonies throughout the year.
Price guide: from £150

Reception

Catering: £15–60pp

STOP PRESS
The Beehive, Cheltenham
01242 579443
The Old Rectory Hotel, Cheltenham
01242 673766
Tewkesbury Park Hotel, Tewkesbury
01684 295405
Wyck Hill House Hotel, Stow on the Wold 01451 831936

Alton House Hotel
Normady Street
Alton
Hants GU34 1DW
Tel: 01420 80033 Fax: 01420 89222
Contact: David Knights, General Manager

Ceremony

Set near the centre of the old market town of Alton, this Victorian built hotel has over two acres of landscaped gardens and an outdoor pool.
Price guide: £60

Reception

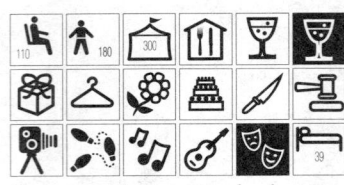

Recommendations can also be given for horse and carriages, cars, video and balloons.
Catering £21.50

Ashburn Hotel
Station Road
Fordingbridge
Hants SP6 1JP
Tel: 01425 652060 Fax: 01425 652150
Contact: Terri Robson, Director

Ceremony

The hotel is set in landscaped gardens. Its Garden Room is licensed for ceremonies and is available on Wednesdays and Saturdays.
Price guide: £100

Reception

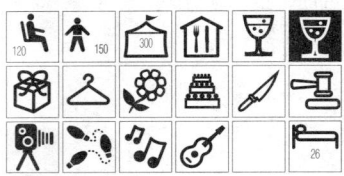

The hotel has an award winning chef and can offer a vegetarian menu, a medieval banquet or an Elizabethan feast.
Catering: Buffets from £7pp Sit down from £12pp

Bartley Lodge Hotel
Cadnam
Hants SO40 2NR
Tel: 01703 812248 Fax: 01703 812075
Contact: Rachel Smith, Manager (Tel: 01703 283717)

Ceremony

This Grade II listed hunting lodge (1759) is set in eight acres of parkland and walled gardens. Interior features include a minstrel's gallery and a grand oak panelled room. Two rooms are available for ceremonies. Only one ceremony is permitted per day.
Price guide: from £200

Reception

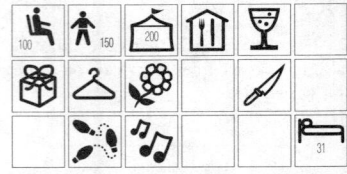

A late night drinking licence will be applied for on request. Special catering features include barbecues and spit roasts. A complimentary bridal suite on the wedding night is part of the wedding package. In the past, couples have had firework displays in the grounds, and one couple even parachuted in for their wedding! The Lodge is part of Care Hotels plc which has four other country houses in the area, offering special rates for guests.
Catering: from £18pp

Botleigh Grange Hotel
Hedge End
Southampton, Hants SO30 2GA
Tel: 01489 787700 Fax: 01489 788535
Contact: Conference co-ordinator

Ceremony

This 17th Century country house is set in parkland with lakes and a sweeping drive. Ceremonies can take place here any day of the week, with a space of 90 minutes left between weddings. Confetti is only allowed outside.
Price guide: £100

Reception

Catering: £18.95

The Burley Manor Hotel
Burley, Ringwood
Hants BH24 4BS

Tel: 01425 403522 Fax: 01425 403227
Contact: Andrew Rogers, GM

Ceremony

This RAC/AA 3 star hotel is set in five acres of landscaped grounds with an outdoor pool. One ceremony per day is allowed on any day excluding Sundays and Bank Holidays.
Price guide: £200

Reception

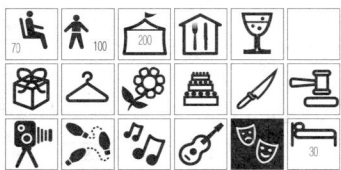

The hotel can help you to arrange balloons, helicopters and horse drawn carriages.
Catering: from £19.75

Celebration Plaza
3 Terminus Terrace
Southampton, Hants SO14 3DT
Tel: 01703 322260/322240
Fax: 01703 366646
Contact: David Onslow, GM

Ceremony

This restaurant and nightclub is owned by Matthew Le Tissier and Mike Osman. The ground floor nightclub and restaurant area is licensed for ceremonies which can take place here on any day except Bank Holidays.
Price guide: POA

Reception

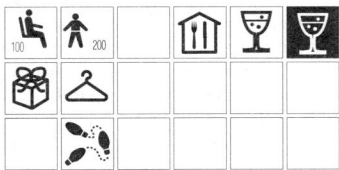

Catering: POA

Chewton Glen Hotel
Christchurch Road
New Milton
Hants BH25 6QS
Tel: 01425 275341 Fax: 01425 273310
Contact: Thierry Lepoinoy, Banqueting Manager

Ceremony

A renowned health and country club with five stars AA and RAC rating, Chewton Glen offers wedding ceremonies on any day of the week and allows up to two ceremonies per day. No confetti is allowed.
Price guide: £350

Reception

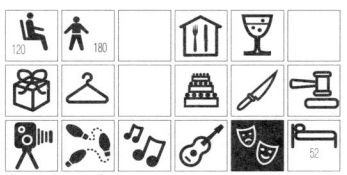

Chewton Glen's catering has earned it one Michelin star. Discos and live music are available upon discussion with the hotel.
Catering: £70pp (fully inclusive)

Elmers Court Country Club
South Baddesley Road
Lymington, Hants SO41 5BZ
Tel: 01590 676011 Fax: 01590 679780
Contact: Banqueting Manager

Ceremony

This Tudor manor is set in 25 acres with lawns sweeping down to the Solent. One room, the Waterford Room is licensed for ceremonies on any day except Christmas Day. There is room in the grounds for helicopters and hot air balloons.
Price guide: £200

Reception

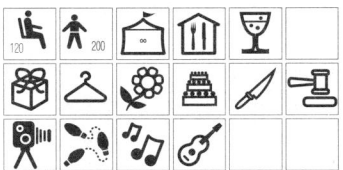

This is a time-share country club, so although it has rooms, these are largely privately owned and would not be available to your wedding guests. However, the venue is able to offer a complimentary suite to the newly weds as part of the wedding package. Elmers Court can provide seasonal menus, and while there is currently no late night drinking licence, this can be applied

---

for. Special entertainments can be arranged.
Catering: £15pp

Essebourne Manor Hotel
Hurstbourne Tarrant
Andover
Hants SP11 0ER
Tel: 01264 736444 Fax: 01264 736725
Contact: I Hamilton, Proprietor

Ceremony

This country house hotel holds a wedding licence for its Dining Room. This is available seven days a week, with one ceremony permitted per day.
Price guide: £200

Reception

Helicopters and hot air balloons may use the grounds.
Catering: POA

The Falcon Hotel
68 Farnborough Road
Farnborough, Hants GU14 6TH
Tel: 01252 545378 Fax: 01252 522539
Contact: Mandy Childs, GM

Ceremony

This town centre hotel has one room licensed for ceremonies, which is available any day except Christmas Day. The ceremony room hire fee is reduced to £35 if you also hold you reception at the venue. A small patio is the only area available for outdoor photography.
Price guide: £75

Reception

While there is no late night drinking licence for non-residents, this can be

applied for if required. The reception package (and price guide below) includes a drink on arrival as well as the room hire.
Catering: £20.65pp

The Forest Park Hotel
Rhinefield Road
Brockenhurst, Hants SO42 7ZG
Tel: 01590 622844 Fax: 01590 623948
Contact: Sales Manager

Ceremony

Originally built as a vicarage, this venue became an hotel in 1902. The hotel, set in four acres, boasts a tennis court, outdoor heated pool, and log cabin sauna. Weddings can take place in the Morant Room on any day of the week, with only one ceremony permitted per day.
Price guide: £125

Reception

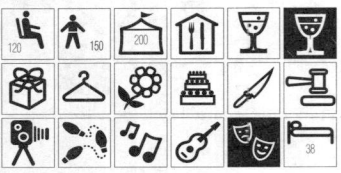

Catering: from £20pp

The Fountain Court Hotel
Frost Lasne, Hythe
Southampton, Hants SO45 3NE
Tel: 01703 846310 Fax: 01703 847295
Contact: Mrs V Harris, Proprietress

Ceremony

Built in 1856, the hotel boasts intricate decor, a garden fountain and an under-garden chamber. The Garden Room holds the wedding licence and is available any day except Christmas Day and Good Friday. There is no ceremony room hire fee if your reception is also held at the hotel.
Price guide: FOC (with reception)

Reception

The hotel offers a wide vegetarian menu, as well as a children's menu, with cuisine ranging from Cajun to oriental, French and American. Helicopters and hot air balloons can use the site.
Catering: Buffets from £5pp Sit down from £12.50pp

The Grange Hotel
London Road
Alton
Hants GU34 4EG
Tel: 01420 86565   Fax: 01420 541346
Contact: Sandra Ford,
Function and conference co-ordinator

Ceremony

This 3-star, 4-crown, privately owned hotel is set in two acres of gardens. Two rooms are licensed for ceremonies seating a minimum of 20 guests. Ceremonies are not usually available on a Saturday here, depending on the size of the wedding.
Price guide: £100

Reception

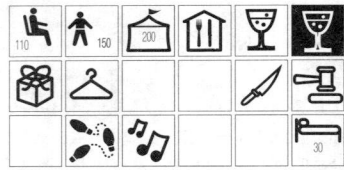

Catering: Buffets from £7.95pp Sit down from £23.50 (inc drinks)

Highclere Castle
Highclere
Hants RG15 9RN
Tel: 01635 253210 Fax: 01635 810193
Contact: Lindsey Giles,
Event Co-ordinator

Ceremony

Highclere Castle is a listed building and is claimed to be the finest Victorian home still in existence. Ceremonies can take place in the Library Room or the Salon. The venue encourages late afternoon civil ceremonies and receptions during the Castle's open season from May to September. Confetti is not permitted.
Price guide: £1000 + VAT

Reception

Catering: POA

HMS Warrior
HM Naval Base
Portsmouth
Hants PO1 2QX
Tel: 01705 291379 Fax: 01705 821283
Contact: Mrs Sorel Mitchell, Special Events Manager

Ceremony

This restored 1860's warship lies within Portsmouth's Historic Dockyard. Ceremonies take place in the Captain's Cabin. Availability on application. Confetti and smoking are not permitted, and ladies are requested not to wear high heels.. Photography is allowed on the upper deck, the main gun deck and in the Captain's Cabin.
Price guide: £500

Reception

Receptions may be held on board after the ship is closed to the pubilc following a late afternoon ceremony. These are held in the Wardroom (20), on the Half Deck (up to 50) or on the Gun Deck for larger numbers. There is a choice of two contract caterers who will obtain the relevant drinks licence and can provide cake stand and knife if required. Advice on local accommodation is available together wih a wide choice of photographers and musicians.
Catering £10-£25

Lainston House Hotel
Sparsholt
Winchester, Hants SO21 2LT
Tel: 01962 863588 Fax: 01962 776248
Contact: Patsy Enright, Sales & Marketing Manager

Ceremony

This William and Mary, 17th Century, country house hotel is set in 63 acres of parkland featuring a lime tree avenue. One ceremony is permitted per day on any day except Christmas and New Year but only with reception
Price guide: from £200

Reception

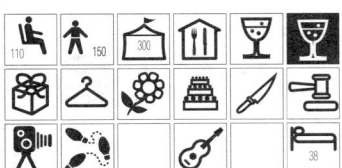

Lainston House offers several rooms for receptions including the Dawley Barn (a 17th Century half-timbered barn). For larger numbers a marquee can be set up on the lawn adjacent to the dining room. Wedding menus include Gourmet and Gastronomique options for a maximum of 16 people. Reception room hire of £775 includes a toastmaster.
Catering: from £28pp

Lismoyne Hotel
Church Road
Fleet, Hants GU11 8NA
Tel: 01252 628555 Fax: 01252 811761
Contact: Marcus Can Hagen, GM

Ceremony

This 4-crown, AA 3-star, hotel can offer ceremonies on any day.
Price guide: £375

Reception

Car hire can also be arranged by the venue.
Catering: £19pp

Lyndhurst Park Hotel
High Street
Lyndhurst
Hants SO43 7NL

Tel: 01703 283923 Fax: 01703 283019
Contact: Sue Cotton, Banqueting Manager

Ceremony

Located on the edge of the New Forest, Lyndhurst Park is set in its own gardens of five acres. The hotel has one room licensed for wedding ceremonies, which can take place on any day of the week. The hotel allows up to four ceremonies per day.
Price guide: from £160

Reception

Marquee only for daylight hours.
Catering: £22pp

Mottisfont Abbey
Mottisfont
Romsey
Hants SO51 0LP
Tel: 01794 340757 Fax: 01794 341492
Contact: Julie Evans, Visitor Services Manager

Ceremony

This National Trust property is set on a tributary to the River Test. Its grounds feature lawns and gardens, (including a collection of old-fashioned roses), while inside the house is a room painted by Whistler. The Morning Room holds the Ceremony licence. This is available from Wednesday to Saturday inclusive. Confetti is not permitted.
Price guide: POA

Reception

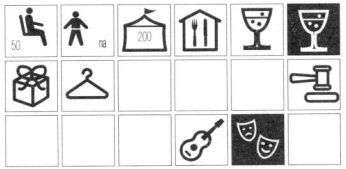

Catering at the Abbey includes fresh local produce such as trout from the River Test.
Catering: POA

New Place Management Centre
High Street, Shirrell Heath
Southampton, Hants SO32 2JH
Tel: 01329 833543 Fax: 01329 833259
Contact: Sue Conduct

Ceremony

This Grade I listed building was designed by Sir Edwin Lutyens and is set in 30 acres of landscaped gardens and woodland. It also has a swimming pool.
Price guide: £150

Reception

Cuisine by Laurent Beaunier, ex-Boulestin. Venue hire for the reception is £1,000.
Catering: from £25pp

Portsmouth Football Club
Fratton Park
57 Frogmore Road
Portsmouth, Hants PO3 8RA
Tel: 01705 731204 Fax: 01705 734124
Contact: Commercial Manager

Ceremony

The club's Board Room is the marriage room. Ceremonies can take place on any day when there is not an afternoon home match.
Price guide: £200

Reception

Catering: POA

Portsmouth Marriott
North Harbour
Portsmouth, Hants PO6 4SH
Tel: 01705 383151 Fax: 01705 388701
Contact: Tiffany Rowe, Meetings Manager

Ceremony

The Mary Rose Suite can take a minimum of 70 guests with only one ceremony allowed per day, on any day except the Christmas period. Ceremonies at the hotel must be followed by reception here. Confetti is only permitted outside.
Price guide: Currently no charge.

Reception

The hotel offers a comprehensive wedding package which includes cake, flowers and disco. Late night drinking licence for residents.
Catering: from £34.50pp

The Potters Heron Hotel
Ampfield
Nr Romsey, Hants SO51 9ZF
Tel: 01703 266611 Fax: 01703 251359
Contact: Jackie Quarrell, Conference & Banqueting Sales Co-ordinator

Ceremony

This thatched building, surrounded by woodland offers its Ampfield Suite for wedding ceremonies. Up to four ceremonies per day may take place on any day of the year.
Price guide: £100

Reception

Catering: from £18pp

Rhinefield House Hotel
Rhinefield Road
Brockenhurst
Hants SO42 7QB
Tel: 01590 622922 Fax: 01590 622800
Contact: Jan Hamon, Conference & Banqueting co-ordinator

Ceremony

The hotel, part of Virgin Hotels, is set in the New Forest. Ceremonies can take place in the Orangery conservatory or the regal style Kings Room. The hotels award-winning gardens have been restored to the original 1890's design, with maze and formal parterres.
Price guide: £250

Reception

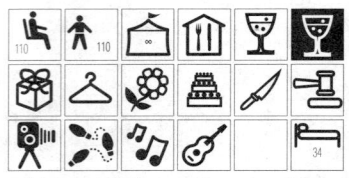

Rhinefield features a model of Westminster Hall, as well as an authentic recreation of prt of the Alhambra Palace in Granada (these are not marriage rooms). It has three AA and RAC stars as well as an AA Rosette. Accommodation discounts are available.
Catering: £23.50-£30pp

The Royal Armouries
Fort Nelson, Down End Road
Fareham, Hants PO17 6AN
Tel: 01329 233734 Fax: 01329 822092
E-mail: nelson@rmplc.co.uk.
Contact: David Waterhouse

Ceremony

Fort Nelson is a scheduled ancient monument and is the Royal Armouries Museum of artillery. Smoking is only allowed in designated areas and confetti is not permitted. Two rooms are licensed for ceremonies: the Officers Mess Ante Room (50) and The Point of the Redan(100). Wheelchair access is limited. Ceremonies may take plac here any day except Bank Holidays, at the discretion of The Keeper.
Price guide: from £300

Reception

A reception may be held at the fort following a late fternoon ceremony.
Catering: Buffets from £7.50pp Sit down from £16.50pp

The Solent Hotel
Rookery Avenue, Whiteley
Fareham
Hants PO15 7AJ
Tel: 01489 880000 Fax: 01489 880007
Contact: Nikki Carpenter, Banqueting Manager

Ceremony

This purpose-built hotel features log fires, polished stone floors and cherry-wood panelling. Two rooms are licensed; the Hambledon Suite and the Carisbrick Suite (the smaller seating up to 100). Up to two ceremonies are permitted per day, but the ceremony must be followed by reception at the hotel.
Price guide: No charge

Reception

There is no room hire charge for the reception at the Solent. Options include a red carpet, menu cards, and a four poster bridal suite with champagne. Reduced rate accommodation is available for wedding party guests.
Catering:£23.50-£32.50

Southdowns Hotel & Restaurant
Trotton, Rogate
Petersfield
Hants GU31 5JN
Tel: 01730 821521 Fax: 01730 821790
Contact: Mr Vedovato

Ceremony

This country hotel has a licence to hold ceremonies in the Lounge or the Harting Suite, offering a minimum capacity of 10 people. Only one ceremony is permitted per day. Only biodegradable confetti is allowed.
Price guide: £250

Reception

The hotel can help to organise cars and more unusual modes of transport such as carriages and helicopters. A 10% discount is offered to guests who stay for two or three nights.
Catering: from £15pp

Tyrells Ford Hotel
Avon, Nr Christchurch
Hants BH23 7BH
Tel: 01425 672646 Fax: 01425 672262
Contact: Collette Birkbeck, GM

Ceremony

This 18th Century family owned manor house is set in ten acres of grounds on the edge of the New Forest. The Lounge (with minstrel's gallery) is licensed for ceremonies and is available all days of the year. Ceremonies here must be followed by reception at the venue. Confetti is not permitted. Helicopters and hot air balloons may use the grounds.
Price guide: £125

Reception

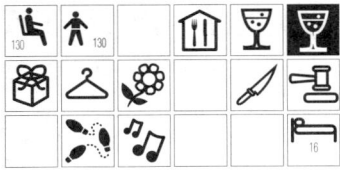

Catering: from £16.85pp

The Vyne
Sherbourne St John
Basingstoke, Hants RG26 5DX
Tel: 01256 881337 Fax: 01256 88120
Contact: Douglas Whyte, Property Manager

Ceremony

This National Trust property holds a licence for two rooms. However, The Vyne is currently undergoing refurbishment. Provisional bookings can be taken for August 1998 onwards. Prices quoted here are for 1996 and will be reviewed when the Vyne reopens.
Price guide: £150-£350

Reception

While in-house catering is available, it is possible to arrange your own caterer.
Catering: from £9.50pp

The Wessex Centre
Sparsholt College
Winchester, Hants SO21 2NF
Tel: 01962 776647   Fax: 01962 776636
Contact: Anne McDonald, Catering & Conference Manager

Ceremony

The Wessex Centre is part of Sparsholt Agricultural College which is set in over 400 acres. One room is licensed; The Jane Austen Suite, to which wheelchair access is limited. The Suite is available on any day of the year except over the Christmas and New Year period. Ceremonies must be followed by reception at the centre.
Price guide: £50

Reception

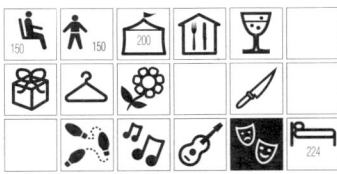

Helicopters and hot air balloons may use the grounds.
Catering: Buffets fr £12.50 Sit down fr £14pp

The Westover Hall
Park Lane
Milford on Sea, Hants SO41 0PT
Tel: 01590 643044 Fax: 01590 644490
Contact: Stewart Mechem/Nicola Musetti, Proprietors

Ceremony

This Grade II listed Victorian mansion overlooks the Solent and the Isle of Wight. The building features a minstrel's gallery and stained glass. The Nuffield Suite, which has limited wheelchair access, is licensed, and ceremonies can take place here on any day of the year. Confetti is not permitted.
Price guide: £250

Reception

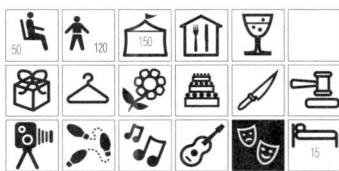

Cuisine at the Hall has a strong Italian influence. The Hall may take the prize for the most romantic wedding, as one couple apparently had dinner on the beach before paddling in the sea.
Catering: from £17.50pp

Winchester Guildhall
The Broadway
Winchester, Hants SO23 9LJ
Tel: 01962 840820 Fax: 01962 878458
Contact: Kelly Vaughan

Ceremony

This listed Victorian building has two marriage rooms; the Mayor's Parlour (seats 20) and the Conference Chamber (seats 150). The latter has limited wheelchair access.
Price guide: £50

Reception

There is one elected contract caterer to the Guildhall. Recommendations can be given for discos and live music.
Catering: POA

STOP PRESS
'68', Fareham
01329 221338
The Beaulieu Hotel, Lyndhurst
01703 293344
Botley Park Hotel, Southampton
01489 780888

Busketts Lawn Hotel, Southampton
01703 292272
Careys Manor Hotel, Brockenhurst
01590 623551
Chilworth Manor, Chilworth
01703 767333
The Game Larder, Stockbridge
01264 810414
Montague Arms Hotel, Beaulieu
01590 612324
Old Thorns Hotel, Liphook
01428 724555
Parkhill Country House Hotel,
Lyndhurst 01703 282944
Romans Country House Hotel,
Silchester 01734 700421
Stanwell House Hotel, Lymington
01590 677123
Tylney Hall, Hook 01256 764881

The Marine Hotel
5-7 The Front
Seaton Carew, Hartlepool
Tel: 01429 266244 Fax: 01429 864144
Contact: Wedding Co-ordinator

Ceremony

This Victorian town house, a listed
building, has a licence for its ground
floor restaurant and first floor
Rennaisance Suite. Ceremonies can
take place on any day except Christmas
Day, and there is no charge by the
hotel for the ceremony if the reception
is also held in house.
Price guide: F.O.C. (with reception) -
£200

Reception

The hotel offers a traditional four
course menu, although other menus
can be arranged through the manager.
The hotel will offer reduced price
accommodation for wedding guests.
Catering: £8.25 - £16.75pp

Avoncroft Museum of Historic
Buildings
Stoke Heath, Bromsgrove
Worcs B60 4JR
Tel: 01527 831363/831886
Fax: 01527 876934
Contact: Judy Lines, Manager

Ceremony

The Museum of Historic Buildings,
Guesten Hall, has a medieval roof set
within a modern, specially designed
building. On site is a Victorian 'tin'
church which can be used for blessings.
The New Guesten Hall holds a ceremony licence and weddings can take
place here on any day except Bank
Holidays. Confetti is not permitted.
Price guide: £300

Reception

Helicopters and hot air balloons may
use the grounds.
Catering: Buffets from £5pp Sit down
from £15pp

Aylestone Court Hotel
Hereford
Herefordshire
Tel: 01432 341891 Fax: 01432 267691
Contact: Mrs Holloway, Owner

Ceremony

This Georgian hotel is set in one acre
of gardens. Ceremonies are held in The
Orangery on any day of the year.
Price guide: P.O.A.

Reception

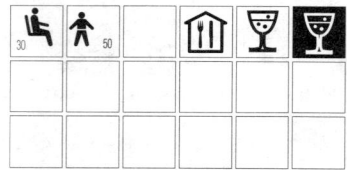

Price guide: P.O.A.

Berrington Hall
Leominster, Hereford HR6 0DW
Tel: 01568 615721 Fax: 01568 613263
Contact: Mrs Y Osborne, Manager

Ceremony

This National Trust owned, Grade I
listed building was designed by Henry
Holland and is set above the River
Lugg with views to the Black
Mountains and Brecon Beacons.
Capability Brown created the lake in
the grounds which features an artificial
island. Three rooms hold ceremony
licences, but these have limited wheelchair access. They are, however, available all year. Only biodegradable confetti is permitted, and photography cannot be allowed inside the house.
Price guide: from £300

Reception

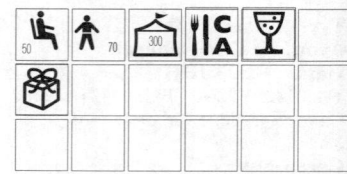

Reception facilities are offered from
November 1st to March 15th.
Dancing and music is permitted in a
marquee.
Price guide: POA

Burford House
Burford
Nr Tenbury Wells
Worcestershire WR15 8HQ
Tel: 01584 810777 Fax: 01584 810673
Contact: Andrew Kinniburgh,
Site Assistant Manager

Ceremony

The House's panelled entrance hall
leads to the Burford House Gardens,
which features four acres of lawns and
is home to the National Clematis
Collection. Ceremonies are available
Monday to Saturday excluding Bank
Holidays. The price guide to hold the
ceremony includes the use of the
grounds for photography.
Price guide: £150

Reception

Reception facilities are not available in
the House itself, although a marquee is
available with a capacity of 500.

Catering is on a contract basis but does not have to be from an approved list.
Catering: P.O.A.

Dormy House Hotel
Willersley Hill
Broadway, Worcs WR12 7LF
Tel: 01386 852711 Fax: 01386 858636
Contact: Nicola Sinclair, Sales Manager

Ceremony

This hotel, a converted 17th Century Cotswold farmhouse, has three marriage rooms, each with limited wheelchair access. These are available on any day except Christmas Day and Boxing Day.
Price guide: £150

Reception

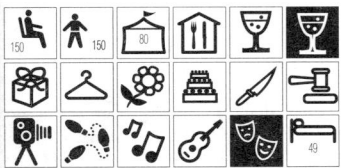

The hotel has two AA Rosettes and is RAC recommended.
Catering: from £19.50pp

Eastnor Castle
Eastnor, Ledbury
Herefordshire HR8 1RL
Tel: 01531 633160 Fax: 01531 631776
Contact: Simon Foster, Administrator

Ceremony

This privately owned 'fairytale' castle is set in the Malvern Hills and surrounded by a deer park and a lake. The Castle's Gothic Drawing Room holds the ceremony licence, and this room has limited wheelchair access. Weddings can take place here on any day except Sundays and Bank Holidays, and every day except Saturday during July and August.
Price guide: £250

Reception

Helicopters and hot air balloons can use the Castle grounds.
Catering: POA

Elms Hotel
Abberley
Nr Worcester WR6 6AT
Tel: 01299 896666 Fax: 01299 896804
Contact: Mrs Pamela Aczel

Ceremony

The hotel's "Gallery Room" is licensed to hold ceremonies which are not available on Sundays and Bank Holidays and has a minimum capacity of 10. Although there is wheelchair access to the hotel, there is no disabled WC. It is not possible to hold ceremonies without reception facilities also.
Price guide: £250

Reception

The hotel's restaurant has been awarded two AA rosettes. In addition to the services indicated, which include free use of an antique cake stand and knife, the hotel is happy to organise any further services for the couple. For instance, menu cards, place names and even bud vases can be provided at no extra cost.
Catering: POA

Grafton Manor
Bromsgrove
Worcs B61 7HA
Tel: 01527 579007 Fax: 01527 575221
Contact: Stephen Morris, Managing Partner

Ceremony

The Manor dates from 1567, but was substantially rebuilt in the early 18th Century. Two rooms (with limited wheelchair access) are available for ceremonies on any day of the year. Ceremonies must be followed by reception at the Manor.
Price guide: £125

Reception

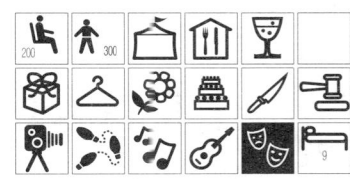

Grafton cater for weddings on an exclusive use basis.
Catering: from £31.50

Granary Hotel & Restaurant
Shenstone, Nr Kidderminster
Worcs DY10 4BS
Tel:01562 777535 Fax: 01562 777722
Contact: Sue Taylor, Wedding Co-ordinator

Ceremony

Up to three ceremonies per day are allowed at the hotel. Ceremonies can only be held here if the reception is also at the hotel.
Price guide: from £125

Reception

A traditional carvery can be offered by the hotel, as well as table plans if required.
Catering: from £14.50pp

Hanbury Hall
School Road
Hanbury
Droitwich
Worcs WR9 7EA
Tel: 01527 821214 Fax: 01527 821251
Contact: Mr JP Blades, Property Manager

Ceremony

This National Trust property offers its Drawing Room, Hall and Library for wedding ceremonies. These are available at any time from November to March but from April to October the Hall is available mornings only from Sunday to Wednesday. There are

restrictions for indoor photography.
Price guide: from £400

Reception

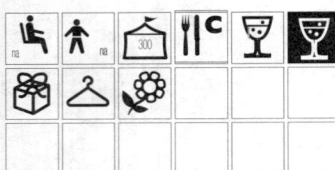

Helicopters and hot air balloons may use the grounds.
Catering: POA

Hereford Town Hall
St Owen Street
Hereford HR12 2PJ
Tel: 01432 362521
Contact: J Arnold, Communications Assistant

Ceremony

This listed building has approval for four rooms, including the Assembly Hall and the Council Chamber. All rooms have limited wheelchair access. Confetti is not permited.
Price guide: from £20

Reception

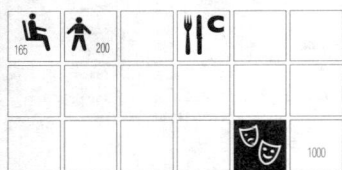

Couples would need to arrange for their own caterers at the Town Hall.

Lygon Arms
Broadway
Worcester WR12 7DU
Tel: 01386 852255 Fax: 01386 858611
Contact: Simon Hancox

Ceremony

This 16th Century coaching inn set in the heart of the village, is situated at the foot of the Cotswolds and features antique furniture and log fires. Only one ceremony is allowed per day.
Price guide: from £300

Reception

A cake maker and photographer can be recommended by the hotel.
Catering: from £20.75pp

New Priory Hotel
Stretton Sugwas
Hereford HR4 7AR
Tel: 01432 760264 Fax: 01432 761809
Contact: KJ Benjamin, Owner

Ceremony

Ths old vicarage, now an hotel and restaurant, is set in over 3 acres of grounds. The Breakfast Bridal Room is available for ceremonies on any day of the year.
Price guide: £50

Reception

The New Priory can offer vegetarian menus. Helicopters and hot air balloons can use the site.
Catering: Buffets from £5pp sit down from £8.50pp

Penrhos Court
Kington
Herefordshire
HR5 3LH
Tel: 01544 230720 Fax: 01544 230754
Contact: Daphne Lambert, Owner

Ceremony

Dating back to 1280 there are three periods to the main house, including the great medieval Cruck Hall and an Elizabethan wing with oak beams. Only one ceremony per day is permitted.
Price guide: £120

Reception

Penrhos prides itself on its organic produce which is grown in the Court's own garden. The Court has 19 bedrooms, two of which have four poster beds.
Price guide: from £20pp

Redditch Town Hall
Alcester Street
Ringway
Redditch
Worcs B98 8AH
Tel: 01527 64252 Fax: 01527 65216
Contact: Mrs Heather Hayes, Room Bookings

Ceremony

Located in the town centre, Redditch Town Hall offers a Wedding Room and the Council Chamber for wedding ceremonies.. These can take place on any day except Bank Holidays. The Mayor of Redditch was the first person to get married here.
Price guide: £50

Reception

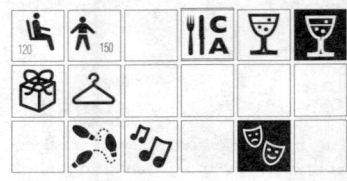

Catering" POA

Salford Hall Hotel
Abbotts Salford
Evesham
Worcs WR11 5UT
Tel: 01386 871300 Fax: 01386 871301
Contact: Sally Pearce, General Manager

Ceremony

This Tudor manor is a Grade I listed building, restored six years ago. Up to two ceremonies are permitted per day, on any day except Christmas Day.

Confetti is not permitted.
Price guide: £100

Reception

The Hotel has two AA Rosettes for its cuisine. It is possible to take over the whole hotel, with a minimum of 30 bedrooms. Catering: from £25pp.

STOP PRESS
Bank House Hotel, Bransford
01886 833551
The Chase Hotel, Ross on Wye
01989 763161
The County Hotel, Hereford
01432 299955
Fownes Hotel, Worcester
01905 613151
Munstone House, Munstone
01432 267122
St Andrews House Hotel, Droitwich
01905 779677
Vale Golf & Country Club, Nr Pershore 01386 462781
Wood Norton Hall, Evesham
01386 420232

Cheshunt Marriott Hotel
Halfhide Lane
Turnford
Broxbourne
Hertfordshire EN10 6NG
Tel: 01992 451245 Fax: 01992 440120
Contact: Andrea Moughan

Ceremony

This modern hotel does not have any restrictions on the number of ceremonies held per day and confetti is permitted. The cost of holding the ceremony varies from £300 during weekdays to £250 at weekends.
Price guide: from £250

Reception

Catering: Packages from £38.50pp

Edgwarebury Hotel
Barnet Lane
Elstree
Herts WD6 3RE
Tel: 0181 953 8227 Fax: 0181 207 3668
Contact: Zandra Fraser, Conf and Banqueting Manager

Ceremony

The hotel is built in the Tudor manor house style featuring big stone fireplaces and carved oak. It is set in 10 acres of grounds. Three rooms hold licences and these are available on any day of the year. Ceremonies here must be followed by reception at the hotel.
Price guide: from £250

Reception

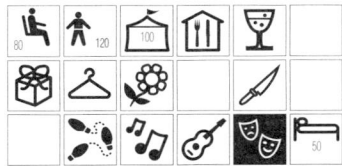

Catering: Buffets from £10.50pp sit down from £26.95pp

Elstree Moat House
Barnet by pass
Borehamwood
Hertfordshire WD6 5PU
Tel: 0181 214 9988 Fax: 0181 207 3194
Contact: Catherine Heaton

Ceremony

The capacity for the ceremony varies from a minimum of 20 to a maximum of 500. Ceremonies are available seven days a week excluding Saturday, subject to management discretion.
Price guide: POA

Reception

Although catering is in-house, the hotel also offers a choice of contract caterers, but from an approved list only.
Catering: Buffets from £8.50pp Sit down from £24.95pp

Fanhams Hall
Fanhams Hall Road
Ware, Herts SG12 7PZ
Tel: 01920 460511 Fax: 01920 469187
Contact: House Manager

Ceremony

Set in 27 acres of gardens, this listed Jacobean style building has a modern pavilion extension which has views over a small landscaped lake. Ceremonies are available throughout the week excluding Sundays, dependent upon conference bookings. The Hall does not accept bookings for ceremonies only.
Price guide: £200

Reception

In addition to the Hall's 85 bedrooms, two honeymoon/VIP suites are available. A late night drinking licence is available until midnight and the Hall is happy to recommend any services you may require.
Catering: £25pp

The Glen Eagle Hotel
1 Luton Road
Harpendon
Hertfordshire AL5 2PX
Tel: 01582 760271 Fax: 01582 460819
Contact: David Hunter, GM

Ceremony

This country house style hotel, is set in award winning gardens, and holds no restrictions on the availability of ceremonies.
Price guide: POA

Reception

The hotel offers reduced rates of

accommodation for those wedding guests wishing to stay on a Friday, Saturday or Sunday night.
Catering: from £21pp

Green End Park Hotel
Dane End
Near Ware, Hertfordshire
Tel: 01920 438344 Fax: 01920 438523
Contact: Valerie Hutcheon, Assistant to the Proprietor

Ceremony

This hotel and restaurant is a listed building and has its Louis Room licensed to hold ceremonies. The room has a seating capacity of 70 and the hotel is more than happy to combine a mixture of seated and standing guests to a maximum of 80. Ceremonies are available without receptions while confetti is permitted outside only.
Price guide: £175-250

Reception

Catering is in-house, and a marquee is available for a maximum of 200 guests.
Catering: £28pp

Hanbury Manor Hotel
Ware, Herts SG12 0SD
Tel: 01920 487722 Fax: 01920 487692
Contact: Josefine Strygstryg

Ceremony

Only one ceremony is available per day, which must be held in conjunction with a reception.
Price guide: from £300

Reception

The hotel provides a complimentary overnight suite for the bride and groom including breakfast. In addition to the services indicated, the hotel offers the bridal party a horse and carriage and use of vintage cars.
Catering: from £30pp

Hatfield Lodge Hotel
Comet Way, Hatfield
Hertfordshire AL10 9NG
Tel: 01707 272661 Fax: 01707 256282
Contact: The Conference Department

Ceremony

This modern hotel has three rooms licensed to hold ceremonies with capacities from 35 to 100. Ceremonies must be followed by reception here.
Price guide: from £110

Reception

Flower arrangements are included in the price of the ceremony.
Catering: from £24.95pp

Hilton National Hotel
Elton Way, Watford
Hertfordshire WD2 8HA
Tel: 01923 235881 Fax: 01923 220836
Contact: Matthew Wykes

Ceremony

Ceremonies are available in the Registrar's suite for up to 30 and in the New Hertford Suite which can only be reserved in conjunction with a wedding breakfast (minimum of 120 guests).
Price guide: from £100

Reception

Although the hotel's catering is in-

house, a list of outside contract caterers is available. However it is acceptable for the couple to supply their own contract caterer. The hotel boasts kosher and ethnic cuisine expertise.
Catering: from £35pp

Jarvis Aubrey Park Hotel
Hemel Hempstead Road
Redbourn, Herts AL3 7AF
Tel: 01582 792105 Fax: 01582 792001
Contact: Claire Healy / Merissa Lohan, Conference & Events Sales Managers

Ceremony

The hotel boasts a complete package of services to make the wedding day as simple as possible for the couple. The package includes, amongst other things, free accommodation for the couple on the night of the wedding, special overnight rates for wedding guests, and fun packs to keep children occupied during speeches.
Price guide: £200

Reception

Catering: £20pp

Jarvis Comet Hotel
301 St Albans Road West
Hatfield, Herts AL10 9RH
Tel: 01707 265411 Fax: 01707 264019
Contact: General Manager

Ceremony

This Grade II listed art deco building has been renovated to its former glory. Southpoint and the Pioneer Suite are both licensed for wedding ceremonies.
Price guide: £245

Reception

Further accommodation should be available from August 1997.
Catering: Buffet from £8pp Sit down from £18pp

Knebworth Park
The Manor Barn
Old Knebworth, Herts SG3 6PY
Tel: 01438 813825 Fax: 01438 813003
Contact: Clive Duffey, Events Manager

Ceremony

This 16th century tithe barn is set in 250 acres of deer park with Knebworth House, Gardens and Barns Banqueting Centre available for the reception and photographs.
Price guide: £300

Reception

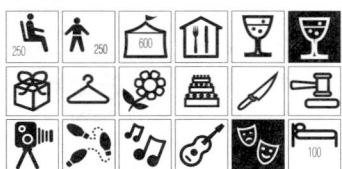

Receptions are undertaken in-house by the award-winning Lytton Catering. Accommodation is available at the Novotel hotel set within the park, and a list of other local accommodation is also available.
Catering: £17.95pp

The Manor
St Michael's Village
Fishpool Street
St Albans, Herts AL3 4RY
Tel: 01727 854444 Fax: 01727 848909
Contact: Helen Jones

Ceremony

The original Manor House was built around 1512 on medieval foundations and is now a Grade II listed building set in five acres of award winning grounds. Only one ceremony per day is permitted.
Price guide: from £175

Reception

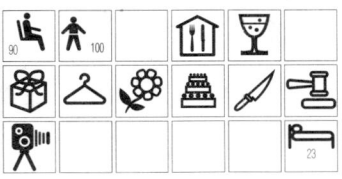

A late night drinking licence is available for residents of the Manor only.
Catering: from £24.50

Offley Place
Kings Walden Road
Great Offley
Hertfordshire SG5 3DS
Tel: 01462 768787 Fax: 01462 768724
Contact: Carrie Horwood, Manager

Ceremony

This conference and training venue is a listed building, with parts dating back to the 16th Century, and was once a stately home. Set in its own grounds with orchards and rose gardens, Offley Place has three rooms licensed with capacities from 25 to 80.
Price guide: £100

Reception

For a fee of £500 Offley Place may be hired on an exclusive basis with exclusive use of the grounds and staff. The couple are offered a complimentary overnight suite while staff are quick to point out that although accommodation is provided, and is clean and comfortable, it is not to hotel standards.
Catering: £16-25pp

The Old Palace
Hatfield Park
Hatfield
Hertfordshire AL9 5NE
Tel: 01707 262055 / 272738
Fax: 01707 260898
Contact: Banqueting Manager

Ceremony

Originally built in the late 15th century, the Old Palace was acquired by King Henry VIII in 1538 and became the childhood home of Queen Elizabeth 1st. The Palace has two room licensed, the Great Hall and the Riding School with capacities varying from 220 to 400. Ceremonies are only available in conjunction with recep-

tions and are not permitted on Sundays, Good Friday and Christmas Day.
Price guide: from £100

Reception

Although the Palace does not have accommodation available on the premises, a list of local accommodation is available. In addition to the services indicated, the Old Palace offers themed receptions; Elizabethan of course.
Catering: £19.50pp

Pearse House, Parsonage Lane
Bishops Stortford, Herts
Tel: 01279 757400 Fax: 01279 506591
Contact: Mrs V McGregor, Deputy Director

Ceremony

Pearse House is a privately owned conference centre with residential facilities, and allows only one ceremony per day. Confetti is permitted outside only.
Price guide: £150-250

Reception

The House prides itself on a 'one stop shop facility' to relieve the couple of any further wedding worries. A children's crèche is available during formalities and preferential rates are offered for guests staying overnight.
Catering: £12.50-33.50pp

The Ponsbourne Park Hotel
Newgate Street Village
Nr Hertford, Herts SG13 8QZ
Tel: 01707 876191 Fax: 01707 875190
Contact: Functions Manager

Ceremony

This old country house, set in 170 acres of grounds, was once the hunting lodge of King Henry VIII. The hotel has two rooms licensed, which are available seven days a week although there is limited availability from Monday-Thursday.
Price guide: from £100

Reception

Catering: from £19pp

The Priory
High Street
Ware
Hertfordshire SG12 9AL
Tel: 01920 460316 Fax: 01920 484056
Contact: Mrs Janet Buttery, Town Clerk, Ware Town Council

Ceremony

The Priory is a Grade I listed building and scheduled ancient monument, and was originally a friary founded in 1338. Confetti is not permitted.
Price guide: from £110

Reception

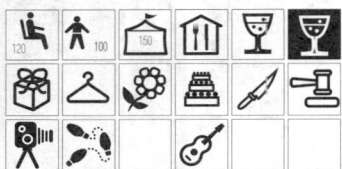

Receptions take place in Byrche's Restaurant, which is situated in the Priory's rebuilt Victorian greenhouse conservatory which overlooks the river and gardens. Although accommodation is not available at the Priory, a list of local accommodation is available which offer preferential rates agreements.
Catering: £20pp (inc. room hire)

Quality Clock Hotel
The Link Road
Welwyn
Hertfordshire AL6 9XA
Tel: 01438 716911 Fax: 01438 714065
Contact: Tina, Conf & Banqueting

Ceremony

The hotel features a clock tower outside the main reception and offers only one ceremony per day if held in conjunction with a reception. Ceremonies are generally conducted between 10am-4pm and are available without receptions.
Price guide: POA

Reception

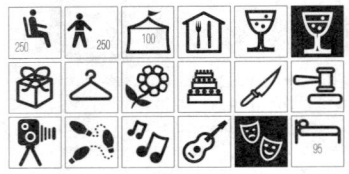

Couples are able to compile their own menu package for maximum flexibility and choice, which may also reduce costs. Children's entertainment such as Punch and Judy shows are available during formalities. A complimentary overnight bridal suite is available as well as preferential rates for guests.
Catering: from POA

Shendish Manor
London Road
Apsley
Hemel Hampstead
Herts HP3 0AA
Tel: 01442 232220 Fax: 01442 230683
Contact: Tom Concannon, GM

Ceremony

Shendish Manor is a large stately listed building offering leisure facilities such as a golf course and health club, as well as conference facilities. Two rooms are licensed for ceremonies and are available any day of the year. Confetti is not permitted.
Price guide: POA

Reception

Shendish Manor has a New Zealand and Asian chef. Helicopters and hot air balloons may use the grounds.
Catering: from £24.95

Sopwell House Hotel
Cottonmill Lane
Sopwell, St Albans
Hertfordshire
Tel: 01727 864477 Fax: 01727 845636
Contact: Jeremy Hollands, Banqueting Manager

Ceremony

This four star, Georgian country house hotel, was once the country home of Lord Mountbatten and is set in 11 acres of gardens and grounds. Two ceremonies are allowed per day. Confetti is permitted.
Price guide: from £300

Reception

The hotel also operates preferential rate agreements with other local hotels and in addition to the services indicated is willing to organise balloons, place cards, menu printing, table plans, car hire, beauty therapy and leisure facilities for the couple.
Catering: from £30pp

Tewin Bury Farm
Near Welwyn
Hertfordshire AL6 0JB
Tel: 01438 717793 Fax: 01438 840440
Contact: Veronica Winterbourne, Functions Manager

Ceremony

This 17th century listed barn, situated on the banks of the river Mimram, is available for ceremonies every day excluding Saturday. Ceremonies are available only in conjunction with receptions.
Price guide: £150

Reception

Receptions are offered in either the tithe barn, stable or the farmhouse itself, with capacities varying from 20 to 200. Some of the farm's accommodation consists of two storey suites which are suitable for families and sleep four people.
Catering: £23.70pp

Vintage Court Hotel
Vintage Corner
Puckeridge
Nr Ware
Hertfordshire SG11 1SA
Tel: 01920 822722 Fax: 01920 822877
Contact: Sue Wright, Banqueting Sales

Ceremony

This modern hotel has two rooms licensed and features small but pleasant gardens suitable for photography.
Price guide: £150

Reception

The hotel has 24 bedrooms all of which are either double or twin bedded.
Catering: from £19.85pp

STOP PRESS
Barley Town House, Royston
01763 849119
Hertford County Hall, 01992 555550
Manor of Groves Hotel,
Sawbridgeworth 01279 600777
Pendley Manor Hotel, Tring
01442 891891
Putteridge Bury, Luton 01582 489092
The Radlett Centre, Radlett
01923 852697
Redcoats Farmhouse Hotel, Nr
Hitchin 01438 729500
The Sun Hotel, Hitchin 01462 436411
Vintage Court Hotel, Puckeridge
01920 822722

Swainston Manor Hotel
Calbourne Road
Newport
Isle of Wight PO30 4HX
Tel: 01983 521121 Fax: 01983 521406
Contact: Mr Woodward, Managing Director

Ceremony

This Grade II listed building is set in 32 acres of grounds and has three rooms available to hold ceremonies with varying capacities from 12 to 120. Ceremonies are available without receptions but costs are dependent on the size of the party. The hotel has its own church which is available for blessings.

Reception

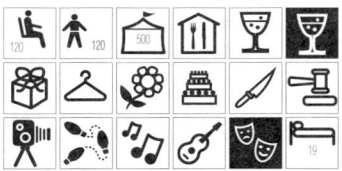

Catering is in-house with a capacity of 120.
Catering: from £12pp

STOP PRESS
Northwood House, Cowes
01983 821000
Sandringham Hotel, Sandown
Tel: 01983 406655

Abbots Barton
36 New Dover Road
Canterbury, Kent CT1 3DU
Tel: 01227 760341 Fax: 01277 785442
Contact: Miss Moore

Ceremony

This is a 17th Century gothic house set in two acres.
Price guide: £80 – 1/2 day/£140 – day

Reception

Catering: £7 (buffet) to £12.50 (waited)

Alexandra Suite
St Mary's Road
Swanley, Kent BR8 7BU
Tel: 01322 613900 Fax: 01322 614998
Contact: Paula Smith, Marketing Manageress

Ceremony

Five suites are available for ceremonies at the Alexandra Suite and The Woodlands. The Alexandra Suite (up to 250 guests itself and the Clocktower Pavilion (30-70 guests) are on the ground floor below the civic centre. The Woodlands, (in Hilda May Avenue), offers the Poplar Suite (100-160 guests), the Linden Suite (80-100 guests) and the Walnut Lounge (60-90 guests), the latter also featuring a conservatory. Marriages can take place on any day of the week.
Price guide: from £104

Reception

Catering at both buildings is operated by Swanley Banqueting.
Catering: £18pp

Boughton Monchelsea Place
Boughton Monchelsea
Nr Maidstone, Kent ME17 4BU
Tel/Fax: 01622 743120
Contact: Jill Harris, Secretary

Ceremony

This is a privately owned, battlemented Elizabethan ragstone manor house with Regency alterations. It is set in a deer park, with views over the Weald of Kent, and has its own walled gardens. Ceremonies can take place on any day except Sundays, with up to four allowed per day.
Price guide: £300 + VAT

Reception

Activites available include standard and laser clay shooting, fishing and quad biking. Firework displays, hot air balloons and entertainers, such as magi-

cians, can also be arranged. Local accommodation list available.
Catering: from £19pp

Brandshatch Place Hotel
Fawkham Valley Road
Fawkham, Kent DA3 8NQ
Tel: 01474 872239 Fax: 01474 879652
Contact: General Manager

Ceremony

A Georgian country house, set in 12 acres, this listed building can play host to wedding ceremonies on any day of the week.
Price guide: £200

Reception

The Head Chef is Mark Cheeseman who holds two rosettes for his skills in modern English cuisine, and has been nominated for a third. Other facilities at the hotel include an indoor heated pool, snooker, beauty centre, gym, and tennis and squash.
Catering: from £20pp

Bridgewood Manor Hotel
Maidstone Road
Rochester, Kent ME5 9AX
Tel: 01634 201333 Fax: 01634 201330
Contact: Conference & Banqueting

Ceremony

This four star AA and RAC hotel (part of Marston Hotels) offers three marriage rooms: the Hythe Suite, Hogarth Suite and Maidstone Suite, for as few as four guests. Not available on Christmas Day and Boxing Day. No confetti.
Price guide: £200 (£150 with reception)

Reception

In addition to the services listed above, the Bridgewood Manor Hotel will also print special wedding menus for receptions held at the venue. If required, children can be catered for separately. The maximum capacity for both waited and buffet style receptions at the hotel is 130, and the site is not suitable for a marquee.
Catering: from £21.50

Broome Park
The Broome Park Estate
Canterbury, Kent CT1 6QX
Tel: 01227 831701 Fax: 01227 831973
Contact: Gwen Willbye,
Food & Beverage Manager

Ceremony

Built in the reign of Charles I, this listed mansion, set in 268 acres, was once the home of Lord Kitchener. It is now a club operated on a time-share basis. Two rooms have been granted a licence for ceremonies: The Green Room, which seats up to 60, and the Gazebo, which is set in the Italian Garden, and seats up to 300. Up to two ceremonies are permitted per day. Wheelchair access is limited.
Price guide: from £50

Reception

The Club has three restaurants including Dizzy's Jazz Bar and Creole Restaurant, and a more formal a la carte restaurant. Other facilities include an 18 hole championship golf course, driving range, tennis courts, squash courts, putting green, outdoor pool and health centre. While accommodation is usually available on site; there are 18 suites in the main building and a further 26 villas in the grounds; availability is variable. The club can recommend numerous services that cannot be offered in-house.
Catering: from £18pp

Chiddingstone Castle
Hill Hoath Road
Nr Edenbridge, Kent TN8 7AD
Tel: 01892 870347
Contact: Functions Manager

Ceremony

One of the historic houses of Kent, and formerly the home of Denys Eyre Bower, Chiddingstone Castle is now maintained by a private charitable trust. Set in its own grounds, with woods and a cascade, the castle is a particularly tranquil setting for a wedding. The oak panelled Great Hall is the marriage room which can be hired on any day of the week except over the Christmas Bank holiday, with only one ceremony permitted per day. Confetti is not allowed, and it should be noted that stiletto heels are prohibited since they irreparably damage the floors.
Price guide: up to £350

Reception

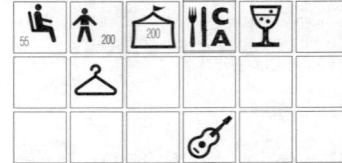

Receptions can take place in one of several rooms, the smallest of which is the Assembly Room, suitable for up to 40 guests. If a marquee is required this is sited in front of the south entrance, which provides a backdrop of towers and battlements. The castle has a restaurant licence for drinks, but you may also provide your own drinks and pay corkage. Personalised wedding stationery is said to be a speciality of the castle. The castle has its own musician; disco music is not permitted. A dressing room is provided for the bride in the 17th Century wing of the castle.
Catering: from £8pp

Chilston Park Hotel
Sandway, Lenham
Kent ME17 2BE
Tel: 01622 859803 Fax: 01622 858352
Contact: Sue Greenwood, Events Manager

Ceremony

This Grade I listed mansion house set in parkland has a marriage licence for its Orangery. The minimum number for a wedding ceremony is six people. Ceremonies cannot be held here on Christmas Day or Boxing Day. Up to three ceremonies are permitted per day.
Price guide: £750

Reception

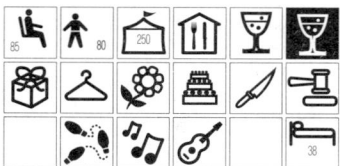

Catering: from £26.50 (3-course meal)

Cobham Hall
Cobham
Kent DA12 3BL
Tel: 01474 824319 Fax: 01474 822995
Contact: Sue Anderson, Development
Director

Ceremony

This 16th Century mansion, former home of the Earls of Darnley and now a girls' school, is set in 150 acres of landscaped parkland and gardens. Ceremonies can take place on any day of the week, in any of three licensed rooms; The Gilt Hall, The Vestibule and Lady Darnley's Gazebo, which is set in a romantic garden. Confetti is not permitted.
Price guide: £600 + VAT

Reception

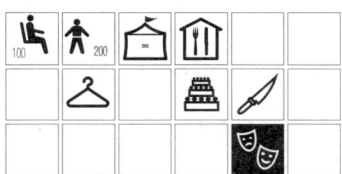

While there is no accommodation on the premises, a list of local accommodation, with preferential rate agreements with the Hall, can be provided. The Hall has its own helicopter landing area.
Catering: £20pp

County Hall
County Road
Maidstone, Kent ME14 1XQ
Tel: 01622 694151 Fax: 01622 694158
Contact: Conference Manager

Ceremony

Ceremonies can only take place on a Saturday or Sunday at County Hall (a listed building), and not on any Bank Holidays. Up to four ceremonies are allowed per day, unless couples are also holding their reception at the Hall, in which case their's will be the only wedding that day and no charge will be made for room hire for the ceremony.
Price guide: from £250 or F.O.C.

Reception

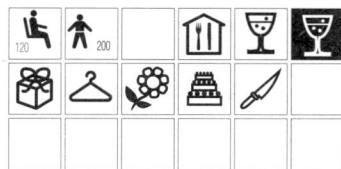

County Hall offers a wedding package, starting at £20.50pp, which includes food and room hire. Drinks packages start at £5 per head. Accommodation is available at Oakwood House, which is also run by Kent County Council.
Catering: from £20.50

Dover Town Hall
Biggin Street
Dover, Kent CT16 1DL
Tel: 01304 201200 Fax: as phone
Contact: Trevor Jones, GM

Ceremony

This listed building offers a choice of two rooms for ceremonies; The Maison Dieu Hall (up to 30 guests) and the Council Chamber (up to 45 guests).
Price guide: £100

Reception

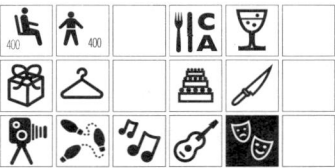

The Victorian Connaught Hall will accommodate up to 400 guests with room for dancing. Catering and bar services are provided by White Horse Caterers.
Catering: from £15pp

Eastwell Manor
Eastwell Park
Boughton Lees
Ashford, Kent TN25 4HR
Tel: 01233 219955 Fax: 01233 635530
Contact: Helen Rushton, Conference & Banqueting Manager

Ceremony

This country house hotel and restaurant offers two marriage rooms: the Bayeaux Room (max 50) and the Rose Garden Room (max 90). Ceremony numbers are limited to one per day.
Price guide: £500

Reception

Catering: £33pp

Finchcocks
Goudhurst
Kent TN17 1HH
Tel: 01580 211702 Fax: 01580 211007
Contact: Mrs Katrina Burnett, Director/Owner

Ceremony

Finchcocks, Grade I listed, was built in 1725, and now houses a collection of over 80 historical keyboard instruments. The house stands in 13 acres of grounds including a recently planted walled garden. Period music can be provided free as part of the ceremony, Wheelchair access is good for the marriage room and gardens, but limited for the toilets and restaurant. Confetti is not permitted. Availability for ceremonies varies considerably, please consult Finchcocks directly to enquire about your chosen day.
Price guide: £350 + VAT

Reception

A special feature of the in-house catering at Finchcocks is the choice of Georgian (18th Century) menus. Accommodation is only occasionally available on the premises (there is a self-contained flat), but a list of other local accommodation can be provided.

Finchcocks has contacts with many musicians who could provide chamber music of all kinds for the wedding.
Catering: from £15

The Garden Hotel
167-169 The Street
Boughton, Faversham
Kent ME13 9BH
Tel: 01227 751411 Fax: 01227 751801
Contact: Karen Carr, Manager

Ceremony

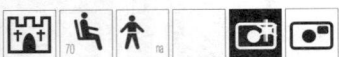

Set in a village location, The Garden Hotel is a 17th Century listed building converted from an antique shop in 1889 and now holds a licence for its Garden Restaurant. This has limited wheelchair access. It is available all days except Christmas Day and Boxing Day.
Price guide: £150

Reception

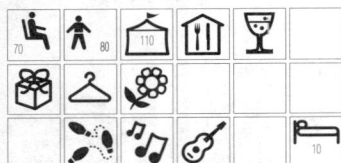

Catering: Buffets from £12.50pp Sit down from £18.50pp

Groombridge Place
Groombridge, Kent TN3 9QG
Tel: 01892 861444 Fax: 01892 863996
Contact: Ann Tesler, Functions Co-ordinator

Ceremony

This Grade I listed moated mansion, set in extensive 17th Century gardens, has featured in many films, including Peter Greenaway's The Draughtsman's Contract. Ceremonies can take place in the oak panelled Baronial Hall on any day of the week.
Price guide: £350

Reception

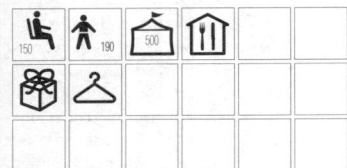

Couples need to organise their own caterers for a reception at Groombridge, but a list of local wedding suppliers is available on request. While there is no overnight accommodation at the house, a list of local hotels, with which Groombridge has arranged preferential rates, can be provided.

Hythe Imperial
Prince's Parade
Hythe, Kent CT21 6AE
Tel: 01303 267441 Fax: 01303 264610
Contact: Jane Burden, Conference & Banqueting Co-ordinator

Ceremony

The Imperial, built in 1880, is sited on the unspoilt seafront at Hythe. Two rooms are licensed for ceremonies; the Garden Room (max 100) and the Elizabeth Room (max 70). Ceremonies can take place here any day of the week, but not between December 24 and 25, New Year's Eve and new Year's Day or the Easter weekend. Confetti is not permitted.
Price guide: £200

Reception

Catering: from £22pp

Jarvis Great Danes
Hotel & Country Club
Maidstone
Kent ME17 1RE
Tel: 01622 631163 Fax 01622 735290
Contact: Wedding Consultant

Ceremony

Originally a manor house, Great Danes has had more recent additions over the years. It is set in 26 acres of landscaped gardens. Wedding ceremonies can take place in one of two rooms (the smaller takes up to 100 guests) on any day of the week. Each wedding is assigned a Wedding Host whose function is to ensure that the event goes smoothly

and that all details are taken into account.
Price Guide: £250

Reception

Great Danes has considerable experience of both Greek and Asian weddings, providing traditional fayre. The hotel's wedding package includes free accommodation for bride and groom on their wedding night, plus breakfast, fruit, flowers, champagne and a gift. Other services that can be offered include a free postal service for your invitations, free table fun packs for children, and free cake boxes.
Catering: from £18pp

The Knowle Restaurant
School Lane, Higham
Rochester, Kent ME3 7HP
Tel: 01474 822262
Contact: Michael Baragwanath, Proprietor

Ceremony

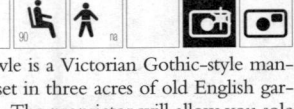

Knowle is a Victorian Gothic-style mansion set in three acres of old English gardens. The proprietor will allow you sole use of the premises for your wedding.
Price guide: £2pp

Reception

Food at Knowle is English and continental style. No charge is usually made for flowers or cake stand and knife. A list of local accommodation, with which the restaurant has preferential rate agreements, is available on request.
Catering: from £24pp

Little Silver Country Hotel
St Michael's
Tenterden, Kent TN30 6SP
Tel: 01233 850321 Fax: 01233 850647
Contact: Mrs Lawson, Proprietor

Ceremony

This mock Tudor style hotel has a marriage licence for its Kent Hall (an octagonal shaped room), which can only be hired for wedding ceremonies if the recption is also at the hotel.
Price guide: £175 + vat

Reception

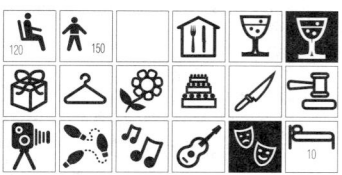

The hotel can also arrange Rolls Royces and video operators.
Catering: £25pp

Lympne Castle
c/o Robert Spicer
52 Lympne Industrial Park
Hythe, Kent CT21 4LR
Tel: 01303 262398 Fax: 01303 261810
Contact: Barrie Marshall, Consultant

Ceremony

Price guide: £375

Reception

Catering: from £4.25 (buffet) to £25.50pp

Nizel's Golf Club
Nizel's Lane
Hildenborough
Kent TN11 8NX
Tel: 01732 833138 Fax: 01732 833764
Contact: Mark Warne, Catering Manager

Ceremony

The recently refurbished Queen Anne House at Nizels is adjacent to formal rose gardens and a summer marquee.

The house overlooks an 18 hole golf course in the heart of the Kentish Weald.
Price guide: POA

Reception

Catering: from £25pp

Oakwood House Training
Centre
Oakwood Park
Maidstone, Kent ME16 8AE
Tel: 01622 764433 Fax: 01622 763704
Contact: Conference Manager

Ceremony

This Victorian house, run by Kent County Council, is set in mature parkland, and is about a mile from the centre of Maidstone. It is only available for ceremonies on Saturdays and Sundays, with only one ceremony permitted per day. Ceremonies here must be followed by reception at Oakwood.
Price guide: See below

Reception

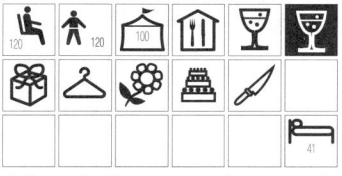

Oakwood offers a comprehensive package, starting at £36 per head, which includes room hire, wedding breakfast, sherry on arrival, a glass of wine with the meal and a glass of wine for taosts. Children under 12 are charged at half price, and children under 4 are catered for free.
Catering: from £36pp

Penshurst Place
Penshurst, Kent TN11 8DG
Tel: 01892 870307 Fax: 01892 870866
Contact: Terri Scott, Banqueting

Ceremony

Dating from the 16th Century and set in extensive grounds with formal gardens, Penshurst Place is a privately owned house with two rooms licensed to hold wedding ceremonies. The smaller of these seats up to 80 guests. Ceremonies can take place on any day of the week and are restricted to one per day. There is limited wheelchair access.
Price guide: from £300

Reception

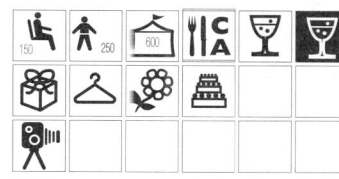

While no accommodation is available on the premises, a list of local accommodation can be provided.
Catering: from £30pp

Quex House & Gardens
Quex Park
Birchington-on-Sea
Kent
CT12 4AG
Tel: 01843 842168 Fax: 01843 346661
Contact: Mrs Sarah Vale, Banqueting Manager

Ceremony

This Regency country manor house, with museum adjacent is set in 250 acres of parkland and gardens. The venue has a ceremony licence for the Dining Hall and the Banqueting Hall. These are available on any day of the year.
Price guide: £250

Reception

The range of buffets available includes a hot fork buffet of home-made spicy and oriental dishes.
Helicopters and hot air balloons may use the grounds.
Catering: Buffets from £4.95pp Sit down from £ 6pp

Read's Restaurant
Painters Forstal
Faversham
Kent ME13 0EE

Tel: 01795 535344 Fax: 01795 591200
Contact: Mrs RC Pitchford, Owner

Ceremony

The restaurant is set in a rural location with gardens and views. The restaurant itself is licensed for weddings and cere-monies can take place here on any day of the year, but must be followed by reception at the restaurant.
Price guide: POA

Reception

Read's is the only Michelin starred restaurant in Kent. Helicopters and hot air balloons may use the grounds.
Catering: from £18pp

Rowhill Grange
Wilmington, Kent DA2 7QH

Tel: 01322 615136 Fax: 01322 615137
Contact: Banqueting Co-ordinator

Ceremony

Extensively refurbished in 1994, Rowhill Grange is a thatched house dating from 1868 and set in 9 acres of woodland and landscaped garden with lake. While cer-emonies can take place here any day of the week, these must be followed by reception at the venue. There is an administration cost for the ceremony, then a room hire fee from £500 which covers the reception through to mid-night. Two rooms have ceremony licences. Confetti is not permitted.
Price guide: £1.50pp

Reception

While there are 18 bedrooms at the grange, only six of these are allocated to each wedding party.
Catering: from £29.95pp

Royal Wells Inn
Mount Ephraim
Tunbridge Wells
Kent TN4 8BG

Tel: 01892 511188 Fax: 01892 511908
Contact: Deana Short, Wedding Co-ordinator

Ceremony

Price guide: £200

Reception

Catering: from £15pp

Salomons Centre
David Salomons Estate
Broomhill Road
Tunbridge Wells
Kent TN3 0TG

Tel: 01892 515152 Fax: 01892 539102
Contact: Dawn Ellingham, Sales & Marketing Manager

Ceremony

This Victorian country mansion is set in 36 acres of landscaped gardens, woodland, parkland and lakes. The Victorian theatre is offered for cere-monies. This is said to have a cathedral like atmosphere (and even has an organ), and is claimed to be the largest licensed room in Kent. For smaller ceremonies, the Gold Room is offered.
Price guide: from £275

Reception

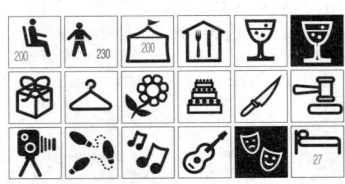

Catering: from £22.25pp

Sevenoaks Town Council Offices
Bradbourne Vale Road
Sevenoaks, Kent TN13 3Q9

Tel: 01732 459953 Fax: 01732 742577
Contact: Ann White, Admin Asst

Ceremony

The town council offices are newly built. The Chamber is licensed for weddings, and is available on Saturdays and Sundays only.
Price guide: POA

Reception

Receptions cannot be held at the premises, but are held at the community centre nearby. Outside caterers can be used for receptions; hence no price guide.

Sharsted Court
Newnham, Nr Sittingbourne
Kent ME9 0JU

Tel: 01795 890343 Fax: 01795 890713
Contact: Mrs Judith Shepley, Owner

Ceremony

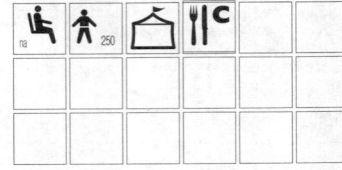

This stately home is Grade I and II listed and dates from the 12th Century. It features ornamental brick and flint walls, gazebos, and clipped yew trees (including a maze). Ceremonies are held in the Ballroom.
Price guide: £500

Reception

Three rooms are available for recep-tions: the Ballroom, the Billiard Room and the Front Hall. Couples have a complete choice of caterer; the follow-ing prices are offered as a guide to reg-ular caterers at the house.
Catering: Buffets from £7.50pp
Sit down from £20pp

Basia Zarzycka

135 Kings Road, Chelsea, London
Tel: 0171 351 7276

Individual Gowns of Distinction

Headdresses, Hats, Veils & Shoes

FAIRY TALE WEDDINGS DO COME TRUE

THE MOST UNRESTRICTED
WEDDING ARRANGERS

01707 251589

WHETHER YOU'RE LOOKING FOR THE COMPLETE LIZ TAYLOR EXTRAVAGANZA

OR THE FULL CINDERELLA EXPERIENCE   OR EVEN A QUIET TRADITIONAL WEDDING

CALL FAIRY TALE WEDDINGS DO COME TRUE

LOCK UP THE HEADACHE TABLETS, TAKE THE PADDING DOWN FROM THE WALLS

RELAX AND LET US DO THE WORK

SEARCH-LINE
FREE
RESEARCH

YOU CALL US
WE CALL THEM
THEY CALL YOU

24 HR
PANIC-LINE
SOLUTIONS TO LAST MINUTE
DISASTERS

"JUST CALL 01707 251 589 24-HRS 365-DAYS A YEAR"

HANNA GOLDMAN

Please send £3 for colour brochure to:
Studio 4, 10-13 Hollybush Place, London E2 9QX Tel: 0171-739 2690

Top: White Swan Water, Little Venice, London. See page 105
Above: Somerhill, Nr Tonbridge, Kent. See page 81

Top: Stafford House, Dorchester, Dorset. See page 46
Above: The Firs, Winchmore Hill, London. See page 95

Top Left: Eastnor Castle, Ledbury, Herefordshire. See page 69   Top Right: Naworth Castle, Brampton, Cumbria. See page 35   Above: Bolton Moat House, Greater Manchester. See page 106

Top: The Old Mill, Aldermaston, Berkshire. See page 12
Above: The Berystede Hotel, Ascot, Berkshire. See page 9

Top Left: Salterns Hotel, Lilliput, Dorset. See page 46   Top Right: Bolholt Country Park Hotel, Bury,
Greater Manchester. See page 106   Above: Fairfield Halls, Croydon, London. See page 95

Top Left: The Spa Hotel, Tunbridge Wells, Kent. See page 81 Top Right: Davenport House, Bridgnorth, Shropshire. See page 126   Above: Tiverton Castle, Tiverton, Devon. See page 44

Top Left: Groombridge Place, Groombridge, Kent. See page 78   Top Right: Elmers Court, Lymington,
Hampshire. See page 63   Above: Northcote Manor, Langho, Lancashire. See page 85

Top Left: Craiglands Hotel, Ilkley, West Yorkshire. See page 149   Top Right: Stragglethorpe Hall, Lincoln, Lincolnshire. See page 93   Above: Headland Hotel, Newquay, Cornwall. See page 30

Above: Alderley Edge Hotel, Alderley Edge, Cheshire. See page 19

Above: Bailiffscourt, Littlehampton, West Sussex. See page 146

Above: Polhawn Fort, Torpoint, Cornwall. See page 30

Top Left: Thurning Hall, East Dereham, Norfolk. See page 114   Top Right: Powderham Castle, Exeter Devon. See page 43   Above: The Cwrt Bleddyn Hotel, Llangybi, Monmouthshire. See page 163

Above: Stanhill Court Hotel, Charlwood, Surrey See page 138

Above: The Phyllis Court Club, Henley-on-Thames, Oxfordshire. See page 124

Top Left: St Brides Hotel, Saundersfoot, Pembrokeshire. See page 165
Top Right: Duncombe Park, Helmsley, North Yorkshire. See page 119
Above: The Grapevine Hotel, Stow-on-the-Wold, Gloucestershire. See page 59

Top: The Richmond Gate Hotel, Richmond, London. See page 101
The Pittville Pump Room, Cheltenham, Gloucestershire. See page 61

Top: Armathwaite Hall Hotel, Keswick, Cumbria. See page 31
Above: The Ravenswood Hotel, Sharpthorne, West Sussex. See page 148

Top: Trevigue, Crackington Haven, Cornwall. See page 31
Above: The Manor House, Castle Combe, Wiltshire. See page 156

Top Left: Cheltenham Racecourse, Gloucestershire. See page 58 Top Right: The Wild Boar Hotel, Tarporley, Cheshire. See page 27 Above: Combe Grove Manor, Monkton Combe, Bath. See page 106

Top: Esseborne Manor Hotel, Andover, Hampshire. See page 63
Above: Chilford Hall, Linton, Cambridgeshire. See page 17

Top Left: Hyatt Carlton Tower, London SW1. See page 97 Top Right: New Priory Hotel, Hereford.
See page 70 Above: Whatley Manor, Malmesbury, Wiltshire. See page 157

Top: The Orangery, Settrington, North Yorkshire. See page 120
Above: Hartford Hall, Hartford, Cheshire. See page 22

Top and above: Fennes, Bocking, Nr Braintree, Essex. See page 54

Above: The Mill House, Swallowfield, Nr Reading, Berkshire. See page 12

Leez Priory

Above: Leez Priory, Hartford End, Nr Chelmsford, Essex. See page 55

Top: Alder House Hotel, Batley, West Yorkshire. See page 148
Above: Bentley Wildfowl & Motor Museum, Halland, East Sussex. See page 50

Above: Curdon Mill,, Wiliton, Somerset. See page 127

Top: The Pear Tree at Purton, Nr Swindon, Wiltshire. See page 156
Above: Mains Hall, Singleton, Lancashire. See page 85

Above: Liverpool Town Hall, Liverpool, Merseyside. See page 111

Somerhill
Five Oak Green Road
Tonbridge
Kent TN11 0NJ
Tel: 01732 352124/01732 368398
Contact: Sarah Byrne, Events Manager

Ceremony

This Grade I Jacobean mansion, set in its own gardens, is now a school. It is available for weddings on Saturdays and Sundays and some week days throughout the year. It is not possible to hold ceremonies without a wedding breakfast here. There are two marriage rooms; the Slaon and the Grand Hall. The hire charge is for exclusive use of the mansion and grounds.
Price guide: £995 (Summer) £695 (Winter)

Reception

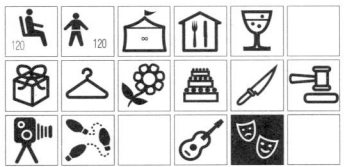

Catering: £21.95pp - £25.99pp

The Spa Hotel
Mount Ephraim
Tunbridge Wells, Kent TN4 8XJ
Tel: 01892 520331 Fax: 01892 510575
Contact: David Collier, James Pritchard

Ceremony

Price guide: £250

Reception

Catering: POA

Swallows Leisure Centre
Central Avenue
Sittingbourne, Kent ME10 4NT
Tel: 01795 420420 Fax: 01795 431324
Contact: David Hughes, Food & Beverage Co-ordinator

Ceremony

The modern Swallows Leisure Centre is situated in the heart of Sittingbourne and offers all round family leisure as well as a suite of function rooms.
Price guide: from £100

Reception

The Centre's Maitre'D has considerable experience of catering for large functions and has catered for the Queen and the Princess of Wales.
Catering: Buffets from £3.50pp Sit down from £12.95pp

Swarling Manor
Petham, Canterbury
Kent CT45 5QW
Tel/Fax: 01227 700377
Contact: C Lamb, Owner

Ceremony

This private manor house, dating from 1750 is located in a rural setting with its own 12 self catering cottages. Interestingly, the licensed room here is the Kitchen, which is available any day of the year except Bank Holidays.
Price guide: £250

Reception

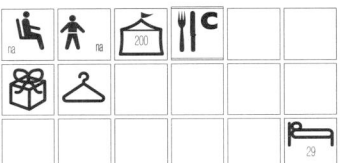

There are no reception facilites on site, but couples may appoint their own caterer, with the reception in a marquee.

Tenterden Town Hall
24 High Street
Tenterden
Kent TN30 6AN
Tel: 01580 762271 Fax: 01580 765647
Contact: Mrs CA O'Neill, Town Clerk

Ceremony

This Grade II listed 18th Century building is available for an unrestricted number of wedding ceremonies on any day of the week. Confetti is not permitted. There is a £50 price reduction on ceremony facilities for residents.
Price guide: from £150

Reception

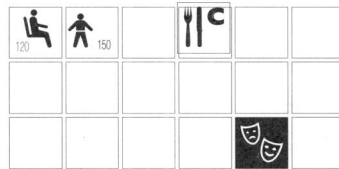

Couples need to arrange their own catering at this venue, but suitable function rooms are available. A list of local accommodation can be supplied.

Tonbridge Castle
Castle Street, Tonbridge
Kent TN9 1BG
Tel: 01732 876333 Fax: 01732 770449
Contact: Sheila Kostyrka, Tourism and Customer Services Manager

Ceremony

This is a motte and bailey castle, with a 13th Century gatehouse. It is local authority owned and an ancient monument. The marriage room is the Mansion House adjoining the Gatehouse. Ceremonies can take place on any day of the week, with only one permitted per day.
Price guide: £200

Reception

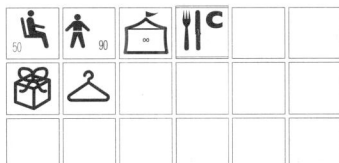

The marriage room can also be used for receptions, but couples must arrange their own catering. A marquee can be erected on the lawn by arrangement. There is no accommodation on the premises, but a list of local establishments with which the castle has preferential rate agreements is available on request.

STOP PRESS

Ashford International Terminal
01233 618501
The Chaucer Hotel, Canterbury
01227 464427
The Coniston Hotel, Sittingbourne
01795 472131
The County Hotel, Canterbury
01227 766266
Mount Ephraim, Nr Faversham
01227 751496
The Shurland, Isle of Sheppey
01795 881100
Windyridge, Whitstable
01227 263506
Yotes Court, Nr Maidstone
01622 814488

The Cornmill Hotel
Mount Pleasant
Holderness Road
Hull HU9 1LA
Tel: 01482 589000 Fax: 01482 586447
Contact: The Duty manager

Ceremony

This converted mill, situated in the heart of the business community and commercial areas of the city, offers ceremonies seven days a week from 9am to 5pm with no restrictions on the number held per day. No confetti.
Price guide: £250

Reception

The Alexandra Restaurant features original timber beams and cast iron columns. In addition to buffets and special menus, the hotel will strive to meet the religious or dietary requirements of wedding guests. Other services available include room decorations, the provision of stationery, cars, a beautician, balloons and children's entertainment.
Catering: Buffets from £5.75 Sit down from £30pp

Forte Posthouse Hull Marina
Castle Street
Hull HU1 2BX
Tel: 01482 225221 Fax: 01482 228926
Contact: Xanthe Carmichael, Meetings and Conference Manager

Ceremony

The hotel is based on the marina and has ceremonies available seven days a week withno restrictions on Bank Holidays. The hotel offers a maximum of four ceremonies per day depending on availability, and must be followed by reception at the hotel.
Price guide: £50

Reception

Catering from £22.50

STOP PRESS

Quality Royal Hotel, Ferensway
01482 323172

Astley Hall
Astley Park
Off Hall Gate
Chorley, Lancs PR7 1NP
Tel: 01257 515555 Fax: 01257 232441
Contact: Laura Morris, Administrator

Ceremony

This Grade I listed house dates back to the Elizabethan period. and is set in parkland. The Great Hall and the Dining Room hold liceces for weddings which can be held here on any day of the year. Confetti is not permitted.
Price guide: from £150

Reception

Reception facilities are not available on site.

Bartle Hall Country Hotel
Lea Lane
Bartle, Nr Preston
Lancs PR4 0HA
Tel: 01772 690506 Fax: 01772 690841
Contact: General Manager

Ceremony

Bartle Hall is a Grade II listed building set in 16 acres of landscaped gardens and woodland. Up to three ceremonies are permitted per day.
Price guide: £300

Reception

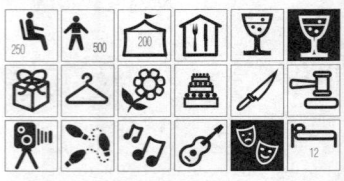

Bartle Hall's wedding package includes free overnight accommodation for bride and groom as well as full English breakfast, plus a reduced accommodation rate for guests.
Price guide: £8 - £30pp

Blackburn Rovers
Ewood Park
Blackburn
Lancs BB2 4JF
Tel: 01254 691919 Fax: 01254 671042
Contact: Carmel Dillon, Conference & Banqueting Manager

Ceremony

The Centenary Suite at the club's stadium is available on any day of the year. Ceremonies here must be followed by reception at the Club. Helicopters and hot air balloons can use the site.
Price guide: £100

Reception

Catering: Buffets from £5.95 Sit down from £15.95

Blackpool Tower Ballroom
Promenade
Blackpool
Lancs
Tel: 01253 22242
Contact: Mel Verren

Ceremony

Probably the major landmark in Blackpool, Blackpool Tower is now a Grade I listed building. The Ballroom is licensed for wedding ceremonies for a minimum of 50 guests. In keeping with the ambience of the building, an organist can be provided if required.
Price guide: POA

Reception

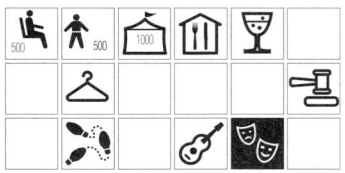

Catering: POA

Blackpool Town Hall
PO Box 77 , Blackpool
Lancs FY1 1AD
Tel: 01253 25212 Fax: 01253 751163
Contact Mr L Herrington, Principal Administrative Officer

Ceremony

Wedding ceremonies are held in the council chamber of this listed building. The chamber is available from Monday to Friday, but not on Bank Holidays. Confetti is only allowed outside.
Price guide: £50

Reception

No reception facilities are available on site, but a list of local accommodation can be provided.

The Crazy Horse Saloon
Frontierland Theme Park
Marine Road West
Morecambe Bay LA4 4DG
Tel: 01524 410024 Fax: 01524 831399
Contact: Sharon Leeson, Marketing Manager

Ceremony

The Crazy Horse Saloon is a western

style saloon bar sited in an American theme park. Ceremonies can take place here on any day of the year.
Price guide: from £100

Reception

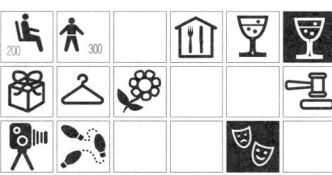

In keeping with the theme, outdoor barbecues are a speciality at the Saloon. The venue can also provide themed characters such as cowboys and Indians for a truly western style wedding.
Catering: Buffets from £5pp Sit down from £10pp

The Dunkenhalgh Hotel
Blackburn Road
Clayton-le-Moors
Accrington
Lancs BB5 5JP
Tel: 01254 398021 Fax: 01254872230
Contact: Gill Sith, Conference Director

Ceremony

The Dunkenhalgh Hotel is a Grade II listed building offering five ceremony rooms. These are available on any day of the year, but ceremonies here must be followed by reception at the hotel.
Price guide: £50

Reception

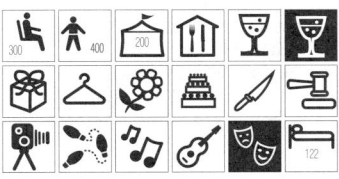

Several all-inclusive menus are offered, with choices within each price bracket. Wedding guests are offered discounts on overnight accommodation.
Catering: Buffets from £7pp Sit down from £24.50pp

The Farington Lodge
Stanifield Lane
Farington, Leyland
Lancs PR5 2QR
Tel: 01772 421321 Fax: 01772 455388
Contact: Steph Brewer, Events/Banqueting Manager

Ceremony

The Farington Lodge is a listed building set in gardens. The Victoria Room, Royal Room and Garden Room are all available for ceremonies on any day of the year. They have limited wheelchair access. Ceremonies here must be followed by reception at the Lodge.
Price guide: £150

Reception

Helicopters and hot air balloons may use the hotel grounds.
Catering: POA

Foxfields Country Hotel
Whalley Road
Billington
Clitheroe, Lancs   BB7 9HY
Tel: 01254 822556 Fax: 01254 824613
contact: Mike G Hill, GM

Ceremony

This is an AA 4-star hotel and part of the Lyric Hotel group. Ceremonies can take place in the Pendle Suite or the boardroom on any day of the year, but must be followed by reception at the hotel.
Price guide: FOC

Reception

Helicopters and hot air balloons may use the hotel grounds.
Catering: from £15pp

Gibbon Bridge Hotel
Forest of Bowland
Nr Chipping, Preston
Lancs PR3 2TQ
Tel: 01995 61456 Fax: 01995 61277
Contact: Janet Simpson, MD

Ceremony

The Gibbon Bridge Hotel is set in award-winning grounds overlooking the Longridge Fells in the heart of the Forest of Bowland. Ceremonies can be held in the Garden Room or in the new bandstand in the gardens. Both seat up to 25 seated guests, and have patio areas for further guests to congregate.
Price guide: £150

Reception

Catering: from £20pp

Harris Park Conference Centre
253 Garstang Road, Preston
Lancs PR2 9XB
Tel: 01772 717621 Fax: 01772 787243
contact: Roz Goodwin, Asst Manager or Jacqui Hateley, Manager

Ceremony

The conference centre is a Victorian building set in 15 acres of grounds. The Main Hall and Conservatory Bar are licensed for ceremonies which can take place here on any day of the year.
Price guide: £200

Reception

In addition to the above services, the centre can provide decorative balloons.
Catering: Buffets from £5.99pp sit down from £15pp

Higher Trapp
Country House Hotel
Trapp Lane
Simonstone
Lancs
Tel: 01282 772781 Fax: 01282 772782
Contact: Warren Marsh, Banqueting

Ceremony

Price guide: P.O.A.

Reception

Catering: P.O.A.

Horncliffe Mansions
Bury Road
Rawtenstall
Lancs BB4 6JS
Tel: 01706 213093 Fax: 01706 222929
Contact :Owner

Ceremony

Price guide: P.O.A.

Reception

Catering: P.O.A.

Inn at Whitewell
Forest of Bowland
Nr Clitheroe
Lancs BB7 3AT
Tel: 01200 448222 Fax: 01200 448298
Contact: Jonty Haighton, Partner

Ceremony

Price guide: £100

Reception

Catering: £17.50 - £22pp

Leigh Town Hall
Market Street
Wigan, Lancs
Tel: 01942 672421
Contact: Halls Manager

Ceremony

Price guide: P.O.A.

Reception

Unfortunately, there are no reception facilities available at Leigh Town Hall. However, wedding receptions can be held nearby at the adjacent Derby Rooms, although separate arrangements will have to be made for ceremony and reception.
For full details of the reception packages that are available at The Derby Rooms, you should telephone 01942 244991.
Catering. P.O.A.

Leyland Masonic Hall
Wellington Park
Burlington Gardens
Church Road
Leyland, Lancs
Tel: 01772 432881 Fax: 01772 453151
Contact: General Manager

Ceremony

This modern building, dating from the late 1980s, has four licensed rooms, which are available seven days per week. Ceremonies and receptions must both be held at the hall. Confetti is allowed. A local accommodation list is available, including preferential rates.
Price guide: F.O.C. (with reception)

Reception

Price guide: from £12.75pp (package)

Mains Hall
Mains Lane
Little Singleton
Poulton-le-Fylde
Lancs FY6 7LE
Tel: 01253 885130 Fax: 01253 894132
Contact: R Yeomans, Proprietor

Ceremony

This was once the home of Prince Regent George IV and is a Grade II listed house built in 1536. It is set in five acres of grounds, with private access to the River Wyre. There are formal walled gardens, featuring old walnut trees, orchards and an ornamental fountain. Two rooms are available for ceremonies: the oak panelled hall, with room for 40 guests, and the Royal Garden Room, which can accommodate up to 150.
Price guide: from £60

Reception

The house has a recently refurbished dining room overlooking the river. For the catering, a discount of 50% is offered for children under 12 years old, while no charge is made for children under 2 years old. A complimentary four-poster suite is offered if all the hotel rooms are booked for the wedding guests.
Catering: from £28pp

Mawdsleys Eating House
Hall Lane
Mawdesley
Nr Ormskirk
Lancs L40 2QZ
Tel: 01704 822552 Fax: 01704 822096
Contact: Michael Gilroy, GM

Ceremony

This former basket works is set in the village of Mawdsley which was recently voted Lancashire's Best Kept Village. Two rooms are licensed for ceremonies and are available any day of the year.
Price guide: £50

Reception

Catering: Sit down from 14pp

The Mill at Croston
Moor Road, Croston, Lancs
Tel: 01772 600110 Fax: 01772 601623
Contact: Max Pierce, GM

Ceremony

The Mill was originally a farm building that has now been converted to a 46 bedroom hotel with restaurant, bar and banqueting complex... Two suites are licensed for ceremonies.
Price guide: £100

Reception

Catering: Sit down from £14.95pp

Mytton Fold Farm Hotel
Whalley Road, Blackburn
Lancs BB6 8BE
Tel: 01254 240662 Fax: 01254 248119
Contact: Mrs Lilian Hargreaves, owner

Ceremony

Set in its own grounds with gardens, featuring a gazebo, and 18 hole golf course Mytton Fold Farm is a privately owned hotel which allows only one ceremony at a time on any day of the week.
Price guide: £150

Reception

The hotel has five rooms suitable for wedding receptions, but will only accept two wedding parties at any one time; these could be for parties as small as 10 guests. The wedding package includes complimentary bridal suite for the wedding night. Flowers, cake stand and knife, piped music and a stage can all be provided free of charge; other services extra.
Catering: £15

North Euston Hotel
The Esplanade, Fleetwood, Lancs
Tel: 01253 876525
Contact: Hilary Johns, Partner

Ceremony

Price guide: P.O.A.

Reception

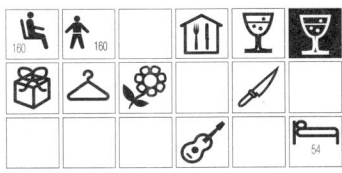

Catering: P.O.A.

Northcote Manor
Northcote Road, Langho
Lancs BB6 8BE
Tel: 01254 240555 Fax: 01254 246568
Contact: Craig J Bancroft, GM

Ceremony

This is a small country house hotel, and winner of the Good Hotel Guide's Country Hotel of the Year for 1995. It has been owned and run by Craig Bancroft and Nigel Haworth since 1983. The Northcote Hotel, which is situated in the Ribble Valley, limits ceremonies to one a day, on any day except Christmas Day and Boxing Day.
Price guide: £200

Reception

Northcote's Chef Patron, Nigel Haworth won Egon Ronay's Chef of the Year for 1995. His cuisine is described as 'British cookery with modern tones', and includes many Lancashire specialities.
Catering: £25-£30pp

Oaks Hotel
Colne Road, Reedley
Burnley
Lancs BB10 2LF
Tel: 01282 414141 Fax: 01282 33401
Contact: Tina Ostler, Banqueting Manager

Ceremony

The Oaks is a Victorian style Grade II listed building featuring a stained glass window in the main lounge. The hotel stands in four acres at the foot of Pendle Hill. Two ceremonies are allowed per day on any day of the week.
Price guide: £150

Reception

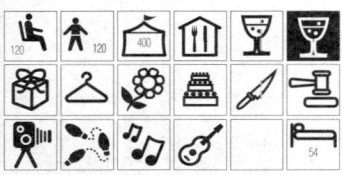

While accommodation is available on the premises, the hotel also has preferential rate agreements with other local establishments.
Catering: from £6.50

Park Hall Hotel
Charnock Richard
Chorley
Nr Preston
PR7 5LP
Tel:-1257 452090 Fax: 01257 451838
Contact: Alison Wilcock,
Wedding Co-ordinator

Ceremony

Park Hall is set in 137 acres of grounds featuring a scenic lake. A wedding licence is held for the medieval banqueting hall, and ceremonies can be held here on any day except Sunday. Ceremonies must be followed by reception at the hotel.
Price guide: £120

Reception

Helicopters and hot air balloons may use the hotel grounds. For those looking for a period feeling, however, the hotel can offer a full medieval banquet with full entertainment.
Catering: Buffets from £9.95pp Sit down from £14.95pp

Pines Hotel
Preston Road
Chorley
Lancs PR6 7ED
Tel: 01772 338551 Fax: 01772 629002
Contact: Clare Seefus,
General Manager

Ceremony

Price guide: P.O.A.

Reception

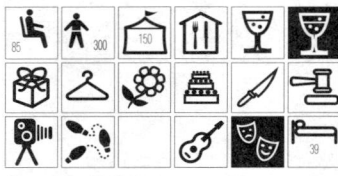

Catering: P.O.A.

Rosehill House Hotel
Rosehill Avenue
Burnley
Lancs BB11 2PW
Tel: 01282 453031 Fax: 01282 455628
Contact: Jacky Doherty, Proprietor

Ceremony

This listed stone mansion features ornate architecture, including highly decorative ceilings. The two restaurants have ceremony licences. While the maximum capacity in these is currently 50, this will double by Spring this year. Weddings can take place here on any day except Sundays, but must be followed by reception at the hotel.
Price guide: FOC

Reception

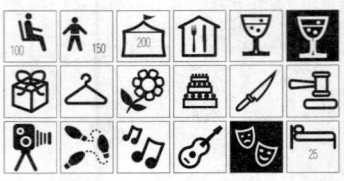

Reception capacites will also double from Spring 1997, when live music and entertainment will also be a possiblity at this venue.
Catering: Buffets from £7.50pp Sit down from £19.50pp

Savoy Hotel
Queens Promenade
Blackpool FY2 9JS
Tel: 01253 352561 Fax: 01253 500735
Contact: Barrie Aspinall, GM

Ceremony

The Savoy is currently the only hotel on the Promenade to hold a wedding licence. Four rooms are licensed and are suitable for a minimum capacity of 50 guests.
Price guide: from £50 - £250

Reception

If a minimum of £7.50 per head is spent on catering, the ceremony room hire fee is waived.
Catering: Buffets from £5.95pp sit down from £14.95pp

Sparth House Hotel
Whalley Road
Clayton-Le-Moors
Accrington BB5 5RP
Tel/Fax: 01254 872263
Contact: Victoria Taylor, PA to owner

Ceremony

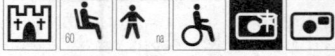

The Sparth House is a listed building (1740)featuring period interiors and gardens. The Oak Room and Regency Room are licensed and ceremonies may take place here on any day of the year

except Christmas Day. Helicopters and hot air balloons may use the grounds.
Price guide:POA

Reception

Catering: Buffets from £6pp Sit down from £16pp

Springfield House Hotel
Wheel Lane
Pilling, Nr Preston
Lancs PR3 6HL
Tel: 01253 790301 Fax: 01253 790907
Contact: Mrs ME Cookson, Proprietor

Ceremony

Two rooms are available for wedding ceremonies in this Grade II listed Georgian building set within walled gardens. Ceremonies are restricted to one per day, on any day except Sunday.
Price guide: £150

Reception

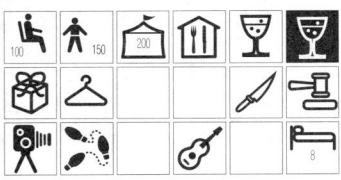

Table decorations form part of the reception package at Springfield. The hotel can also provide a list of other accommodation available locally.
Catering: £18.50pp

Stirk House Hotel
Gisburn
Nr Clitheroe
Lancs BB7 4LJ
Tel: 01200 445581 Fax: 01200 445744
Contact: Mr M Weaving

Ceremony

Originally a 16th Century manor house, Stirk House is located six miles from Clitheroe. The hotel has land-

scaped gardens to the front. Up to two ceremonies are allowed at the venue per day.
Price guide: £100

Reception

Catering: £12.50 - £31

The Tickled Trout
Preston New Road
Salmesbury
Nr Preston PR5 0LJ
Tel: 01772 877671 Fax: 01772463
Contact: Rachel Waters, Banqueting Manager

Ceremony

This hotel enjoys a riverside location with grounds featuring a fountain and kissing arch. The Rainbow and Ribble Suites are licensed for ceremonies which can take place here any day of the year.
Price guide: £50

Reception

Catering: Buffets from £7.75pp Sit down from £14.95pp

Whoop Hall Inn
Burrow with Burrow
Kirby Lonsdale
Carnforth
Tel: 015242 71284 Fax: 015242 72154
Contact: Elaine Dean, GM

Ceremony

The Inn offers its Lonsdale Suite and Ruskin Room for ceremonies which can take place here on any day of the year. There is good wheelchair acess to the Lonsdale Suite.
Price guide: POA

Reception

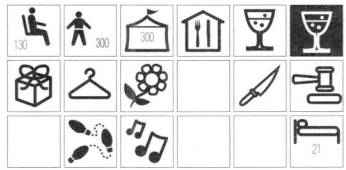

Helicopters and hot air balloons may use the grounds.
Catering: Buffets from £5.95pp Sit down from £13pp

STOP PRESS
Beaufort Hotel, Burscough
01704 892655
Bowers Hotel, Garstang
01995 602120
Burnley Friendly Hotel 01282 427611
Celebrations, Kirkham 01772 671111
Fence Gate Inn, Fence 01282 618101
Hampson House Hotel, Lancaster
01524 751158
Marine Hall, Fleetwood 01253 771141
Olde England Kiosk, Darwen
01254 701530
The Paradise Room, Blackpool,
01253 341033
Seabank Hotel, Blackpool
01253 22717
Shaw Hill Hotel, Chorley
01257 269221
West Tower Country Hotel, Aughton
01695 423328
Whitewalls Restaurant, Lancaster
01524 822768

Barnsdale Country Club
Barnsdale, Exton, Leics LE15 8AB
Tel: 01572 757901 Fax: 01572 756235
Contact: Jane Downs (Tel: 01572 722209)

Ceremony

This hotel and restaurant is also a club and time share site. The Club is set in a 60 acre estate of gardens and woodland on the shores of Rutland Water. Wheelchair access is limited.
Price guide: £150

Reception

The Club offers a choice of rooms for receptions, including one that overlooks Rutland Water.
Catering: from £13.50pp

Barnsdale Lodge Hotel
The Avenue, Rutland Water
Oakham, Leics LE15 8AH
Tel: 01572 724678 Fax: 01572 724961
Contact: John Farrington GM

Ceremony

The hotel offers two marriage rooms: the Barn Suite (max 220 seated) and the Conservatory (max 50 seated). Weddings can take place here any day of the year.
Price guide: £100 + vat

Reception

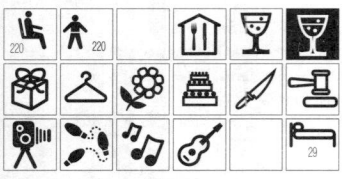

Catering: from £15pp

Beaumanor Hall
Woodhouse, Loughborough
Leics LE12 8TX
Tel: 01509 890119 Fax: 01509 891021
Contact: Liz Funnell, Accommodation Officer

Ceremony

The Hall was originally built in the 1840s for a wealthy landowner. It was purchased by Leicestershire County Council in 1974 as a training and conference centre for council employees. Features include ornate ceilings, wood carvings and elaborate stone and plaster work. There is also a galleries central hall with sweeping staircase and stained glass windows.
Price guide: £190

Reception

While there is no accommodation available on the premises, a list of local establishments with which the Hall has preferential rate agreements can be supplied on request.
Catering Buffets from £4.25pp sit down from £14pp

Belmont House Hotel
De Montfort Street
Leicester LE1 7GR
Tel: 0116 2544773
Contact: Sally Summerscales, Conference & Banqueting

Ceremony

Several rooms are licensed for ceremonies taking from 6 to 75 guests. Weddings can take place here on any day except Sundays and Bank Holidays. Ceremonies must be followed by reception at the hotel.
Price guide: POA

Reception

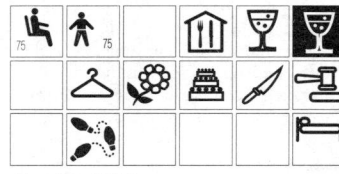

Catering: POA

The Castle Hotel
Main Street
Kirby Muxloe
Leicester LE9 2AP
Tel: 0116 239 5337
Fax: 0116 238 7868
Contact: Mr T Doblander, GM

Ceremony

The Castle Hotel is set in a quiet village, just four miles from Leicester city centre. At the back of the hotel is the remains of a 14th Century castle, with wooden bridge (a suitable location for photographs). The hotel also has large award-winning gardens. Helicopters and hot air balloons may use the grounds. Ceremonies can take place in the Hastings Suite on any day except Sunday, Christmas Day and New Year's Day. At weekends, ceremonies should be followed by reception at the hotel.
Price guide: £200

Reception

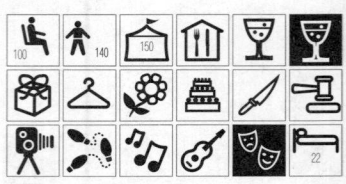

Cuisine at the hotel is described as 'English/Continental'.
Catering: Buffets from £9.50pp Sit down from £19.50pp

Charnwood Arms Hotel
Beveridge Lane
Bardon, Coalville
Leics LE67 2TB
Tel: 01530 813644 Fax: 01530 815425
Contact: Jim Conway GM

Ceremony

This modern, recently refurbished, hotel and public house offers wedding ceremonies on any day of the week, but limits these to one per day. It is not possible to hold the ceremony here without the reception.
Price guide: FOC (with wedding breakfast and evening function)

Reception

Catering: from £15pp

Hambleton Hall
Hambleton
Oakham, Rutland
Leics LE15 8TH
Tel: 01572 756991 Fax: 01572 724721
Contact: Sue Perkin, House Manger

Ceremony

Hambleton has a starred Michelin restaurant and is a member of the Relais & Chateaux collection of exclusive hotels. It was originally built in 1881 as a hunting box, and has views over Rutland Water. Three rooms are licensed for ceremonies; The Study (max 12 people), the Private Dining

Room (max 20 people) and The Restaurant (max 40 people).
Price guide: from £250

Reception

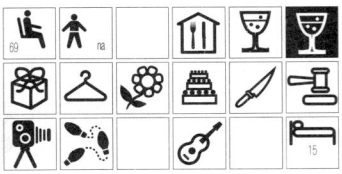

The head chef here is Aaron Patterson. Professional service and an interesting selection of wines are boasted as top priorities at this friendly hotel.
Catering: from £35pp

Hotel St James
Abbey Street
Leicester
Leics LE1 3TE
Tel: 0116 251 0666 Fax: 0116 575 183
Contact: Heather Doldie

Ceremony

This modern city centre hotel offers one marriage room; the French Suite. Weddings can take place here on any day except Christmas Day with only one ceremony per day.
Price guide: £100

Reception

A complimentary room is provided for bride and groom to change in during the day.
Catering: from £12.50pp

Leicester City Football Club
City Stadium
Filbert Street
Leicester LE2 7FL
Tel: 0116 291 5000
Fax: 0116 247 0585
Contact: Nickie Howard,
Conference Development Manager

Ceremony

Team supporters will be delighted that the Club is now licensed for wedding ceremonies. These can take place in the Boardroom or the Bradgate Suite on any day except when matches are played at home. Photos can, of course, be taken on the pitch, and the Club can arrange for a player to be present.
Price guide: £180

Reception

The Club has established banqueting facilities, and says it can be very flexible, depending upon requirements.
Catering: from £15pp

Leicester Town Hall
Town Hall Square
Leicester
Tel: 0116 254 9922 Fax: 0116 285 5681
Contact: Andrew Bubb, Administration Buildings Manager

Ceremony
Whilst the City Council holds a licence to hold civil wedding ceremonies at Leicester Town Hall, bookings for wedding are not currently being taken as possible building and refurbishment worked is planned. Contact the property services division for an update.

Leicestershire Museum
& Art Gallery
New Walk
Leicester
LE1 1EA
Tel: 0116 255 4100 Fax: 0116 247 3005
Contact: Mrs Helene Kelly, Commercial Services Officer

Ceremony

This is a major regional museum and art gallery featuring local and national collections including many romantic Victorian fine art pieces. Ceremonies can take place in the Victorian Gallery on any day except Sunday, and Bank Holidays. Confetti is not permitted.
Price guide: £155

Reception
There are no reception facilities on site.

Melton Mowbray Council Offices
Nottingham Road
Melton Mowbray
Leics LE12 8TX
Tel: 01664 67771 Fax: 01664 410283
Contact: Chief Technical Officer

Ceremony

Three marriage rooms are offered for weddings at the council offices; the Council Chamber (up to 250), the Egerton Room (up to 80) and the Warwick Room (up to 40). Weddings can take palce on any day except Bank Holidays.
Price guide: POA

Reception
There are no reception facilities at the offices.

Normanton Park Hotel
Rutland Water
South Shore
Oakham, Leics LE15 8RP
Tel: 01780 720315 Fax: 01780 721086
Contact: General Manager

Ceremony

The hotel was originally the stable block to the Georgian Normanton Manor House. It is only 50 yards from the edge of Rutland Water and set in five acres of parkland. Weddings can take place here on any day of the year.
Price guide: £170

Reception

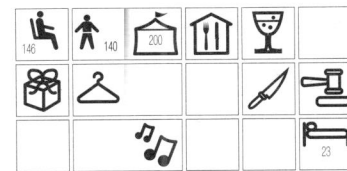

A late night drinking licence can be applied for if required. Catering arrangements are flexible.
Catering: from £32pp

Oakham Castle
Market Place
Oakham
Leics
LE15 6JW
Tel: 01572 732654 Fax: 01572 757576
Contact: Mr Tim Clough, Keeper

Ceremony

This 12th Century scheduled ancient monument is Grade I listed and houses the Court of Justice on a Monday – hence no ceremonies allowed on this day. Christmas Day, Boxing Day and New Year's Day are also not available. Two rooms have marriage licences; The Great Hall, adorned with over 200 presentation horseshoes!, and the Court Room (30 people max). While there is reasonable disabled access, there are no disabled toilet facilities. Confetti is not permitted.
Price guide: Tues-Sat £145 Sunday or Bank Holiday £175.

Reception

There are no reception facilities at the Castle.

Prestwold Hall
Prestwold, Loughborough
Leics LE12 5SQ
Tel: 01509 880236 Fax: 01636 812187
Contact: Annabel Weldon, GM

Ceremony

Prestwold Hall was largely remodelled in 1843 and has been in the Packe family for 350 years. It is now a conference centre, still owned by a descendant of the Packe family and not open to the general public. Ceremonies take place on any day except Christmas Day and must be followed by reception at the house.
Price guide: £150

Reception

The Hall offers home-made food using home grown ingredients where possible.
Catering: from £21pp

Quality Friendly Hotel
New Ashby Road
Loughborough, Leics LE11 0EX
Tel: 01509 211800 Fax: 01509 21868
Contact: Conference & Banqueting Manager

Ceremony

This modern hotel offers weddings in the Beaumanor Suite, which comprises four rooms. It is not possible to hold ceremonies here without also booking the reception facilities. Confetti is not permitted. Outdoor photography is limited.
Price guide: no charge at present

Reception

A late night drinking licence can be applied for if required. Kosher and Asian caterers can be permitted on discussion with the hotel.
Catering:buffets from £6.75pp Sit down from £14.45pp

Quorn Country Hotel
66 Leicester Road, Quorn
Loughborough, Leics LE12 8BB
Tel: 01509 415050 Fax: 01509 415557
Contact: Debby Robinson, Sales Manager or Heather Brewin, Sales Executive

Ceremony

This hotel and restaurant permits one ceremony per day on any day except Sundays and Bank Holidays.
Price guide: POA

Reception

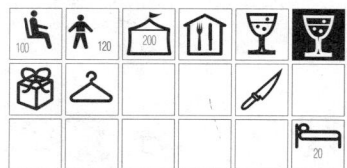

The hotel has been awarded an AA Rosette for the quality of its cuisine.
Catering: POA

Sketchley Grange Hotel
Sketchley Lane
Burbage,, Hinckley
Leics LE10 3HU
Tel: 01455 251133 Fax: 01455 631384
Contact: Sales Manager

Ceremony

The hotel permits up to two ceremonies per day on any day of the year.
Price guide: £300

Reception

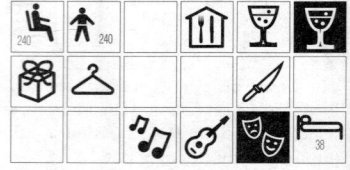

Several rooms are available for receptions, including the Bradgate Suite, with its own bar, lounge and foyer; the Willow Room (up to 100 guests), overlooking the garden; and the Warwick Room (up to 50 guests). The catering has recently received an AA Rosette.
Catering: from £16pp

Stage Hotel
299 Leicester Road
Wigston Fields
Leicester
LE18 1JW
Tel: 0116 288 6161 Fax: 0116 281 1874
Contact: Michelle Warner, Sales Manager

Ceremony

The Stage Hotel is situated south of the city centre near to the ring road. Two rooms are licensed; the Knighton Suite (up to 50 guests), and the Oadby Suite (up to 100 guests). The price guide allows for one hour's use. There is an additional charge of £50 per half hour for any extra time required. Ceremonies can take place on any day except Sunday.
Price guide: POA

Reception

Asian weddings can be catering for at the hotel. A 10% discount is given for all Monday to Friday or Sunday wedding receptions.
Catering POA

Stapleford Park Country House Hotel, Stapleford
Melton Mowbray
Leics LE14 2EF
Tel: 01572 787522 Fax: 01572 787332
Contact: Mrs Annabel Eley, Wedding & Banqueting co-ordinator

Ceremony

This well-known Grade II listed building, is set in grounds designed by Capability Brown. The Drawing Room (max 50) and the Morning Room (max 20) are available for ceremonies on any day of the year except Christmas and New Year. Receptions at the hotel must follow ceremonies here. Confetti is not permitted.
Price guide: from £250 + vat

Reception

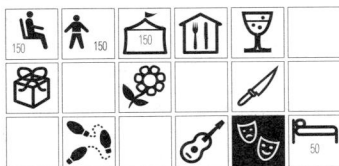

Helicopters and hot air balloons may use the grounds of the hotel.
Catering: from £35pp

The Three Swans Hotel
High Street
Market Harborough
Leics LE16 7NJ
Tel: 01858 466644 Fax: 01858 433101
Contact: General Manager

Ceremony

Up to two ceremonies per day are permitted at this 16th Century coaching inn. These can take place in the Cygnet Room on any day except Good Friday and Christmas Day. Some assistance would be required with wheelchairs.
Price guide: from £85

Reception

The hotel can offer a selection of well-persented banqueting menus. As well as the above service, the hotel can offer personalised menus, a 'good luck' token and bedrooms with four poster beds.
Catering: from £16.85pp

STOP PRESS
Donnington Manor Hotel, Castle Donnington 01332 810253
Fernie Lodge Hotel, Husbands Bosworth 01858 880551
Hermitage Park Hotel, Coalville 01530 814814
Olde Stocks Restaurant, Grimston 01664 812255
Quorn Grange Hotel, Loughborough 01509 412167

Brackenborough Arms Hotel
Cordeaux Corner
Brackenborough
Louth, Lincolnshire LN11 0SZ
Tel: 01507 609169 Fax: 01507 609413
Contact: Rosemary, Duty Manageress

Ceremony

The hotel is situated in the heart of the Lincolnshire Wolds in its own landscaped grounds. Ceremonies are available seven days a week.
Price guide: £175

Reception

Catering is in-house and the hotel prides itself on 35 years of cuisine experience. Although the hotel can not provide the wedding cake and photography themselves, they can organise them externally.
Catering: from £12pp

Comfort Friendly Inn
Bicker Bar Roundabout
Boston, Lincolnshire PE20 3AN
Tel: 01205 820118 Fax: 01205 820228
Contact: Chris Crowfoot

Ceremony

This modern building built in 1993 is situated in limited grounds and is available to hold ceremonies seven days a week on any day of the year excluding Christmas Day and New Years Eve. It is possible to hold your wedding ceremony without a reception at the Comfort Friendly Inn.
Price guide: POA

Reception

Catering is in-house and although there is no area available to display wedding gifts there is a room for the bride and groom to change in.
Catering: from £7pp.

Fydell House
South Square
Boston
Lincs PE21 6HU
Tel: 01205 351520 Fax: 01205 358363
Contact: David Jones, Christine Wright, Julie Smith

Ceremony

This is a university adult education centre set in a Grade I listed building. The 18th Century house is set in the centre of town and has its own gardens. Two rooms (American and Green) are licensed for weddings and are available on any day of the year, but booking are usually easier for out of term time.
Price guide: £50

Reception
Couples have a choice of caterer for this venue.

The George Hotel
71 High Street
St Martins, Stamford PE9 2LB
Tel: 01780 755171 Fax: 01780 757070
Contact: Wedding Co-ordinator

Ceremony

The George offers three ceremony rooms which are available on any day of the year. Ceremonies here must be

followed by reception at the hotel.
Price guide: POA

Reception

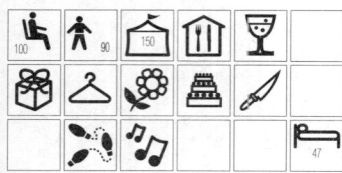

Catering: from £16.50pp

Golf Hotel
The Broadway
Woodhall Spa
Lincolnshire LN10 6SG
Tel: 01526 353535 Fax: 01526 353096
Contact: Rose Thomson, Deputy
Manager

Ceremony

This Tudor-style building is set in
seven acres of grounds and features a
terraced area to the front of the hotel.
Ceremonies are available seven days a
week excluding Christmas Day and
Boxing Day, with two permitted per
day.
Price guide: £150

Reception

Catering costs range from £4.25 to a
maximum of £16.95pp. Children
under five years of age are catered for
free of charge while those aged
between five and 12 are half price.
The couple is offered a complimentary
bridal suite, while special room rates are
available for wedding guests. In addition to the services indicated, the hotel
is happy to organise celebratory fireworks. The rear lawn is suitable to act
as a helicopter landing pad.
Catering: Buffets from £4.25pp Sit
down from £23pp

The Judges Lodgings
Castle Hill
Lincoln LN1 3AA
Tel: 01522 511068 Fax: 01522 512150
Contact: Peter Allen, Manager

Ceremony

This historic building, located between
Lincoln Castle and the Cathedral, is still
used as the judge's lodging when the
Judge is sitting at the Crown Courts.
The Sitting Room is licensed for cere-
monies and is available every day of the
year.
Price guide: £200

Reception

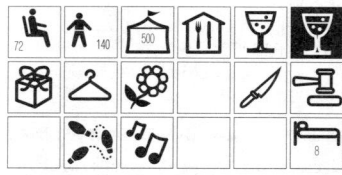

Catering: Buffets from £6.50pp Sit
down from £18.50pp

Kenwick Park
Hotel & Leisure Club
Kenwick Park, Louth
Lincolnshire LN11 8NR
Tel: 01507 608806 Fax: 01507 608027
Contact: Craig Dowie, GM

Ceremony

This country house is set in 500 acres
of grounds and allows a maximum of
three ceremonies per day.
Price guide: £250

Reception

Catering costs average between £15
and £40pp. The hotel offers a full
honeymoon package including accommodation in the luxury suite at an additional cost of £65 providing the reception is also held at the hotel.
Catering: from £15pp.

Petwood House Hotel
Stixwold Road, Woodhall Spa
Lincolnshire LN10 6QF
Tel: 01526 352411 Fax: 01526 353473
Contact: Linda Chalmers, Conference
& Banqueting Co-ordinator

Ceremony

The House is set in 30 acres of woodland with extensive lawns and was built
at the turn of the century for Lady
Weigall. It was also the war-time
home of 617 Squadron, the
"Dambusters", and features extensive
oak panelling with a carved main staircase. Ceremonies are not available on
Christmas Day and New Year's Eve.
Price guide: £150

Reception

A late night drinking licence is held for
residents only. The House also operates preferential rate agreements with
local hotels and guest houses.
Price guide: from £20pp.

Stoke Rochford Hall
Stoke Rochford, Grantham
Lincolnshire NG33 5EJ
Tel: 01476 530337 Fax: 01476 530534
Contact: Conference Department

Ceremony

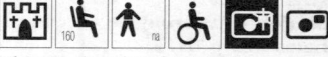

This Grade I listed Victorian mansion
house is set in 28 acres of gardens and
over 1,000 acres of parkland. The Hall
has five rooms licensed to hold ceremonies with varying capacities from 30
to 160. Although the Hall will consider holding ceremonies any day of the
week, it prefers to hold them at weekends only. Ceremonies can only be
held in conjunction with receptions.
Price guide: £150

Reception

The Hall offers a reception package
costing £32pp which includes all food
and drink but not an evening function.
Included in the package is an overnight

stay for the couple, with a champagne breakfast.
Catering: Buffets from £5.95pp Sit down from £18.25pp

Stragglethorpe Hall
Lincoln LN5 0QZ
Tel: 01400 272308 Fax: 01400 273816
Contact: Mrs Michael Rook, Proprietor

Ceremony

This former monastic buiding is Grade II listed and set in gardens. The Great Hall and Dining Room are both licensed for weddings which can take place here on any day except Christmas Day and Easter..
Price guide: £400

Reception

Discos and live modern music are only feasible in a marquee. Helicopters and hot air balloons can use the grounds.
Catering: from £18pp

STOP PRESS
Branston Hall Hotel, Branston
01522 793305
Fantasy Island, Ingoldmells
01754 872030
Lady Anne's Hotel, Stamford
Tel: 01780 481184
Northope Hall, Gainsborough
Tel: 01724 764848

Alexandra Palace
Alexandra Palace Way
Wood Green,London N22 4AY
Tel: 0181 365 2121 Fax: 0181 883 3889
Contact: Sarah Freds, Sales Co-ordinator

Ceremony

This impressive Victorian Palace can accommodate even the largest of weddings in style. Only one room, The Londesborough Room, is available seven days a week for marriage ceremonies, with one wedding permitted

per day. Confetti is permitted indoors only.
Price Guide: £950

Reception

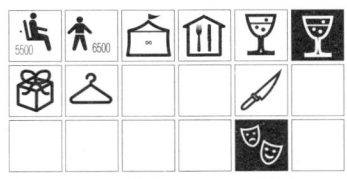

Reception facilities are available in several rooms including The Palm Court (with seating for 170), The Palace Restaurant (seating 300), The West Hall (seating 2,000) and The Great Hall (seating 5,500 or accommodating 6,500 for a buffet style reception). A marquee of unlimited capacity can be sited in nearby parkland. Catering is provided in-house. Accommodation at local hotels, at preferential rates, can be arranged.
Catering: approx £29.50pp

Berkeley Hotel
Wilton Place
London SW1
Tel: 0171 235 6000 Fax: 0171 823 1743
Contact: Rosemary Russell, Banqueting Co-ordinator

Ceremony

The Berkeley Hotel in Knightbridge is an ideal choice for a prestigious wedding. Ceremonies are currently permitted on any day, though the hotel is restricted to one wedding per day. Three rooms are available for the reception, namely the Waterloo Room, which seats 20, the Belgravia room (40) and the Ballroom (250).
Price Guide: POA

Reception

The Berkeley Hotel, member of the Savoy group, boasts five red stars and two rosettes. The hotel can cater for up to 450 guests for a buffet style reception, and 120 for a seated dinner. Both in-house and contract catering from an approved list is offered and the hotel is

able to provide a wide variety of cuisine including Kosher.
Catering: from £18.50pp

The Bridge
Kangley Bridge Road
Lower Sydenham
London SE26 5AQ
Tel: 0181 778 7158 Fax: 0181 659 2680
Contact: Manager

Ceremony

The Bridge is the community leisure centre of Lower Sydenham, and has three licensed rooms for wedding ceremonies, seating 110, 70 and 25 people respectively. A perfect choice for sports enthusiasts, who can even tie the knot in the centre's Training Room. Availability is subject to demand only, as the centre is open every day of the week and is not restricted to a maximum number of ceremonies per day. Confetti is permitted outside the building only.
Price Guide: from £50

Reception

Three rooms are available for the reception, namely the Sports Hall (with a seated capacity of 200), the Functions Room (100) and the Conference Room (40). Both in-house and contract catering is available, and self-catering facilities are also offered.
Catering: from £4- £15pp

Burgh House
New End Sqaure
Hampstead NW3 1LT
Tel: 0171 431 0144
Contact: Pauline Pleasance, Administrator

Ceremony

This Grade I listed Queen Anne house (1703) is run by an independent trust, and is a popular venue for meetings, concerts and exhibitions. Its garden was designed after the style of Gertrude

Jekyll. The panelled Music Room is licensed for ceremonies and is available Wednesday to Saturday inclusive.
Price guide: £125

Reception

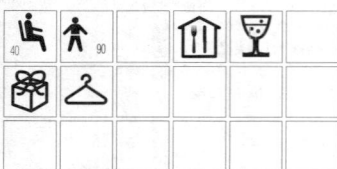

Catering here is generally finger buffet or fork buffet, with Scandinavian food a speciality.
Catering: £10-£20pp

Cambridge Cottage
37 Kew Green
Royal Botanic Garden
Kew, Richmond TW9 3AB
Tel: 0181 332 5616 Fax: 0181 332 5632
Contact: Sarah Corser, Events Manager

Ceremony

Cambridge Cottage, a Grade II listed 18th century building, is set in over 300 acres of the famous Kew Gardens. The Lounge is licensed to hold the wedding ceremony, and can accommodate up to 50 guests, seated or standing. Weddings can be held any day of the week, except between 23rd December and 2nd January. Confetti is not allowed.
Price Guide: POA

Reception

The Gallery at Cambridge Cottage can house receptions of up to 80 for a seated dinner and 120 for a buffet. The venue has a list of approved caterers. Guests can enjoy an intimate reception here surrounded by and exhibition of fine botanical paintings.
Catering: P.O.A.

Cannizaro House
West Side, Wimbledon Common
London SW19 4UE
Tel: 0181 879 1464 Fax: 0181 879 7338
Contact: Lucy Robinson, Banqueting

Ceremony

Cannizaro House, a Georgian mansion on the edge of Wimbledon Common, claims to be London's first country house hotel. The Queen Elizabeth Room alone is licensed to hold wedding ceremonies, and can seat up to 60 guests. Standing spaces are not allowed by the venue during the ceremony. Weddings are currently permitted every day except Sundays and are only available in conjunction with a reception.
Price Guide: £750

Reception

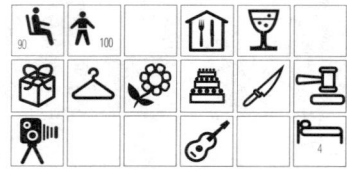

Receptions can be held in the elegant drawing room, which overlooks the terrace and Cannizaro Park. Drinks can be served outside if weather permits. Alternatively, a choice of private dining rooms is available. These can seat up to 90 guests for waited service, or 100 for a buffet reception. Smaller rooms, for around 40 guests, can also be hired. Award winning in-house chefs provide catering.
Catering: approx. £25pp

Chelsea Football Club
Fulham Road, London SW6 1HS
Tel: 0171 385 5545 Fax: 0171 381 4831
Contact: Debra Ware

Ceremony

The perfect wedding site for fans, Chelsea FC even offers tours of the ground for interested wedding visitors. Two rooms are licensed to hold ceremonies. Weddings are not permitted on match days and Sundays.
Price Guide: £300

Reception

Chelsea FC can cater for 200 guests for

a seated banquet and up to 350 for a seated buffet. A marquee, seating up to 200, is also available. The Leith's trained chef can provide catering for any type and scale of event, from basic buffets and pub-style food to a five course silver service dinner. A children's menu at lower rates is also offered.
Catering: £10 - £35pp

Chelsea Old Town Hall
Kings Road
London SW3 5EE
Tel: 0171 361 2220 Fax: 0171 938 3468
Contact: Maxine Howitt, Sales Conference Executive

Ceremony

The Main Hall can seat up to 480 guests in theatre style, whilst the Small Hall is suitable for smaller weddings, seating 120. Marriages can be held on any day except Christmas Day.
Price Guide: from £400

Reception

The Main Hall can cater for up to 400 guests for a cocktail style reception, or 250 for a seated dinner. Likewise, the Small Hall is suitable for 150 and 100 respectively.
Catering: P.O.A.

Claridge's Hotel
45/57 Brook Street
London, W1A 2JQ
Tel: 0171 629 8860 Fax: 0171 872 8092
Contact: Louise Clarke, Deputy Banqueting Manager

Ceremony

One of London's most famous hotels, Claridge's has eight rooms which are licensed for wedding ceremonies: the Royal Suite (25), the Ballroom (125), the Drawing Room (100), The French Salon (75) and The Mirror Room (75). They all boast superb interiors, some with original Art Deco from the 1930s.

Weddings can be held every day of the week.
Price Guide: from £1,200

Reception

Claridge's offers the same selection of rooms for wedding receptions, capable of seating up to 240 for a silver service dinner, or 400 for a cocktail party. Catering is in-house, but Claridge's use contract caterers to provide for special requirements such as Kosher.
Catering: from £25pp(canapes) from £30pp (lunches)

Dorchester Hotel
Park Lane
London W1A 2HJ
Tel: 0171 629 8888 Fax: 0171 317 6363
Contact: Victoria Gillespie, Conference Administration Manager

Ceremony

Built in 1931, the hotel's accolades include Egon Ronay 'Hotel of the Year'. Seven rooms are licensed including the Orchid room, the Ballroom and the Pavilion. Ceremonies are available seven days a week. No confetti.
Price guide: from £300+VAT

Reception

The hotel features in-house catering although contract caterers may be brought in providing they are from an approved list.
Catering: from £32pp

Duke's Hotel
St Jame's Place
London SW1
Tel: 0171 491 4840 Fax: 0171 493 1264
Contact: Nicky Glynn, Private Dining Co-ordinator

Ceremony

Duke's Hotel, almost adjacent to St James's Palace, is a traditional London Hotel. It has recently undergone extensive restoration and now offers its Marlborough Suite for wedding ceremonies.
Price Guide: £300 (with reception)

Reception

The Marlborough Suite is also available for wedding receptions. The room can cater for up to 60 guests for dinner or 75 for a buffet. Guests can enjoy the benefit of complete privacy with their own bar. Alternatively, The Dining Room may be used.
Catering: from £30pp

Dulwich College
Dulwich, London SE21 7LD
Tel: 0181 299 9284 Fax: 0181 693 6319
Contact: Julia Field, Enterprise Manager

Ceremony

Dulwich College was built in 1866. Today, it is an elegant combination of classical, mediaeval and contemporary architecture, with spacious grounds. Weddings can be held any day of the week outside school hours.
Price Guide: from £190

Reception

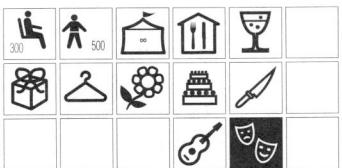

A number of rooms is available for the wedding reception, including The Great Hall, The Lower Hall, the Pavilion Salle, the Cloisters and the Christison Hall which seats a maximum of 300 guests. The majority of catering is undertaken by the in-house team. Wheelchair access is limited.
Catering: £9 - £25pp

Fairfield Halls
Park Lane, Croydon
Surrey CR9 1DG
Tel: 0181 681 0821 Fax: 0181 760 0835
Contact: Jackie Laidlaw, Food and Beverage Manager

Ceremony

Fairfield Halls in Croydon offers four rooms including The Concert Hall, complete with gallery, tiered seating and oak panelling (up to 1,800). Smaller rooms are The Maple Room, (120), and The Arnhem Gallery (500).
Price Guide: £200 to £2,000 (reduced rate or FOC if reception held here)

Reception

The Halls can cater for parties of up to 400 for a formal dinner and up to 600 for a buffet. Own caterers allowed for a fee of £2,075+.vat
Catering: from £10pp

The Firs
890 Green Lanes
Winchmore Hill
London N21 2RS
Tel: 0181 360 6788 Fax: 0181 364 2446
Contact: John Thorpe, GM

Ceremony

The Firs Conference and Banqueting Centre can take wedding ceremonies for up to 80 guests in its Grovelands Room. Weddings may be held every day of the week, but may only be held in conjunction with a reception. Confetti is allowed.
Price Guide: from £110

Reception

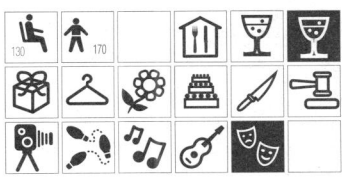

Two rooms, The Grovelands Room,

and the larger Winchmore Room, can house 130 guests for a seated dinner, and 170 for a buffet. European-style catering is in-house. There are preferential rate agreements with local hotels. Catering: from £25.95pp (inclusive package)

Four Seasons Hotel
Hamilton Place, Park Lane
London W1A 1AZ
Tel: 0171 499 0888 Fax: 0171 499 5572
Contact: Charlotte Doherty, Banqueting Manager

Ceremony

The Four Seasons offers a choice of four rooms for the ceremony: the newly refurbished Pine Room with its painted ceiling, the Oak Room, the Garden Room and the Ballroom for up to 400 seated or 750 standing.
Price Guide: POA

Reception

Receptions can be held in one of the remaining three rooms, depending on the number of guests. Summer weddings may also wish to enjoy the Garden room, which opens out on to the patio. In-house catering is provided by executive chef Eric Deblonde, who won the 1995 Banqueting Award from the Craft Guild of Chefs.
Catering: fPOA

Fulham Town Hall
Fulham Road
London SW6 1HS
Tel: 0181 576 5008 Fax: 0181 576 5459
Contact: Dee Little, Civic Facilities Manager

Ceremony

Fulham Town Hall is a late Victorian, early Edwardian, listed building, which has recently been completely refurbished. Internally the building is highly decorative with stained glass panels and marble painted columns. There is no

wheelchair access to Fulham Town Hall. The ceremonies rooms are available any day of the year except Christmas Day and Good Friday. Confetti is not permitted.
Price guide: from £192

Reception

Catering Buffets from £4pp sit down from £12.50pp

Goring Hotel
Beeston Place
London SW1W 0JW
Tel: 0171 396 9000 Fax: 0171 834 4393
Contact: David Morgan Hewitt, Deputy General Manager

Ceremony

This is one of the best known, and well respected, privately owned and family run hotels in London. (The hotel holds many accolades from hotel guides and individuals) Set in the centre of London, the hotel enjoys a peaceful location with its own gardens. The Drawing Room and Garden Lounge are licensed for weddings which can take place here on any day of the year. Ceremonies here must be followed by reception at the hotel. Confetti is not permitted.
Price guide: £250

Reception

The Goring offers traditional British cuisine, and is one of a handful of hotels in London to have a Michelin Red Turret.
Catering: from £25pp

Grosvenor House Hotel
Park Lane, London W1
Tel: 0171 499 6363 Fax: 0171 493 3341
Contact: Hugh Harris, Conference and Banqueting Sales Manager

Ceremony

This is one of the oldest and largest hotels on Park Lane, with facilities to accommodate up to 1500 people. Numerous rooms hold ceremony licences allowing for wedding for 10 to 1500 people. These rooms are available on all days of the year except Christmas Day. Ceremonies here must be followed by reception at the hotel. Confetti is not permitted.
Price guide: POA

Reception

Numerous styles of cuisine can be offered by the Grosvenor, and Kosher caterers can be brought in. Nico Laudenis also operates a restaurant within the building.
Catering: from £30pp

Hammersmith Town Hall
King Street, London W6 9JU
Tel: 0181 576 5008 Fax: 0181 576 5459
Contact: Dee Little, Civic Facilities Manager

Ceremony

Hammersmith Town Hall dates from the 1930s and is a listed building. The Hall's Assembly Hall is claimed to be one of the largest halls in west London and features a Canadian sprung dance floor which has been meticulously maintained. Weddings can take place here on any day of the year except Christmas Day and Good Friday.
Price guide: from £192

Reception

Catering: Buffets from £4pp Sit down from £12.50pp

Holiday Inn London - Nelson Dock
265 Rotherhithe Street
London SE16 1EJ
Tel: 0171 865 1914 Fax: 0171 417 7048
Contact: Alexandra Frankpitt, Assistant
Conference & Banqueting Manager

Ceremony

This purpose-built hotel and conference centre incorporates original wharf buildings, as well as Nelson Dock itself; the only dry dock left in London, now housing a full size replica of a 3-masted French barque. The hotel enjoys views over the Thames. Five rooms are licensed, and these are available on any day of the year except Christmas Day.
Price guide: from £250

Reception

Couples can arrive and depart from this venue by boat.
Catering: from £25pp

Hyatt Carlton Tower
2 Cadogan Place
London SW1X 9PY
Tel: 0171 235 1234 Fax: 0171 823 1708
Contact: Tracey Gibbs, Banqueting Manager

Ceremony

The Hyatt Carlton Tower, a five star hotel in the centre of Knightsbridge, offers its Drawing Room and Ballroom for wedding ceremonies. The Drawing Room, which seats 50 theatre style, offers excellent views of the gardens. The Ballroom is more suitable for large weddings.
Price Guide: from £150

Reception

The hotel offers to arrange any form of entertainment, theming and room decoration for wedding receptions, in either The Drawing Room or The Ballroom (which has recently been refurbished). Children can be catered for separately.
Catering: £38pp

Hyde Park Hotel
66 Knightsbridge
London SW1X 7LA
Tel: 0171 235 2000 Fax: 0171 235 4552
Contact: Mr Knut Ketterman, Banqueting Manager

Ceremony

This well known hotel located in the heart of Knightsbridge offers four rooms for ceremonies, including the Ballroom, which overlooks Hyde Park. All rooms have natural daylight. Ceremonies can take place here on any day of the year.
Price guide: from £500

Reception

Not only does the hotel offer all the above services, it can also provide printing, room themeing, and even babysitting.
Catering: from £35pp

Kensington Town Hall
Hornton Street
London
W8 7NX
Tel: 0171 361 2220 Fax: 0171 938 3468
Contact: Maxine Howitt, Sales Conference Executive

Ceremony

Kensington Town Hall offers two rooms for wedding ceremonies. The Small Hall can seat up to 190, theatre style, while The Great Hall is suitable for up to 600 guests. Weddings can be held every day of the year except Christmas Day.
Price Guide: from £422

Reception

For many the ideal solution is a wedding in The Small Hall followed by the reception in The Great Hall. Kensington Town Hall has preferential rates with local hotels.
Catering: from £22pp

The Lambourne Room
Ilford Town Hall
High Road, Ilford
Essex IG1 1DD
Tel: 0181478 9071 Fax: 0181 478 9190
Contact: Halls Lettings Officer

Ceremony

The Lambourne Room is in the same complex as Ilford Town Hall, which also has a ceremony licence. The Lambourne Room has a maximum capacity for 180, while the Town Hall itself has room for over 590. Wheelchair access is limited to the Lambourne Room. Both rooms are available on Saturdays and Sundays only. Confetti is not permitted.
Price guide: POA

Reception

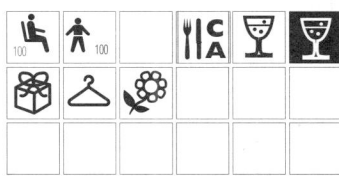

Catering: POA

The Landmark London Hotel
222 Marylebone Road
London NW1 6JQ
Tel: 0171 631 8000 Fax: 0181 630 8097
Contact: Michael Flatter, Conference & Banqueting Manager

Ceremony

Dating from 1899, this Grade II listed Edwardian hotel has many original features including the clock tower. It

offers several rooms for wedding ceremonies: The Ballroom (seating 400), The Music Room (330), The Empire Room (200) the Drawing Room (200) and The Tower Suite (30). .
Price Guide: from £550

Reception

The same set of five rooms is also available for the reception, and can comfortably cater for parties from around 30 to 360 guests for a seated dinner, and up to 500 for a standing buffet. Small receptions in the 5th floor Tower Room are afforded views of the clock tower through its glass roof.
Catering: from £36.95pp

The Lanesborough
No. 1 Lanesborough Place
Hyde Park Corner
London SW1X 7TA
Tel: 0171 259 5599 Fax: 0171 259 5606
Contact: Alexandra Hurley, Director of Banqueting

Ceremony

The Lanesborough, a listed building close to Hyde Park Corner, provides a traditional setting for a London wedding. The hotel offers five rooms for wedding ceremonies. The largest of these, The Belgravia, seats 100 (250 standing). Other rooms are The St. George's, The Wellington, The Westminster and the Wilkins which seats 35. All, except the St George's, are located on the lower ground floor of the hotel.
Price Guide: from £125

Reception

The same suite of five rooms are also available for reception purposes. The largest capacity for a waited service dinner is 100, and the hotel can cater for

up to 150 with a fork buffet.
Catering: Buffets from £24pp Sit down from £43pp

The Langham Hilton
1 Portland Place
Regent Street
London W1 3AA
Tel: 0171 636 1000 Fax: 0171 436 7418
Contact: Melina Becket, C & B Manager

Ceremony

Opened by the Prince of Wales in 1865, but badly damaged during the war, the hotel was painstakingly restored by Hilton in the 1980s. From the marble floor and pillars of the lobby upwards, the Langham is once more one of the finest places to dine and stay in the capital. Full details of the services were not made available to the guide. Please phone for details.
Price Guide: from £1200

Reception

Catering: from £35pp

Lee Valley Leisure Centre
Picketts Lock Lane
Edmonton, London N9 0AS
Tel: 0181 345 6666 Fax: 0181 884 4975
Contact: Rick Garvey

Ceremony

The Great Hall at Lee Valley Leisure Centre can seat up to 1,900 guests. Weddings can be held every day except Christmas Day and New Year's Day but only with a reception.
Price Guide: POA

Reception

Other than The Great Hall, which can cater for 1,500 for a formal dinner and 2,000 for a buffet, other rooms at the venue are The Sports Hall, catering for 1,000 and 1,200 respectively (weekends only), The Bowls Hall (600 and 1,000), The Golf Bar (60 and 200) and the smaller Conference Room (40 and 60).
Catering: P.O.A.

The London Mayfair Hotel
Stratton Street
London W1
Tel: 0171 629 7777 Fax: 0171 629 1459
Contact: Ashley Meyerowitz, Conference & Banqueting Manager

Ceremony

The London Mayfair Hotel offers a wide range of facilities including a spa club and a theatre. The building itself dates from 1927 and became part of the Inter-Continental Group in 1982. Five rooms, including The Theatre (seating 292), The Crystal Room (100) The Danziger Room (90), The Berkeley Room (45) and The Curzon Room (40) are licensed.
Price Guide: P.O.A.

Reception

The London Mayfair Hotel can cater for receptions of up to 250 for a seated dinner and 350 for a buffet in one of the five rooms listed above. All catering is undertaken in-house under the supervision of Michael Coaker, Executive Chef. Michael has won two gold medals at Hotelympia and is a member of the Academie Culinaire de France.
Catering: from £28pp

London Zoo Hospitality
The Outer Circle
Regents Park, London NW1 4RY
Tel: 0171 586 3339 Fax: 0171 722 0388
Contact: Sales Manager

Ceremony

London Zoo is a wedding location with a difference. The ceremony can be held in either The Regency Suite, which seats a maximum of 200 guests, or The Raffles Suite which seats around 40. The bride and groom can arrive at London Zoo by canal boat and travel to the wedding by pony and trap. The Raffles Suite only is accessible for wheelchairs. Both the ceremony and the reception must be held at the venue.
Price Guide: P.O.A.

Reception

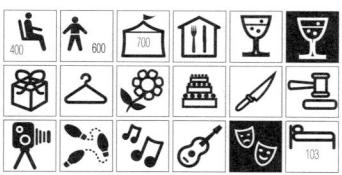

Receptions at London Zoo can also be held in either The Regency or The Raffles Suite, although afternoon weddings are able to enjoy reception drinks in one of the Zoo's animal houses. A marquee for up to 1,000 guests is a possibility. Catering is provided by Letheby & Christopher.
Catering: £30pp

Middx and Herts Country Club
Old Redding
Harrow Weald
Harrow HA3 6SD
Tel: 0181 954 7577 Fax: 0181 954 3466
Contact: Banqueting Manager

Ceremony

Price Guide: £250

Reception

Catering: from £30pp

Mosimann's
11b West Halkin Street
London
SW1X 8JL
Tel: 0171 235 9625 Fax: 0171 245 6354
Contact: Charles Morgan, Club Manager, or Saskia Phillips

Ceremony

Ceremonies must be held with a reception.
Price guide: All-in price with reception

Reception

Availability is on request. Late night licence can be obtained if required. The club's main claim to fame is the renowned cooking of celebrity chef Anton Mossiman. The opportunities for outdoor photography are limited.
Catering: £85pp

New Connaught Rooms
Covent Garden Exhibition Centre
Great Queen Street
London WC2B 5DA
Tel: 0171 405 7811 Fax: 0171 831 1851
Contact: Tracey Worrall, Mekala Ambrose, or Robert Minott

Ceremony

This listed building in the centre of Covent Garden was once a Masonic house. The Drawing Room is licensed, and this takes a minimum of 30 guests. It is available any day of the year. Outside photography is approximately five minutes walk away at Garden Square.
Price guide: POA

Reception

A choice of caterer is offered at this venue. Price guide: buffets from £24pp Sit down from £27.50pp

Oak Lodge Hotel
80 Village Road
Enfield, London EN1 2EU
Tel: 0181 360 7082
Contact: John Brown, Proprietor

Ceremony

Weddings can be held every day of the week except for the Christmas and New Year period.
Price Guide: £100

Reception

Catering: from £20pp

Park Lane Hotel
Piccadilly, London W1A 4UA
Tel: 0171 499 6321 Fax: 0171 499 1965
Contact: Mr Gareth Bush, Banqueting

Ceremony

The hotel has five rooms licensed to hold ceremonies including the Drawing Room, Orchard Room and Tudor Rose Room, which have varying capacities from a minimum of 25 to a maximum of 500 guests. Ceremonies are available seven days a week with a maximum of two a day. The price guide to hold the ceremony is dependent upon the number of guests in the party, the size of the room booked and the time of year; on some occasions there may be no charge. Wheelchair access is limited and the hotel stresses that Green Park proves a popular choice for outdoor photography.

Reception

The catering guide for a luncheon reception starts at £32 a head and increases to a minimum of £40 a head for an evening sit down meal. The hotel holds a Kosher licence and offers a room for the bride and groom to change in which may be subject to a charge. The hotel also charges for the services listed above.
Catering: from £32pp

The Pump House
Battersea Park
London SW18 4NJ
Tel: 0171 350 0523
Contact: Kristine Scarff, Manager
(0171 350 0523)

Ceremony

This Grade II listed building was recently restored by English Heritage and Wandsworth Borough Council and serves as a gallery and function rooms. Set in parkland with views of the lake and surrounding greens, the house has a seated ceremony capacity of 100, provided guests are housed within the marquee. Ceremonies are available Monday to Saturday inclusive, but not on Christmas Day, Sundays in Summer, and after opening hours from Wednesday to Saturday. The price quoted below excludes the Registrar's fee. There is wheelchair access to the ground floor only.
Price guide: £125+VAT

Reception

Catering is on a contract basis which does not have to be from an approved list although the house is in a position to provide a list of names if required. For this reason, it is not possible to give a catering price guide. Although accommodation is not available on the premises, the house provides a list of local hotels and guest houses. The house states it can provide names of suppliers of any service the couple requires, from a horse and carriage to a laser show. A multi-media console is available which projects video images onto the wall.
Catering: P.O.A.

Queen Elizabeth II Conf Centre
Broad Sanctuary, Westminster
London SW1P 3EE
Tel: 0171 798 4017 Fax: 0171 798 4200
Contact: Marketing Department

Ceremony

Three rooms are licensed to hold ceremonies at the conference centre, with varying capacities of 50 to 750. Ceremonies are available seven days a week and the price is available on application. Confetti is permitted.

Reception

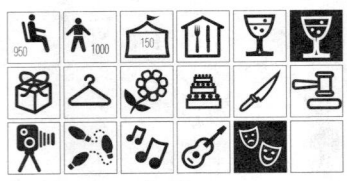

Catering is undertaken on a contract basis by Leith's and the price per head is available on application. Although accommodation is not available on the premises, a list of local hotels is available. The centre also operates preferential rates agreements with a selection of local hotels. In addition to the services indicated above the centre provides videos, lighting and themed weddings.

The Queens House
National Maritime Museum
Romney Road
Greenwich SE10 9NF
Tel: 0181 858 4422 Fax: 0181 312 6632
Contact: Anna Kingsley-Curry

Ceremony

The Queen's House was designed in 1616 by Inigo Jones as a small Palace for royal entertainment. It has recently been restored to its original glory. It is set next to the Maritime Museum and backs onto Greenwich Park. The ceremony room is the south west parlour in the Van de Velde Suite and this is available any day of the year except 24th - 26th December. Ceremonies here must be followed by reception at the venue. Confetti is not permitted.
Price guide: from £1000

Reception

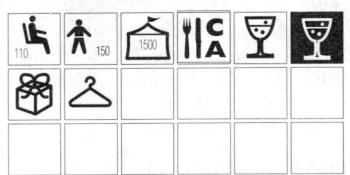

Couples can arrive or depart from Greenwich pier which is five minutes walk away.
Catering: Dependent on caterer chosen.

Radisson Edwardian Hotel
140 Bath Road
Hayes, Middx
Tel: 0181 759 6311 Fax: 0181 759 4559
Contact: Gavin Sanders, Director of Conference & Banqueting

Ceremony

Voted 'The Best New Business Hotel in the World' by Business Traveller Magazine, the hotel offers ceremonies seven days a week with a maximum of three per day. Ceremonies are not available without reception facilities, and the price guide below indicates the cost of the room hire based on 100 guests being present.
Price guide: £2,000

Reception

Although catering is in-house, contract catering is also available providing it is from an approved list. The hotel's health spa is open to all guests, and offers sauna, gymnasium, steam rooms with spa and plunge pools and solarium; beauty treatments are also available. Of the 459 bedrooms at the hotel, 17 are suites, 62 are executive King size doubles, and 54 are King size doubles.
Catering: £30pp

Raddisson SAS Portman Hotel
22 Portman Square
London W1H 9FL
Tel: 0171 208 6000 Fax: 0171 208 6001
Contact: Helmut Polt, Banqueting

Ceremony

The Raddisson SAS Portman Hotel, located in Portman Square close to Marble Arch and Oxford Street, offers a choice of six rooms for either the wedding ceremony or the reception. The largest of these, The Ballroom, seats 400 theatre style or 700 standing. The smallest room, The Bryanston Suite, is more suitable for weddings with less than 100 guests.
Price Guide: POA

Reception

Catering is generally provided by the in-house chef, although approved contract caterers may also be used by arrangement. Guests can easily be accommodated overnight in the hotel's 279 rooms.
Catering: from £50pp

Ravens Ait
Portsmouth Road
Surbiton
London KT6 4HN
Tel: 0181 390 3554 Fax: 0181 399 7475
Contact: Keith Hartog, MD

Ceremony

Being an island situated on the Thames, Ravens Ait is a charming setting to hold a wedding. There are two rooms licensed to hold ceremonies; the Thames Suite which holds a minimum of 35 and a maximum of 120, and the Lambourne Room which holds a maximum of 40 and a minimum of five for a more intimate wedding.
It is possible to hold a ceremony without reception facilities although a reduction of £60 will be made if the reception is also held on the island. The guide below includes a complimentary drink.
Price guide: £250

Reception

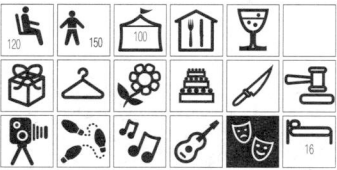

Accommodation on the island takes the format of 10 twin bedrooms and six bedded cabins which each sleep six. In addition to the services indicated above, the island may provide decorating services including floral arrangements and balloons, and a registered child minder for attending children during the formalities.
Catering: £8-30pp

The Regent Banqueting Suite
331 Regents Park Road
Finchley
London N3 1DP
Tel: 0181 343 3070 Fax: 0181 343 3010
Contact: Susan Damary, Banqueting Manager or Lynda Scrinminger, Conference Events Manager

Ceremony

This banqueting suite was built at the turn of the century, and still retains all its original features including decorative ceilings and chandelier. The Regency Suite is licensed for ceremonies and is available any day except Saturday and Jewish religious holidays.
Price guide: £250

Reception

The prices below are for a fully inclusive package. This venue employs a Thai chef who prepares reception food, hors d'oeuvres and fruit carvings.
Catering: from £55pp

The Rembrandt Hotel
11 Thurloe Place
London SW7 2RS
Tel: 0171 589 8100 Fax: 0171 225 3363
Contact: Sarah Cox, Banqueting Co-ordinator

Ceremony

Built in 1906 as Harrods apartments, the hotel features Georgian architecture and ornate pillars. Ceremonies are available seven days a week excluding Christmas Eve, Christmas Day, and New Year's Day. Confetti is permitted.

Reception

In addition to the services indicated the hotel has full banqueting facilities.
Catering: from £25pp

Ceremony

The hotel is a country house overlooking the Royal Park and is RAC and AA recommended. Three private rooms are available for ceremonies each featuring period furnishings and decor. These rooms are available seven days a week.

Reception

Catering is in-house and the hotel boasts a speciality of international cuisine and vegetarian dishes. Over 100 world wines are also on offer.
Catering: £42pp

Richmond Hill Hotel
Richmond
Greater London
TW10 6RW
Tel: 0181 940 2247 Fax: 0181 940 5424
Contact: Jane Smeeton or Sue Roberts, Conference & Banqueting Co-ordinators

Ceremony

This Grade II listed building has original Georgian remains forming the central part of the hotel, which date back to 1726. The Georgian decor and much of the original architecture has been conserved. There are four rooms licensed to hold ceremonies with fees from £300 for the smallest to £3,000 for the largest (the Ballroom). The hotel is also RAC and AA recommended.
Price guide: from £300

Reception,

The hotel's Chef de cuisine, Jean-Claude Seraille, insists that the finest, freshest foods from around Britain are used in the restaurant. Although there is no specifically allocated area for indoor photography, the terrace opposite the hotel with views of the river and the city proves to be ever-popular.
Catering: £35- £47pp

Richmond Theatre
The Green, Richmond, TW9 1QJ
Tel: 0181 940 0220 Fax: 0181 948 3601
Contact: Kate Littlewood, Theatre Manager

Ceremony

The theatre was built in 1899 and restored in 1991. Both the auditorium (max 850) and the Matcham Room (max 20) are licensed for ceremonies which can only take place here on a Friday..
Price guide: from £300

Reception

Catering is buffet style.
Catering: from £15pp

Ritz Hotel
150 Piccadilly
London W1V 0BR
Tel: 0171 493 8181 Fax: 0171 499 7487
Contact: Paul Chamberlain, Banqueting Manager

Ceremony

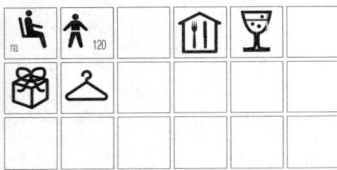

The hotel has two rooms licensed to hold ceremonies; the Marie Antoinette Suite which has a sitting capacity of 50 and a standing capacity of 80, and the Trafalgar Suite with a capacity of 20. Ceremonies are available seven days a

week with no restriction on the number permitted per day. An area for outside photography is available by arrangement.
Price guide: from £500

Reception

Personalised menus are created for each occasion and complimentary cards and place cards are also provided. A toastmaster and room for the bride and groom to change in are provided by prior arrangement.
Catering: £80pp

The Roof Gardens
99 Kensington High Street
London W8 5ED
Tel: 0171 937 7994 Fax: 0171 938 2774
Contact: Peter Insall, General Manager

Ceremony

This Grade I listed English Heritage roof garden club is set in 1.5 acres of landscaped gardens and fountains. Ceremonies are available seven days a week excluding Christmas Day and Thursday and Saturday evenings. Ceremonies are not available without receptions.

Reception

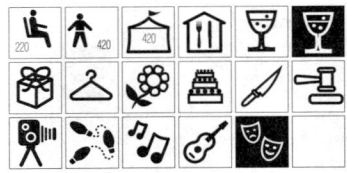

The Gardens pride themselves on their barbecues and buffets and are more than happy to provide marquees, fireworks and themed receptions in addition to the services indicated.
Catering: £40pp

Royal Garden Hotel;
2-24 Kensington High Street
London W8 4PT
Tel: 0171 937 8000 Fax: 0171 361 1921
Contact: Mr Philip Sacker, Banqueting Manager

Ceremony

This well known hotel situated in the heart of Kensington offers four rooms for ceremonies on any day of the year except Sundys and Bank Holidays. Ceremonies here must be followed by reception at the hotel.
Confetti is not permitted.
Price guide: £350

Reception

Catering: from £30pp

Royal Society of Arts
8 John Adam Street
London WC2N 6EZ
Tel: 0171 930 5115 Fax: 0171 321 0271
Contact: Christine Bond, Conference Manager

Ceremony

The house of the RSA (the Royal Society for the encouragement of Arts, Manufactures & Commerce) was designed in the 1770s by Robert Adam specifically for the Society. After a complex £4.5 million refurbishment programme, the terrace of five 18th Century vaults are now fully equipped for receptions and private dining. Ceremonies are available seven days a week excluding Bank Holidays.
Price guide: from £500+VAT

Reception

Although the Society does not hold a late night drinking licence, it does have a late supper certificate. All food is prepared in the Society's kitchen by Catering & Allied Services Ltd. Although accommodation is not available on the premises, the Society has a list of local accommodation, with some of whom it operates preferential rate agreements.

Catering: £40 - £60pp (package)

Savoy Hotel
The Strand
London WC2R 0EU

Tel: 0171 836 4343 Fax: 0171 872 8894
Contact: Chris Hamilton, Banqueting

Ceremony

The hotel has 10 rooms licensed to hold ceremonies including the Sorcerer, Iolanthe, Lancaster, Abraham Lincoln, Beaufort, Pinafore, Mikado and Gondoliers suites. These have varying capacities from a minimum of four guests to a maximum of 300. Ceremonies are available seven days a week with only one permitted per day. Confetti is not allowed.
Price guide: from £250

Reception

The hotel boasts Anton Edelmann as Maitre Chef des Cuisines. Although the hotel has a total of 202 bedrooms, they would like to point out that it is not possible to hire them all on an exclusive basis.
Catering: from £38pp

Searcy's
Searcy Tansley & Co Ltd
30 Pavilion Road
London SW1X 0HJ

Tel: 0171 823 9212 Fax: 0171 823 8694
Contact: Matthew Black, GM

Ceremony

30 Pavilion Road was created specifically by Searcy's for the purpose of entertaining, and must be hired on an exclusive basis. The Georgian town house features log fires, antique furniture and chandeliers and is available seven days a week to hold ceremonies excluding the period from Christmas Eve to the 4th of January. As the building is hired on an exclusive basis

---

only, ceremonies are not available without receptions and for this reason no price guide is given as this is part of the overall hire charge.

Reception

The capacity varies from 140 for a seated buffet, 200 for a fork buffet and increases to 250 for a finger buffet. Pavilion Road boasts a speciality in French, English and Oriental cuisine and in addition to the services indicated, is happy to provide a full event management service. At the top of the house there are 12 bedrooms with en-suite facilities.
Catering: POA

Sheraton Skyline Hotel
& Conference Centre
Bath Road, Hayes
Middx UB3 5BP

Tel: 0181 759 2535 Fax: 0181 750 9150
Contact: Edwin Wijkhuys,
Food & Beverage Manager

Ceremony

The hotel offers ceremonies seven days a week with a maximum of two held per day. There are no restrictions on Bank Holidays. Confetti is permitted.
Price guide: £500 - £2000

Reception

The hotel prides itself on its chef who has also worked at London's Dorchester Hotel.
Catering: from £15pp

Sutton House
2 Homerton High Street
Hackney, London E9 6JQ

Tel: 0181 986 2264 Fax: 0181 533 0556
Contact: Carol Mills, Property Manager

Ceremony

This Tudor brick built house, dating back to 1535, is said to be the oldest domestic house in London, built by a courtier of King Henry VIII. It is now National Trust owned, and run as an arts education, cultural centre. Three rooms are licensed to hold ceremonies; the Linen Fold Parlour, which features 16th Century carved panelling and a Tudor fireplace which can be lit, the Wenlock Barn featuring an inglenook fireplace and balcony, and the Marriage Suite. Ceremonies are available Thursday, Friday and Saturday excluding Bank Holidays and the house is closed in January. There is no wheelchair access to the Marriage Suite. The house does not have gardens but features an enclosed paved courtyard.
Price guide: from £50

Reception

A marquee is available for drinks only, to a capacity of 30, and buffet catering prices range from £10-25 per person and increase to £15-30 per person for a sit down meal. Cuisine is traditional English. Photography is not permitted during the ceremony itself. The Wenlock Barn has a Steinway concert grand piano which may be used for a re-tuning fee of £30. The house has held in the past a Scottish wedding which featured bagpipes at the reception.
Catering: from £10pp

Templeton
118 Priory Lane
Roehampton, London SW15 5JW

Tel: 0181 878 1672 Fax: 0181 876 2753
Contact: Jill Leney, Functions Secretary

Ceremony

This Grade II listed mansion, set in ornate grounds on the edge of Richmond Park, dates back to 1778 and was the home of Winston Churchill in the 1920s. The public room on the ground floor and the for-

mal garden have recently been opened for a wide range of both private and commercial functions. The hire of the premises includes sole use of the complete ground floor and gardens. This comprises an entrance lobby, marble hall, large ballroom, two sitting rooms and a panelled dining room.
Price guide: £180 (£100 with reception)

Reception

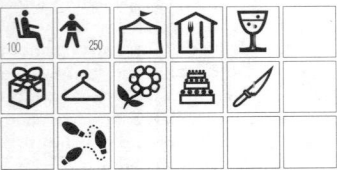

The house's kitchens have been recently renovated and Clare Johnston, of Clare's Fare, is happy to advise on any menu requirements you may have, the house also offers a Bride's Room for the day of the wedding from 10am until the event concludes.
Catering: £20 - £25pp

Tower Thistle Hotel
St Katherine's Way
London E1 9LD
Tel: 0171 481 2575 Fax: 0171 480 5487
Contact: Craig Ambury, Conference & Banqueting Manager

Ceremony

The hotel is actually situated in St Katherine's dock and is surrounded by water, with views of Tower Bridge and across the City of London. Two rooms are licensed to hold ceremonies, the Tower Suite with a maximum capacity of 250, and the Neville Suite with a capacity of 60. Ceremonies are available seven days a week and it is possible to hold a ceremony without reception facilities.
Price guide: £600

Reception

Catering prices per head start from £14 for a buffet style reception up to £27 for a sit down meal. A complimentary

room is available for the bride and groom to change in and, in addition to the services indicated the hotel features a jetty which allows the bride to arrive by boat if she wishes. The hotel may also provide fireworks on the river. The hotel's restaurant has been RAC and AA recommended.
Price guide: from £14-27pp

Trafalgar Tavern
Park Row
Greenwich
London SE10 9NW
Tel: 0181 858 2437 Fax: 0181 858 2507
Contact: Marcus Child, Banqueting co-ordinator

Ceremony

This riverside pub was the 1996 Evening Standard Pub of the Year. Couples can arrive and depart by boat. The pub is set in a listed building and was once frequented by Dickens, Thackery and Gladstone as well as Dr Crippen! The Nelson room is the ceremony room and this is available any day of the year, but ceremonies here must be followed by reception at the pub.
Price guide: POA

Reception

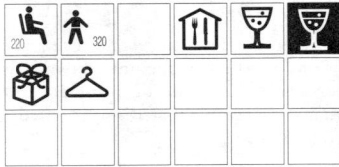

Whitebait is a speciality of the house!
Catering: from £19pp

Waldorf Hotel
Aldwych
London WC2B 4DD
Tel: 0171 836 2400 Fax: 0171 240 9277
Contact: Kate Signy, Conference & Banqueting Sales Manager

Ceremony

This famous hotel, set in the heart of London's theatreland is a traditional five star Edwardian hotel with authentic decor. The Charter, Adelphi and Palm Court Rooms are licensed for ceremonies and are available any day

of the year. Sadly these rooms do not have wheelchair access. Confetti is not permitted.
Price guide: from £3,000

Reception

The minimum number of guests catered for for a wedding reception is 15. Kosher caterers are allowed to use the kitchens if required. Couples can arrive and depart by boat as Charing Cross Pier is five minutes walk away.
Catering: from £26pp

West Lodge Park Hotel
Cockfosters Road
Hadley Wood
London EN4 0PY
Tel: 0181 440 8311 Fax: 0181 449 3698
Contact: Jane Wakenell, Conference & Banqueting Manager

Ceremony

The hotel offers ceremonies seven days a week excluding Christmas Day with a maximum of two permitted per day. Ceremonies are only available when held in conjunction with receptions and confetti is allowed.
Price guide: £150

Reception

Although the hotel does not hold a late night drinking licence, it does have a late night supper licence. The hotel's head chef, Peter Leggat, is a Chef of the Year semi-finalist.
Catering: POA

West Thames College
London Road
Isleworth TW7 4HS
Tel: 0181 568 0244 Fax: 0181 569 7797
Contact: Ian Butlin, Business Centre Manager

Ceremony

The building housing the West Thames College was originally owned by Captian Cook's botanist, Joseph Banks. The Winter Gardens Room holds the wedding licence, and ceremonies can take place here on any day except Sundays and Bank holidays. Confetti is not permitted.
Price guide: FOC

Reception

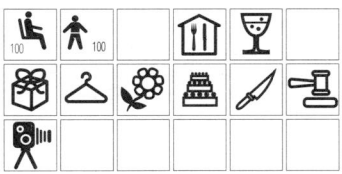

Rock and Roll weddings and Indian Weddings have both featured at the College.
Catering: from £10pp

White Swan Water
The Pool of Little Venice
London W9 2PF
Tel: 0171 266 1100 Fax: 0171 266 1926
Contact: Emma Hartley, Assistant General Manager

Ceremony

This permanently moored 1935 Regents Canal barge is situated in the conservation area of Little Venice. Wheelchair access is limited. The barge can host weddings for 4 to 40 guests on any day of the year.
Price guide: POA

Reception

This venue is striving to offer couples a 'truly unique wedding day', and 'aims to meet every culinary requirement'. Space on the barge allows for a two piece band only if live music is required. As a special feature, White Swan can offer Aromastream.
Catering: from £20 - £50pp

York House
146 Petersham Road
Richmond, TW10 6UX
Tel: 0181 831 6108 Fax: 0181 940 7568
Contact: Janet Pattenden, Senior Lettings Officer

Ceremony

York House, a listed civic building which dates from the 17th Century, sits amid gardens overlooking The Thames. Two rooms are offered for wedding ceremonies; The Terrace Room and The Salon. The Salon, an ornate stuccoed room overlooking the driveway, seats 40 guests, or 50 to stand. The Terrace Room, which opens out onto the Terrace and Gardens, is large enough for 40 seated or 50 standing guests.

Reception

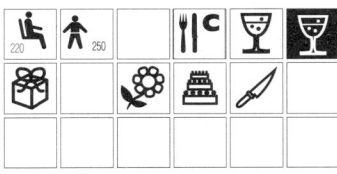

In addition to The Terrace Room and The Salon, York House offers The Hyde Room and Clarendon Hall for receptions. The Hyde Room can cater for 80 seated guests, and up to 100 for a buffet, while Clarendon Hall can cater for 200 and 250 respectively. Contract caterers are used, or self-catering facilities are available.
Catering: negotiated with contract caterers

STOP PRESS

Apollonia Restaurant, Harrow
0181 954 5060
Avenue House, Finchley
0181 3592000
BAFTA, Piccadilly 0171 734 0022
Belvedere Restaurant, W8
0171 602 1238
Berners Hotel, W1 0171 636 1629
Browns Hotel, Dover St
0171 493 6020
Cafe Royal, Regents St
0171 437 9090
Carnarvon Hotel, Ealing
0181 992 5399
Churchill Hotel, W1 0171 486 5800
The Comedy Store, SW1
0171 839 6642
Epping Forest Moat House Hotel
Woodford Green 0181 787 9988

Excelsior Hotel, West Drayton
0181 759 66_1
Grims Dyke Hotel, Harrow Weald
0181 954 4227
Ham House, Richmond TW10
0181 940 1950
Harrow School 0181 422 2196
The Hawker Centre, Kingston
0181 546 2121 (see Surrey entries)
Heathrow Park Hotel 0181 759 2400
Highgate School N6
0181 342 8323
The Lodge, Havering 01708 220730
Heathrow Hilton Hotel 0181 759 7755
Hilton on Park Lane
0171 208 4015
Madonna Hayley Hotel, Edgware
0181 951 5959
Market House, Kingston
0181 296 9747 (see Surrey entries)
Packfords Hotel, Woodford Green
0181 504 2642
Prince Regent Hotel,
Woodford Bridge 0181 505 9966
Quayside Restaurant, E1
0171 481 0972
Ramada Hotel, Harlington
0181 897 6353
Regents Park Marriott 0171 722 7711
Royal Geographical Society,
Kensington, 0171 589 5466
Scandic Crown Hotel SE16
0171 231 1001
Sheraton Heathrow 0181 759 2424
Soho House W1 0171 734 5188
Stakis London, SW1
0171 222 7838
TS Queen Mary, WC2
0171 240 9404
Wandsworth Town Hall SW18
0181 871 6394

The Acton Court Hotel
187/189 Buxton Road
Stockport, SK2 7AB
Tel: 0161 483 6172 Fax: 0161 483 0147
Contact: Tom McKee, GM

Ceremony

Price guide: F.O.C. (only with reception)

Reception

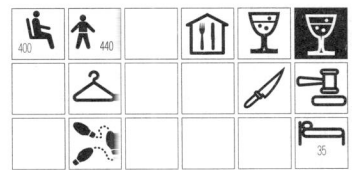

Catering: POA

The Albany Hotel
87/89 Rochdale Road East
Heywood, Rochdale OL10 1PX
Tel: 01706 369606 Fax: 01706 627914
Contact: Peter or Michael Rush

Ceremony

The Albany is an hotel (AA 2 star), restaurant and public house that will allow ceremonies on any day of the week.
Price guide: POA

Reception

The wedding package includes four poster honeymoon suite for the wedding night, plus full English breakfast. The hotel can also offer preferential rate agreements for other local accommodation. The hotel has a resident DJ.
Catering: Buffets from £5pp Sit down from ££10pp

The Albert Halls
Victoria Square
Bolton BL1 1RU
Tel: 01204 522311 Fax: 01204 399928
Contact: Sue Wilkinson or Rene Hall, Sales Executives

Ceremony

The Albert Halls are housed within Bolton Town Hall, a fully refurbished (1985) Victorian building with Grade I listing. Up to two ceremonies can take place on any day of the week, but not on Christmas Day, Boxing Day, New Year's Day, Good Friday, Easter Sunday or Easter Monday. Various rooms are available, the smallest taking 20 guests.
Price guide: from £50

Reception

While there is no accommodation on the premises, a list of local accommodation is available, and the Hall has preferential rate agreements with many local hotels.
Catering: from £6.50

The Belmore Hotel
143 Brooklands Road
Sale, Trafford M33 3QU
Tel: 0161 973 2538 Fax: 0161 973 2665
Contact: Carol Deaville, Proprietor

Ceremony

This privately owned Victorian style hotel is set in mature gardens. Ceremonies can only be held here if the reception is also booked at the hotel.
Price guide: F.O.C.

Reception

The hotel is happy to cater for any special dietary requirements. While a residents' supper drinking licence is already in place, a late night licence can be applied for if required.
Catering: £5pp -£20pp

Birch Hotel
Manchester Road, Birch,
Heywood, Nr Rochdale
Tel: 01706366137 Fax: 01706 621000
Contact: Mrs Purchon, Proprietor

Ceremony

Once a local mill owner's house, this first became an hotel in the early 1970s and is set in over three acres of woodlands and fields.
Price guide: FOC

Reception

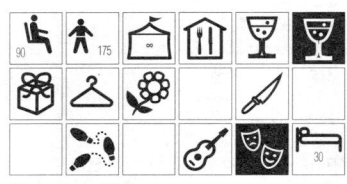

Catering: £15

Bolholt Country Park Hotel
Walshaw Road, Bury
Greater Manchester
Tel: 0161 764 3888 Fax: 0161 763 1789
Contact: Tracey Whaley, Conference Co-ordinator

Ceremony

Set in its own private estate (of 50 acres), just two miles from Bury, one of the claims to fame for this listed building is that it is the birthplace of the first Dean of Harvard University. The original building has been added to over the years, with a leisure centre and tennis courts completed in 1996.
Price guide: F.O.C. (only with reception)

Reception

Catering: from £13pp

Bolton Moat House
1 Higher Bridge Street, Bolton
Greater Manchester BL1 2EW
Tel: 01204 879988 Fax: 01204 380777
Contact: Sue Howell, Banqueting Sales Manager

Ceremony

The Moat House is sited in the centre of town on the former site of the Temperance Hall. The hotel's Cloisters restaurant was formerly St Mary's Catholic church and still features the stained glass windows.

Reception

The hotel offers several rooms for receptions, some providing intimate dining for 10 to 18 guests. For Saturday bookings in the Ashton Suite or Cloisters restaurant there is mini-

mum requirement of 50 guests for the wedding breakfast and 120 for the evening reception. The hotel provides a comprehensive wedding package that includes wine, flowers, changing room, overnight accommodation and breakfast for the bride and groom, plus special overnight rates for guests attending the reception.
Catering: from £14.95

Bramall Hall, Bramall Park, Stockport SK7 3NX

Tel: 0161 485 3708 Fax: 0161 486 6959
Contact: Wedding Co-ordinator

Ceremony

This Grade I listed Tudor building is available for wedding ceremonies on Saturdays only, with up to four permitted per day.
Price guide: £400 - £500 + VAT

Reception

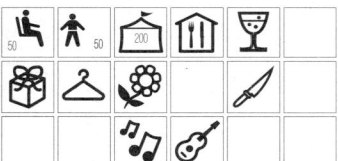

While there are in-house catering facilities at the Hall, other caterers are also permitted. A list of local accommodation can be provided by Bramall Hall.
Catering: £25pp - £350pp

Bredbury Hall Hotel
Goyt Valley, Bredbury, SK6 2DH

Tel: 0161 430 7421 Fax: 0161 430 5079
Contact: Margaret Anne Stone, Sales

Ceremony

Ceremonies can take place at the Club on any day except Sundays and Bank Holidays. Up to three are permitted per day. Confetti is not allowed.
Price guide: £75 + VAT

Reception

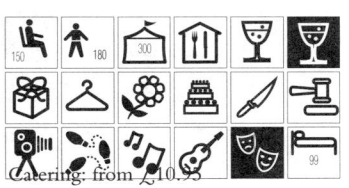

Catering: from £10.95

Bury Town Hall, Bury
Greater Manchester

Tel: 0161 253 5111
Contact: Graeme Ramsden, Superintendent Registrar

Ceremony

This is a 1937 Art Deco civic building with many original features. The marriage room itself, on the ground floor of the building, is also Art Deco in style. Up to eight wedding ceremonies can be performed in a day, mornings and afternoons Monday to Friday, and up to 12.30pm on a Saturday. Ceremonies cannot take place on Christmas Day and other Bank Holidays. Confetti is only permitted outside.
Price guide: F.O.C. (plus registrar's fees)

Reception

The Town Hall has four function suites on the first floor, which can cater for wedding parties of up to 400: the catering for which is operated by Bury Contract Catering. In addition to standard fayre, they are able to provide vegetarian and kosher dishes. While there is no accommodation on the premises, a list of local accommodation is available.
Catering: POA

The Cricketer
Keats Avenue
Poolstock, Wigan WN3 5UB

Tel: 01942 824555
Contact: Mr Rutter, Manager

Ceremony

Price guide: F.O.C. (with reception)

Reception

Catering: from £2.75pp

Deanwater Hotel
Wilmslow Road
Woodford SK7 1RJ

Tel: 01625 522906 Fax: 01625 536626
Contact: Jackie Smith

Ceremony

Parts of this hotel, restaurant and public house date back to the 16th Century. The hotel offers two marriage rooms; the Gold Suite (max 120) and the Balmoral Suite (max 250). These are available any day except Sundays and Bank Holidays, with a maximum of four weddings permitted per day.
Price guide: £120-£160

Reception

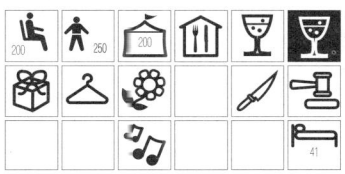

Catering: from £7pp (buffets) £15pp (waited)

Egerton House Hotel
Blackburn Road
Egerton, Bolton BL7 9PC

Tel: 01204 307171 Fax: 01204 593030
Contact: General Manager

Ceremony

Price guide: from £50

Reception

Catering: from £16pp (waited)

Georgian House Hotel
Manchester Road, Blackrod
Bolton BL6 5RU

Tel: 01942 811598 Fax: 01942 813427
Contact: Banqueting

Ceremony

The Georgian House (AA 4 star) dates back to to the 1700s, and has been added to more recently. Several rooms are suitable for the wedding ceremony with varying capacities from 50 guests upwards. It is only possible to have ceremonies at the hotel with a reception. There is only a room hire charge made if the ceremony and reception rooms differ. Up to two ceremonies are permitted per day, on any day of the week.
Price guide: from £200

Reception

Reception capacities depend upon the choice of room. The smallest can house a sit down meal for 34 and a buffet for 50. Personalised menu cards, red carpets, and colour co-ordinated table linen can all be provided.
Catering: from £25pp (package)

Granada Studio Tours
Bonded Warehouse
Water Street
Manchester M60 9EA
Tel: 0161 832 9090 Fax: 0161 834 3684
Contact: Jenny Smith (0161 828 5244)

Ceremony

Ceremonies can take place at the Studios' Baskerville Suite on any day of the year except Christmas Day.
Price Guide: £600 + VAT

Reception

Receptions can take place on the Baker Street set (from Sherlock Holmes), in the Rover's Return and Stables Restaurant, in the Baronial Hall, or the Starlight Theatre - (sadly not in the mock of the House of Commons). The Studios have a preferential rate agreement with the nearby Victoria & Albert Hotel for those seeking

---

overnight accommodation.
Catering: from £9pp

The Hacienda Club
13 Whitworth Street West
Manchester M1 5WG
Tel: 0161 236 5051 Fax: 0161 236 0518
Contact: Jon Drape, Production Manager

Ceremony

This popular live music venue and nightclub features an award winning interior design by Ben Kelly. Up to two ceremonies are permitted here per day, on any day of the year.
Price guide: £200

Reception

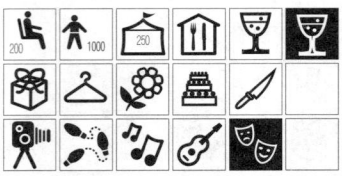

In addition to the list of services above, the Club can also design and print your invitations. The club can also supply a list of local accommodation with which it has preferential rate agreements.
Catering: from £2pp

Haigh Hall
Haigh
Wigan WN2 1PE
Tel: 01942 832895 Fax: 01942 831081
Contact: Ms Stazicker, Manager

Ceremony

This is a Georgian house overlooking a golf course and the valley of the River Douglas. The Cocktail Bar (up to 35) and the Grand Ballroom (up to 150) are licensed for ceremonies which can take place on any day except Saturday and Sunday.
Price guide: £30-£150

Reception

It is possible for hot air balloons and

---

helicopters to use the grounds, upon discussion. Couples can arrive and depart by boat from the Leeds/Liverpool Canal.
Catering: Buffets from £5pp Sit down from £8pp

Holiday Inn Crowne Plaza
Midland Hotel, Peter Street
Manchester M60 2DS
Tel: 0161 236 3333 Fax: 0161 932 4100
Contact: Elizabeth Holmes, Conference Network Manager

Ceremony

Built in 1903 and a Grade I listed building, the Crowne Plaza can host wedding ceremonies on any day of the year. Confetti is not permitted.
Price guide: from £175

Reception

Catering: from £20pp

Kilhey Court Hotel
Chorley Road
Standish
Wigan WN1 2XN
Tel: 01257 472100 Fax: 01257 422401
Contact: Jane Maton, Wedding & Banqueting Co-ordinator

Ceremony

The original part of this hotel is Victorian (1884), but it has since been extended. The hotel is set in its own grounds of around 10 acres. There are no restrictions on the number of ceremonies that can be held per day.
Price guide: £135

Reception

The hotel has a drinking licence extension to midnight, but a further extension could be applied for if required.
Catering: £18

Manchester Town Hall
Albert Square, Manchester
Gtr Manchester M60 2LA
Tel: 0161 234 3243 Fax: 0161 234 3242
Contact: Lis Monson, Sales Facilities
Co-ordinator or Avril Chang, Assistant

Ceremony

This Grade I listed civic building has a wedding licence for seven rooms ranging from the smaller committee rooms (for 50 people) to the Lord Mayor's Parlour, Banqueting Room, Reception Room and Conference Hall (all for 150 people), and The Great Hall (for 500 people). The Great Hall features a 70 foot high ceiling bearing the arms of the principal countries and towns with which Manchester has traded. The walls are adorned with murals by Ford Maddox Brown. Weddings can take place here on any day of the year.
Price guide: from £200

Reception

All catering requests can be provided apart form Kosher cuisine.
Catering: from £10.95

Norton Grange Hotel
Manchester Road
Castleton, Rochdale,
Greater Manchester OL11 2XZ
Tel: 01706 30788 Fax: 01706 49313
Contact: Conference & Banqueting
Manager

Ceremony

Ceremonies can be performed in the Hopwood Suite (max 135 people) and the Restaurant (max 50 people).Up to two ceremonies per day can take place on any day of the week except Sundays. Confetti is not permitted.
Price guide: £75

Reception

Catering: from £22.95

Quaffers Theatre Restaurant
Stockport Road West
Bredbury, Stockport
Greater Manchester SK6 2AR
Tel: 0161 494 0234 Fax: 0161 406 6372
Contact: Norma Levy

Ceremony

This well known Northern venue has its own hydraulic stage system, which presents the most unusual and dramatic opportunities for the imaginative staging of wedding receptions, such as bringing the couple's wedding car up on stage. Various rooms at Quaffers have the marriage licence, seating from 50 to 850, but wheelchair access is only available to the Cheshire Suite. The only days that the venue is not available for ceremonies are Sundays and Bank Holidays.
Price guide: £150

Reception

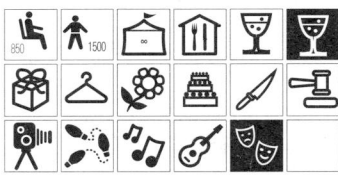

Contract caterers are allowed in to cater for ethnic weddings.
Catering: from £5.75pp

Rochdale Town Hall
The Esplanade
Rochdale
Gtr Manchester OL16 1AB
Tel: 01706 864797 Fax: 01706 59475
Contact: The Manager

Ceremony

This Victorian gothic style civic building has three marriage rooms including the Great Hall, the main banqueting hall which has a feature stained glass window and a balcony. Ceremonies can take place here on Saturdays and Sundays only, and not on Christmas Days or Bank Holidays. It is not possible to hold ceremonies here without also booking the reception at the Town Hall. Confetti is not permitted. While there is nowhere to take outdoor photographs immediately outside the building, there is a park across the road.
Price guide: from £200

Reception

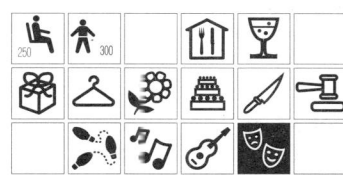

The Town Hall specialises in large scale banqueting. Outside caterers can only be brought in for Kosher or Halal catering. Recent weddings included one on an American theme.
Catering: from £3.74 (buffet) –£10.20 (waited)

Royal Northern College of Music
124 Oxford Road
Manchester
Gtr Manchester M13 9RD
Tel: 0161 273 6283 Fax: 0161 273 7611
Contact: Mandy Flude, Events
Manager

Ceremony

This arts centre and college of music has a licence for its main concert hall and can provide use of a Steinway grand piano and organ. Choir balconies and orchestral seating can also be made available. Ceremonies can take place here on Fridays, Saturdays and Sundays, but not during term time. Only one ceremony is permitted per day.
Price guide: £500

Reception

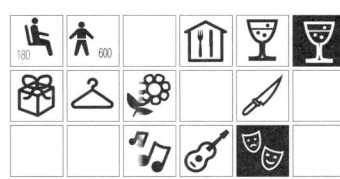

The College can create personalised desserts with the initials of the couple. A red carpet can also be provided in the

main venue. While there is no accommodation on the premises, a list of establishments with which the College has preferential rate agreements can be provided on request. Receptions can also take place at Hartley Hall, the college's Victorian style hall of residence situated 10 minutes from the main concert halls.
Catering: from £7 (buffets)

Saddleworth Hotel
Huddersfield Road, Delph
Saddleworth, Oldham
Greater Manchester OL3 5LX
Tel: 01457 871888 Fax: 01457 871889
Contact: Anthony, Owner

Ceremony

The Saddleworth Hotel was originally built in 1800 as a pack horse station. It is set in nine acres which includes woodlands and landscaped gardens. The hotel has a marriage licence for one room which has a conservatory at one end. Up to two ceremonies can take place here each day, on any day except Good Friday and Christmas Day.
Price guide: £200

Reception

The hotel offers wedding packages, the most basic of which caters for 15 people and includes use of the hotel's Rolls Royce, ceremony, flowers and a three course meal with coffee and toasting drink. This costs £550. Each additional person is charged at £17.50pp. Banqueting is a speciality of the hotel which offers English and French style cuisine.
Catering: £550 (15 people)

Stockport Town Hall
Stockport, Manchester SK1 3XE
Tel: 0161 474 3259 Fax: 0161 477 9530
Contact: Ann Cullen, Reception Services

Ceremony

The Town Hall can cater for between 30 and 350; the latter accommodated in the Large Hall. Ceremonies can take place on any day of the week.
Price guide: P.O.A.

Reception

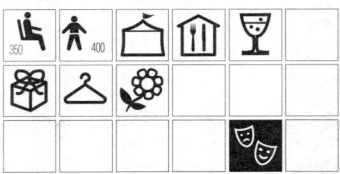

A late night drinking licence can be applied for. While there is no accommodation on the premises, a list of local establishments can be supplied. The services above can be organised in house or by the wedding party themselves.
Catering: P.O.A.

STOP PRESS
Bowdon Hotel, Trafford
0161 928 7121
The Bower Hotel, Oldham
0161 682 7254
Buile Hill Banqueting Suite ,Salford
0161 737 6277
Cresta Court Hotel, Altincham
0161 927 7272
East Lancs Masonic Hall M3
0161 832 6256
Flixton House, Urmston
0161 912 3000
Last Drop Village Hotel, Bolton
01204 591131
Longfield Suite, Prestwich
0161 773 3769
Manchester United Football Club
0161 872 3331/7722
The Oaks, Salford
0161 703 8694
Pack Horse Hotel, Bolton
01204 527261
Queen Elizabeth Hall, Oldham
0161 911 4071
Radcliffe Civic Hall, Radcliffe
0161 723 2917
Ramsbottom Civic Hall, Ramsbottom
0161 253 5894
Royals Hotel, Wythenshaw
0161 945 7593
Smithills Coaching House, Bolton
01204 844442
Worsley Court Hotel, Salford
0161 794 5760

The Alicia Hotel
3 Aigburth Drive
Liverpool L17 3AA
Tel/Fax: 0151 727 4411
Contact: Brian Bennett, GM

Ceremony

The Alicia has two ceremony rooms, the Park Lounge and the Zodiac Suite. These are available on any day except Christmas Day and Good Friday.
Price guide: from £160

Reception

The Alicia has hosted a Somali wedding (which is quite a noisy affair with a lot of whooping) which included the-meing the room Somali style. This demonstrates the hotel's flexibility and puts stock behind their claim that they will cater as required.
Catering: Buffets from £6pp sit down from £15pp

Bowler Hat Hotel
2 Talbot Road, Oxton
Birkenhead L43 2HH
Tel: 0151 652 4931 Fax: 0151 653 8127
Contact: Greg Ballasty, Gen Manager

Ceremony

The hotel is a Grade II listed building and is set in 1.5 acres of gardens. Three rooms are licensed to hold ceremonies; the restaurant, the Oxton Suite and the Garden Suite (which are both function rooms). Ceremonies are available without reception facilities but an extra charge of £100 will be made. Confetti is permitted.
Price guide: £150 or £250 (without recep)

Reception

Buffet style receptions begin at a price of £9.45 per person, and rise to a maximum of £20.95 for a sit down five course meal. The hotel is AA recommended.
Catering: Buffets from £9.45pp sit down from £16.95

The Cavern
8/10 Mathew Street
Liverpool L2 6RE
Tel: 0151 236 9091 Fax: 0151 236 8081
Contact: Dave Jones, Director

Ceremony

A must for all Beatles fans, The Cavern is probably one of the most famous clubs in the country, if not the world. One ceremony room is available here, (with limited wheelchair access), and this is available any day except August Bank Holiday Monday.
Price guide: £300

Reception

Catering here is buffet style.
Catering: from £3.50pp

Hulme Hall
Bolton Road
Port Sunlight Village
Wirral L62 5DH
Tel: 0151 644 8797
Contact: Mr P Mortimer, Proprietor

Ceremony

This Grade I listed building is home to the banqueting hall which is available to hold ceremonies Monday to Saturday with a maximum of two to be held a day. Ceremonies are only available in conjunction with reception facilities and confetti is permitted.
Price guide: P.O.A.

Reception

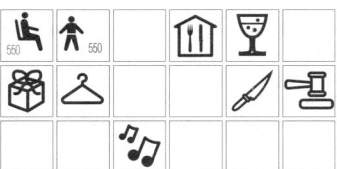

The hall states that children may be catered for separately and although no accommodation is offered on the premises, the hall has a list of local accommodation. Preferential rates are available from some of these hotels.
Catering: from £14pp

Huyton Suite
Poplar Bank
Huyton, Merseyside L36 9TP
Tel: 0151 443 3761 Fax: 0151 443 3573
Contact: Mrs Jan Scully, Manager

Ceremony

The Huyton Suite is located in the centre of Huyton and offers three rooms for ceremonies. One of which is the Octagon Room with its octagonal dance floor. Ceremonies can take place here on any day except Sundays and Bank Holidays, but must be followed by reception at the venue.
Price guide: £150

Reception

This venue can offer an all inclusive package, including disco and evening buffet.
Catering: Buffets from £4.50pp Sit down from £12.45pp

The Kirkby Suite
Cherryfield Drive
Kirkby, Knowsley L32 1TX
Tel: 0151 442 4063
Contact: Mrs Cathy Weir, Manager

Ceremony

This central Kirkby venue offers two ceremony rooms; the Eagle Room and the Falcon Room, which are available on any days except Sundays and Bank Holidays. Ceremonies here must be followed by reception at the Suite.
Price guide: £150

Reception

All inclusive arrangements are possible, to include all food and drink, room hire and disco.
Catering: Buffets from £4.50pp sit down from £12.45pp

Leasowe Castle Hotel
Moreton, Wirral L46 3RF
Tel: 0151 606 9191 Fax: 0151 678 5551
Contact: Mr Carruthers, GM

Ceremony

This listed building is 400 years old and set in five acres of land. One room is licensed to hold ceremonies which are available seven days a week with a maximum of two permitted per day. It is not possible to hold ceremonies without reception facilities.
Price guide: £125

Reception

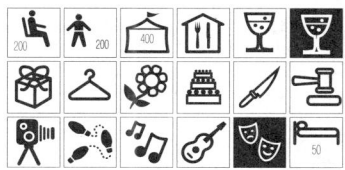

The catering costs range from £15.50 a head, for a sit down meal up to a starting price of £19 a head for a buffet style reception, although the hotel does not recommend buffet receptions at weddings.
Catering: from £15.50pp

Liverpool Town Hall
High Street, Liverpool L2 3SW
Tel: 0151 707 2391 Fax: 0151 709 2252
Contact: Simon Osborne, Manager

Ceremony

The Town Hall is a listed building and offers ceremonies seven days a week with no restrictions on Bank Holidays. Only two ceremonies are allowed per day.
Price guide: £200

Reception

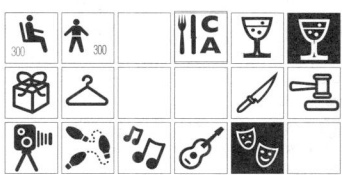

Although the Town Hall does not have accommodation on the premises, a list of local hotels is available and preferential rate agreements are operated with some of the guest houses.
Catering: £17pp

The Scarisbrick Hotel
Lord Street
Southport
Merseyside
PR8 1NZ
Tel: 01704 543000 Fax: 01704 533335
Contact: Carol Taylor, Sales
& Banqueting Co-ordinator

Ceremony

The hotel is a Grade II listed building and is situated in the centre of the famous Lord Street. With the promenade just one minute's walk away, the hotel is also a short distance from the Marine Lake and several top class golf courses. Ceremonies are available seven days a week excluding Christmas Day. Confetti is permitted.
Price guide: £300

Reception

The hotel offers executive bedrooms and four poster mini-suites in addition to its regular rooms.
Catering: £15-20pp

Thornton Hall Hotel
Neston Road
Thornton Hough
Wirral L63 1JF
Tel: 0151 336 3938 Fax: 0151 336 7864
Contact: Sue Rushton,
Conference & Banqueting Co-ordinator

Ceremony

The hotel is a period hall set in three acres of grounds, with a modern accommodation block. Ceremonies only permitted with receptions.
Price guide: POA

Reception

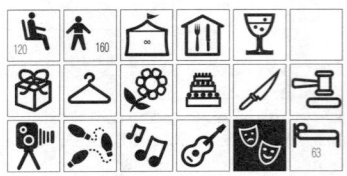

The hotel achieved a Les Routier award in 1995 and although a late night drinking licence is not permanently held, it can easily be obtained. The hotel has 63 bedrooms, all of which are en-suite. 1996 catering prices started at £12pp.
Catering: POA

Tree Tops Country House Hotel
Southport Old Road
Formby, Merseyside L37 0AB
Tel: 01704 879651 Fax: 01704 879651
Contact: Ann Marie Jackson

Ceremony

This listed building was the former dower house to Formby Hall and is set in three acres of woodland. Although ceremonies are available Monday to Saturday the hotel would like to stress that Fridays and Saturdays are already proving extremely popular during April to September, but is happy to discuss requirements for 1997 and 1998. One ceremony a day is permitted and it is not possible to hold ceremonies without reception facilities.
Price guide: £25

Reception

The hotel is keen to stress that each wedding is adapted to suit the individual requirements of the couple and every effort is made to tailor reception and ceremony facilities to suit the party. For this reason most services and facilities are open to negotiation. The hotel boasts a speciality in French and traditional English cuisine while the price indicated below is for a weekend reception and may be reduced at other times of the week. A late night drinking licence may be obtained.
Catering: from £25pp

STOP PRESS
Aintree Racecourse
0151 522 2935
Haydock Thistle Hotel, St Helens
01942 272000
Liverpool Marina, Liverpool
0151 709 0578
Liverpool Moat House
0151 471 9988
Logwood Mill Hotel, Knowsley
0151 449 2341
Lyceum Library Restaurant, Liverpool
0151 709 7097
Solna Hotel, Liverpool
0151 281 7595

The Appleyard
Banham Zoo
The Grove
Norfolk, NR16 2HB
Tel: 01953 887 384 Fax: 01953 888 427
Contact: Mr David Barber, Manager

Ceremony

This is one of only two zoos currently registered for ceremonies (the other being London Zoo). The ceremony room here (no wheelchair access) is available on any day except Sunday.
Price guide: POA

Reception

Helicopters and hot air balloons can use the grounds here. Horse drawn carriage and zoo train can be made available to the marriage couple. You can even have your pictures taken by the penguin pool.
Catering: Buffets from £3.75pp Sit down from £7.50pp

Congham Hall Country House
Grimston
King's Lynn
Norfolk PE32 1AH
Tel:01485 600250 Fax: 01485 601191
Contact: Mr Trevor Forecast,
Proprietor

Ceremony

This Georgian manor house, situated only six miles from King's Lynn, stands in 40 acres of parkland and formal gardens. One ceremony can take place here per day, on any day except Bank Holidays.
Price guide: £250

Reception

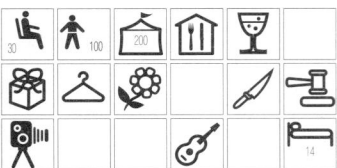

The head Chef, Jonathon Nicholson, has created several menus specially for wedding celebrations. The Hall has an attractive restaurant, the Orangery, with full length windows overlooking the lawns. Large doors open onto the terrace from here. Smaller dinner parties can be catered for in the Board Room.
Catering: £17.50pp - £30pp

**The Highwayman
Hermanus Leisure Centre
Winterton on Sea, Gt Yarmouth**
Tel: 01493 393607
Contact Mr Malcolm Lake, Manager

Ceremony

This venue overlooks the beach. The wedding room (with limited wheelchair access) is available on any day of the year. Ceremonies here must be followed by reception at the venue.
Price guide: POA

Reception

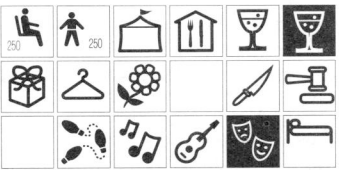

Helicopters and hot air balloons can land on site. Firework displays have also been held here as part of wedding celebrations.
Catering: Sit down from £10pp

**King's Lynn Town Hall
Saturday Market Place
King's Lynn
Norfolk PE30 1EX**
Tel: 01553 777259
Contact: Miss Brenda Hall, Assistant Administrative Officer

Ceremony

The Town Hall was built in 1421 and features ornate decoration, portraits and decorative mirrors. Confetti is not permitted here.
Price guide: from £75 + an hourly rate or £50 with reception

Reception

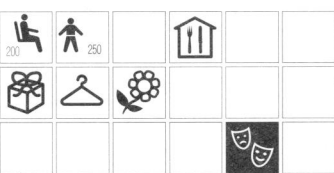

Couples may use their own choice of caterer for a reception at the Town Hall. A list of local accommodation can be provided.
Catering: P.O.A.

**Lynford Hall
Lynford
Thetford
Norfolk
IP26 5HW**
Tel: 01842 878351 Fax: 01842 878252
Contact: Gerald F Rand, Owner

Ceremony

This is a Grade II listed mansion house (English Heritage), formerly the seat of the Montagu family. The grounds include Italian gardens designed by Nesfield, and an ornamental lake. The park and gardens have been featured in Country Life and on TV. Ceremonies can take place here on any day of the year.
Price guide: £250 + VAT

Reception

One of the claims to fame for Lynford Hall is that its caterers hold a Royal Warrant. Accommodation can be provided by the Hall's own motel, which offers a four poster bridal suite.
Catering: £20pp - £40pp

**Norwich City Football Club
Carrow Road
Norwich NR1 1JE**
Tel: 01603 76 126 Fax: 01603 628373
Contact: Dawn Beasley,
PA to Marketing Manager

Ceremony

Undoubtedly the first choice venue for keen Canary fans, the Club has gained marriage licences for four rooms; The Boardroom, The Players Room, The Carvery and the Executive Suite. These are suitable for wedding parties of 75 to 300. Only one ceremony is permitted per day on any day except match days. All ceremonies must be followed by a reception at the Club.
Price guide: P.O.A.

Reception

A list of local accommodation, with which the Club has preferential rate agreements, can be provided.
Catering: from £6.95pp

**Sprowston Manor Hotel
Sprowston Park, Wroxham Road
Norwich, NR7 8RP**
Tel: 01603 410871 Fax: 01603 423911
Contact: S Pepworth, Conf Co-ordinator

Ceremony

This 4-star hotel is set in 10 acres of parkland, which can be used by helicopters and hot air balloons. Three rooms are licensed (one has no wheelchair access), and these are available any day of the year.
Price guide: from £150

Reception

Catering: from £18pp

Stakis Norwich
Amsterdam Way
Cromer Road
Norwich, Norfolk NR6 6JA
Tel: 01603 410544 Fax: 01603 478801
Contact: Ann Eagle, Conference and
Banqueting Sales Manager

Ceremony

The hotel offers its City Penthouse as
the ceremony room. This is available
on any day of the year, but ceremonies
here must be followed by reception at
the venue. Confetti is not permitted.
Price guide: £50 (over 30 guests FOC)

Reception

Catering: from £14.95pp

St Andrews & Blackfriars Hall
S Andrews Plain, Norwich
Norfolk NR3 1AU
Tel: 01603 628477 Fax: 01603 762182
Contact: Tim Aldous, Halls Manager

Ceremony

This Grade I, Scheduled Ancient
Monument is claimed to be 'The most
complete Friary complex in the UK'.
Ceremonies can take place in St
Andrew's Hall (max 900) or in
Blackfriars Hall (max 400). Up to four
ceremonies a day can take place here,
on any day of the year.
Price guide: from £75

Reception

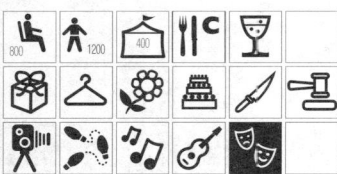

Despite its ability to cater for large
numbers, the Hall can also cater for
parties with as few as 10 people. A late
night drinking licence can be applied
for, if required. As well as the above
services, the venue can also arrange

vehicles for your wedding party.
Catering: £5pp - £50pp

Thurning Hall
East Dereham NR20 5QY
Tel: 01263 587200
Contact: Pauline Harrold, Owner

Ceremony

This private house is a remote mid 18th
Century Georgian hall, set in woodland
and approached via a canopied drive. It
was recently used for the filming of
Mill on the Floss. Ceremonies can take
place here on any day except Christmas
Day, Boxing Day and Good Friday.
The licensed room is attractively furnished. Large windows provide clear
views of the lawn and lake.
Price guide: £100

Reception

Couples may choose their own caterers
for the reception at Thurning Hall. A list
of local accommodation can be provided.
Price guide: P.O.A.

The Wensum Lodge Hotel
Bridge Street
Fakenham NR21 9AY
Tel: 01328 862100 Fax: 01328 863365
Contact: Dawn Woods, Manageress

Ceremony

The hotel is a former grain store which
stands on the banks of the River
Wensum by the original mill house.
Price guide: from £120

Reception

The hotel's chef is said to draw his
inspiration from the finest seasonal pro-

duce sourced locally. The bar offers a
wide selection of malt whiskies and
cask-conditioned ales. The hotel can
also offer a four-poster bedroom.
Catering: P.O.A.

Woodland Comfort Inn
Thetford Road
Northwold IP26 5LQ
Tel: 0500 61 62 63 Fax: 0500 00 5000
Contact: Conference co-ordinator

Ceremony

This is part of the Friendly Hotels
group, and is set in its own 7 acres.
Ceremonies here must be followed by
reception at the Inn.
Price guide: POA

Reception

Catering: from £9.95pp

STOP PRESS
Caistor Hall, Caistor St Edmund
01603 624406
Gissing Hall, Diss
01379 677291
Quality Friendly Hotel, Norwich
01603 744535
Sculthorpe Mill, Fakenham
01328 862726
South Walsham Hall, South Walsham
01603 270378
Taverham Hall School, Taverham,
01603 868206

Castle Ashby House
Castle Ashby
Northampton NN7 1LQ
Tel: 01604 696696 Fax: 01604 696516
Contact: Andrea Fawkes, Sales Manager

Ceremony

Castle Ashby was built in 1574 to
entertain Queen Elizabeth I. It is now
owned by the Marquess of
Northampton, and run as a special
event venue with accommodation.
Price guide: P.O.A.

Reception

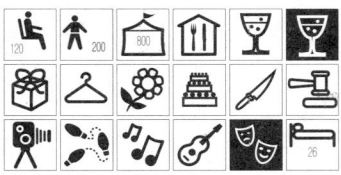

Catering is in-house for smaller receptions, but contract caterers are brought in if the number of guests exceeds 500. This would also mean the erection of a marquee, which can accommodate up to up to 800
Catering: POA

Kettering Park Hotel
Kettering Parkway
Kettering NN15 6XT
Tel: 01536 416666 Fax: 01536 416171
Contact: Janine Thorne, Banqueting

Ceremony

The Kettering Park Hotel offers a price which includes room hire in conjunction with a wedding breakfast.
Price guide: £100 (with breakfast)

Reception

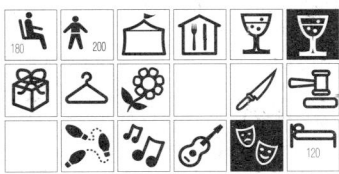

The hotel can cater for any dietary requirements. The maximum capacity for buffets of 200 refers to evening receptions only.
Catering: from £18pp (wedding breakfast)

Rushden Hall
Rushden, Northants
Tel: 01933 412000 Fax: 01933 410564
Contact: Mike Bowerman, Rushden Centre Manager

Ceremony

This Grade II listed period building is set in a public park in the town centre. Ceremonies can take place here on any day of the year. Confetti is not permitted.
Price guide: £160

Reception

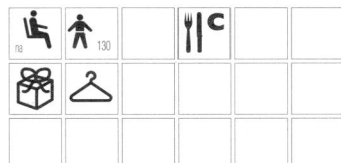

Catering: POA

Sunley Management Centre
Nene College, Park Campus
Boughton Green Road NN2 7AL
Tel: 01604 791907 Fax: 01604 712413
Contact: Paula Towers, Conference Administrator

Ceremony

The ceremony room at the Centre is the Sir William Shapland Lecture Theatre. This is available on Saturday or Sunday only. Ceremonies here must be followed by reception at the Centre.
Price guide: POA

Reception

Catering: Buffets from £12.95pp Sit down from £16.25pp

STOP PRESS

Bentleys, Towcester
01327 857335
The Diamond Centre, Irthlingborough
01933 650345
Hellidon Lakes, Daventry
01327 262550
The Hind Hotel, Wellingborough
01933 222827
Lamport Hall, Lamport
01604 686272
The Talbot Hotel, Oundle
01832 273621

NORTH EAST LINCOLNSHIRE STOP PRESS

Forte Posthouse, Gt Grimsby
01472 350295
The Oaklands Hotel, Nr Grimsby
01472 872248
Stallingborough Grange Hotel
01469 561302

Wortley House Hotel
Rowland Road
Scunthorpe
North Lincolnshire
DN16 1SU
Tel: 01724 842223 Fax: 01724 280646
Contact: Caroline Hutson, Conference Co-ordinator, or James Main, Deputy Manager

Ceremony

This modern hotel is situated in the middle of town and has three rooms licensed to hold ceremonies; the Sergeant Suite, with a capacity of 250, and the Rolling Mill, with a capacity of 100, and the hotel restaurant for the smaller wedding of 15-30 people. Ceremonies are available seven days a week with no restrictions on the number held per day or on Bank Holidays. Ceremonies are only available in conjunction with receptions and are free of charge.

Reception

Although no specifically allocated area exists for outdoor photography, the hotel recommends the use of a park, just two minutes walk away.
Catering: £18.50-25.50pp

Ashton Court Mansion
Ashton Court Estate
Long Ashton, Bristol
North Somerset BS18 9JN
Tel: 0117 9633438 Fax: 0117 9530650
Contact: Christopher Wood, Operations Manager

Ceremony

This is a Grade I listed 16th Century mansion house set in 900 acres of parkland, which helicopters and hot air balloons may use. The Music Room and panelled lounges are licensed for ceremonies which can take place here on any day of the year, but must be followed by reception at the house.
Price guide: £200

Reception

Testimony to the organisational skills of this venue, the first wedding held here was organised by fax with an Australian couple who arrived in the UK one week prior to the big day. All types of ethnic cuisine can be provided.
Catering: Buffets from £5.95pp + vat sit down from £18pp + vat

Cadbury House Country Club
Frost Hill
Congresbury
N Somerset BS19 5AD
Tel: 01934 834343 Fax: 01934 834390
Contact: Deputy Manager

Ceremony

This is an 18th Century house set in 14 acres of private parkland. It is currently a restaurant and leisure club. Ceremonies can take place here on any day of the year.
Price guide: £75

Reception

Catering for children under 14 will be quoted at a reduced rate, although the club would not normally provide separate catering for children.
Catering: from £16pp

Leigh Court
Abbots Leigh
North Somerset BS8 3RA
Tel: 01275 373393 Fax: 01275 374681
Contact: Sally Barker, GM

Ceremony

An early 19th Century, Greek revival style Grade II listed mansion set in 25 acres of parkland, Leigh Court is two miles from the M5 and 3 miles from the centre of Bristol.
Price guide: £300

Reception

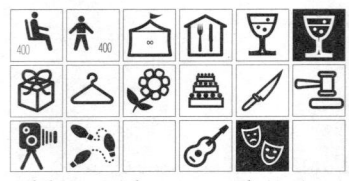

While overnight accommodation is not available on the premises, special rates have been negotiated with local hotels. Leigh Court has nine rooms for hire; a cellar, which can take up to 50, five rooms on the ground floor, and a further three rooms on the first floor.
Catering: from £19.50pp

STOP PRESS
Beachlands Hotel, Weston-Super-Mare
01934 621401
Winter Gardens Pavilion, Weston-Super-Mare 01934 417117

Cragside Hall
Rothbury, Morpeth NE65 7PX
Tel: 01669 620333 Fax: 01669 620150
Contact: Tracey Carnaby, Estate Secretary

Ceremony

This National Trust building is open to the public from April to October. Wedding ceremonies are available March to mid December. Recognised as the first house to be lit by hydro-electricity in 1878, this listed building is set in approximately 1,000 acres of grounds. One room at the Hall is licensed to hold ceremonies, which are available on Friday and Saturday mornings during the open season, and all week during the closed season. Only one ceremony per day is permitted.
Price guide: £300+ VAT

Reception
Reception facilities are not available at Cragside Hall but flowers may be arranged in the ceremony room itself.

Embleton Hall
Longframlington, Morpeth
Northumberland NE65 8DT
Tel: 01665 570249 Fax: 01665 570056
Contact: Lindsey

Ceremony

Price guide: F.O.C. (with reception)

Reception

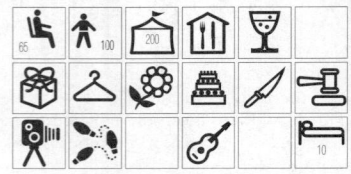

Catering: from £16.00pp

Espley Hall
Morpeth
Northumberland NE61 3DJ
Tel: 01670 513986
Contact: Mr J Kenworthy, Owner

Ceremony

This Victorian merchant's house is available for hire on an exclusive basis only; thereby ensuring total privacy and personal attention. It features 15 acres of lawns and flower beds surrounded by trees. Ceremonies are available seven days a week. Confetti is not permitted.
Price guide: £40 - £125

Reception

There are three types of menus to choose from: a formal hot meal with all courses being served at the table for 90, a finger buffet, a more informal gathering up to a maximum of 120 guests, and a cold fork buffet, whereby guests are seated in a formal arrangement and are shown to the buffet table, to a maximum of 90 guests. The Hall operates preferential rate agreements with other local hotels.
Catering: £28 - £31 (including drinks)

Langley Castle Hotel
Langley on Tyne, Hexham
Northumberland NE7 5LU
Tel: 01434 688888 Fax: 091434 684019
Contact: Anton Phillips, General Manager

Ceremony

This 14th Century castle is a Grade I listed building and has only limited wheelchair access to the ceremony room. Ceremonies are available seven days a week with only one permitted a day.
Price guide: £275

Reception

Catering: from £18pp

Longhirst Hall
Longhirst, Morpeth NE61 3LL
Tel: 01670 791348 Fax: 01670 791 385
Contact: The Wedding Co-ordinator

Ceremony

This 19th Century building is set in 55 acres of grounds. Now used as a management training and conference centre, the Hall offers ceremonies seven days a week with restrictions over the Christmas period. The capacity of the Joicey room is 45 and standing is discouraged. Ceremonies with receptions only.
Price guide: £50

Reception

Catering: £20 - £27.50pp

Marshall Meadows Country
House Hotel
Berwick upon Tweed TD15 1UT
Tel: 01289 331133 Fax: 01289 331438
Contact: Matthew Rudd, GM

Ceremony

Just a quarter of a mile South of the Scottish border, this Georgian mansion was converted in to a country house hotel in 1991 and is set in 15 acres of woodland and matured gardens, bordered by open farmland with sea views.
Price guide: £50-150

Reception

The hotel states that fresh local produce plays an important part when creating its traditional home cooking. This includes fresh fish and shell fish caught daily at the nearby Scottish fishing village of Eyemouth.
Catering: from £5.20pp (buffet) to £14.20pp

The Ramblers Country House
Restaurant
Farnley, Corbridge
Northumberland NE45 5RN
Tel: 01434 632424 Fax: 01434 633656
Contact: Mrs Jennifer Herrmann, Owner

Ceremony

This 19th Century country house is run by husband and wife team Jennifer and Heinrich Herrmann. The restaurant is available to hold ceremonies from Tuesday to Sunday, excluding Bank Holidays, Christmas Day and Boxing Day. During the "wedding season", May to October, the restaurant cannot accept bookings for wedding parties of less than 50 guests on Saturdays. Prices to hold the ceremony range from £50, Tuesday to Friday, up to £100 on Saturday and Sunday.
Price guide: from £50

Reception

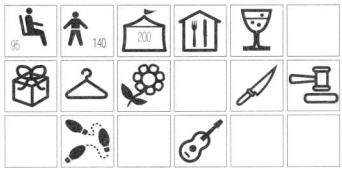

Chef/proprietor Heinrich states that menus can be individually planned for each reception. The couple pride themselves on the quality of the in-house cuisine. Although a late night drinking licence is not held permanently, the restaurant is more than happy to apply for one. Piano music is a feature of the restaurant.
Catering: from £17.35pp

Tillmouth Park Hotel
Cornhill on Tweed
Northumberland TD12 4UU
Tel: 01890 882255 Fax: 01890 882540
Contact: Charles Carroll, General Manager

Ceremony

This Grade II listed building offers ceremonies seven days a week and holds no restrictions during Bank Holidays or other times of the year. Only one ceremony a day is permitted and confetti is allowed.
Price guide: £150

Reception

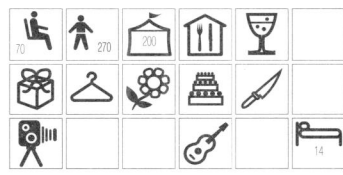

Buffet-style catering is available for a maximum of 200 guests. Couples requiring this format must hire a marquee in order to house this number of guests, as the hotel itself can only accommodate up to 70. It may, however, be hired on an exclusive basis and features a portable dance floor. Children can be catered for separately.
Catering: £25pp

STOP PRESS
Anglers Arms, Morpeth 01665 570271
Ashington Leisure Centre, Ashington 01670 813254
Chillingham Castle, nr Alnwick 01668 215359
Linden Hall Hotel Morpeth 01670 516611
Northumberland County Hall, Morpeth 01670 533030
Otterburn Hall, Otterburn 01830 520663
Slaley Hall, Hexham 01434 673350
Tynedale Farmer Function Suite, Hexham 01434 605444
Wallington Hall, Morpeth 01670 774691

Aldwark Manor Golf Club
Aldwark, York YO6 2NF
Tel: 01347 838146 Fax: 013-7 838867
Contact: Richard Harrison, CM

Ceremony

The Club is housed in a listed building, dating back to 1865, and allows only one ceremony per day, but this must be booked in conjunction with the reception.
Price guide: from £50

Reception

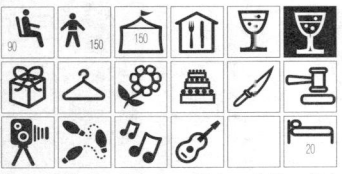

The Club offers traditional English fayre, and has a range of complete packages on offer.
Catering: from £29.90

Allerton Park
Nr Knaresborough
N Yorks HG5 0SE
Tel: 01423 330927 Fax: 01423 330632
Contact: Mike Farr, Administrator

Ceremony

This Grade I listed Gothic revival stately home can be hired out on an exclusive use basis. Only one ceremony is permitted here per day, on any day except Sunday. Confetti is only permitted outside.
Price guide: £2000

Reception

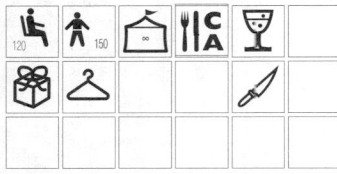

Catering: from £17.50 + VAT pp

Beningbrough Hall
Shipton by Beningbrough
York, North Yorks YO6 1DD
Tel: 01904 470666 Fax: 01904 470002
Contact: Assistant Property Manager

Ceremony

This National Trust property is a Georgian hall set in 365 acres. It features many pictures on loan from the National Portrait Gallery, as well as a cantilevered staircase, fine furniture and porcelain. Croquet is available for hire. Ceremonies can take place in the Great Hall on Thursdays, Fridays and Saturdays (after 5pm for exclusive use), but not on Bank Holidays. Only one ceremony is permitted per day.
Price guide: £350 + VAT

Reception

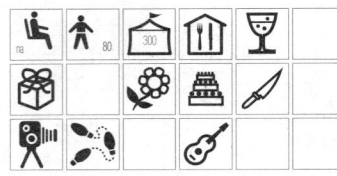

Catering: from 18pp

The Carlton Lodge
Bondgate, Helmsley YO6 5EY
Tel: 01439 770557 Fax: 01439 770623
Contact: Chris Parking, MD

Ceremony

The Lodge is situated on the edge of 12th Century Helmsley within the North York Moors National Park. Three rooms are licensed for ceremonies and are available any day of the week.
Price guide: from £150

Reception

The Lodge uses local produce whenever possible. It is also able to put themed packages together if requested.
Catering: Buffets from £12.50pp Sit down from £13.95pp

Croft Spa Hotel
Croft on Tees
N Yorks DL2 2ST
Tel: 01325 720319 Fax: 01325 721252
Contact: Mr Lawrence

Ceremony

Up to two ceremonies per day are permitted in this listed building, on any day of the year.
Price guide: P.O.A.

Reception

Catering: from £8.75

Crown Hotel
Crown Place, Harrogte
N Yorks HG1 2RZ
Tel: 01423 567755 Fax: 01423 502284
Contact: Laura Isherwood

Ceremony

The Crown has been a hotel since 1740. One of its claims to romantic fame is that Lord Byron wrote his ode "To a beautiful Quaker' whilst staying here. Ceremonies can take place here on any day of the year.
Price guide: from £150

Reception

Catering: P.O.A.

Devonshire Arms Country House Hotel, Bolton Abbey
Skipton, N Yorks BD23 6AJ
Tel: 01756 710441 Fax: 01756 710564
Contact: Sarah Graham-Harrison, Sales, Conference & Banqueting Manager

Ceremony

Originally a 17th Century coaching inn, the Devonshire Arms is now owned by the Duke and Duchess of Devonshire and enjoys a splendid set-

ting in the Yorkshire Dales national parkland. Although ceremonies are usually available on any day of the year, they are not available from 24 to 26 December inclusive or on New Year's Eve. Up to four ceremonies can be held per day, depending upon availability. Confetti is only allowed outside
Price guide: £150 – £500

Reception

The Devonshire Arms holds two AA rosettes for its cooking.
Catering: £25 – £32pp

Duncome Park
Helmsley, York, YO6 5EB
Tel: 01439 770213 Fax: 01439 771114
Contact: Sally Potter, Visitor Co-ordinator

Ceremony

Duncombe Park is a Baroque style stately home, built around 1713 and set in extensive grounds. Three rooms are offered for wedding ceremonies, all of which are richly decorated; The Saloon and The Stone Hall (100 max), and the Ladies Withdrawing Room ((seats 25). Weddings can take place here on any day except event days, and are restricted to one per day.
Price guide: from £450 + VAT

Reception

Accommodation is not available on the premises, but a list of local establishments can be supplied.
Catering: £33pp

Dunsley Hall Hotel
Whitby
N Yorks YO21 3TL
Tel: 01947 893437 Fax: 01947 893505
Contact: Mr Steven Talbot, Assistant Manager

Ceremony

Dunsley Hall is a country house hotel set in 4 acres of grounds. Three rooms are licensed for ceremonies, with only one ceremony permitted here per day.
Price guide: POA

Reception

Catering: from £12.50pp

Falcon Manor Hotel
Skipton Road
Settle, N Yorks BD24 9BD
Tel: 01729 823814 Fax: 01729 822087
Contact: Elizabeth Weatherby,
Event Manager

Ceremony

The Falcon Manor is a listed building and is set in its own landscaped gardens. One ceremony is permitted here per day on any day of the year.
Price guide: £175

Reception

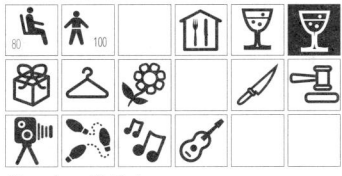

Catering: P.O.A.

Galtres Centre
Market Place, Easingwold
N Yorks YO6 3AD
Tel: 01347 822472
Contact: Major RM Crees, Vice Chairman Management Committee

Ceremony

The Galtres Centre is a community centre within a Victorian house, and is run by volunteers. Four rooms have marriage licences; two on the ground

floor, for which catering is available, and two on the first floor (no catering). The Centre hopes to install a lift to improve disabled access to the first floor. Ceremonies can take place here on any day of the year. Confetti is not encouraged.
Price guide: £50

Reception

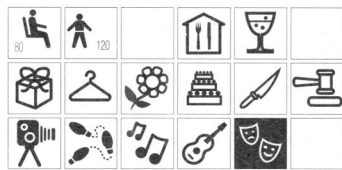

Couples may choose their own caterers for receptions, with prices varying accordingly. In addition to the Centre itself, a large leisure hall is adjacent, which will accommodate up to 250 for a disco or dinner dance. Other facilities at the Centre include a rifle range and tennis courts. List of local accommodation is available.
Price guide: P.O.A.

Hotel St Nicholas
St Nicholas Cliff
Scarborough, N Yorks YO11 3EU
Tel: 01723 364101 Fax: 01723 500538
Contact: Sue Chapel, Conference & Banqueting Co-ordinator

Ceremony

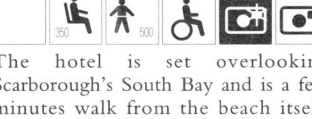

The hotel is set overlooking Scarborough's South Bay and is a few minutes walk from the beach itself. Ceremonies can take place here on any day of the year except Christmas Day and New Year's Day, but must be in conjunction with a reception at the hotel.
Price guide: F.O.C.

Reception

Flowers on the tables are provided as part of the wedding package, as is a first anniversary dinner for the happy couple. Wedding guests are also offered special overnight rates.
Catering: from £6.50 (buffet) – £15pp (waited)

National Railway Museum
Leeman Road
York, N Yorks YO2 4XJ
Tel: 01904 621261 Fax: 01904 611112
Contact: Mandy MacGrath, Events
Executive

Ceremony

Three ceremony rooms are available at
the museum; the Conference Room,
the Stephenson Room and the South
Hall. Weddings can take place here
any day of the week except Sunday.
Confetti is not permitted.
Price guide: £175

Reception

A list of local accommodation with
which the museum has preferential
rates can be supplied if requested.
Catering: £9.95 – £24.50pp

Nidd Hall Country House Hotel
Nidd, Harrogate
N Yorks HG3 3BN
Tel: 01423 771598 Fax: 01423 770931
Contact: Stephen Watson, Manager

Ceremony
While the Nidd Hall hotel holds a
licence for civil ceremonies, it is not
keen to hold ceremonies here except in
exceptional circumstances. The hotel
will be closed throughout 1997.

The Orangery
Settrington, Malton
N Yorks YO17 8NP
Tel: 01944 768 345 Fax: 01944 768 484
Contact: Mandy Atkinson, Administrator

Ceremony

This former riding school features a
large pillared hall. It is a classical building set in extensive grounds.
Ceremonies (only one per day) can
take place here on any day of the year,
but must be followed by a reception at
the venue.
Price guide: £450

Reception

A list of local accommodation can be
provided.
Catering: £11 – £15pp

Ripley Castle
Ripley
Nr Harrogate
N Yorks HG3 3AY
Tel: 01423 770152 Fax: 01423 771745
Contact: Mrs Harriet Crossley
Weddings and Special Events
Administrator

Ceremony

Ripley Castle itself is a Grade I listed
building and a member of the Historic
Houses Association. It has been home
to the Ingilby family for over 670 years
and stands in extensive grounds featuring a Capability Brown landscaped deer
park, lakes and valley. Ceremonies
can take place here on any day of the
year, but must take place after 4.30pm
between April and October when the
castle is open to the public.
Price guide: £500

Reception

A marquee is available for use all
Summer. This is usually used for
any events involving dancing. In
addition to the above services, the
castle can also arrange for a horse
and carriage, hot air balloon or
helicopter. Exclusive tours of the
castle and its walled gardens (home
of the National Hyacinth
Collection) can also be arranged.
Accommodation is available in the
Castle's adjacent hotel, the Boar's
Head Hotel, a Grade II listed
building located in a conservation
area.
Catering: Complete packages start at
£51pp

Rudding House
Rudding Park, Follifoot
Harrogate, N Yorks HG3 1JH
Tel: 01423 871350 Fax: 01423 872286
Contact: Joanne McBratney, Weddings
Co-ordinator

Ceremony

Rudding House is a Grade I listed
Regency house, set in 230 acres and
designed by Wyatt in 1806. It is now a
non-residential conference and banqueting centre, with grounds featuring
woodlands and ornamental lakes and a
herb garden. Ceremonies can take place
on any day of the year. Confetti is not
permitted.
Price guide: from £175

Reception

While no accommodation is available
on the premises, a list of local establishments, with which Rudding has preferential rate agreements, can be provided.
Catering: £20 – £30pp

Scotch Corner Hotel
Nr Richmond
N Yorks DL11 6ED
Tel:01748 850900 Fax: 01748 825417
Contact: Alison Boys, GM

Ceremony

The hotel permits wedding ceremonies
on any day of the year, allowing only
one per day. Confetti is not permitted.
Price guide: from £170

Reception

A late night drinking licence can be
applied for as required.
Catering: from £6.95 – £25pp

Solberge Hall
Newby Wiske DL7 9ER
Tel: 01609 779191 Fax: 01609 780472
Contact: Wedding co-ordinator

Ceremony

Once a Victorian country house, Solberge Hall sits in 16 acres overlooking the moors and dales. Ceremonies must be followed by reception at the Hall. Price guide: F.O.C. (with reception)

Reception

The Hall offers two main function suites; the Garden Suite (max 100) and the Clock Tower Suite (max 120). As part of the wedding package, bride and groom are offered complimentary use of a four-poster bedroom on their wedding night. Reduced rates are offered for children under 10 years old. Personalised menus can also be provided.
Catering: POA

Tan Hill Inn
Keld, Nr Richmond DL11 6ED
Tel: 01833 628246
Contact: Maureen Keating, Manager

Ceremony

The Tan Hill Inn claims to be the highest pub in Britain (1732ft), and the first pub in the country to hold a wedding (televised). The pub is also a listed building and dates back to the 13th Century. Ceremonies can take place on any day except Bank Holidays, although in high season, Saturdays and Sundays availability can be limited. Price guide: £75

Reception

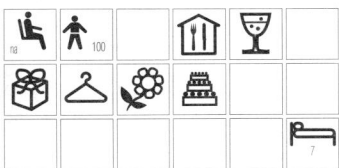

Catering: from £4.25pp

Waterford House
Middleham, N Yorks D28 4PG
Tel: 01969 622090 Fax: 01969 624020
Contact: Everyl M Madell, Joint Proprietor

Ceremony

This Grade II listed building, with its own walled garden, is set in Middleham, a major racecourse training centre in the Yorkshire Dales. Internally the house features period and antique furnishings and four poster beds. The Dining Room (limited wheelchair access) is licensed for ceremonies on any day of the year. Ceremonies must be followed by reception at the house. Price guide: £20- £100

Reception

The hotel features in many guides, including the Good Food Guide. Guests can go on a racing stable visit during their stay if requested. Catering:Buffets from £10pp Sit down from £19.50pp

Wood Hall Hotel
Trip Lane, Linton LS22 4JA
Tel: 01937 587271 Fax: 01937 584353
Contact: Elaine Hardy, Conference & Banqueting Co-ordinator

Ceremony

Four marriage rooms are available in this Grade II listed building. Ceremonies can take place here on any day of the year except Easter Monday.   Only biodegradable confetti is permitted. Price guide: from £100

Reception

Catering: £27pp - £35pp

Wrea Head Country House
Barmoor Lane
Scalby, Scarborough
N Yorks YO13 0PB
Tel: 01723 378211 Fax: 01723 371780
Contact: Mike Turner, Sales Director

Ceremony

This Yorkshire country house is set in acres of grounds and gardens, which can be used by helicopters and hot air balloons.   The ceremony room is the Library which is available any day of the year. Vintage cars can also be provided by this venue.
Price guide: £200

Reception

The marquee is set up permantnely throughout the summer – April to November.
Catering: Buffets from £15pp Sit down from £20pp

STOP PRESS
Angel Inn, Thirsk
01845 577237
Ayton Hall, Gt Ayton
01642 723595
Bedale Hall, Bedale
01677 423797
Bolton Castle, Leyburn
01969 623981
Bridge Inn, Wetherby
01937 580115
Cairn Hotel, Harrogate
01423 504005
Crathorne Hall Hotel Nr Yarm
01642 700398
Gateforth Hall Hotel, Gateforth
01757 228225
Grantley College, Ripon
01765 620259
Larpool Hall, Whitby 01947 602737
Newburgh Priory, Newburgh
01347 868372
Old Swan Hotel, Harrogate
01423 500055
Pavilions of Harrogate, Yorks Showground 01423 561536
Raven Hall, Ravenscar 01723 870353
Ripon Spa Hotel 01705 602172
Royal Hotel, Scarborough
01723 364333

Cotgrave Place
Golf & Country Club
Stragglethorpe, Notts
Tel: 0115 9333344 Fax: 0115 9334567
Contact: Melissa Read, Banqueting

Ceremony

The golf club is set in 250 acres of parkland. The venue is available for ceremonies seven days a week, with weekday weddings qualifying for a 15% discount. The Club can cater for up to 200 with dancing. Confetti is permitted. The Club suggests couples telephone to arrange a visit.
Price guide: £100

Reception

All wedding bookings include a complimentary flower arrangement for the head table.
Catering: from £6pp (buffet)

Indian Community Centre
Rawson Street, New Basford
Nottinghamshire N67 7FR
Tel: 0115 9785 985 Fax: 0115 9791 500
Contact: Raj Jogia, Manager

Ceremony

The Indian Community Centre has recently been refurbished and extended. It now offers two halls which are licensed to hold ceremonies. The smaller hall is offered at a rate of £30 for four hours, while the large hall is offered at a cost of £50 for four hours. Each additional hour is charged at an additional £10 per hour. Each of the halls has adjoining rooms for receptions.
Price guide: from £30

Reception

Catering facilities are undertaken on a contract basis, and although the Community Centre can recommend a selection of caterers (specialising in ethnic cuisine), couples are welcome to supply their own contract caterers which will incur a kitchen hire fee. A list of local accommodation which operate rate agreements with the Centre is available.
Catering: from £4.50pp

Langar Hall Hotel
Langar
Nottinghamshire NG13 9HG
Tel: 01949 860559 Fax: 01949 861045
Contact: Mrs Imogen Skirving, Proprietor/Manager

Ceremony

This Grade II listed building offers ceremonies seven days a week excluding Saturday afternoons unless the House is booked as a whole. Only one ceremony per day is permitted and confetti is allowed. The ceremony fee includes the marriage room, private meeting room, changing room for the bride and flowers.
Price guide: £200

Reception

The buffet capacity indicated is on the basis of a plated buffet or finger buffet only. If a seated meal for more than 50 guests is required, the marquee and both dining rooms will need to be used. For weekday lunchtime marriages, a 25% discount will be offered for parties of 15 guests or less.
Catering: POA

Mansfield Civic Centre
Chesterfield Road South
Mansfield
Nottinghamshire
Tel: 01623 656766 Fax: 01623 635764
Contact: Ring & Brymer

Ceremony

The Centre has two rooms licensed to hold ceremonies, one of which has a capacity of 600 in a seated, theatre style. Ceremonies are available seven days a week with only one per day permitted in the Banqueting Suite. However, ceremonies can be held as and when required in the Council Chamber. Maximum capacity is 700. All enquiries from combined weddings and receptions should be made to the in-house contract caterers, Ring & Brymer. Contact Carol Grant or Pam Potter, General Manager, on 01623 656766. Anyone interested in holding their ceremony in the Oakham Room or Council Chamber without any catering or reception at the venue, should contact James Spray of Mansfield District Council on 01623 656766.
Price guide: £100

Reception

Catering is in-house and the Centre boasts a speciality in Ethnic cuisine. The Centre operates preferential rate agreements with local hotels and guest houses.
Catering: from £9pp

Newstead Abbey
Linby
Basford, Nottinghamshire
Tel: 01623 793557 Fax: 01623 797136
Contact: Brian Ayres, Custodian

Ceremony

This Grade I listed monument was originally a 12th Century monastery, which later became the country residence of Lord Byron. The Abbey is set in 320 acres of parkland, with 28 acres of Japanese, Rose and French gardens. There is also an orangery, which is the only interior space suitable for wedding photography. Nottinghamshire City Council took over ownership of the Abbey in 1939. A loop system is also offered in the ceremony room for the hard of hearing. Ceremonies are available seven days a week, excluding the period from Christmas Eve until New Year's Day.
Price guide: £350.50

Reception

The Abbey features a separate restaurant, the White Lady Restaurant, which is run by an independent caterer. For further information please contact Mrs Crisp on 01623 797392. The Abbey is keen to stress that various wedding packages are available, including items such as flowers, car, etc.
Catering: P.O.A.

West Retford Hotel
East Retford
Nottinghamshire
Tel: 01777 706333 Fax: 01777 709951
Contact: Craig Dowie, GM

Ceremony

The hotel offers ceremonies seven days a week with a maximum of four permitted a day. Confetti is allowed.
Price guide: £150

Reception

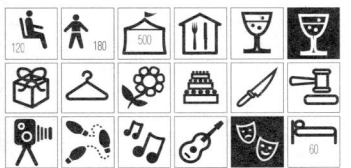

In addition to the hotel's 60 bedrooms, it also operates preferential rate agreements with other local hotels and guest houses. The hotel takes particular pride in its grounds.
Catering: Buffets from £10.50pp sit down from £13.95

STOP PRESS
The Charnwood Hotel, Worksop
01909 591610
Clumber Park Hotel, 01623 835333
Kelham Hall, Newark 01636 605111
Newark Town Hall 01636640100
Trent Lock Golf Centre, Long Eaton
0115 9464398

Abingdon Four Pillars Hotel
Marcham Road
Abingdon, Oxon OX14 1TZ
Tel: 01235 553456 Fax: 01235 554117
Contact: Sue Randall, GM

Ceremony

This modern hotel is set in limited grounds, and has two rooms licensed to hold ceremonies with capacities varying from 30 to 80. Ceremonies are permitted without receptions and confetti is allowed.
Price guide: £100

Reception

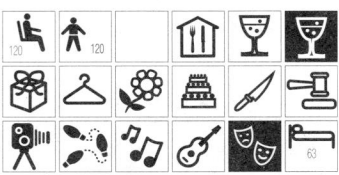

Buffet receptions are available from £7.50 with sit down meals increasing to a minimum of £14. A complimentary overnight suite for the couple is offered if the reception is also held at the hotel.
Catering: from £7.50pp

The Garth
Launton Road
Bicester, Oxon OX6 0JB
Tel: 01869 252915 Fax: 01869 324554
Contact: Mrs A Graham, Town Clerk

Ceremony

The Garth, operated by Bicester Town Council, is available to hold ceremonies seven days a week. Confetti is not permitted.
Price guide: £130

Reception
No reception facilities or accommodation are offered at The Garth, although a list of local hotels and guest houses is available.

Hawkwell House Hotel
Church Way
Iffley Village, Oxon OX4 4DZ
Tel: 01865 749988 Fax: 01865 748525
Contact: Lisa Williams, Sales & Conference Co-ordinator

Ceremony

The hotel was originally a family home dating back to 1856 and features two houses on the same site. The hotel is 1.5 miles from the centre of Oxford and is set in three acres of grounds. The hotel has five rooms licensed to hold ceremonies, the smallest of which, the Windrush Suite, accommodates 20 guests, while the largest room, the Ballroom, accommodates a maximum of 200.
Price guide: from £275

Reception

Receptions maybe held in the same five rooms as the ceremonies, with the hotel particularly recommending the conservatory room. The hotel specialises in modern English cuisine, and the price indicated below includes a drink for guests on arrival, two glasses of wine with the meal, a glass of Champagne for the toast, and flower arrangements. In addition to the 27 bedrooms, the hotel also has two honeymoon suites available which feature a jacuzzi, champagne, flowers and chocolates.
Catering: £37pp

Le Manoir Aux Quat' Saisons
Church Road
Great Milton, Oxon OX44 7PB
Tel: 01844 278881 Fax: 01844 278847
Contact: Julia Saunders, Conference & Banqueting Co-ordinator

Ceremony

Raymond Blanc's 15th Century manor house is a listed building set in 30 acres of grounds with a water garden. The Cromwell Room, the Manor's private dining room, is licensed to hold ceremonies with only one permitted a day. There is no guaranteed area suitable for indoor photography but the Manor's grounds more than make up for this. No confetti.
Price guide: £750

Reception

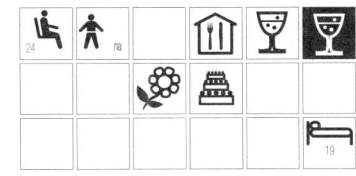

The manor's famous restaurant (two Michelin stars, five Egon Ronay

123

rosettes and four AA red stars) offers three menu packages: all on a waited service basis. Buffets are not available. In addition to the services indicated the Manor can recommend toastmaster, photographer, piped music, live music and other entertainments.
Catering: from £45-65pp

Phyllis Court Club
Marlow Road,
Henley on Thames
Oxon RG9 2HT
Tel: 01491 574366 Fax: 01491 410725
Contact: Roger Best, Banqueting Manager

Ceremony

This club with its Grade II grandstand pavilion stands on the banks of the Thames, opposite the winning post of the Royal Regatta. The Club has a long history dating back as far as 1301, while the re-built part of the building has been nominated for a British Construction Industry Award. Three rooms are licensed with varying capacities of 30 to 300.
Price guide: £100 (Oct – Mar) £150 (Apr – Sep)

Reception

Catering: £25.00pp

Rivers and Boaters
1 St Helen's Avenue
Benson
Oxon OX10 0PY
Tel: 01491 838331 Fax: 01491 826353
Contact: C J Price, General Manager or Mike Allen, Promotions Manager

Ceremony

Both Rivers (nightclub and restaurant) and Boaters (bar and restaurant) are licensed to hold ceremonies, with capacities ranging from 50 to 400. Available Tuesday to Sunday, inclusive, but not Christmas or New Year's Day.
Price guide: from £175

Reception

Although accommodation is not available on site, a list of local hotels is available.
Catering: from £14pp

Studley Priory Hotel
Horton cum Studley
Oxon
Tel: 01865 351203 Fax: 01865 351613
Contact: Mr Bright, Manager or Mr Parke, Owner

Ceremony

This Elizabethan manor house was converted from a 12th Century nunnery, and is situated in 13 acres of wooded grounds with views to the West of the Cotswolds and, to the East, along the line of the Chilterns. The hotel has been awarded three AA stars and is ETB four crown commended and Egon Ronay recommended.
Price guide: from £250

Reception

The hotel has three wedding packages available, The Regal, The Grand and The Traditional: all of which aim to facilitate planning arrangements. These packages may be adapted to suit individual requirements. All include a complimentary overnight stay for the couple on their first wedding anniversary.
Catering: £25pp

Woodstock Town Hall
The Market Place
Woodstock
Oxon OX20 1SL
Tel/Fax: 01993 811216
Contact: Mrs Marian Moxon, Town Clerk

Ceremony

The Town Hall is a Grade II listed building built by William Chambers in 1766. It commands a view over Woodstock market place and is adjacent to Blenheim Palace and estate. The Mayor's Parlour is the marriage room, and is available on all days except Sundays, Christmas Day and Boxing Day. Outdoor photography can be taken in the Museum gardens.
Price guide: £125

Reception

Reception at the Town Hall take place in the Assembly Room. This room is also covered by a Public Entertainments Licence. Receptions larger than 60 could use the nearby Community Centre off New Road. Caterers for the reception would be your own choice of contract caterers, the price below is therefore an average price.
Catering: Buffets from £5pp Sit down from £10pp

Wroxton House
Banbury
Oxon OX15 6QB
Tel: 01295 730777 Fax: 01295 730800
Contact: Jessica Pickup, Conference & Banqueting Co-ordinator

Ceremony

The hotel is a thatched, country house, dating back to the 17th Century. Ceremonies are available seven days a week excluding the Christmas and New Year period. Confetti is permitted.
Price guide: £155

Reception

Catering is in-house with a speciality in French and English cuisine. A list of local accommodation with preferential rates is available.
Catering: from £31pp (package)

Rushpool Hall Hotel
Saltburn Lane
Saltburn by Sea TS12 1HD
Tel: 01287 624111 Fax: 01287 625255
Contact: Functions Manager

Ceremony

The hotel is a listed building dating back to 1863 and has one room licensed to hold ceremonies. Ceremonies can take place here fom Monday to Saturday inclusive and are free if reception is also held at the hotel.
Price guide: FOC (with reception)

Reception

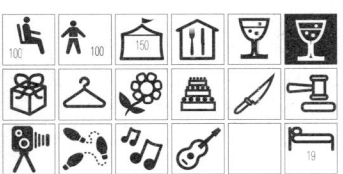

The hotel offers a complimentary bridal suite to the bride and groom.
Catering: from £5.95pp

STOP PRESS
The Park Hotel, Cleveland
01642 491233

Albrighton Hall Hotel
Albrighton
Shrewsbury
Shropshire SY4 3ag
Tel: 01939 291000 Fax: 01939 291123
Contact: Maria Roberts, Conference & Banqueting Co-ordinator

Ceremony

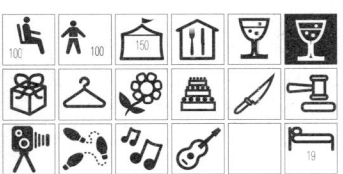

Albrighton Hall is a listed building, built in 1603. It is set in 14 acres of grounds that include an ornamental lake and a croquet lawn. Ceremonies can take place here on any day except Sundays and Bank Holidays. Ceremonies must be followed by a reception at the hotel.
Price guide: P.O.A.

Reception

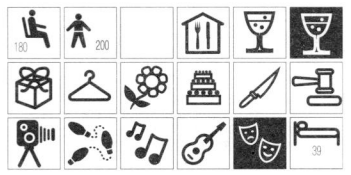

The wedding package (for over 50 guests), includes complimentary accommodation for bride and groom on their wedding night, choice from a selection of menus, and discounts on accommodation for wedding guests.
Catering: POA

Bourton Manor
Bourton
Nr Much Wenlock
Shropshire TF13 6QE
Tel: 01746 785531 Fax: 01746 785683
Contact: Chris Stewart, Manager

Ceremony

Bourton Manor is set in its own grounds and is a listed country house dating from the 16th Century. Internal features include oak panelling and a Queen Anne staircase. Weddings can take place here on any day of the year.
Price guide: £100

Reception

A special overnight rate of £25 per person (B&B) is available for your wedding guests.
Catering: £12pp - £25pp

Buckatree Hall Hotel
The Wrekin, Wellington
Telford, Shrops TF6 5AL
Tel: 01952 641821 Fax: 01952 247540
Contact Mr MacKay, General Manager

Ceremony

This Best Western hotel has two rooms with licences: The Champagne Suite and The Terrace Restaurant. These take minimum numbers of 25 and 60

guests respectively. Fall below these numbers and a room charge will be incurred. Otherwise, the room hire for the ceremony is free, although ceremonies can only be held with a reception.
Price guide: F.O.C. (with reception)

Reception

Tailor-made menus will be created on request. Children can be catered for separately, on request. A marquee taking up to 100 can be erected in the gardens, which feature a lake.
Catering: from £16.50

Castle Lodge
Castle Square, Ludlow
Shropshire SY8 1AY
Tel: 01584 878098
Contact: Mr W Pearson, Owner

Ceremony

This is a Grade II listed Tudor mansion style building which features oak panelling and stained glass. Ceremonies can take place on any day except Sundays. Other facilities available for your ceremony include flowers, photography, live or piped music. A list of local accommodation is also available.
Price guide: £100

Reception

Reception facilities are not available.

Combermere Abbey
Nr Whitchurch
Shropshire SY13 4AJ
Tel: 01948 871537 Fax: 01948 871293
Contact: Mrs Eric Wilkinson, Administrator

Ceremony

Weddings take place in the Combermere Room which is housed in the Grade II listed restored 19th Century stable block in the grounds of the 12th Century Grade I listed abbey. One ceremony is permitted here per

day on any day of the year. Confetti is not permitted, but rice is accepted. Blessings can take place in the walled garden or the pleasure garden (which has a fruit tree maze), or by the 143 acre lake.
Price guide: POA

Reception

Accommodation can be provided by the 10 Combermere self-contained cottages, which are tastefully decorated from collections by Laura Ashley, Jane Churchill, Nina Campbell and other well-known designers.
Catering: POA

Davenport House
Worfield, Bridgnorth WV15 5LE
Tel: 01746 716221/345
Fax: 01746 716021
Contact: Roger G R Murphy, Proprietor

Ceremony

This 18th Century Grade I listed country house is privately run. Only one wedding party is ever accommodated on one day, so you have the house to yourselves. The emphasis here is on a relaxed, friendly ambience. Ceremonies can take place here on every day of the year, with the exception of Sundays and Bank Holidays. Confetti is not permitted. Physical assistance would be required for wheelchair access.
Price guide: £150

Reception

Catering: £27 - £30pp

Delbury Hall
Diddlebury, Craven Arms
Shropshire SY7 9DH
Tel: 01584 841267 Fax: 01584 841441
Contact: Patrick Wrigley, Owner

Ceremony

This stately home is a Grade II listed Georgian country house (c1750), with attractive gardens. Only one ceremony is permitted per day, every day except Sunday and Bank Holidays.
Price guide: £150

Reception

Receptions will sometimes take place in the house, but usually a marquee is erected. Catering may be in-house or contract depending on the size of party, but there is no choice of caterer.
Catering: £15pp - £25pp

The Longmynd Hotel
Cunnery Road
Church Stretton
Shropshire SY6 6AG
Tel: 01694 722244 Fax: 01694 722718
Contact: Max Chapman, Manager

Ceremony

Longmynd is a Regency style building, with more recent additions, set in 15 acres of private landscaped grounds, and is set against the backdrop of the South Shropshire Hills. The hotel has two restaurants and its own leisure club including outdoor swimming pool. Ceremonies can take place here on any day of the week.
Price guide: £100

Reception

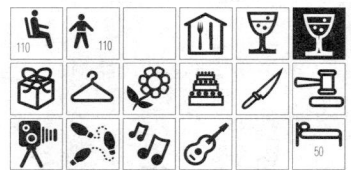

In addition to the services above, the hotel can also make a Rolls Royce available for use by the wedding couple.
Catering: £12pp - £25pp

Newport Guildhall
High Street, Newport
Shropshire TF10 7TX
Tel: 01952 814338
Contact: Jayne Parnham, Projects Officer

Ceremony

The Guildhall dates from the late 15th Century, with additions made up to 1860. It has been restored with help from English Heritage. Weddings can take place here on all days except Sundays and Bank Holidays. A room can be made available for bride and groom to change in, and a list of local accommodation can also be provided. There are, however, no reception facilities at the Guildhall.
Price guide: £50

The Parkhouse Hotel
Park Street
Shifnal
Shropshire TF11 9BA
Tel: 01952 460128 Fax: 01952 461658
Contact: Sharon Roberts or Karen Ryder, Conference & Banqueting Co-ordinators

Ceremony

The hotel offers three marriage rooms, taking a minmum of 20. The rooms are: The Garden Suite, The Stephen Dobson Suite and the Assac Suite. Ceremonies ca take place here any day except Sundays and Bank Holidays. Ceremonies must be followed by reception at the hotel.
Price guide: POA

Reception

A late night licence can be obtained.
Catering: £17.95pp

Shrewsbury Castle
Shrewsbury
Shropshire SY1 2AT
Tel: 01743 358516
Contact: Steve Martin

Ceremony

The Castle is a scheduled ancient monument set in its own grounds in the heart of Shrewsbury. It now houses a regimental museum. Ceremonies can take place here on any day except Sundays. Confetti is not permitted. A list of local accommodation can be provided. There are no reception facilities at the Castle.
Price guide: £75

The Telford Moat House
Forgegate
Telford Centre
Telford, Shrops TF3 4NA
Tel: 01952 429988 Fax: 01952 292012
Contact: Sally Felton, Conference & Banqueting Admin Manager or Sarah Corbett, Co-ordinator

Ceremony

The Moat House is in the centre of Telford and offers its Ironbridge and Telford Suites as marriage rooms. These are available any day of the year.
Price guide: POA

Reception

Catering: from £19.95pp

The Walls
Eating House & Dining Room
Welsh Walls
Oswestry
Shropshire SY11 1AW
Tel: 01691 670970 Fax: 01691 653820
Contact: Sarah Oliver, Weddings Organiser

Ceremony

This building is a spacious converted Victorian school. Only one wedding can take place here at any one time, on any day except Sunday.
Price guide: P.O.A.

Reception

As well as the above services, the venue will also print menu cards and name cards for you, and can provide a list of local overnight accommodation if requested.
Catering: £15pp - £25pp

STOP PRESS
Adcote School, Shrewsbury
01939 260202
The Feathers Hotel, Ludlow
01584 875261
The Lion Hotel, Shrewsbury
01743 353107
Lord Hill Hotel, Shrewsbury
01743 232601
Madeley Court Hotel and Mill, Madeley 01952 680068
Radbrook Hall Hotel, Shrewsbury
01743 236676
Rowton Castle Hotel, Shrewsbury
01743 884044
The Shropshire, Telford 01952 677800
Tern Hill Hall Hotel, Market Drayton
01630 638310

Carnarvon Arms Hotel
Dulverton
Somerset TA22 9AE
Tel: 01398 323302 Fax: 01398 324022
Contact: Mrs Jones, Proprietor

Ceremony

The hotel is a Victorian building set in 50 acres. Its features include lounges with log fires and a billiard room. One ceremony per day can take place in one of three marriage rooms. Ceremonies can take place on any day of the year, but must be followed by a reception at the hotel.
Price guide: F.O.C. (with reception)

Reception

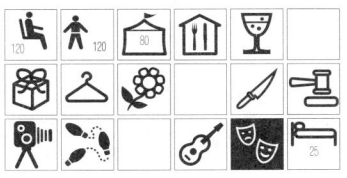

A late night drinking licence can be applied for as required. As well as the above services, the hotel can help couples arrange cars, horse and carriage, helicopters and hot air balloons.
Catering: from £8.50 (buffet) from £10.50 (sit down)

Curdon Mill
Lower Velloe, Williton
Somerset TA4 4LS
Tel: 01984 656522 Fax: 01984 656197
Contact: Daphne Criddle

Ceremony

Curdon is a sandstone watermill set amidst acres of farmland at the foot of the Quantock Hills. Ceremonies are restricted to one per day on any day of the year except Christmas Day.
Price guide: P.O.A.

Reception

The Mill specialises in home made food using local produce. A wide selection of menus is available to help bridal parties choose the ideal food for their function.
Catering: £12pp (buffet) - £16.40pp (menu)

Dillington House
Ilminster
Somerset TA19 9DT
Tel: 01460 52427 Fax: 01460 52433
Contact: Carol Slinger, Conference Manager

Ceremony

This Grade II listed house was once the home of Lord North, Prime Minister to George III. Somerset County Council took responsibility for Dillington in 1949. The grounds feature a croquet lawn and putting green, while the back terrace looks out across the rose garden to parkland. Ceremonies can take place here on any day of the year. Confetti is not permitted.
Price guide: £120

Reception

There is a room hire charge of £475 for the use of the appropriate function rooms in the main house. Discounts on food and accommodation are available for children.
Catering: from £9pp (main course dish)

Farthings Hotel
Hatch Beauchamp
Taunton
Somerset TA3 6SG
Tel: 01823 480664 Fax: 01823 481118
Contact: Marie Barker, Owner

Ceremony

Farthings is a family owned Georgian country hotel set in three acres of gardens, which includes a croquet lawn. Up to two ceremonies can take place here on any day on any day of the year. All of the bedrooms are en-suite and feature the usual extras one would expect in a well-appointed establishment.
Price guide: £150

Reception

The hotel's restaurant, specialising in modern English cuisine, is Egon Ronay recommended and has two AA Rosettes.
Catering: £12pp - £22pp

The Holbrook House Hotel
Holbrook
Nr Wincanton BA9 8BS
Tel: 01963 32377 Fax: 01963 32681
Contact: Giovanni Cestagrossa, GM

Ceremony

This country house hotel offers two marriage rooms; the Kent Room and the Drawing Room. Ceremonies must be followed by a reception at the hotel, but only one wedding is permitted per day. Ceremonies can take place on any day of the year except the Christmas and New Year's Bank Holidays.
Price guide: £100

Reception

Catering: £12.95pp - £50pp

The Old Muncipal Buildings
Corporation Street
Taunton TA1 4AQ
Tel: 01823 356356 Fax: 01823 356329
Contact: Peter Cottell, Admin Officer

Ceremony

The Old Muncipal Hall is an ancient monument (1522) and listed building right in the centre of Taunton. The marriage rooms are the Municipal Hall and the Committee Room, and are available on any day except Sundays, Bank Holidays, or when the council offices are normally closed.
Price guide: from £60

Reception

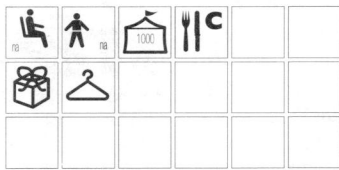

Hirers are to arrange their own caterers at this venue.

The Shrubbery Hotel
Ilminster
Somerset TA19 9AR
Tel: 01460 52108 Fax: 01460 536600
Contact: Stuart Shepherd, Managing Director

Ceremony

This country house hotel and restaurant offers four rooms licensed for civil ceremonies. Weddings can take place here on any day of the year.
Price guide: £125

Reception

Preferential overnight rates can be offered to wedding guests.
Catering: £25-£30pp (Packages)

STOP PRESS
The Centurion Hotel, Midsomer Norton 01761 417711
Crewkerne Town Hall,
01460 74001
Haynes Motor Museum, Yeovil
01963 440804
Hornsbury Mill, Chard
01460 63317
The Old Rectory, Frome
01373 836265
Rumwell Manor Hotel, Taunton
01823 461902
The Walnut Tree Hotel, Bridgwater
01278 662255

Forte Crest
Filton Road, Hambrook
South Glos BS16 1QX
Tel/Fax: 0117 956 4242
Contact: Chris Swire, Banqueting Manager

Ceremony

The hotel is set in its own extensive landscaped grounds which feature two ornamental ponds. It has two rooms with licences to hold weddings, the smaller of which can accommodate up to 25 guests. Up to two ceremonies are permitted per day on any day of the week.
Price guide: £100

Reception

The wedding package is an all-inclusive price which includes drinks on arrival, with meal and for toasts, plus flowers and complimentary overnight accommodation for bride and groom. The hotel recently hosted a show business wedding complete with opera singer.
Catering: from £29.50pp

Thornbury Castle
Thornbury,
South Gloucestershire,
BS12 1HH
Tel: 01454 281182 Fax: 01454 416188
Contact: Janine Black

Ceremony

This former Tudor castle is now run as an award-winning hotel and restaurant. It still retains a vineyard and walled gardens within its 15 acres. The restaurant has two, baronial style, dining rooms.
Price guide: £175-£250

Reception

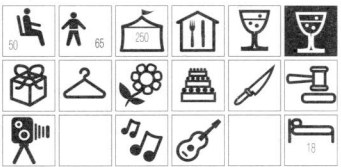

The top catering package here includes 8 courses with dishes such as smoked salmon and caviar.
Catering: £24.75 - £58.75pp

STOP PRESS
Chipping Sodbury Town Hall
01454 852223
Park Hotel & Restaurant, Falfield
01454 260550

Mosborough Hall Hotel
High Street, Mosborough
Sheffield
South Yorkshire S19 5AE
Tel: 01142 484353 Fax: 01142 477042
Contact: Tracy, Banqueting Manager

Ceremony

This Grade II listed building has two rooms licensed to hold ceremonies; the Stables and the hotel restaurant. These have varying sitting and standing capacities from 75 to 150. Ceremonies are

available seven days a week, excluding Christmas Day, with a maximum of two ceremonies permitted per day. The hotel does allow confetti.
Price guide: from £150

Reception

Reception capacities are to a maximum of 150 while the site is also suitable for a marquee with a capacity of 200. Although the hotel has 24 rooms it also operates preferential rate agreements with other local hotels and guest houses.
Catering: £25pp

Mount Pleasant Hotel
Great North Road, Rossington,
Doncaster DN11 0HP
Tel: 01302 868219 Fax: 01302 865130
Contact: Helen Pitts, Sales & Marketing

Ceremony

The hotel has two rooms available to hold ceremonies, although the conservatory is generally chosen in preference. The conservatory has a maximum capacity of 45 standing, and 35 sitting. Up to 10 ceremonies are available, seven days a week excluding Christmas Day.
Price guide: POA.

Reception

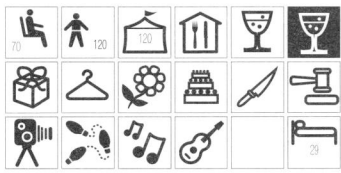

The hotel offers reception catering facilities to a maximum of 120 guests, while the hotel's grounds are suitable for a marquee of a similar capacity.
Catering: from £16pp

Sheffield Wednesday Football Club
Penistone Road
Hillsborough
Sheffield S6 1SW
Tel: 0114 2212310 Fax: 0114 12212122
Contact: Lesley Adyer, Facilitator

Ceremony

A must for Wednesdayites, the Club has three marriage rooms, two of which overlook the pitch. These rooms are available on any day except match days. Confetti is not permitted.
Price guide: POA

Reception

Catering: Buffets from £6pp sit down from £16pp

Swallow Hotel
Kenwood Road
Sheffield S7 1NQ
Tel: 0114 2533811 Fax: 0114 500138
Contact: Maxine Clark, Sales Manager

Ceremony

The hotel is set in 11 acres of landscaped gardens with its own ornamental lake. Helicopters and hot air balloons may use the grounds. The marriage rooms are the Raffles and Meadow rooms which are available on any day of the year. Ceremonies here must be followed by reception at the hotel.
Price guide: POA

Reception

Catering: Buffets from £14.70pp Sit down from £17pp

Whitley Hall Hotel
Elliott Lane, Sheffield S30 3NR
Tel: 0114 245 4444 Fax: 0114 245 5414
Contact: Ian Davies, General Manager

Ceremony

This Elizabethan manor house is a Grade II listed building and is available to hold ceremonies seven days a week with a maximum of three per day. The price guide to holding ceremonies increases to £325 on a Saturday. Confetti is not permitted. The hotel would like to stress that ceremonies are only available in conjunction with reception facilities.
Price guide: POA

Reception

Catering capacities are to a maximum of 100 guests, while a marquee may be made available to a capacity of 250. The hotel prides itself on the quality of its traditional English cuisine.
Catering: POA

The Bass Museum
PO Box 220
Horninglow Street
Burton on Trent,
Staffs DE14 1YQ
Tel: 01283 511000 Fax: 01283 513509
Contact: Mrs S Stokes

Ceremony

The Bass Museum of Brewing is housed in brewery buildings dating from 1835. Shire horse stables are also on the site. The museum's Worthington Suite (max 170) and Charrington Room (max 120) are licensed for ceremonies, which can take place on any day of the year, and are restricted to one per day.
Price guide: P.O.A.

Reception

Catering is by contract caterers from an approved list. A list of local accommodation with which the museum has rate agreements can be provided on request.
Catering: P.O.A.

Biddulph Town Hall
High Street
Biddulph
Staffs ST8 6AE
Tel: 01782 513231 Fax: 01782 523980
Contact: Mrs K Thacker, Administrator

Ceremony

Biddulph Town Hall is located in the town centre and holds a licence for ceremonies in its Council Chamber. This is available any day of the year except Sundays and Bank Holidays. Confetti is not permitted.
Price guide: £25

Reception

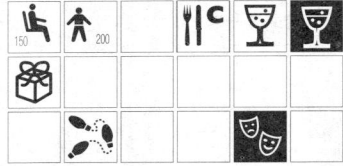

A list of local accommodation can be provided.
Catering: POA

The Borough Arms Hotel
King Street
Newcastle Under Lyme
Staffs ST5 1HX
Tel: 01782 629421 Fax: 01782 712388
Contact: Mr S N Sheikh, GM

Ceremony

The Borough Arms is an English Heritage, listed, building which offers two marriage rooms. These are the King Room (max 100) and the Baker Room (max 45). These are available for ceremonies on any day of the year, but ceremonies must be followed by a reception at the hotel.
Price guide: £50 - £125

Reception

Vegetarian menus are available on request. The hotel can also cater for ethnic cuisine, such as Indian and Pakistani food, if required.
Catering: £8pp - £16pp

Dovecliff Hall Hotel
Stretton
Burton upon Trent
Staffs DE13 0DJ
Tel: 01283 531818 Fax: 01283 516546
Contact: Mr Leigh MA Frost
Restaurant Manager

Ceremony

This Georgian listed building set in seven acres features gardens overlooking the River Dove. The Lounge is licensed for ceremoneis and is available on all days except Sunday, Monday and Bank Holidays.
Price guide: POA

Reception

Helicopters and hot air balloons may use the grounds.
Catering: POA

Hotel Rudyard
Lake Road
Rudyard
Nr Leek, Staffs ST13 8RN
Tel/Fax: 01538 306208
Contact: Mr R W Lloyd, Owner

Ceremony

The hotel is licensed to hold ceremonies in the Lake Carvery Room and the Rudyard Room. These are available on any day except Sunday.
Price guide: from £50

Reception

Catering: Buffets from £7.50pp Sit down from £16pp

Keele Conference Park
Darwin Building
Keele University, Keele ST5 5BG
Tel: 01782 584025 Fax: 01782 713058
Contact: Kim Iisley, Events Organiser

Ceremony

This Grade II listed building featuring lakes and Italian gardens, was originally owned by the Sneyd family.   The Great Hall and the Old Library are both licensed for ceremonies which can take place here on any day except Sunday, Christmas and New Year.
Price guide: £150

Reception

Helicopters and hot air balloons can use the grounds, and couples can arrive and depart by boat around Keele Lake. Other services offered by the Hall include balloon arrangements, table decorations, printed menus and table plans, and flexible menus.
Catering: Buffets from £5.95pp Sit down from £13.90pp

The Moat House Hotel
Festival Way, Festival Park
Stoke on Trent, Staffs ST1 5BQ
Tel: 01782 609988 Fax: 01782 284500
Contact: Jane Findler

Ceremony

The hotel is a listed building (in part) and was the former family home of Josiah Wedgwood. Up to four ceremonies a day can take place here on any day except Sundays and Bank Holidays.
Price Guide: POA

Reception

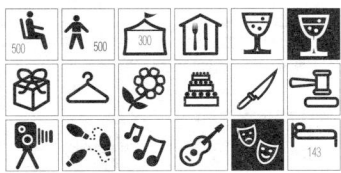

Catering: POA

The Moat House Restaurant
Lower Penkridge Road
Acton Trussell
Nr Stafford
Staffs ST17 0RQ
Tel: 01785 712217 Fax: 01785 715344
Contact: Christopher Lewis, Manager

Ceremony

The Moat House was formerly the home of the de Trussell family and is a listed building. It is set in six acres of landscaped grounds. The moat flanks the Colin Lewis Suite, and the restaurant overlooks the Staffordshire and Worcestershire Canal. Ceremonies can take place here on any day except Monday and Sunday.
Price guide: £200 (F.O.C. with reception)

Reception

The Colin Lewis Suite is an oak beamed room that dates from 1480. It has its own bar and is suitable for parties of up to 66. The Trussell Room and Restaurant, meanwhile, has a Victorian style conservatory overlooking the gardens and canal, and can take parties of up to 86. For receptions, children can be eligible for discounts. A list of local accommodation with which the restaurant has negotiated special rates is available on request.
Catering: £16pp - £25pp

Port Vale Football Club
Vale Park, Burslem
Stoke on Trent
Staffs ST6 1AW
Tel: 01782 835524 Fax: 01782 836875
Contact: Brian Toplass,
Commercial Manager

Ceremony

Port Vale will restrict wedding ceremonies to one per day if the reception is also held on the premises. Ceremonies can take place here on any day except Christmas Day. Confetti is not permitted.
Price guide: £200

Reception

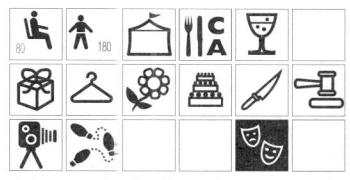

A late night drinking licence can be applied for if required. While there is no overnight accommodation on the premises, the Club has a list of local establishments with which it has preferential rate agreements.
Catering: £5pp (buffet) - £11pp (sit down)

The Riverside Hotel
Riverside Drive
Branston, Burton on Trent
Staffs DE14 3EP
Tel: 01283 511234 Fax: 01283 511441
Contact: Duty Manager

Ceremony

The Riverside hotel is situated in a garden setting overlooking the River Trent. Only one ceremony is permitted here per day.
Price guide: POA

Reception

Catering: from £15pp

Seedy Mill Golf Club
Elmhurst, Lichfield
Staffs WS13 8HE
Tel: 01543 417333 Fax: 01543 418098
Contact: Craig Rogers, Marketing

Ceremony

The Clubhouse derives from an old seed mill, and its surrounding buildings are Grade II listed. The Millcroft Suite is licensed for ceremonies which can take place here on any day of the year. Ceremonies here must be followed by reception at the venue.
Price guide: FOC

Reception

The prices below are for packages which include drinks on arrival, cake stand, menu, etc. Apparently grooms have, in the past, managed to get in 18 holes of golf before the ceremony - perhaps the ultimate in relaxation!
Catering: Buffets from £6pp Sit down from £28pp

Shugborough Estate
Shugbrough
Milford
Stafford
Staffs ST17 0XB
Tel: 01889 881388 Fax: 01889 881323
Contact: Anne Wood, Promotions & Events Manager

Ceremony

Shugborough is a National Trust property, and is the 900 acres seat of the Earls of Lichfield. One wedding can take place here per day and only on a Saturday. Confetti is not permitted, nor is indoor photography. Lists of entertainers and other services can be provided.
Price guide: £500

Reception

Reception facilities are not available at Shugborough.

Stoke City Football Club
Victoria Ground
Stoke on Trent
Staffs ST4 4EG
Tel: 01782 845840 Fax: 01782 846422
Contact: Lorraine Hampson

Ceremony

Three marriage rooms are available at the Club: the Sir Stanley Matthews Suite, the Club Members' Room and the Executive Suite. These will accommodate from 20 to 200 guests. Ceremonies must be followed by reception at the Club.
Price guide: £152.50

Reception

Marquees can be the 'size of a football pitch' if required! Players and management may also be available for your wedding, as may celebrities such as Frank Bruno. Helicopters may also land at the Club.
Catering: from £12pp (sit down)

Trentham Leisure Ltd
Trentham Gardens
Stone Road
Trentham
Stoke on Trent ST4 8AX
Tel: 01782 657341 Fax: 01782 644536
Contact: Karen Nixon, Sales Co-ordinator

Ceremony

This conference and leisure centre is set in a 750 acres estate featuring Italian gardens. Three rooms are available (from 50 to 1,000 guests), on any day of the year.
Price guide: from £100

Reception

Helicopters and hot air balloons may use the grounds.
Catering: Buffets from £6pp sit down from £15pp

Uttoxeter Racecourse
Wood Lane
Uttoxeter
Staffs ST14 8BD
Tel: 01889 562561 Fax: 01889 562786
Contact: Janet Womby, Marketing Manager

Ceremony

The racecourse offers views across the Dove Valley. The Staffordshire Room is licensed for ceremonies which can take place here on any day, although there are certain restrictions on race days.. The venue says there is no area suitable for outdoor photography.
Price guide: £300

Reception

The racecourse offers 'extreme flexibility of menus and numbers' and can even provide a behind the scenes tour. Helicopters and hot air balloons can also use the site.
Catering: Buffets from £7.50pp Sit down from £12pp

STOP PRESS
Blakelands, Bobbington
01384 221464
Ford Green Hall, Stoke on Trent
01782 534771
Fox Hotel, Rushton Spencer
01260 226692
Garth Hotel, Stafford
01785 256124
Haling Dene Centre, Penkridge
01785 714157
Hatherton Country Hotel, Penkridge
01785 712459
Pendrell Hall College, Codsall Wood
01902 842398
Queens Hotel, Burton upon Trent
01283 564993
Red Lion Inn, Thorncliffe
01538 300325
Stakis Stoke on Trent Hotel
01782 202361
Stone House Hotel, Stone
01785 815531
Swinfen Hall Hotel, Swinfen
01543 481494
Upper House, Barlaston
01782 373790
Uttoxeter Town Hall
01889 564085

The Angel Hotel
Angel Hill, Bury St Edmunds
Suffolk IP33 1LT
Tel: 01284 753926 Fax: 01284 750092
Contact: Mrs Adi Ellis, Conf & Banq

Ceremony

This 14th century, creeper-clad listed building, was immortalised by Dickens as the hostelry where Mr Pickwick enjoyed an evening meal. The hotel allows two ceremonies per day and is situated opposite the award winning Abbey Gardens, which provides a picturesque location for photography.
Price guide: approximately £150

Reception

Catering is in-house with prices ranging from £7.50 to £25 per head. The hotel prides itself on its English and French cuisine. Special accommodation rates are offered to wedding guests staying overnight.
Catering: from £7.50.

The Brook Hotel
Orwell Road
Felixstowe, Suffolk IP11 7PF
Tel: 01394 278441 Fax: 01394 670422
Contact: Peter Whalley, Functions

Ceremony

This 4-Crown Victorian-style hotel offers ceremonies free of charge if in conjunction with a waited service reception. Ceremonies cannot be at Christmas or the New Year holiday.
Price guide: F.O.C. (with waited reception)

Reception

Catering is in-house and Chinese cuisine is available. Waited meals start at around £15 per head.
Catering: POA

Hill Lodge Hotel
8 Newton Road
Sudbury, Suffolk CO10 6RL
Tel: 01787 377568 Fax: 01787 373636
Contact: Jim or Anita French, Owners

Ceremony

The original part of the hotel is 70 years old and has a sympathetic modern extension. Set in nearly two acres of grounds, the hotel has two rooms licensed to hold ceremonies which are free of charge if in conjunction with receptions. Ceremonies are available without receptions upon discussion only. Ceremonies can be performed on any day of the year except Christmas Day.
Price guide: P.O.A.

Reception

Catering is in-house with a capacity of 80, whether for a formal seated meal or a buffet-style. Although formal wheelchair access is not available assistance is at hand. The hotel has 17 bedrooms. Its garden is a suitable site for wedding photography or the erection of a marquee.
Catering: P.O.A.

Hintlesham Hall
George Street, Hintlesham
Ipswich, Suffolk IP8 3NS
Tel: 01473 652268 Fax: 01473 652463
Contact : Function Co-ordinator

Ceremony

This Grade I listed Manor House features a Georgian façade and has Tudor origins. The Carolean Room is licensed to hold ceremonies for up to 50. It features plasterwork ceilings dating from the end of the 17th Century. The Hall is also available for hire on an exclusive basis. Ceremonies must be held in conjunction with receptions.
Price guide: £200

Reception

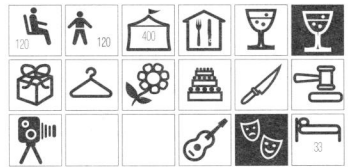

Catering facilities are extended from the Carolean Room into the dining room up to a capacity of 120. A room for the bride and groom to change in is offered depending on availability.
Catering: from £25pp.

Hatfield Hotel
The Esplanade
Lowestoft, Suffolk NR33 0QP
Tel: 01502 565337 Fax: 01502 511885
Contact: Ibraham Mohammed, GM

Ceremony

The hotel stands next to the 'best beach in Britain' for 1995 and 1993. The hotel has four rooms licensed for ceremonies with capacities ranging from 4 to 200.
Price guide: £150 – £200

Reception

Catering: from £14.50pp

Ipswich Guildhall
Hadleigh, Ipswich, IP7 5DT
Tel: 01473 823884
Contact: Mrs J Townsend, Bookings Clerk/Mr R Stevens, Clerk to the Charity

Ceremony

This 15th century Grade I listed building is situated just off Hadleigh High Street, and contains many of its original architectural features. It has three licensed rooms.
Price guide: £75

Reception

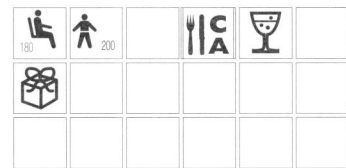

Catering is on a contract basis and must be selected from an approved list. An area for the display of wedding gifts is available by arrangement.

Ipswich Moat House
London Road
Copdock
Ipswich IP8 3JD
Tel: 01473 209988 Fax: 01473 730801
Contact: Peter Coney, Operations
Manager

Ceremony

The Constable Suite and the Lucas
Room are licensed for ceremonies
which can take place here on any day
of the year.
Price guide: POA

Reception

Helicopters and hot air balloons may
use the site.
Catering: from £10pp

Marlborough Hotel
Henley Road
Ipswich
Suffolk IP1 3SP
Tel: 01473 257677 Fax: 01473 226927
Contact: Karen Gough, Owner

Ceremony

This small, family owned and family
run hotel, is set in it own secluded
floodlit garden, and may be hired for
weddings on an exclusive basis.
Ceremonies are not permitted without
receptions facilities also.
Price guide: from £100

Reception

The hotel's catering is in-house and
boasts two AA rosettes. There are 22
bedrooms in total, all of which are en-
suite, and a late night drinking licence
is available for residents only.
Catering: £15 - £30pp

Orwell Park
Nacton, Ipswich IP10 0ER
Tel: 01473 659140, Fax: 01473 659140
Contact: Mrs Ungate

Ceremony

Orwell Park was originally a Georgian
stately home and now acts as a prepara-
tory school which overlooks the river
Orwell and is set in 80 acres of
grounds. There are four rooms
licensed to hold ceremonies with varying capacities of 50 (in the
Headmaster's drawing room) to 200.
Although the school is interested in
enquiries throughout the year, ceremonies would be more convenient
during holiday time.
Price guide: from £250

Reception

Catering capacities vary from a waited
service of 110 to 150 for a stand up buffet, while children are offered reduced
catering rates. Orwell Park prides itself
on the quality of its chef's cuisine.
Price guide: £31.50-50pp.

Priory Barn, Priory Farm,
Preston St Mary, Sudbury, CO10 9LT
Tel: 01787 247251
Contact: Mr and Mrs Adrian Thorpe, Owners

Ceremony

Preston Priory Barn, a renovated traditional Suffolk timber-framed barn, featured in BBC's Lovejoy. It is available
for hire for a three-day period, at a cost
of £800, with a small extra charge for
the hire of the kitchen.
Price guide: £800 for three days

Reception

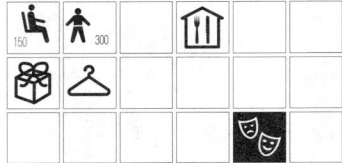

The Barn features a large caterer's
kitchen. A list of local accommodation
can be provided.
Catering: POA

Ravenwood Hall
Country Hotel & Restaurant
The Pavilion
Rougham
Bury St Edmunds IP30 9JA
Tel: 01359 270345 Fax: 01359 270788
Contact: Richard Clayfield,
Conference & Banqeting Manager

Ceremony

This Grade II listed house is over 400
years old and is set in 40 acres of
grounds. It has one room licensed to
hold weddings.
Price guide: £125

Reception

The Pavilion at Ravenwood Hall specialises in traditional English food and
will cater for children separately.
Catering: from £8.50pp - £16.95pp

The Smoke House
Beck Row
Mildenhall
Suffolk IP28 8DH
Tel: 01638 713223 Fax: 01638 712202
Contact: Matthew Cooke,
Restaurant Manager

Ceremony

The Sunderland Lounge holds the
licence.
Price guide: FOC with reception

Reception

Catering: from £7.50

Somerleyton Hall & Gardens
Somerleyton NR32 5QQ
Tel: 01502 730224 Fax: 01502 732143
Contact: Ian Pollard, Administrator

Ceremony

This stately home and historic house is a member of the Historic Houses Association and is set in 12 acres featuring a maze. Helicopters and hot air balloons may use the grounds. Four rooms are licensed with capacities for 56 to 206. Ceremonies can take place here on any day except Christmas and New Year. Bahai faith wedings have also taken place here, in the gardens.
Price guide: from £300

Reception

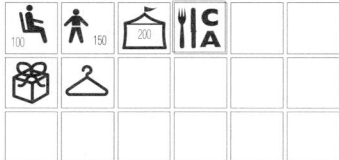

Wedding reception drinks can be served at the centre of the 150 year old maze - guests have to find their way to the champagne! Formerly part of the Victorian Winter Garden , the Hall also boasts a Loggia which can serve as a function room and be used for evening dancing and extra guests. The Loggia leads out into the sunken garden on one side. Evening receptions should be concluded by midnight.
Catering: POA

Stoke By Nayland Golf Club
Keepers Lane, Leavenheath
Nr Colchester, Suffolk CO6 4PZ
Tel: 01206 262836 Fax: 01206 263356
Contact: Duty Manager

Ceremony

Just one ceremony permitted per day, and only when the reception is also at the club.

Reception

A list of local accommodation is available, including preferential rate agreements with hotels and guest houses. The club also boasts a trained florist as part of the wedding package.
Price guide: from £12pp.

The Westerfield House Hotel
Humber Doucy Lane
Ipswich
Suffolk IP4 3QG
Tel: 01473 231344 Fax: 01473 213709
Contact: Frank Howard, MD

Ceremony

Ceremonies must be held with reception.
Price guide: £150

Reception

Catering: £16.50pp + vat

Woodbridge Town Council
Shire Hall
Woodbridge
Suffolk IP12 4LU
Tel: 01349 383599
Contact: P Cotton or Y Schofield,Clerk

Ceremony

This listed building is unable to hold ceremonies on Tuesdays and Thursdays and permits a maximum of four ceremonies a day. Confetti is not allowed.
Price guide: £50 for local residents (£75 others).

Reception
Facilities are not available.

STOP PRESS
Cornwallis Arms, Eye
01379 870326
Courtyard by Marriott, Ipswich
01473 272244
Swan Hotel, Lavenham
01787 247477
Ufford Park Hotel, Woodbridge
01394 383555

Anugraha Hotel
Wick Lane, Englefield Green
Surrey TW20 0XN
Tel: 01784 434355 Fax: 01784 430596
Contact: Conference & Banqueting Department

Ceremony

This hotel and conference centre is housed in a Grade II listed building set in attractive grounds. Ceremonies can take place here on any day of the year.
Price guide: £350

Reception

Catering: from £28pp

Bourne Hall
Spring Street, Ewell
Epsom , Surrey KT171UF
Tel: 0181 393 9571 Fax: 0181 786 7265
Contact: Sandra Dessent, Facilities Manager

Ceremony

Bourne Hall is a restaurant, museum and library which can offer several marriage rooms. Only one ceremony is permitted here per day on any day of the year.
Price guide: £60 - £100

Reception

A list of local accommodation can be provided on request.
Catering: P.O.A.

Clandon Park
West Clandon, Guildford
Surrey GU7 7RQ
Tel: 01483 222482 Fax: 01483 223479
Contact: Sonia Ashworth, Administrative Assistant

Ceremony

This 18th Century stately home, is set in parkland and gardens which include a parterre, grotto, Dutch garden and Maori House. Clandon is available for ceremonies on any day of the week, but not during Christmas, Easter, January or February. A maximum of two ceremonies are allowed per day. No confetti is allowed.
Price guide: from £600 + vat

Reception

There is currently no late night drinking licence, but this can be applied for if required. There is no accommodation on the premises, but a list of local accommodation can be provided. The grounds are suitable for a helicopter to land if desired.
Catering: £8.95 - £29.75 + vat

Epsom Downs Racecourse
Epsom Downs
Surrey KT18 5LQ
Tel: 01372 726311 Fax: 01372 748258
Contact: Marilyn Watkinson, Sales & Marketing

Ceremony

The two marriage rooms at Epsom are in the Queen's Stand. Weddings may take place here Monday to Saturday, but not during Christmas, New Year's or Easter Holidays, or race days.
Price guide: £400 (£350 with reception) + vat

Reception

The Epsom wedding package (and price guide shown below) includes drinks, floral table arrangements and room hire for the day. Evening room

hire starts at £200. The Racecourse has its own helipad, and hot air balloons can also take off from here (all with permission). The venue will be holding a Wedding Fair on 21st September 1997, which will include a wedding exhibition and fashion show. A list of local accommodation can be provided, if required.
Catering: from £37pp

Frensham Heights
Rowledge
Farnham
Surrey GU10 4EA
Tel: 01252 793845/792299
Fax: 01252 794369
Contact: Toby Turl

Ceremony

This Edwardian, neo-Elizabethan style, country house (now a school) stands in 100 acres on the Heights of Frensham, looking south towards the Blackdown Hills. Ceremonies can be held in the Ballroom, Jacobean Gallery, Blue Drawing Room or Old Orangery. The suite of rooms, as well as terrace and lawns, is available 7 days a week, with or without reception.
Price guide: £450 without reception
£350 with reception

Reception

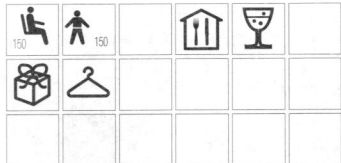

Menus of your choice are provided by a specialist firm and up to 150 can be seated in the Ballroom. Sole occupation is guaranteed, with full drinks licence.
Catering: from £16pp

The Hawker Centre
Lower Ham Road
Kingston Upon Thames KT2 5BH
Tel: 0181 296 9747 Fax: 0181 296 9759
Contact: Malcolm North, Facilities Manager

Ceremony

This sport and leisure facility enjoys a

riverside location with large car park and licensed bar on site.. The main hall, small hall and studio are all licensed for ceremonies which can take place here on any day of the year.
Price guide: from £20

Reception

Couples need to organise their own catering at this venue.

Inn on the Lake
Ockford Road, Godalming
Surrey GU7 1RH
Tel: 01483 415575 Fax: 01483 860445
Contact: James Ginders, GM

Ceremony

The Inn on the Lake (which claims to be an inn, not a hotel) is a part Tudor building with a listed Georgian frontage. It is set in two acres of landscaped grounds overlooking is own lake. The building has limited wheelchair access. Ceremonies can take place here on any day of the year.
Price guide: P.O.A.

Reception

The venue has a lakeside restaurant as well as a bar which features a log fire and real ale.
Catering: from £32pp

Jarvis Thatcher's Hotel
Epsom Road, East Horsley
Nr Leatherhead KT24 6TB
Tel: 01483 284291 Fax: 01483 284222
Contact: Alex Power, Conference & Banqueting Managr

Ceremony

This is a Tudor style building set in its own landscaped gardens. Ceremonies can take place here on any day except Christmas Day and New Year's Day, with up to five ceremonies permitted per day. Price guide: £250

Reception

The hotel holds an AA Rosette for its cuisine. Wedding packages start at £21.70pp, which includes a three course meal, toastmaster, invitations sent out for you, table plan and cards, cake boxes and a double room at any Jarvis hotel for the wedding night. Drinks packages start at £9.70pp. Other packages offered by the hotel have also been well thought out and include things such as fun packs for children, 'favours' for all the ladies, and a dinner for two at Thatcher's on your first anniversary.
Catering: from £21.70pp - £6.85pp (buffets)

La Bonne Auberge
Tilburstow Hill
South Godstone
Surrey RH9 8JY
Tel: 01342 892318 Fax: 01342 893435
Contact: Claire Shay, Manager

Ceremony

This privately owned Victorian country house restaurant is set in its own 14 acres with a lake. There are two marriage rooms, which can be used only if the reception is to follow at the restaurant. They are available any day except Bank Holidays.
Price guide: from £95

Reception

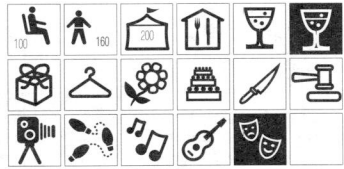

The restaurant specialises in classical French cuisine, but was once asked to cater for a 'Kiwi barbecue' for which a specialist was brought in. Helicopters and hot air balloons may use the grounds of the restaurant, and it is possible to have use of a gondola on the lake. Fireworks have also been organised in the past.
Catering: from £19.90 (waited) - £10pp (buffet)

Leatherhead Golf Club
Kingston Road, Leatherhead
Surrey KT22 0EE
Tel: 01372 843958 Fax: 01372 843966
Contact: Terry

Ceremony

The club allows one ceremony per day on any day of the week, but not on Bank Holidays. No confetti is allowed.
Price guide: from £250

Reception

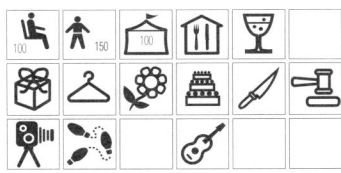

Catering: P.O.A.

Lythe Hill Hotel
Petworth Road, Haslemere
Surrey GU27 3BQ
Tel: 01428 651251 Fax: 01428 644131
Contact: K Lorimer, General Manager

Ceremony

Three rooms are available for ceremonies within this cluster of buildings, the oldest of which dates from 1475. The hotel's 20 acres of grounds includes a lake, a floodlit tennis court, a croquet lawn, games room and even a jogging track. Two ceremonies are permitted per day at the Lythe Hill Hotel, and can be held on any day of the week.
Price guide: from £50.

Reception

The hotel's wedding package includes a room to use during the day, and a complimentary room for the night. An accommodation discount is offered to all wedding guests. For the reception the hotel specialises in traditional English and French cuisine. Children under 10 are charged at half price.
Catering: £45.50 (wedding package)

The Manor
Newlands Corner
Guildford, Surrey GU4 8SE
Tel: 01483 222624 Fax: 01483 211389
Contact: David Hill, GM

Ceremony

The Manor is a country house hotel set in nine acres of parkland, and within easy reach of Heathrow and Gatwick airports.. Three rooms are available for weddings, but ceremonies can only take place Sunday to Friday throughout most of the year. Saturdays are only available in November, January and February. Only one ceremony per day is permitted at The Manor. As part of its standard wedding package, The Manor offers a complimentary room for the bride and groom, or transport for the couple to their evening destination within the local area
Price guide: Registrar's fees only

Reception

The Manor has a late night drinking licence for Thursday, Friday and Saturday only. For the reception, children under 12 are charged at half price, while those under 4 are free.
Catering: from £23pp

The Market House
Market Place
Kingston upon Thames
Tel: 0181 296 9747 Fax: 0181 296 9759
Contact: Malcolm North, Facilities Manager

Ceremony

This is the old Kingston town hall and is a Grade II listed building. The main hall and ante chamber are licensed for ceremonies which can take place here on any day of the year.
Price guide: from £40

Reception

There is currently no catering on site, so couples may arrange their own.

Oatlands Park Hotel
Oatlands Drive, Weybridge
Surrey KT13 9HB
Tel: 01932 847242 Fax: 01932 821413
Contact: Barbara Harris, Sales & Marketing Manager

Ceremony

Three marriage rooms are available in this Grade II listed building which is set on the original estate where Henry VIII built a palace for Anne of Cleves. The rooms are The York Suite (120 -220 people), The Broadwater Restaurant (80-160 people), and the Drawing Room & Garden room (up to 60 people). Ceremonies can take place here on any day of the year.
Price guide: £100

Reception

Cake stand and knife and typed menus are provided free for the day, and a complimentary changing room is offered for the bride and groom. Overnight accommodation is also offered free of charge for the newlyweds.
Price guide: from £22pp

Sandown Park
Portsmouth Road, Esher
Surrey KT10 9AJ
Tel: 01372 464790 Fax: 01372 465205
Contact: Sales Manager

Ceremony

Opened as a racecourse in 1875 Sandown Park offers a choice of seven suites in its main building.
Price guide: F.O.C. (with reception)

Reception

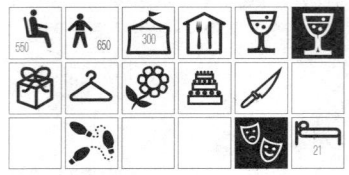

Sandown has a marquee erected from May to August. Accommodation is offered in the Ostler's Lodge, a modern hotel set in the grounds of the Park. The park also has a golf centre, a squash club and three artificial ski slopes.
Catering: from £18pp

Stanhill Court Hotel
Charlwood
Horley, Surrey RH6 0EP
Tel: 01293 862166 Fax: 01293 862773
Contact: Leonie Hudson, Manager

Ceremony

This Victorian country hosue was built in 1881 in the Scottish Baronial style. It is set in 35 acres of ancient wooded countryside and grounds which feature an open-air ampitheatre and a walled garden. The Morning Room is licensed for ceremonies. But ceremonies here must be followed by reception at the venue.
Price guide: £150

Reception

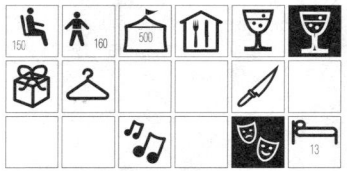

Stanhill holds English Tourist Board Awards (1995/96) for food, hospitality and service.
Catering: from £22pp

STOP PRESS
Bramley Grange Hotel, Bramley
01483 893434

The Burys, Godalming
01483 869221
The Bush Hotel, Farnham
01252 715237
Ewell Court House, Epsom
0181 393 9571
Farnham House Hotel, Farnham
01252 716908
Forte Posthouse, Guildford
01483 574444
Great Fosters, Egham
Tel: 01784 433822
Nonsuch Mansion, Cheam
0181 393 4922
Nutfield Priory Hotel, Redhill
01737822066
Preston Cross Hotel, Bookham
01372 456642
Ramster, Godalming
01428 644422
The Wentworth Club, Virginia Water
01344 842201
Woodlands Park Hotel, Cobham
01737 780200

Close House Mansion
Heddon on the Wall
Newcastle upon Tyne NE15 0HT
Tel: 01661 852255 Fax: 01661 853322
Contact: Jane Thompson

Ceremony

This conference and banqueting centre is an English Heritage, Grade II listed building, set in 179 acres of wooded grounds and parkland and features an 18 hole private golf course and helipad. Just 10 minutes from Newcastle city centre, the mansion dates back to 1779 and was once the property of a former Mayor of Newcastle. Ceremonies are permitted seven days a week with only one permitted per day.
Price guide: £300

Reception

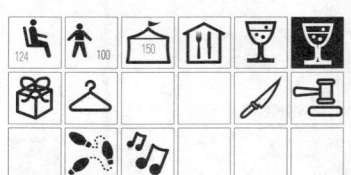

The Bolbec and Bewicke Rooms are considered spacious and light and ideal for larger wedding breakfasts. The Bewicke Room features a marble fireplace and a bay window which opens out on the the east lawn. The Rococo Room, decorated in the Italian Rococo style, features a marble fireplace as a

centrepiece and is suitable for smaller wedding parties. The mansion's grounds and lawns provide excellent surroundings for exterior photography. Pre-arranged wedding packages include amongst other services, menu and drinks of your choice, table plans, hire of the function room and a private changing room for the bride and groom. Although bedrooms are not available on the premises, a list of local accommodation is available which operate preferential rate agreements with the mansion.
Catering: from £16pp

County Thistle Hotel
Neville Street, Newcastle NE99 1AH
Tel: 0191 232 2471 Fax: 0191 232 1285
Contact: Mary Thornton, GM

Ceremony

The hotel has three rooms licensed to hold ceremonies, which are not available on Bank Holidays or over the period 24th - 27th December. Ceremonies are free of charge when held in conjunction with receptions, while the price without a reception is available upon application, depending on the room required and the time of year.
Price guide: P.O.A.

Reception

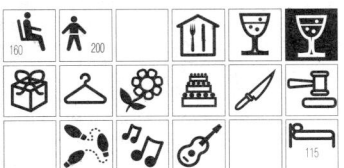

A buffet style reception can hold a maximum of 200 standing guests, while the price guide below includes a sit down luncheon, red carpet, drinks for the reception, wine with the meal, sparkling wine for the speeches, flower and overnight accommodation for the bride and groom.
Catering: £23pp

Dissington Hall, Dalton
Newcastle Upon Tyne NE18 0AD
Tel: 01661 886063 Fax: 01661 886896
Contact: Michael Brown, Proprietor

Ceremony

This Georgian mansion was designed in 1794 and is set in 18 acres of grounds. Three rooms are licensed to hold ceremonies, the Garden room which features a sweeping staircase and has a seated capacity of 90 people; the Old Library, which features a large book case and fireplace, which seats 50; and the Billiards room which is the main banqueting room and has a seated capacity of 100. Ceremonies are not available during the Christmas and New Year holiday and are only available with reception facilities. There is wheelchair access to the ground floor.
Price guide: POA

Reception

The Hall takes pride in its high standard of cuisine and specialises in home-made food. If required, children can be catered for separately. The Admiral's bedroom is available for the bride and groom to change in, and the Hall can also provide a list of local hotels and guest houses. However, there are no preferential rate agreements with any of these establishments. The grounds are suitable for a marquee for up to 200 guests.
Catering: from £21pp

Jarrow Town Hall
Grange Road, Jarrow
Newcastle upon Tyne NE32 3LE
Tel: 0191 489 1141 Fax: 0191 455 0208
Contact: Mr Graham Jarvis, Assistant Director (Administration)

Ceremony

The Town Hall is a listed building and is licensed to hold ceremonies in the Council Chamber, on Saturdays and Sundays only. Confetti is permitted.
Price guide: £225

Reception

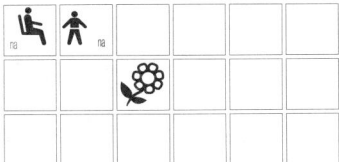

Although no reception facilities are offered at the Town Hall, a list of local accommodation is available and background music can be provided.

Newcastle United Football Club
St James' Park
Newcastle upon Tyne NE1 4ST
Tel: 0191 201 8525 Fax: 0191 201 8611
Contact: Conference & Banqueting

Ceremony

Newcastle United Football Club, established over 100 years ago, now play in one of the world's most modern sporting arenas. Situated in the heart of Newcastle, St James' Park offers panoramic views over the River Tyne and the City, and has extensive parking facilities. Four rooms at St James' Park are now licensed to hold marriage ceremonies; the St James' Suite, the Boardroom Club, the Centenary Suite and the United Suite. These rooms offer varying capacities from between 80 to 180. Ceremonies are available seven days a week, excluding match days of course.
Price guide: POA

Reception

Although it is not possible to hold the ceremony or take photographs actually on the pitch, the grounds are available to take outside photography. The club boasts a speciality in Northumbrian cuisine in the Magpie Room, thanks to chef, John Blackmore of Alnwick, and Barry Johnson is featured as head chef. There are a total of eight function rooms in which to hold receptions and although accommodation is not available on the premises, the Club does operate preferential rate agreements with local hotels.
Catering: from £9pp

South Shields Town Hall
Westoe Road, South Shields
Newcastle upon Tyne NE33 2RL
Tel: 0191 427 1717 Fax: 0191 455 0208
Contact: Mr Graham Jarvis, Assistant Director (Administration)

Ceremony

The Town Hall has four rooms licensed to hold ceremonies, with varying capacities; the Reception Room is the largest with a capacity of 145, the Ante-room to the Council Chamber seats 50 while the two Committee rooms seat each seat 30. Ceremonies are available Saturday and Sunday only and confetti is permitted.
Price guide: £225

Reception

Although accommodation is not available on the premises, the Town Hall provides a list of local hotels and guest houses. In addition to the services indicated above, the Hall provides background music if requested.
Catering: £9.50-15pp

Temple Park Centre
John Reid Road, South Shields
Newcastle upon Tyne
Tel: 0191 456 9119 Fax: 0191 456 6621
Contact: Harry Blackett, Manager

Ceremony

The leisure centre has three rooms licensed to hold ceremonies; the Function Suite, which seats 140, Parkers Bar, which seats 100 guests and the Main Hall which is for larger weddings, with a maximum capacity of 600 seated and up to 3,000 standing. Ceremonies are available seven days a week with a maximum of four per day, with an interval of 1.5 hours in between each. Confetti is permitted.
Price guide: £225

Reception

Although accommodation is not avail-

able on the premises, the leisure centre offers a list of local hotels and guest houses. In addition to the services indicated the centre offers champagne for guests on arrival and past weddings have featured a horse and carriage for the bridal party.
Catering: £9.50-15pp

Tuxedo Royale
Hillgate Quay
Gateshead
Tyne & Wear NE8 2QS
Tel: 0191 477 8899 Fax: 0191 477 3297
Contact: Thelma Barnes

Ceremony

The Tuxedo Royale is actually a ship berthed on the river Tyne and has been moored here for approximately six years. The room licensed to hold ceremonies is the Commodore Suite which has a minimum capacity of four guests for a more intimate wedding. Although it is possible to hold a ceremony without reception facilities, ceremonies are free of charge if held in conjunction with receptions. Confetti is permitted.
Price guide: £500

Reception

Catering is in-house and children can be catered for separately. Although accommodation is not available on the premises, preferential rate agreements are operated with local hotels and guest houses.
Catering: from £10.95pp(buffet)

Washington Old Hall
The Avenue
Washington Village
Newcastle upon Tyne NE38 7LE
Tel: 0191 416 6879
Contact: Wedding Co-ordinator

Ceremony

Owned by the National Trust, the Hall is a Jacobean manor house which was

home to the direct ancestors of George Washington in the latter part of the 12th Century, and incorporates many of the medieval remains of the original building. Largely rebuilt in the 17th Century the house is furnished with contemporary paintings and furniture. Ceremonies take place in the Great Hall, which has a seated capacity of 36, although additional standing room is available at the back of the Hall. Ceremonies are available seven days a week from the beginning of November to the end of March, but only on Fridays and Saturdays during summer time. Smoking is not permitted in any part of the building.
Price guide: £100 (£235 wedding + day time reception).

Reception

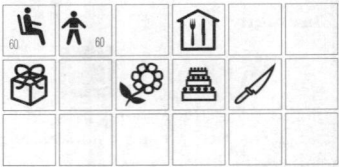

In order to tailor your wedding to your exact preferences, the Hall has a list of three recommended contract caterers so couples may choose everything to suit their own requirements. The Hall does not insist that couples buy a drinks package, by offering the bridal party the opportunity to supply guests with their own wines and spirits, without incurring a corkage fee. Receptions are permitted during the daytime only, and the Hall operates preferential rate agreements with local hotels and guest houses. The Hall has recently held a 17th Century themed wedding whereby guests, bride and groom were in period costume. The price below indicates the cost of a hot meal per head.
Catering: from £9-25pp

STOP PRESS
The Grand Hotel, Tynemouth
0191 293 6666
The Park Hotel, Tynemouth
0191 257 1406
The Pulman Lodge Hotel, Sunderland
0191 529 2020

007 Bond Street
Bond Gate, Nuneaton
Warwickshire CV11 4DA
Tel: 01203 347563 Fax: 01203 352458
Contact: Heather Clelland, Wedding Co-ordinator

Ceremony

This is a themed venue based on the James Bond character. Ceremonies are available seven days a week with one permitted per day. Although there is no specific area for outdoor photography, the venue is only five minutes walk away from a park.
Price guide: £215

Reception

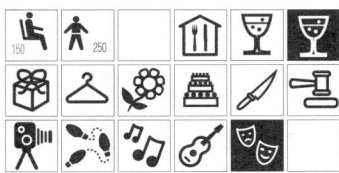

The venue prides itself on the ability to provide any service the couple may require, from videos and horse and carriages to organising the honeymoon for them. As an extra special touch, the venue can organise a James Bond lookalike for the reception. The venue operates special rate agreements with local hotels and guest houses. The price guide indicates the cost per head of a buffet reception, which rises to £12.50 for a sit-down meal.
Catering: from £7.50pp

The Alveston Manor
Stratford-upon-Avon
Warwicks CV37 7HP

Tel: 01789 204581 Fax: 01789 414095
Contact: Pat Hollis Business Development Manager

Ceremony

This riverside hotel and restaurant offers ceremonies seven days a week with a maximum of two to be held per day.
Price guide: £150

Reception

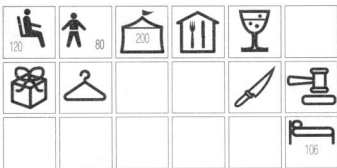

The grounds are suitable for a marquee with a capacity for accommodating up to 200 people.
Catering: from £27pp

The Arden Thistle Hotel
44 Waterside
Stratford upon Avon CV37 6BA

Tel: 01789 294949 Fax: 01789 415874
Contact: Jeremy Mason or Claire Gale, Conference & Banqueting Administrators

Ceremony

This Regency built hotel is opposite the Royal Shakespeare & Swan theatres and is available seven days a week.
Price guide: £195

Reception

The hotel has 63 bedrooms, some of which are executive rooms and two of which feature four poster beds. The hotel's Bard's restaurant features traditional English and continental cuisine, while the terrace is a relaxing location to enjoy drinks with guests.
Catering: £25.50-36.50pp

The Ardencote Manor Hotel
Lye Green Road, Claverdon
Warwickshire CV35 8LS

Tel: 01926 843111 Fax: 01926 842646
Contact: Paul Williams, GM

Ceremony

This hotel and country club, originally a Victorian manor house residence, is set in 40 acres of parkland and features a fishing lodge with a seven acre trout lake. Three rooms are licensed at the hotel with varying capacities; the Palms Conservatory which overlooks the grounds, the Henley Suite and the Oak Room, which is a classical dining room with oak panelling and has a capacity of 46.
Price guide: £170

Reception

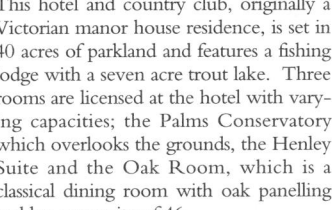

The hotel prides itself on a European approach to cuisin offers special accommodation rat wedding guests.
Catering: from £35pp (wedding packag

The Belfry
Lichfield Road, Wishaw
N Warwickshire B76 9PR

Tel: 01675 470301 Fax: 01675 470178
Contact: Rita Cooper, Sales

Ceremony

The Belfry is a four star hotel set in 500 acres of parkland and offers ceremonies seven days a week with a maximum of two to be held per day.
Price guide: from £250 - £1500

Reception

The hotel prides itself on the ability to meet any catering requirements the couple may have. In addition to the services indicated, the hotel stresses that any request may be arranged.
Catering: from £37.75pp

Courtyard by Marriott Hotel
London Road
Ryton On Dunsmore CV8 3DY

Tel: 01203 301585 Fax: 01203 301610
Contact: Des Richardson, Conference & Banqueting Manager

Ceremony

The hotel is RAC and AA recommended. A maximum of one ceremony a day is permitted, on any day of the week.
Price guide: from £475

Reception

The hotel stresses that however formal or informal your reception requirements may be, they will provide the necessary arrangements. The price guide indicates the starting price of a standing finger buffet. Of the services indicated, the cake stand, toastmaster and piped music are all provided free of charge, a fee will be charged for the remaining services.
Catering: from £7pp

De Montfort Hotel
The Square, Kenilworth CV8 1ED
Tel: 01926 855944 Fax: 01926 857830
Contact: Kerry Holmes, Conference
Co-ordinator

Ceremony

This modern hotel is situated in the town centre and has recently undergone a £2 million refurbishment. The hotel does not feature any gardens but has parking for up to 70 cars. Four rooms are licensed to hold ceremonies with varying capacities from 20 to 130. Ceremonies are available without reception facilities but the hotel would like to avoid this if possible. No charge is made by the hotel for the hire of the ceremony room but a fee of approximately £135 will be made by the registrar.

Reception

The hotel has a lounge area suitable for indoor photography and offers a complimentary overnight suite for the bride and groom on the night of the wedding. Wedding breakfast prices start at approximately £17 per person, reducing to £7 a head for an evening buffet reception. The hotel operates preferential rate agreements with local guest houses for wedding guests.
Catering: from £7pp

Eathorpe Park Hotel
**The Fosse, Leamington Spa
Warwickshire CV33 9DQ**
Tel: 01926 632632 Fax: 01926 632481
Contact: Carol or Rodney Grinnell,
Directors

Ceremony

Ceremonies are available any day of the week with no cap on the number held per day.
Price guide: FOC

Reception

In addition to the hotel's 16 bedrooms, it also operates special rate agreements with other local hotels and guest houses.
Catering: POA

Falstaff Hotel
**16-20 Warwick New Road
Leamington Spa CV32 5JQ**
Tel: 01926 312044 Fax: 01926 450574
Contact: John Seeger, GM

Ceremony

This 18th Century building, converted into three Regency mansions is now home to this 63 bedroom hotel. One room is available to hold ceremonies, with a capacity of 46. Ceremonies are not available without reception facilities.
Price guide: £150

Reception

The hotel features traditional English and continental cuisine with a focus on fresh produce. The charge for the changing room for the bride and groom is included in the price of the evening reception.
Catering: from £11.25pp

Kingsbury Country Club
**Coventry Road
Kingsbury, Tamworth B78 2LP**
Tel: 01827 872404
Contact: Martin Shakespeare, Manager

Ceremony

This modern building is surrounded by a public recreation area with gardens and is available to hold ceremonies seven days a week. Ceremonies are only permitted when held in conjunction with receptions.
Price guide: F.O.C. (with reception)

Reception

The club prides itself on home cooked, traditional cuisine.
Catering: Buffets from £4.95pp Sit down from £12.50pp

Lea Marston Hotel
**Haunch Lane, Lea Marston
Warwickshire B76 0BY**
Tel: 01675 470468 Fax: 01675 470871
Contact: Sharon Smith, Sales
Co-ordinator

Ceremony

The hotel is set in 20 acres of grounds and features a nine hole golf course. Three rooms are licensed at the hotel: the Atrium Room which is in the hotel's conservatory, which has a marble floor and holds 80 guests; the Octagon Suite which overlooks the golf course and has a capacity of 100; and the Perry-Barton room, which has a capacity of 80 people. Ceremonies are permitted without reception facilities although the room hire charge rises to £100 in these circumstances.
Price guide: from £75 (£150 without reception)

Reception

There is a reception room hire fee of £195.
Catering: Buffets from £6.95pp Sit down from £19.95pp

The Manor House Hotel
Avenue Road
Leamington Spa CV31 3NJ
Tel: 01926 423251 Fax: 01926 425933
Contact; Jan Deeming, Banqueting

Ceremony

Said to be home of the first Lawn Tennis Club, this listed building features smooth landscaped lawns and was opened in 1847. Included in the wedding package for a minimum of 45 guests, the hotel includes amongst other things, afternoon room hire, table posies, changing room and overnight accommodation for the bride and groom.
Price guide: from £80

Reception

The hotel offers special overnight rates to wedding guests including a traditional English breakfast. Of the services indicated, the hotel includes the flowers and cake stand in the reception price.
Catering: from £12.90pp Drinks packages from £5.55pp

Nuthurst Grange Country House
Hotel & Restaurant
Nuthurst Grange Lane
Hockley Heath B94 5NL
Tel: 01564 783972 Fax: 01564 783919
Contact: Karen J Seymour, Manager

Ceremony

The hotel has been awarded four ETB Crowns, three AA Red Stars and three Rosettes for its restaurant. Ceremonies are available any day of the week with only one permitted per day.
Price guide: £195

Reception

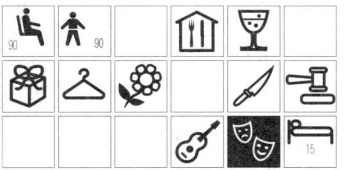

The hotel prides itself on using only the freshest foods in its award winning restaurant.
Catering: from £29.90pp

Salford Hall Hotel
Abbotts Salford
Evesham WR11 5UT
Tel: 01386 871300 Fax: 01386 871301
Contact: Sally Pearce, General Manager

Ceremony

This Tudor manor is a Grade I listed building, restored six years ago. Up to two ceremonies are permitted per day, on any day except Christmas Day. Confetti is not permitted.
Price guide: £100 (FOC with reception)

Reception

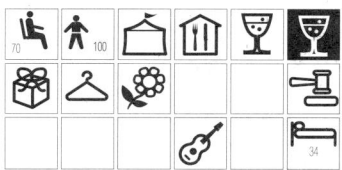

The Hotel has two AA Rosettes for its cuisine. It is also possible to take over the whole hotel, including a minimum of 30 bedrooms.
Catering: from £27.50pp.

STOP PRESS
Billesley Manor Hotel, Alcester
01789 279955
Brandon Hall Hotel, Brandon
01203 542571
Brownsover Hall Hotel, Rugby
01788 546100
Charlecote Pheasant, Charlecote
01789 279954
Marston Farm Hotel, Sutton Coldfield
01827 872133
Moxhull Hall Hotel, Wishaw
0121 329 2056
Riverside Hotel, Kenilworth
01926 858331
Southam Community Hall, Southam
01926 813933
Woodhouse Hotel, Princethorpe
01926 632131

Aston Villa Football Club
Villa Park
Birmingham B6 6HE
Tel: 0121 327 5308 Fax: 0121 328 1351
Contact: Carol Deakin, Sales
& Marketing Co-ordinator

Ceremony

This famous football club and restaurant is licensed to hold ceremonies in the McGregor restaurant seven days a week excluding match days. Two ceremonies per day are permitted and confetti is allowed.
Price guide: £250

Reception

Although accommodation is not available on the premises, the football club has a list of local hotels and guest houses, some of which operate preferential rate agreements with the club. In addition to the services indicated, the club allows photographs to be taken on the pitch and prides itself on offering a full wedding package. The price guide indicated below is for a sit down meal.
Catering: from £15pp

The Chace Hotel
London Road
Toll Bar End
Coventry CV3 4EQ
Tel: 01203 303398 Fax: 01203 301816
Contact: Trisha Hennessy-Cooper, Room Sales Manager

Ceremony

The hotel dates back to the late 19th Century and features traditional wood panelling, a large open fireplace and an imposing foyer. The foyer leads to a sweeping staircase which features stained glass windows. One room is licensed to hold ceremonies at the hotel which is available seven days a week with no restrictions on Bank Holidays. Ceremonies are free when held in conjunction with receptions. The hotel also has the Abbey Room, a luxury bedroom complete with four-poster bed and spa bath, which is popular for both newly weds and anniversary couples. All bedrooms have colour TV and other amenities.
Price guide: F.O.C. (with reception) or £100

Reception

Of the 66 bedrooms, 17 are located in the original building. The hotel boasts traditional English cuisine but is willing to discuss any specific catering requirements.
Catering: from £16.95pp

The Chamberlain Hotel
Alcester Street
Birmingham B12 0PJ
Tel: 0121 627 0627 Fax: 0121 627 0628
Contact: Jacqueline A Perkins,
Banqueting Sales Executive

Ceremony

This Grade II listed building has four rooms licensed to hold ceremonies, one of which, the Rowton Suite, features Victorian skylights, ornate pillars and specially imported wood panels. The Suite also includes an extensive sound and light system and a dance floor at no extra cost. Ceremonies are not available on Good Friday or Christmas Day. Confetti is not permitted.
Price guide: from £150

Reception

The hotel is happy to discuss any special dietary requests and in addition to the reception services indicated the hotel provides a car service, video photography and a stationery contact.
Catering: Buffets from £7pp sit down from £24pp

Coombe Abbey Hotel
Coombe Abbey Park
Brinklow Road
Binley
Coventry CV3 2AB
Tel: 01203 450450 Fax: 01203 635101
Contact: Paul Gossage, Wedding Co-ordinator

Ceremony

This 12th Century Abbey, which is set in 550 acres of grounds, has been tastefully restored into a luxury hotel, which has medieval, 18th century and Victorian features. Two rooms are licensed to hold ceremonies: the De-Canville room, which has a capacity of 23 guests; and the Abbeygate room with a capacity of 138. The hotel prides itself as being "no ordinary hotel" and consequently plans "no ordinary weddings".
Price guide: £200 - £400

Reception

The hotel boasts a speciality in the best of English cuisine, with a touch of European flair. In addition to the services indicated, the hotel offers a complimentary overnight stay for the bridal couple and may also provide medieval themed weddings and in-house opera singers for the reception. There is a room hire fee if only a buffet is required.
Catering: from £24.50pp

Coventry City Football Club
Highfield Road Stadium
King Richard Street
Coventry
CV5 4FW
Tel: 01203 234000 Fax: 01203 630318
Contact: Raj Athwal or Val Wright

Ceremony

The club has a total of 30 hospitality and conference rooms which are capable of catering for as few as two to 24,000 people. There are six rooms licensed to hold ceremonies, one of which is the restaurant, which actually overlooks the pitch. Ceremonies are available seven days a week including match days, and are available without reception facilities if required. Outdoor photography includes the use of the pitch.
Price guide: FOC

Reception

The site is suitable for a marquee which may be constructed on the pitch itself upon discussion. For 1996 we were quoted buffets from £10pp at the Club, with wedding breakfasts starting at £15pp. The Club is now keen to state that catering prices vary according to requirements, which demonstrates their flexibility. The club operates preferential rate agreements with various local hotels and offers a limousine service for the bride and groom to travel to the hotel. A late night drinking licence may be easily obtained.
Catering: POA

Friendly Hotel
20 Wolverhampton Road West
Bentley
Walsall WS2 0BS
Tel: 01922 724444 Fax: 01922 723148
Contact: Mandy Chagger, Banqueting Co-ordinator

Ceremony

This modern hotel has two rooms licensed for ceremonies; the Oliver Cromwell Suite and the King Charles Suite, both of which can be divided into three sections and used individually or as a whole. Each section has a capacity for approximately 50 people seated, which rises to a maximum of 180 when using all three sections.
Price guide: £100 - £360

Reception

The hotel operates special themed receptions which have in the past included an Indian theme and a Halloween theme. A late night drinking licence may easily be obtained and a complimentary overnight room is available for bride and groom.
Catering: from £5.95pp (buffet)

Highbury
Yew Tree Road
Moseley
Birmingham B13 8QG
Tel: 0121 449 6549 Fax: 0121 442 4782
Contact: Mrs J Tanner

Ceremony

Highbury's secluded parkland setting challenges its situation just three miles from Birmingham city centre. Originally built as the home of Joseph Chamberlain MP, in 1878, Highbury features a central Hall with a first floor minstrel's gallery while the Drawing Room is licensed to hold ceremonies. Leading from the Hall the Drawing Room looks out over Highbury's South facing terrace, grounds and surround parkland. Ceremonies are only available when held in conjunction with reception facilities.
Price guide: POA

Reception

Although Highbury features seven bedrooms these are only available for wedding guests upon discussion.
Catering: from £17pp

Jarvis International Hotel
The Square
Solihull
West Midlands B91 3RF
Tel: 0121 711 2121 Fax: 0121 711 3374
Contact: Amanda Hillier, Helen Wallace

Ceremony

English Tourist Board recommended, the hotel specialises in the production of wedding packages, and has three specific packages, the cheapest of which is the Sandringham package at £29 - £42pp. There are three rooms licensed to hold ceremonies with capacities varying from 25 to 100. Ceremonies are available seven days a week with discounts available on Sundays, Fridays and Bank Holidays.
Price guide: £50 - £200

Reception

The Sandringham wedding package includes room hire charge for the reception, a drink for guests on arrival, a choice of three menus (one of which must be chosen before the wedding day), 1.5 glasses of wine for guests with their meal, a glass of sparkling wine for the toast, top table flowers, a changing room for the couple on the day, and a town house overnight suite for the bride and groom.
Catering: packages from £29pp

Nailcote Hall Hotel
Nailcote Lane
Berkswell
Coventry CV7 7DE
Tel: 01203 466174 Fax: 01203 470720
Contact: Karen Bentley, Conference Manager

Ceremony

This 17th Century country house hotel, is a Grade I listed building and is set in 15 acres of grounds. There are no restrictions to hold ceremonies on Bank Holidays but it is not possible to hold ceremonies without using reception facilities.
Price guide: £150

Reception

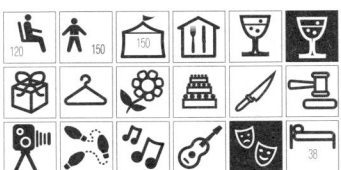

The hotel offers complimentary overnight accommodation for the bride and groom.
Catering: from £35.50 (wedding package)

Quality Norfolk Hotel
257-267 Hagley Road
Edgbaston
Birmingham B16 9NA
Tel: 0121 454 8071 Fax: 0121 455 6149
Contact: Lynn Evans Conference & Banqueting Manager

Ceremony

The hotel is two miles west of the city centre and is set in its own gardens. Ceremonies are available seven days a week excluding Good Friday and Christmas Day.
Price guide: POA

Reception

The hotel states it is well recognised as a venue for wedding receptions and social functions. In addition to the above services the hotel has contacts with the suppliers of cakes, photographers and live music. A complimentary bedroom is offered to the bride and groom on their wedding night and special rates are available for wedding guests.
Catering: from £10pp

Solihull Conference &
Banqueting Centre
Homer Road
Solihull
B91 3QW
Tel: 0121 704 0088 Fax: 0121 711 3157
Contact: Pauline Perla, Conference and Banqueting Admin Manager

Ceremony

This town centre conference centre features tree lined lawns. Its Aylesford and Shenstone rooms are licensed for ceremonies which can take place here on any day of the year.
Price guide: £100 - £200

Reception

The centre is able to provide Asian cuisine if required.
Catering: Buffets from £6.50pp   Sit down from £12.50pp

WEST MIDLANDS - WEST SUSSEX

St Mary's Guildhall Complex
Council House
Bayley Lane
Coventry CV1 5RR
Tel: 01203 833327 Fax: 01203 833329
contact: Roma Stone, Conference &
Banqueting Manager

Ceremony

This Grade I listed medieval guildhall
has four rooms licensed with a minimum capacity of four guests.
Price guide: £60 - £255

Reception

The Guildhall has a hotel situated
nearby which can arrange accommodation for guests.
Catering: from £7.20pp

Sutton Coldfield Town Hall
Upper Clifton Road
Sutton Coldfield B73 6AB
Tel: 0121 355 8990 Fax: 0121 355 8255
Contact: Lynette Skinner, Manager

Ceremony

Three rooms are licensed to hold cere-
monies at the Town Hall: the Council
Chamber,, the Vesey Lounge and the
Vesey Suite. Ceremonies are not avail-
able on Christmas Day and Good
Friday.
Price guide: £100 - £200

Reception

Although the Town Hall does not hold
a late night drinking licence this can be
applied for if required. Ethnic cuisine is
a speciality. A list of local accomoda-
tion is available, some with preferential
rate agreements.
Catering: from £12.50pp

Sutton Court Hotel
60-66 Lichfield Road
Sutton Coldfield B74 2NA
Tel: 0121 355 6071 Fax: 0121 355 0083
Contact: Steve Welch

Ceremony

This Victorian buiding is set in its own
grounds with a gazebo featured in the
garden. Three rooms are licensed to
hold ceremonies: the Wyvern Room,
decorated in brick-effect with stained
glass windows; the Wallace Room, the
main function room; and the
Restaurant, whch is lit by chandelier.
There is wheelchair access to the
Wallace Room.
Price guide: £250

Reception

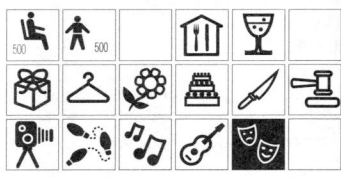

The hotel boasts a wide selection of
three course meals and a speciality
gourmet buffet.
Catering: from £14.95pp

Westmead Hotel
Redditch Road
Hopwood B48 7AL
Tel: 0121 445 1202 Fax: 0121 445 6163
Contact: Tracy Murphy, Conference
and Banqueting Co-ordinator

Ceremony

The hotel is available for ceremonies on
any day of the year, but ceremonies
must be followed by reception at the
hotel. There is limited wheelchair
access.
Price guide: £100

Reception

Catering: Buffets from £6.25pp Sit
down from £20pp

STOP PRESS
Birmingham Botanical Gardens
0121 454 1860
Birmingham Metropole Hotel, NEC
0121 780 4242
Clarendon Suites, Edgbaston
0121 454 2918
Fairlawns Hotel, Walsall
01922 55122
Hyatt Regency Birmingham
0121 643 1234
Jarvis Penns Hall Hotel, Sutton Coldfield
0121 351 31111
Moor Hall Hotel Sutton Coldfield
0121 308 3751
Quality Cobden Hotel, Birmingham
0121 454 6621
West Bromich Moat House
0121 609 9988

Bailiffscourt Hotel
Climping
Littlehampton
West Sussex
BN17 5RW
Tel: 01903 723511 Fax: 01903 723107
Contact: Amanda Cox, Banqueting
Manager

Ceremony

This listed building is the recreation of a medieval manor house
and features oak beams, log fires
and four poster beds. It is set in 22
acres adjacent to the sea and has
two tennis courts and an outdoor
swimming pool. The hotel is available for ceremonies on any day
except Christmas Day.
Price guide: POA

Reception

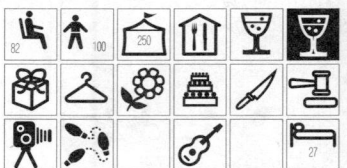

Reception facilities include a
walled courtyard filled with climb-
ing roses which is suitable for al
fresco dining. The hotel has also
been awarded three AA rosettes for
its French/English style cuisine. As
well as the above services, a harpist
can be arranged if required. There
is also a 12th Century chapel on
site, which is available for blessings
if required.
Catering: from £25pp

146

East Court
College Lane, East Grinstead
West Sussex RH19 3LT
Tel: 01342 323636 Fax: 01342 327823
Contact: Mrs Rudin, Facilities Manager

Ceremony

East Court Mansion is an 18th Century Grade II listed manor house to which the Meridian Hall was a recent addition. The Mansion's Cranston Suite (max 40) and the Meridian Hall (max 100) have views over East Court gardens and Ashdown Forest. Meridian also has its own private patio. Confetti is permitted outside only. Ceremonies can take place on any day except Christmas Eve, Christmas Day, Boxing Day and Good Friday.
Price guide: from £60

Reception

Couples may bring in their own caterers for a reception in the Mansion. A list of local accommodation can be provided if required.

Goodwood House
Goodwood, Chichester
W Sussex PO18 0PX
Tel: 01243 774107 Fax: 01243 774313
Contact: Sally Lower, Sales Executive

Ceremony

This famous stately home is only available on an exclusive use basis. Three marriage rooms are available, and ceremonies must be followed by reception. No confetti or stiletto heels.
Price guide: from £1500

Reception

Goodwood does not have a set menu, but will tailor your meal to your specific requirements. Helicopters can use the grounds if required.
Catering: from £45pp

Little Thakeham
Merrywood Lane, Storrington
W Sussex RH20 3HE
Tel: 01903 744416 Fax: 01903 745022
Contact: Fiona Watson or Jenny Ratcliff

Ceremony

This Grade I listed house was design by Edwin Lutyens, as were the five acres of gardens. One room is available for marriage ceremonies. While wheelchair access around the house is not difficult, there are steps up to the house itself. Confetti is not permitted. Ceremonies can take place on any day except Christmas Day and New year's Day.
Price guide: from £250

Reception

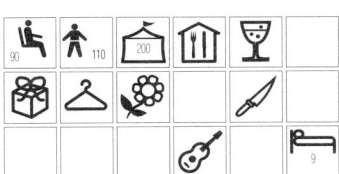

Thakeham is most suited to small dinner party style receptions in the house itself. A pianist can be arranged, and the grounds are suitable for hot air balloons and helicopters. The house has an outdoor swimming pool and tennis courts, and can arrange a spit roast in the gardens. A horse and carriage can also be arranged. The house regrets that reception facilities are limited for children.
Catering: from £21.50 (buffet)

The Mansion House
High Down Towers
Littlehampton
Worthing
West Sussex BN12 6PF
Tel: 01903 700152 Fax: 01903 245387
Contact: Tracy Cotton, Manager

Ceremony

The Mansion House, originally owned by the Lyon family, features famous chalk gardens. The Edward Suite is licensed for ceremonies (limited wheelchair access), which may take place here on any day of the year. Ceremonies here must be followed by reception at the venue. Helicopters and hot air balloons may use the site.
Price guide: £100

Reception

Catering: from £10.30pp

Marle Place
Leylands Road
Burgess Hill
West Sussex RH15 8JD
Tel: 01444 248275 Fax: 01444 871269
Contact: Heather Williamson, Administrator

Ceremony

Marle Place is an Edwardian house and is set in a quiet location near Burgess Hill. Among its prominent features is an original sweeping staircase. Wedding ceremonies are conducted in the ground floor Hall, which is south facing and therefore makes the most of natural light. It also has French doors that lead directly on to the verandah and well-stocked garden. Up to four ceremonies are permitted here per day on any day of the year.
Price guide: £250 (including Registrar's fees)

Reception

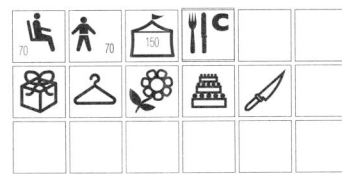

This venue offers a wedding breakfast, including ceremony and finger buffet reception for up to 70 people for under £1,000. A sit-down reception can be catered for in a marquee in the grounds. Stationery can also be arranged by the venue.
Catering: from £6.95 (finger buffet)

Millstream Hotel & Restaurant
Bosham, Chichester
West Sussex PO18 8HL
Tel: 01243 573234
Contact: Aris Tzonis, Restaurant Manager

Ceremony

The original building of this hotel and restaurant dates back to 1701. Only one ceremony is permitted here per day, on any day of the year.
Price guide: £150

Reception

The restaurant holds an AA Rosette for its cuisine, and is said to be famous for its buffets.
Catering: from £18pp

The Ravenswood
Horsted Lane, Sharpthorne
West Sussex RH19 4HY
Tel: 01342 810216 Fax: 01342 811393
Contact: Mr Stephen McArthur, Owner

Ceremony

Ravenswood is a manor house dating from the 15th Century, and is set in grounds and gardens overlooking its own lake. Inside the house has minstrel's galleries and a panelled baronial hall. Weddings can be held here on any day of the year, and their numbers are not restricted. Confetti is allowed, but only in certain areas.
Price guide: £200

Reception

Two rooms are available for receptions ranging from the smallest gathering to 350 guests.
Catering: £18 - £25pp

Southdowns
Hotel & Restaurant
Trotton Rogate, Petersfield
West Sussex GU31 5JN
Tel: 01730 821521 Fax: 01730 821790
Contact: Dominic Vedovato, Owner

Ceremony

This country hotel is set in spacious grounds, with its own croquet lawn and leisure club. Up to two ceremonies can take place here on any day of the year.
Price guide: £250

Reception

The restaurant has an AA Rosette for its cuisine. Wedding guests are offered a 10% discount on a two or three day break.
Catering: £15pp - £25pp

The Spread Eagle Hotel
South Street, Midhurst,
West Sussex GU29 9NH
Tel: 01730 816911 Fax: 01730 815668
Contact: Karen Edgington, Conference & Banqueting Manager

Ceremony

This is a Grand Heritage Hotel dating from 1430. Period features include Flemish stained glass windows, inglenook fireplaces, tudor bread ovens and four poster beds. The Hotel's Edward VII Room is licensed to hold wedding ceremonies for 30, on any day of the year. Ceremonies here must be followed by reception at the hotel.
Price guide: £550

Reception

Catering: from £21pp

Wiston House
Steyning
West Sussex BN44 3DZ
Tel: 01903 815020 Fax: 01903 815931
Contact: Roger Barr, Deputy Manager

Ceremony

Wiston House is a Grade I listed conference centre. The Library is licensed for marriages. Ceremonies are restricted to one per day on any day of the year, and must be followed by a reception at the house.
Price guide: P.O.A.

Reception

Catering: from £30pp

STOP PRESS
Amberley Castle, Nr Arundel
01798 831002
Cathedral Clubhouse, Chichester
01243 536666
Copthorne Hotel, Gatwick
01342 7149711
Great Ballard Scholl, Chichester
01243 814236
Highley Manor, Balcombe
01444 811711
Horsham Museum
01403 254959
Inglenook Hotel, Pagham
01243 262495
Ockenden Manor, Cuckfield
01444 416111
South Lodge Hotel, Nr Horsham
01403 891711
Wimpole Hotels, Haywards Heath
01273 846028

Alder House Hotel
Towngate Road
Healy Lane
Batley
West Yorkshire WF17 7HR
Tel: 01924 444777 Fax: 01924 442644
Contact: Clive Sowler, GM

Ceremony

This privately owned Georgian House

hotel set in over 2 acres, has a licence for its York Suite (wheelchair access is limited). Ceremonies can take place here on any day of the year except Bank Holidays. Saturday weddings, however, must be followed by reception at the hotel.
Price guide: £125 - £175

Reception

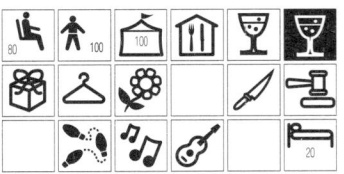

Catering: Buffets from £6.95pp Sit down from £15.95pp

Bagden Hall Hotel
Wakefield Road
Scissett
Huddersfield
West Yorkshire HD8 9LE
Tel: 01484 865330 Fax: 01484 861001
Contact: Charles Storr, GM

Ceremony

This country house hotel, previously a mill owner's mansion, is set in 40 acres of parkland. Three rooms are available for ceremonies. These are not available on Sundays, and a maximum of one ceremony is permitted per day. A minimum of 45 guests is permitted for Saturday ceremonies.
Price guide: £225

Reception

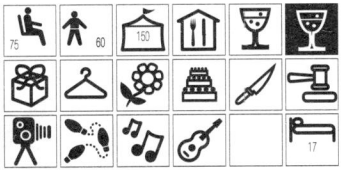

The hotel achieved runner up status in the 1994/95 White Rose Award, Hotel of the Year, and won the 1993 Yorkshire and Humberside Best Newcomer to Tourism award.
Catering: from £21pp.

Batley Town Hall
Market Place, Batley
Tel: 01484 442019 Fax: 01484 446842
Contact: Julia Robinson, Senior Development Officer

Ceremony

Batley Town Hall is also a concert hall and council chamber and has a ceremony capacity of between 10 and 300. Ceremonies are permitted Monday to Saturday inclusive.
Price guide: from £100

Reception

Catering may be provided either in-house or contract, although the Town Hall specifies an approved list of contract caterers. A late night liquor licence is available upon application. A list of local accommodation is available.
Catering: P.O.A.

Bertie's Banqueting Rooms
Brook Street
Elland
Halifax
West Yorkshire HX5 9AW
Tel: 01422 371724 Fax: 01422 372830
Contact: Brett Woodward, Proprietor

Ceremony

This stone-built, listed and converted chapel, offers ceremonies seven days a week with no restrictions. Confetti is permitted and an unlimited number of ceremonies can be held each day.
Price guide: £250 (FOC with reception)

Reception

Catering: POA

Cartwright Hall
Lister Park
Bradford
West Yorkshire BD9 4NS
Tel: 01274 493313 Fax: 01274 481045
Contact: Administration Assistant

Ceremony

This Grade II listed Edwardian baroque art gallery in a park setting, was opened by the Prince and Princess of Wales in 1904. Situated approx 1 mile from the centre of Bradford, ceremonies are only possible on Saturdays with a maximum of three per day.
Price guide: £250

Reception

Reception facilities are not available, although local hotels can offer accommodation and reception services.

Cleckheaton Town Hall
Bradford Road, Cleckheaton
Tel: 01484 513808 Fax: 01484 446842
Contact: Julia Robinson, Senior Devt Officer

Ceremony

The Town Hall also acts as a concert hall and has a ceremony capacity of between 10 and 500. Ceremonies are permitted Monday to Saturday inclusive, with a maximum of two ceremonies allowed per day.
Price guide: from £100

Reception

Catering may be provided either in-house or contract, although the Town Hall specifies an approved list of contract caterers. A late night liquor licence is available upon application. A local accommodation list is available.
Catering: P.O.A.

Set amidst spectacular scenery, this Victorian building stands adjacent to the famous Ilkley Moor. Up to five ceremonies can be held per day: seven days a week. Confetti is permitted.
Price guide: from £125

Reception

Receptions for as few as a dozen to as many as 400. Specialities include French cuisine. There are 70 en-suite bedrooms, with discounts available for wedding party guests.
Catering: from £17.50pp

Dewsbury Town Hall
Wakefield Road
Dewsbury, West Yorkshire
Tel: 01484 226300 Fax: 01484 446842
Contact: Julia Robinson, Senior Devt Officer

Ceremony

This Grade II listed Victorian building is also a concert hall and old court house with cells. Up to two ceremonies per day are possible Monday to Saturday inclusive. Confetti is permitted by arrangement.
Price guide: from £100

Reception

Catering may be provided either in-house or by an approved list of contract caterers. A late night liquor licence is available upon application. A list of local accommodation is available.
Catering: P.O.A.

Forte Posthouse Leeds/Bradford
Bramhope, Nr Leeds
West Yorkshire LS16 9JJ
Tel: 01977 682711
Contact: Julie Clark, Venue Guarantee Co-ordinator

Ceremony

With a ceremony seating capacity of 120 and standing capacity of 150, the hotel offers ceremonies seven days a week throughout the year. Confetti is permitted at the hotel.
Price guide: from £185

Reception

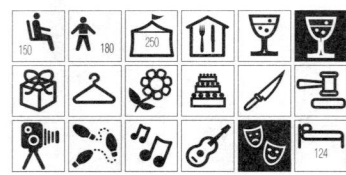

As part of the wedding package, a complimentary overnight suite is provided for the bride and groom.
Although the hotel has 124 bedrooms of its own, a list of alternative local accommodation is also available. All catering at the hotel is carried out in house. Children can be catered for separately, on request.
Catering: £13.75pp

The George Hotel
St George's Square
Huddersfield
West Yorkshire HD1 1JA
Tel: 01484 515444 Fax: 01484 435056
Contact: June Thompson, Sales Manager

Ceremony

This Grade II listed Victorian building offers ceremonies seven days a week with a maximum of four per day. No area is available for outdoor photography, but confetti is permitted.
Price guide: £150

Reception

Reception facilities include a waited service capacity of 150, with a 200 capacity for a buffet style reception. The hotel has 60 bedrooms and also operates preferential rate agreements with other local hotels and guest houses.
Catering: £15pp

The Glenmoor Centre
Wells Road, Ilkley LS29 9JF
Tel: 01943 436272 Fax: 01943 436273
Contact: Marianne Cairns, Manager

Ceremony

This Victorian building is a residential training and conference centre that allows one ceremony to be held per day on any day of the week, excluding Sundays and Bank Holidays.
Price guide: £120

Reception

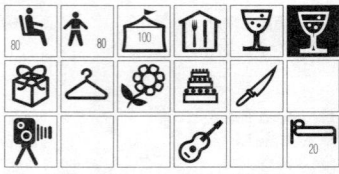

Catering is in-house with specialities including halal, vegetarian and vegan options.
Catering: from £16.50pp

The Guide Post Hotel
Common Road
Low Moor, Bradford BD12 0ST
Tel: 01274 607866 Fax: 01274 671085
Contact: Mr Day, Owner

Ceremony

The hotel has two rooms available to hold a ceremony, one with a sitting capacity of 80, and one with a capacity of 100. Ceremonies are available seven days a week, excluding Christmas and New Year.
Price guide: F.O.C. (with reception)

Reception

Catering: from £13.95pp

Haley's Hotel & Restaurant
Shire Oak Road
Headingley, Leeds LS6 2DE
Tel: 0113 278 4446 Fax: 0113 275 3342
Contact: Pauline Cowie, Conference Co-ordinator

Ceremony

Set in the Headingly conservation area, just two miles from Leeds city centre, Haley's was the first hotel in Leeds to be granted a licence. Ceremonies may be held in the hotel's Bramley Room, Library or Restaurant. One ceremony allowed per day, any day of the week.
Price guide: POA

Reception

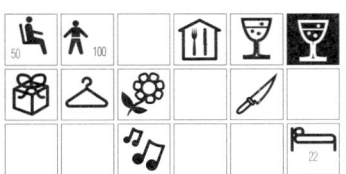

Haley's Hotel & Restaurant is a member of the Virgin Collection Consortium and won the Good Food Guide County Restaurant of the Year in 1994. The late night drinking licence is permitted for residents only.
Catering: from £20pp

Hilton National
Wakefield Road
Garforth, Leeds LS25 1LH
Tel: 0113 2866556 Fax: 0113 2868326
Contact: Mrs Jean Gray, Conference and Banqueting Services Manager

Ceremony

The hotel has four rooms licensed to hold ceremonies with varying capacities from the intimate to the more social gathering. The Magnet room holds a maximum of 120 seated guests, the Yorkshire room 80, the Stamford room 40, and the Boardroom 15. Ceremonies are possible seven days a week.
Price guide: from £180

Reception

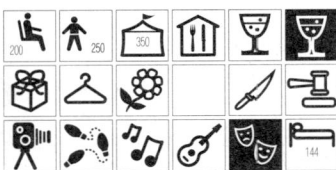

Reception facilities vary in capacity from 60 to 200 for both waited service and buffet options.
Catering: from £16.95pp

Holdsworth House
Holdsworth, Halifax
West Yorkshire HX2 9TG
Tel: 01422 240024 Fax: 01422 245174
Contact: Sue Pickles, Conference and Banqueting Co-ordinator

Ceremony

This 17th Century Jacobean manor house is set in its own grounds, and has two rooms licensed to hold ceremonies. Ceremonies are possible seven days a week, with one permitted per day. The hotel is closed for a couple of days over the Christmas period.
Price guide: Available only as part of a reception package.

Reception

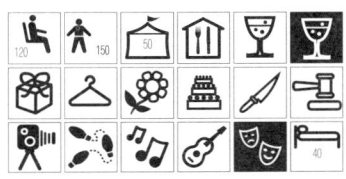

This three star hotel features a two AA rosette restaurant. The bride and groom are offered a complimentary suite for the night, while wedding guests are offered preferential room rates.
Catering: from £20pp

Hoyle Court
Otley Road
Baildon
Shipley
West Yorkshire BO17 6JS
Tel: 01274 584110
Contact: Mr & Mrs DT Blair, Managers

Ceremony

This is a Grade II Edwardian/Baroque house with a south facing terrace and stone steps leading to a sunken rose garden. The house was once owned by one of Bradford's successful mill owning families. Two rooms are licensed; the Lounge and the Dining Room, which are available on Fridays and Saturdays only. Ceremonies must be followed by reception at the house. This venue claims to be one of the UK's most prestigious Masonic premises.
Price guide: £125

Reception

A traditional Danish wedding was recently held at this venue.
Catering: from £15.45pp

Huddersfield Town Hall
Ramsden Street
Huddersfield
West Yorkshire HD1 2TA
Tel: 01484 442019
Contact: Julia Robinson, Senior Devt Officer

Ceremony

The Town Hall has three rooms available to hold ceremonies: the largest, the concert hall, has a capacity of 400. Ceremonies are available Monday - Saturday inclusive, with up to two permitted per day.
Price guide: from £100

Reception

Catering may be provided either in-house or by an approved list of contract caterers. A late night liquor licence and a list of local accommodation are available on request.
Catering: P.O.A.

Jarivs Bankfield Hotel
Bradford Road, Bingley BD16 1TU
Tel: 01274 567123 Fax: 01274 551331
Contact: Helen Kirk, Conference & Events Sales Manager

Ceremony

The hotel offers two ceremony rooms which are available on any day of the year. Ceremonies here must be followed by reception at the hotel.
Price guide: £175

Reception

Helicopters and hot air balloons may use the site.
Catering: Buffets from £8.50pp sit down from £16pp

Leeds Civic Hall
Leeds LS1 1UR
Tel: 0113 247 4055 Fax: 0113 247 4772
Contact: Steven Mason, Lord Mayor's Secretary

Ceremony

This is a Grade I listed building, claimed to be one of the finest civic buildings in the country. Four rooms are licensed for ceremonies which can take place here on any day of the year except Christmas Day.
Price guide: POA

Reception

All types of cuisine are available except Kosher.
Catering: Bufets from £5pp Sit down from £12pp

Linton Springs Hotel
Sicklinghall Road, Wetherby
West Yorkshire LS22 4AF
Tel: 01937 585353 Fax: 01937 587579
Contact: Linsey Rowbury, Wedding Co-ordinator

Ceremony

Set in 14 acres of park and woodland, the hotel offers three ceremony rooms. Ceremonies are not available on Saturdays and Sundays or Christmas Day. One ceremony is permitted per day.
Price guide: £150

Reception

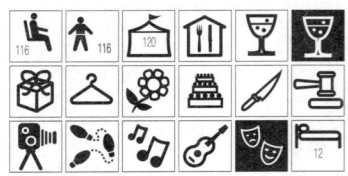

Catering: £23pp

Marsden Mechanics Hall
Peel Street
Marsden
Huddersfield HD7 6BW
Tel: 01484 844587
Contact: Janet Maude, Bookings Officer

Ceremony

This is a listed building in the centre of a Pennine village. The Hall is close to the river and the Village stocks! The Main Hall is licensed and available on any day of the year. Bank Holiday bookings are available at extra cost. Confetti is not permitted.
Price guide: from £60

Reception

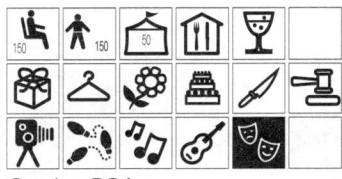

Catering: POA

Oakwell Hall Country Park
Nutter Lane
Birstall
Nr Batley WF17 9LG
Tel: 01924 326240 Fax: 01924 326249
Contact: Karen Jewell, Administrative Officer

Ceremony

This 17th Century Elizabethan Manor (with Bronte connections) is Grade I listed. It is furnished to the year 1690 and also features period gardens. The Great Hall is licensed for ceremonies which can take place here on any day except Bank Holidays and Sundays.
Price guide: £400

Reception

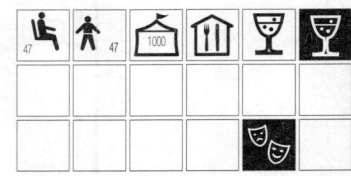

Receptions take place in the Oakwell Barn which is a separate building. This must be arranged separately by the hirer.

The Queens
City Square
Leeds LS1 1PL
Tel: 0113 243 1323 Fax: 0113 242 5154
Contact: Claire Ryan, Venue Guarantee Manager

Ceremony

The Queens hotel is situated in the centre of Leeds, adjacent to the main railway station. The Ark Royal Suite and the Ballroom are licensed for ceremonies which can take place here on any day of the year. Ceremonies here must be followed by reception at the hotel.
Price guide: from £425

Reception

Catering Buffets from £4.50pp Sit down from £14.95pp

The Rock Inn Hotel
Holywell Green
Halifax
West Yorkshire HX4 9BS
Tel: 01422 379721 Fax: 01422 379110
Contact: Robert Vinsen, Proprietor

Ceremony

Set in four acres of breathtaking Yorkshire countryside, The Rock is situated in its own serene rural valley close to Brontë country. Dating back to the 17th Century, the Rock has recently undergone extensive refurbish-

ment. Special areas are available for outdoor photography.
Price guide: from £50

Reception

Special bridal suite for the bride and groom with reduced accommodation rates for guests. Dance floor and disco also available.
Children can be catered for separately.
Catering: £14.00pp

Rogerthorpe Manor Hotel
Thorpe Lane
Badsworth
Pontefract
West Yorkshire WF9 1AB
Tel: 01977 643839 Fax: 01977 641571
Contact: Laeley Denton

Ceremony

This Jacobean Grade II listed building has been restored to create a hotel of 12 bedrooms, an oak panelled restaurant and large function room. There is an unlimited amount of ceremonies permitted per day, and ceremonies are permitted seven days a week, excluding Christmas Day.
Price guide: £250

Reception

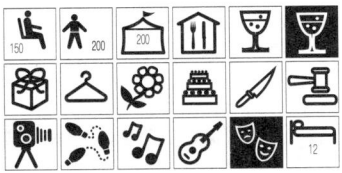

In addition to buffets and special menus, the hotel will strive to meet the religious or dietary requirements of wedding guests. Sample menus are readily available. The hotel also operates preferential rate agreements with local guest houses and other hotels. Other services offered by the Rogerthorpe Manor Hotel include room decorations, fireworks, the provision of stationery, cars, balloons and children's entertainment. No confetti is permitted.
Catering: from £5.75pp

Sacha Court
Park Road, Elland HX5 9HP
Tel: 01422 377232 Fax: 01422 310408
Contact: Andrea Allen, Wedding Co-ordinator

Ceremony

The Sacha Court hotel and restaurant is actually an extended and fully renovated Victorian mill owner's house and is English Tourist Board four crown commended. Ceremonies are available seven days a week.
Price guide: from £50

Reception

The reception facilities include a large purpose-built disco area and free car parking for up to 90 cars.
Catering: from £6.95pp

Springfield Park Hotel
Penistone Road, Kirkburton
Huddersfield HD8 0PE
Tel: 01484 607788 Fax: 01484 607961
Contact: Treda Shotton, Sales Co-ordinator

Ceremony

Ceremonies are available 7 days a week.
Price guide: £200

Reception

The hotel has preferential rate agreements with local guest houses and hotels.
Catering: £15pp

Under the Clock Tower
The Town Hall, Wood Street
Wakefield WF1 2HQ
Tel: 01924 305121 Fax: 01924 305293
Contact: Simon Hartley, General Manager

Ceremony

'Under the Clock Tower' is actually the banqueting and restaurant complex within Wakefield Town Hall. The Victorian Town Hall was first opened in 1880 and is now a Grade I listed building. All 11 rooms within the Town Hall may be used for marriage ceremonies, with the rich wood panelling, ornate plasterwork and chandeliers making it an attractive venue. Ceremonies may be held any day of the year, excluding Bank Holidays.
Price guide: from £70.00

Reception

Fully inclusive reception packages are offered, with a 50% discount on room hire if the reception is held here also. Alternatively, the Clock Tower Restaurant may be used for the smaller party to celebrate after the ceremony.
Catering: from £14.50pp

Waterton Park Hotel
Walton Hall
Walton, Wakefield WF2 6PW
Tel: 01924 257911 Fax: 01924 240082
Contact: Debbie Taylor, Conference and Banqueting Manager

Ceremony

This Georgian listed mansion is situated on an island surrounded by 26 acres of lake and is accessed by an iron bridge. Ceremonies are available all days of the week excluding Saturdays, apart from January-March when Saturdays are also available.
Price guide: £175

Reception

Buffet capacity is to a maximum of

150, increasing to 175 during evening buffets, while a marquee is suitable for a maximum of 175 seated guests. A complimentary honeymoon suite is available for the bride and groom.
Catering: from £21pp.

Weetwood Hall
Otley Road
Far Headingley, Leeds
West Yorkshire LS16 5PS

Tel: 0113 2306000 Fax: 0113 2306095
Contact: Maxine Porter, Business Administration Manager

Ceremony

Set in 9 acres of wooded seclusion on the outskirts of Leeds, this purpose-built centre has been developed around a Grade II listed Tudor manor house. One ceremony per day is permitted, seven days a week. Confetti is not permitted.
Price guide: from £180

Reception

In addition to the 108 en-suite bedrooms, Weetwood Hall offers 14 deluxe rooms and a four poster honeymoon suite.
Catering: from £17.00pp

STOP PRESS
Baildon Masonic Hall, Shipley
01274 584110
Bradford City Hall, Bradford
01274 752222
Bretton Hall College, Wakefield
01924 830261
Briar Court Hotel, Huddersfield
01484 519902
Clay House, Halifax
01422 378586
The Grove, Pontefract
01977 642159
Hilton National, Leeds
0113 244 2000
Hollings Hall Hotel, Shipley
01274 530053
Imperial Crown Hotel, Halifax
01422 342342
Leeds Forte Posthouse, Leeds
0113 243 1323

Leeds Marriott Hotel, Leeds
0113 236 6366
Leed United Conference & Banqueting Centre, Leeds
0113 226 1166
Moorland Lodge, Huddersfield
01484 843398
Oakwood Hall Hotel, Bingley
01274 564123
Stakis Bradford Hotel, Bradford
01274 734734
Swallow Hotel, Wakefield
01924 372111
Todmorden Town Hall, Todmorden
01706 813597
Wentbridge House Hotel, Pontefract
01977 620444
Woolley Hall, Wakefield
01226 382500

Blunsdon House Hotel
Blunsdon
Swindon
Wiltshire SN2 4AD

Tel: 01793 721701 Fax: 01793 721056
Contact: Philip Dodds, Sales and Marketing Manager

Ceremony

Three rooms are licensed within the hotel to hold wedding ceremonies, with seated capacities varying from 60 to 250 and standing capacities from 70 to 300. Ceremonies are available seven days a week with no restrictions on the number permitted per day.
Price guide: £150

Reception

Waited service reception facilities are to a maximum of 250 with buffet service offering a maximum of 300. The site is also suitable for a marquee.
Catering: from £11.50pp

Bowood Golf & Country Club
Derry Hill
Calne
Wilts SN11 9PQ

Tel: 01249 822228 Fax: 01249 822218
Contact: Liz Schofield, Marketing Manager

Ceremony

This Grade I listed building is part of the Bowood estate which covers 2000 acres. The park itself was designed by Capability Brown. Three rooms (limited wheelchair access) are licensed for ceremonies which can take place here on any day of the year except Christmas Day. Helicopters and hot air balloons can use the grounds.
Price guide: £250

Reception

Receptions can take place in the Fitzmaurice Room (up to 50), or in the club's marquee.
Catering: from £15pp

Box House
Bath Road
Box, Wiltshire SN13 8NR

Tel: 01225 744447 Fax: 01225 744333
Contact: Manager

Ceremony

The Box House is a Grade II Georgian Manor set in nine acres of grounds and situated next door to the village church. Ceremonies are available seven days a week with a maximum of two permitted per day. Confetti is allowed.
Price guide: £150

Reception

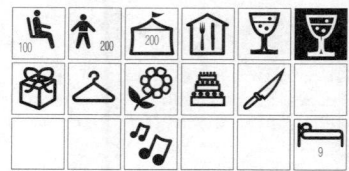

Reception catering facilities vary from finger buffets to sit down banquets with prices adjusted accordingly. The manor house presently features nine bedrooms but is scheduled to increase this to 20 at the end of summer 1996. A 1950's vintage bus is also available for the exclusive use of the manor house guests.
Catering: from £6.50pp

Chiseldon House Hotel
New Road, Chiseldon
Nr Swindon, Wiltshire SN4 0NE
Tel: 01793 741010 Fax: 01793 741059
Contact: Christine Farnell, Wedding
Co-ordinator

Ceremony

This Grade II listed building offers ceremonies from Monday to Saturday with no restrictions on the amount permitted a day. Confetti is allowed.
Price guide: £80

Reception

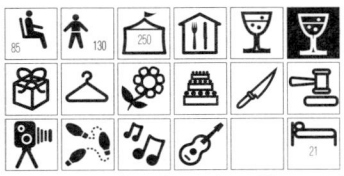

The hotel offers themed weddings and receptions which in the past have included a Medieval theme and a Caribbean wedding featuring a steel band around the hotel's swimming pool. In addition to the services indicated below the hotel can organise cars, stationery, balloons and a video. Some of the bedrooms feature four poster beds.
Catering: from £12.50pp

Cricklade Hotel & Country Club
Common Hill, Cricklade
Wiltshire SN6 6HA
Tel: 01793 750751 Fax: 01793 751767
Contact: Mrs Kearney, General
Manager

Ceremony

This Cotswold manor house, set in its own grounds, features a nine hole golf course. There are five rooms available to hold ceremonies at the hotel with capacities from 30 to 80. Prices vary according to room capacity.
Price guide: from £100

Reception

Reception facilities offer a waited service and buffet service capacity of 120. The main function room features views of a walled garden and a gazebo. The hotel includes flowers in the price of the ceremony.
Catering: from £18.50pp

Crudwell Court Hotel & Restaurant
Crudwell, Nr Malmesbury
Wiltshire SN16 9EP
Tel: 01666 577194 Fax: 01666 577853
Contact: Nick Bristow, Joint
Proprietor

Ceremony

This 17th Century rectory has three rooms available to hold ceremonies, seven days a week. The hotel is situated in three acres of garden and features a heated outdoor swimming pool for use during the summer. The restaurant and ceremony room, but not the bedrooms, have wheelchair access. No fee is charged for the ceremony if the reception is also held at the hotel.

Reception

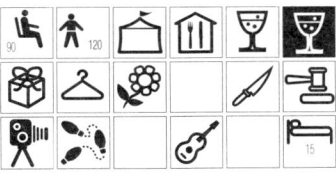

Reception facilities feature a waited service capacity of 90, finger buffets for up to 120 and a seated buffet capacity of 90 also. The site is suitable for a marquee with a capacity of between 150 and 200. The hotel has, in the past, held a Scottish theme wedding, featuring tartan decorations and Scottish music.
Catering: from £15.50pp

Grasmere House Hotel
Harnham Road
Salisbury
Wilts SP2 8JN
Tel: 01722 338388 Fax: 01722 333710
Contact: Dale Naug, Manager

Ceremony

This Victorian hotel and restaurant set in 1.5 acres of gardens, offers four

---

licensed rooms which are available any day of the year except Sundays. Confetti is not permitted.
Price guide: £200

Reception

Catering: Buffets from £8.50pp Sit down from £16.50pp

Grittleton House
Grittleton
Chippenham
Wiltshire SN14 6AP
Tel: 01249 782434 Fax: 01249 782669
Contact: Adrian Shipp, Owner

Ceremony

Situated in its own grounds, this Grade II listed building is available to hold up to two ceremonies, seven days a week. The price is just £25 if the reception is also held at the venue.
Price guide: £150

Reception

Reception facilities include a marquee, with a maximum capacity of 1,000. A list of local accommodation is available.
Catering: £15pp

Guyers House
Guyers Lane
Pickwick, Corsham
Wiltshire SN13 0PS
Tel: 01249 713399 Fax: 01249 712801
Contact: Martin Bevis, Manager

Ceremony

    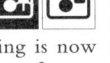

This Grade II listed building is now operating as a training and conference centre. Seating capacity for ceremonies is 50 in one room and a further 65 in

adjoining rooms. Ceremonies are available on Saturdays only with a maximum of one per day. The price guide for ceremonies is £175 plus the hire of the house at £1,000. Confetti is restricted to inside the building only.
Price guide: £175 + vat

Reception

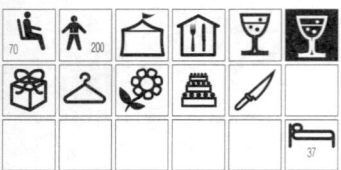

Reception catering may be in-house or from an approved list of contract caterers. The ballroom features a sprung dance floor.
Catering: from £18pp

Kington Manor
Kington St Michael
Chippenham
Wiltshire SN4 6JA
Tel: 01249 750655 Fax: 01249 750651
Contact: Peter Le Grys

Ceremony

Kington Manor stands in 15 acres of parkland, featuring grounds terraced with fountains and herbaceous borders leading to a large lake. The standing capacity for the ceremony is in excess of 180. Ceremonies may be held every day of the week. Ceremonies may only be held in conjunction with receptions.

Reception

The Manor offers buffet receptions for over 400, and boasts a speciality in home cooking.
Catering: £20pp

Leigh Park Hotel
Leigh Road West
Bradford on Avon BA15 2RA
Tel: 01225 864885 Fax: 01225 862315
Contact: Pamela Duckett,
Assistant Manager

Ceremony

This Georgian country house hotel stands in five acres of grounds with its own walled garden and vineyard. Three rooms are available to hold ceremonies, all with varying capacities, from 20 to 120. Ceremonies are available throughout the week excluding Sundays, Christmas Day, Boxing Day and other Bank Holidays.
Price guide: from £75.00

Reception

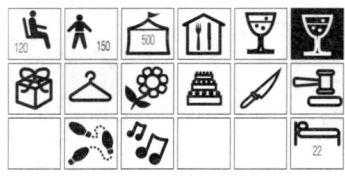

The hotel offers a complimentary overnight stay for the bride and groom in an executive room on the night of the wedding, while special rate overnight accommodation is available for wedding guests.
Catering: from £26.95pp (package)

Lucknam Park Hotel
Colerne
Wiltshire SN14 8AZ
Tel: 01225 742777 Fax: 01225 743536
Contact: James Gormley

Ceremony

This imposing Palladian mansion was built in 1720 and is set in 500 acres of grounds. While wedding ceremonies can be held at the Lucknam Park Hotel seven days a week, only one ceremony is permitted per day. The price guide shown below indicates the cost of hiring the ceremony room. This is a package price that also includes the charge for hiring the room in which the wedding reception is held.
Price guide: £1,000

Reception

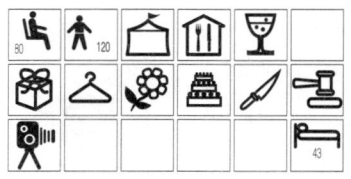

Catering capacities are to a maximum

of 50, although the site is suitable for a marquee with a capacity of 100. A late night drinking licence is held for residents only.
Catering: from £24.50pp.

The Manor House
Castle Combe
Chippenham
Wiltshire
SN14 7HR
Tel: 01249 782206 Fax: 01249 782159
Contact: Lynne Lawton, Sales and Marketing Manager

Ceremony

This Grade II listed building is set in 26 acres of grounds with an additional 200 acres of golf course. Two rooms are licensed to hold ceremonies with capacities varying from 30 to 90. Ceremonies are available seven days a week with one ceremony permitted per day. The price guide increases to £500 for use of the larger room. Confetti is not permitted.
Price guide: from £200

Reception

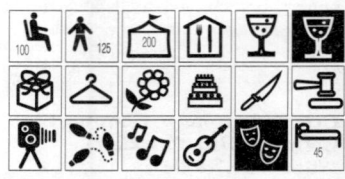

Although a room is available for the bride and groom to change in, a charge will be made.
Catering: from £26pp

The Pear Tree at Purton
Church End
Purton
Swindon
Wiltshire SN5 9ED
Tel: 01793 772100 Fax: 01793 772369
Contact: Francis Young, Proprietor.

Ceremony

This Cotswold stone hotel set in 7.5 acres of grounds has achieved the RAC's highest award: The Blue Ribbon. Ceremonies are available seven days a week, with one permitted per day. Confetti is allowed.
Price guide: £200

Reception

The hotel's chef, Catherine Berry, has been awarded two AA rosettes.
Catering: £30pp

The Royal Oak
Wootton Rivers
Marlborough
Wiltshire SN8 4NQ

Tel: 01672 810322 Fax: 01672 811267
Contact: Mr and Mrs Jones, Proprietors or G Lewis, Administration Manager

Ceremony

This 16th Century, thatched free house is available to hold ceremonies seven days a week with a maximum of two per day. No charge is made for the ceremony providing the reception is also held at The Royal Oak.

Reception

Reception catering is in-house although the proprietors would be happy if couples preferred to organise their own contract catering. The pub features three self-contained cottages for wedding guests, providing a total of nine rooms.
Catering: £10pp

Rudloe Hall Hotel
Hinton Grange
Leafy Lane
Nr Corsham
Wiltshire SN13 0PA

Tel: 01225 810555 Fax: 01225 811412
Contact: Melanie Crick, Assistant Manager.

Ceremony

This listed Gothic building is situated in

four acres of award winning gardens and features oak panelling and high corniced ceilings. It offers a choice of 11 bedrooms. Ceremonies are available seven days a week with two permitted per day.
Price guide: £200

Reception

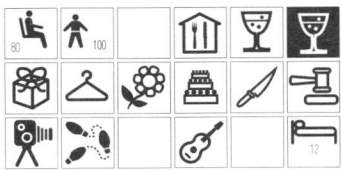

Catering is in-house with a buffet capacity of 100. Subject to availability, a room will be provided for the bride and groom to change in.
Catering: from £19.50pp

Swindon Borough Council
Civic Offices
Euclid Street
Swindon SN1 2JH

Tel: 01793 526161 Fax: 01793 490420
Contact: Carole Woods, Mayor's Office

Ceremony

The civic offices are in the centre of Swindon with (on Saturdays) ample on site parking. The Coucil Chamber is licensed for ceremonies and is available on Saturdays Weekdays wold become available in exceptional circumstances, as the building is used as offices.
Price guide: £100

Reception

No reception facilities are available on the premises.

Tottenham House
Savernake Forest
Nr Marlborough
Wiltshire

Tel: 01980 670160 Fax: 01980 670160
Contact: Katherine Dover, Proprietor

Ceremony

This Grade I Palladian mansion has three rooms available to hold ceremonies with a capacity of up to 280. Ceremonies are available seven days a week, excluding August Bank Holiday,

with one ceremony allowed per day. All bookings are made via Bows Events of Pewsey on the above number.
Price guide: from £100

Reception

Tottenham House provides a list of three recommended contract caterers although it does allow couples to provide their own catering. A liquor licence and late night licence may be arranged through an outside bar, while a marquee is available with an unlimited capacity. The venue can provide a list of local accommodation that offers preferential rates. Linen, china and special furniture may also be provided. The Manor is keen to stress that the reception price guide is entirely dependent on the client's wishes.

Whatley Manor
Nr Easton Grey
Malmesbury
Wiltshire SN16 0RB

Tel: 01666 822888 Fax: 01666 826120
Contact: Peter Kendall, General Manager

Ceremony

This Grade II listed building dates back to the 17th Century and is set in extensive gardens. Ceremonies are available seven days a week, excluding Christmas Day, Boxing Day and New Year. One ceremony per day is permitted and confetti is not allowed.
Price guide: POA

Reception

There are 18 bedrooms in the Manor House and Tudor and Terrace Wings, with a further 11 rooms in the Court House situated 70 yards across the courtyard. The waited service capacity for the reception is 80, although the

Manor may consider a stand-up finger buffet for a maximum of 100. Dancing and live music are possible when guests take exclusive use of the whole hotel.
Price guide: from £18pp

STOP PRESS
Bishopstrow House Hotel, Warminster
01985 212312
De Vere Hotel, Swindon
01973 878785
Limpley Stoke Hotel, Nr Bath
01225 723333
Marlborough Golf Club, Marlborough
01672 512147
Moormead Country Hotel, Swindon
01793 814744
Old Bell, Malmesbury
01666 822344
Salisbury Guildhall, Salisbury
01722 412144
Wiltshire County Hall, Trowbridge
01225 713097

Grange Hotel
1 Clifton
York, YO3 6AA
Tel: 01904 644744 Fax: 01904 612453
Contact: Shara Ross, GM

Ceremony

The Grange is a Regency townhouse with two marriage rooms; the Green Room and the Library (which does not have wheelchair access). Ceremonies can take place any day except Christmas Day.
Price guide: £200 (£100 with reception)

Reception

The Library and Drawing Room with French windows, or the Green Room with small dance floor can be used for receptions. Alternatively guests may have exclusive use of the Restaurant.
Catering: from £10.50pp

Merchant Adventurers' Hall
Fossgate
York YO1 2XD
Tel/Fax: 01904 654818
Contact: Mr Wheatley, Clerk
to the Company

Ceremony

This medieval building is situated right in the centre of York, within the city walls, and has its own garden with river frontage. This means that bride and groom could arrive or depart by boat. Wheelchair access is on the ground floor only, but help can be given to get to the first floor. Weddings can take place here on any day of the year. Confetti is not permitted.
Price guide: from £75

Reception

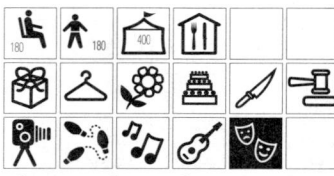

There is a choice of caterer. Themes may include a medieval banquet in keeping with the setting. Drinking licences can be applied for as required. Local accommodation can be recommended.
Catering: from £5pp

National Railway Museum
Leeman Road
York YO2 4XJ
Tel: 01904 621261 Fax: 01904 611112
Contact: Mandy McGrath, Events Executive

Ceremony

Three ceremony rooms are available at the museum; the Conference Room, the Stephenson Room and the South Hall. Weddings can take place here on any day of the week except Sunday. Confetti is not permitted.
Price guide: £175

Reception

A list of local accommodation with which the museum has preferential rates can be supplied.
Catering: Buffets from £9.95pp Sit down from £24.50pp

Swallow Hotel York
Tadcaster Road, York, YO2 2QQ
Tel: 01904 412204 Fax: 01904 702308
Contact: Business Development Manager

Ceremony

The hotel allows only one ceremony per day on any day of the year.
Price guide: P.O.A.

Reception

Catering: P.O.A.

STOP PRESS
Forte Post House, York
01904 707921
Merchant Taylor's Hall, York
01904 608218

WALES

Coed-y-Mwster Hotel
Coychurch, CF35 6AF
Tel: 01656 860621 Fax: 01656 863122
Contact: Andrea Scholefield, Conference & Banqueting Co-ordinator

Ceremony

Ceremonies can take place here on any day of the year.
Price guide: £150

Reception

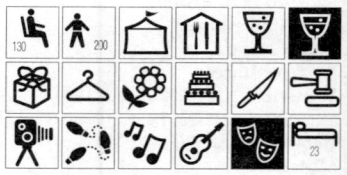

The Head Chef at the hotel is Scott Morgan, who will cater to your requirements, such as catering separately for children or developing a menu to suit your budget, dietary or religious requirements.
Catering: from £1300 (sit down)

Court Colman Hotel
Court Colman
Penyfai
Tel: 01656 720212 Fax:01656 724544
Contact: June Davies, GM

Ceremony

Court Colman is set in 6 acres of grounds and was the seat of the Llewellyn family at the turn of the century. Internally, the hotel features a wide sweeping staircase, oak panelled walls, and a fireplace in the hall that is a replica of the one at the Doges Palace in Venice. The Ballroom is modelled on the Crystal Room at the Palace of Versailles. Ceremonies can take place here any day except Sunday.
Price guide: £50 - £150

Reception

The hotel offers several rooms for receptions; the Ballroom and the Garden Room (up to 200). the Llewellyn Room (up to 75) and the Priory Suite (up to 120).
Catering: Buffet from £4.95pp Sit down from £17.50pp

Caerphilly Castle
Caerphilly CF83 1JS
Tel: 01222 500200 (bookings)
Fax: 01222 500300 (bookings)
Contact: Phillip Stallard, Site Facilities Officer
Tel: 01222 883143 (monument)
Contact: Mr D Radford, Head Custodian

Ceremony

This Medieval Castle is said to be the largest in Wales and is operated by Cadw Welsh Historic Monuments. The Great Hall is licensed for ceremonies which can take place on Saturdays and Sundays only, but must be followed byreception at the Castle. The Castle is not available on Bank Holidays.
Price guide: £100 + vat

Reception

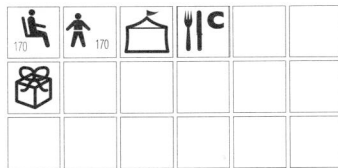

Catering and bar facilities must be organised by the hirer.

Cardiff Castle
Castle Street
Cardiff
CF1 2RB
Tel: 01222 878100 Fax: 01222 231417
Contact: Mrs Jean Brown,
Tours/Functions Co-ordinator

Ceremony

Cardiff Castle is a Grade I listed building and an ancient monument. Ceremonies (for parties of 16-100), can take place in one of three rooms on any day of the week, but not on Bank Holidays, or before 6pm from April to September. Confetti is not permitted.
Price guide: POA

Reception

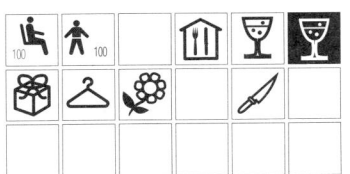

Catering: POA

Cardiff City Hall
Cathays Park
Cardiff
CF1 3ND
Tel: 01222 872000 Fax: 01222 871695
Contact: Ivor Mallett, Function Manager

Ceremony

Up to two ceremonies per day are permitted at this listed building. These can take place on any day of the week, but not on Christmas Day, Boxing Day or New Year's Day.
Price guide: POA

Reception

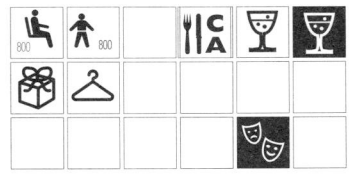

Cateing: POA

Castell Coch
Tongwynlais
Cardiff CF4 7JS
Tel: 01222 500200 (bookings)
Fax: 01222 500300 (bookings)
Contact: Phillip Stallard, Site Facilities Officer
Tel: 01222 810101 (monument)
Contact: Miss AM Peterson, Head Custodian

Ceremony

Castell Coch is described as a fairytale Victorian folly and is operted by Cadw Welsh Historic Monuments. The Banqueting Room and the Drawing Room are licensed for ceremonies which can take place here on any day of the year except Bank Holidays.
Prce guide: £120 + vat

Reception
There are no reception facilities at this venue.

Friendly Hotel
Merthur Road
Tongwynlais CF4 7LD
Tel: 01222 529988 Fax: 01222 529977
Contact: Claire Watkins, Conference & Banqueting Co-ordinator

Ceremony

Ceremonies can take place here on any day of the year. Confetti is not permitted.
Price guide: POA

Reception

Catering: from £16pp

Manor Parc Hotel & Restaurant
Thornhill Road
CF1 5UA
Tel: 01222 693723 Fax: 01222 614624
Contact: Mr Salvatore Salimeni or Mr
Efisio Cinus, Partners

Ceremony

The Manor Parc can offer ceremonies
o any day of the week except
Saturdays, wih a maximum of two ceremonies per day.
Price guide: POA

Reception

Catering: £18pp - £35pp

New House Country Hotel
Thornhill Road CF4 5UA
Tel: 01222 520280 Fax: 01222 520324
Contact: Mr Stephen Banks, GM

Ceremony

This country hotel is housed in a Grade
II listed building with views to Cardiff
and the Bristol Channel. One ceremony is permitted here per day on any
day of the year.
Price guide: £150

Reception

The hotel has two AA Rosettes for its
cuisine. Receptions can take place in
any of three function rooms. A complimentary rom is offered to the bride
and groom on their wedding night.
Catering: from £16pp

STOP PRESS
Cardiff International Arena
01222 234500
Park Hotel, Cardiff
01222 383471

Ashburnham Hotel
Ashburnham Road, Pembrey
Llanelli SA16 0TH
Tel: 01554 834343 Fax: 01554 834483
Contact: Susan Thomas, Manager

Ceremony

This hotel, restaurant and public house
is set in its own grounds overlooking
the Ashburnham Championship Golf
Links and the Gower Penninsula.
Ceremonies can take place here on any
day except Sunday.
Price guide: F.O.C. (with reception)

Reception

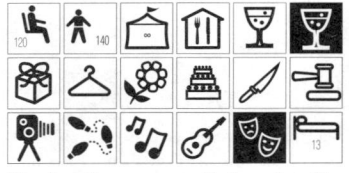

The hotel's restaurant, Rebecca's, offers
Welsh cuisine, while the Conservatory
Bar offers a choice of local ales.
Catering: from £13.95pp

Diplomat Hotel
Felinfoel, Llanelli SA15 3PJ
Tel: 01554 756156 Fax: 01554 751649
Contact: Mr JB Jenkins, Managing
Director

Ceremony

Up to two ceremonies per day can take
place at The Diplomat on any day of
the year.
Price guide: P.O.A.

Reception

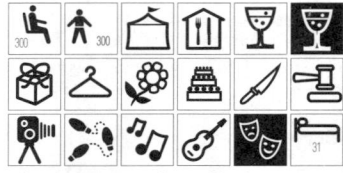

The hotel can also offer beauty and
leisure facilities.
Price guide: £12.50pp - £18pp

STOP PRESS
Gwellian Court Hotel, Kidwelly
01554 890217
Gwesty Plas Pant-Yr-Athro, Carmarthen
01267 241515

Ty Penlan, Llandelio
01558 822644
Undercliff, Ferryside
01267 267270

Tyglyn Aeron
Ciliau Aeron
Lampeter
Tel/Fax: 01570 470625
Contact: Mrs Thomas, Proprietor

Ceremony

One ceremony per day is permitted at
this hotel on any day except Christmas.
Price guide: £30

Reception

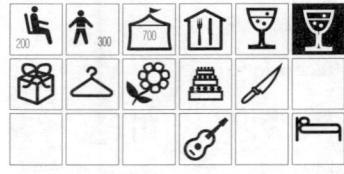

Catering: £15pp

STOP PRESS
The Cliff Hotel, Cardigan
01239 613241
Falcondale Hotel, Lampeter
01570 422910
Ynyshir Hall Hotel, Machynlleth
01654 781209

Conwy County Borough Council
Bodlondeb
Conwy LL32 8DU
Tel: 01492 574000 Fax: 01492 592114
Contact: Gwenda Ells, Superintendent
Registrar on 01492 592407

Ceremony

The council offices building was constructed in 1877 as a private residence
and is located in a public park. The
area registered to hold ceremonies
include the Council Chamber, an
adjoining Committee Room and the
Members' Room. The initial point of
contact must be Mrs Ells on the number above.
Price guide: £70

Reception
Reception facilities are not available at
this venue.

Gwydir Castle
Llanrwst LL26 0PN
Tel: 01492 641687
Contact: Judy Corbett/Peter Welford
Owners

Ceremony

This historic, 16th Century castle is set in Grade I listed gardens. The Solar Hall is licensed for ceremonies (limited wheelchair access) on any day of the year.
Price guide: POA

Reception

Helicopters and hot air balloons may use the grounds.
Catering: POA

Hopeside Hotel
West End, Colwyn Bay LL29 8PW
Tel: 01492 533244 Fax: 01492 532850
Contact: Paul Cliffe, Proprietor

Ceremony

This three star AA and RAC hotel offers two marriage rooms, the Penrhos suite (50 guests) and the Prince's Suite (100 guests). Ceremonies can take place here any day except between December 27th and January 10th.
Price guide: from £65

Reception

Cuisine at the hotel is French/English in style and holds an RAC award.
Catering: from £12.95

Plas Maenan
Country House Hotel
Conwy Valley
Llanwrst
Tel: 01492 660232 Fax: 01492 660551

Contact: James Graham Turner, Proprietor
or Marsha Kendall, Manager

Ceremony

Ceremonies are available seven days a week throughout the year. Although there is no formal wheelchair access, hotel staff members are always willing to help.
Price guide: £65

Reception

The hotel has a buffet capacity of 175, unfortunately children cannot be catered for separately.
Catering: from £8.50pp

St Georges Hotel
The Promenade
Llandudno
LL30 2LG
Tel: 01492 877544 Fax: 01492 878477
Contact Judy Window/ Karen Burns, Conference & Banqueting

Ceremony

This period building dating from 1854 features a protected classic facade, and is located on the seafront. The Conwy Suite is licensed for ceremonies which may take place here on any day of the year. Wheelchair access is limited.
Price guide: £200 (£100 with reception)

Reception

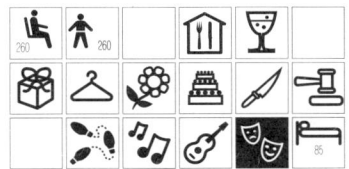

Couples may arrive and depart from the venue by boat. Receptions may also feature Welsh themed menus.
Price guide: Buffets from £6.50pp Sit down from £14.95pp

STOP PRESS
Colwyn Bay Hotel
01492 516555
The Grand Hotel, Llandudno
01492 876245
Imperial Hotel, Llamdudno
01492 877466
Kinmel Manor Hotel, Abergele
01745 832014
Priory Hotel, Llamwrst
01492 660247
Taylors Restaurant, Upper Colwyn Bay
01492 533360

Bodidris Hall
Llandegla
Wrexham
Denbighshire
LL11 3AL
Tel: 01978 790434 Fax: 01978 790335
Contact: Tudor Williams, Manager

Ceremony

This venue allows only one ceremony per day on any day of the year except Sundays and Bank holidays.
Price guide: £50

Reception

Catering: From £20pp

Chainbridge Hotel
Llangollen
Denbighshire
LL20 8BS
Tel: 01978 860215 Fax: 01978 861841
Contact: Mr VN Baker, Proprietor

Ceremony

The hotel sits on the banks of the River Dee and is about three minutes walk from the Horseshoe Falls. The hotel takes its name from the bridge which spans that river at this point. The hotel is also surrounded by the Berwyn and Eglwysig mountains.
Only one ceremony is permitted here per day on any day of the year.
Price guide: £100 or FOC with reception

Reception

The hotel's honeymoon suite is included with all reception reservations, subject to availability.
Catering: from £6.50pp

Ruthin Castle
Ruthin LL15 2NU
Tel: 01824 702664 Fax: 01824 705978
Contact: Mr Clayton, Manager

Ceremony

Ruthin Castle offers two ceremony rooms, which are available on any day of the week except Sundays. Ceremonies here must be followed by reception at the castle. Confetti is not permitted.
Price guide: £50 - £95

Reception

Catering: £10pp - £30pp

STOP PRESS
Bryn Howel Hotel, Llangollen
01978 860331
Bryn Morfydd Hotel, Denbigh
01745 890280
Faenol Fawr Country Hotel, St Asaph
01745 591691
Tyddyn Llan Country Hotel, Corwen
01490 440264
The White House Hotel, St Asaph
01745 582155

All Seasons Lodge Hotel
Northop HallCH7 6HB
Tel: 01244 550011 Fax: 01244 550763
Contact: Ms Jennifer Smith, GM

Ceremony

Up to two ceremonies can be held on any day of the week at the All Seasons lodge.
Price guide: £125

Reception

Catering: Buffets from £6.95 Sit down from £15.95

The Cornist Hall
Flint
Clwyd CH6 5RA
Tel: 01352 733241 Fax: 01352 731710
Contact: Mrs S Napier, Proprietor or Paula Williams, Wedding Co-ordinator

Ceremony

The Cornist Hall is a Jacobean mansion set in parkland and featuring an original walled rose garden. One ceremony per day can take place here on any day of the year.
Price guide: £75

Reception

In addition to the above services, the Hall can provide cars – a Daimler, Rolls or Mercedes, at special rates. While accommodation is not available on the premises, a list of local accommodation can be provided.
Catering: Buffets from £6pp Sit down from £12pp

Highfield Hall Hotel
Northop
Clwyd CH7 6AX
Tel & Fax: 01352 840 221
Contact: Virginia Smith or Molly Millar, Owners

Ceremony

This Georgian Grade II listed building is set in nine acres of mature gardens. The hotel was established in 1982, is family owned, and specialises in weddings. Up to two ceremonies are permitted here per day on any day of the year except Christmas Day.
Price guide: £150

Reception

The hotel's wedding package includes flowers for each table, a decorated cake table, a cake stand and knife, and a changing room for the day. Corkage is charged if you bring our own wine.
Catering: from £16.50pp

Plas Hafod Country House Hotel
Gwenymynydd
Mold CH7 5JS
Tel: 01352 700177 Fax: 01352 755499
Contact: Mrs Buckley, Manager

Ceremony

Hafod Hall was built in the 1730s and features an imposing entrance and stone staircase, and a romantic garden setting of around nine acres. Only one ceremony is permitted per day, on any day of the year.
Price guide: £120

Reception

Catering: from £16.95pp

Soughton Hall Country House Hotel
Northop CH7 6AB
Tel: 01352 840811 Fax: 01352 840382
Contact: Rosemary Rodenhurst, Event Banqueting Manager

Ceremony

This Georgian country house hotel is set in parkland with a half mile long 150 year old lime tree avenue, which can feature in wedding photographs. The house retains many original period fittings, and is full of antiques assembled for generations. Surprisingly, then, the owners of Soughton Hall welcome young children. The hotel offers a video of its wedding services. Only one wedding is permitted here per day, on any day of the year.
Price guide: P.O.A.

Reception

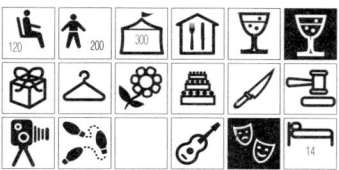

As well as the above, services offered by the hotel include menu printing, stationery, and personalised serviettes.
Catering: from £23pp

STOP PRESS
Kinsale Hall, Holywell
01745 560001
Springfield Hotel, Pentre Halkyn
01352 780503
St Davids Park Hotel, Ewloe
01244 520800

Gwynedd STOP PRESS
Bontddu Hall Hotel, Dolgellau
01341 430661
Castell Cidwn Hotel, Caernarfon
01286 650243
Hotel Maes-y-Neuadd, Harlech
01766 780200
Penmaenuchaf Hall Hotel, Dolgellau
01341 422129
Royal Victoria Hotel, Llanberis
01286 870253
Seiont Manor Hotel, Llanrug
01286 673366

Tre-ysgawen Hall
Capel Coch
LLangefni
Isle of Anglesey LL77 7UR
Tel: 01248 750750 Fax: 01248 750035
Contact: Mr Neil Rowlands, Assistant Manager

Ceremony

This restored country mansion dates

from 1882. Three rooms are available for ceremonies, ranging in capacity from 35 to 150. These are available on all day of the week except the Christmas and New Year's holidays. Ceremonies here must be followed by reception at the Hall.
Price guide: £100

Reception

The Hall offers European cusine, and is Egon Ronay recommended.
Catering: Buffets from £6.95 Sit down from £16.95

Victoria Hotel
Menai Bridge
Anglesey
Gwynedd LL59 5DR
Tel: 01248 712309 Fax: 01248 716774
Contact: Anne Smeaton (proprietor) or Simon Owen (Manager)

Ceremony

This Grade II listed Victorian building, overlooks the Menai Straits and has two rooms licensed to hold ceremonies with capacities of 80 and 120. Ceremonies are permitted without receptions.
Price guide: £50

Reception

The hotel offers a complimentary overnight stay for bridal couples, and will arrange special rates for wedding guests.
Catering: Buffets from £5.50pp
Sit down from £12pp

STOP PRESS
Bulkeley Hotel, Beaumaris
01248 810146
Bwyty Glantraeth Restaurant, Bodorgan
01407 840401
Henllys Hall Hotel, Beaumaris
01248 810412

Trearddur Bay Hotel, Holyhead
01407 860301

Cwrt Bleddyn Hotel
Llangybi, Nr Usk
Tel: 01633 450521 Fax: 01633 450220
Contact: Adrian Puckey, General Manager

Ceremony

The hotel offers three ceremony rooms which are available seven days a week with restrictions on Christmas Day and New Year's Day.
Price guide: £100 -£150

Reception

The hotel boasts accolades including Welsh Chef of the Year 1994 and Young Welsh Chef of the Year 1994 and 1995.
Catering: from £19pp

Glen-Yr-Afon House Hotel
Pontypool Road
Usk NP5 1SY
Tel: 01291 672302 Fax: 01291 672597
Contact: Mrs J A Clarke, Proprietor or Mr A Brown, Manager

Ceremony

The hotel was built in 1868 as a private residence and is set in its own grounds, with plenty of space for parking. Two rooms are licensed to hold ceremonies with varying capacities from 30 to 100. The hotel will consider booking ceremonies without receptions upon application.
Price guide: £100

Reception

Children cannot be catered for separately. The hotel holds a late night drinking licence until midnight.
Catering: from £21.95pp

STOP PRESS
Caldicot Castle, Newport
01291 424447

Glyn Clydach Hotel
Longford Road, Neath SA10 7AJ
Tel: 01792 813701 Fax: 01792 815612
Contact: Mr Rico Rabaiotti, Manager

Ceremony

The hotel is set in its own grounds and features a nine hole golf course. Two rooms are licensed to hold ceremonies which are available seven days a week excluding Christmas Day. A maximum of two ceremonies per day are permitted and confetti is allowed.
Price guide: £50

Reception

Three course wedding breakfasts start at approximately £18.50 a head, while buffets which include the room hire, DJ and an overnight bridal suite, start at £8.50 per person. Of the hotel's seven bedrooms, five are en-suite, and a 10% discount is offered to wedding guests staying overnight at the hotel.
Catering: Buffets from £8.50pp Sit down from £18.50pp

Margam Orangery
Margam Country Park
Margam
Port Talbot SA13 2TJ
Tel: 01639 881635 Fax: 01639 895897
Contact: Rosemary Lloyd

Ceremony

This award-winning orangery, set in acres of ornamental gardens, was originally built in 1786 and is the biggest of its kind in Britain. Following extensive restoration work the orangery was opened by the Queen in 1977. Ceremonies are available any day of the week excluding Christmas Day and Good Friday and are only available when held in conjunction with receptions. The Orangery does not make any charge for ceremonies.

Reception

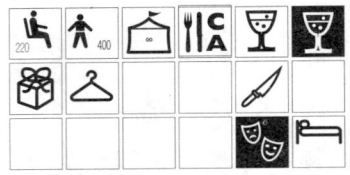

All catering is in-house, undertaken by the Orangery's own contract caterers, West Glamorgan Catering Services. A list of local hotels and guest houses is provided, some of which operate preferential rate agreements with the Orangery.
Catering: £10 – £30pp

Celtic Manor Hotel
Golf and Country Club
Coldra Woods, Newport NP6 2YA
Tel: 01633 413000 Fax: 01633 412910
Contact: Nicola Chattam, Wedding Co-ordinator

Ceremony

This former manor house offers two rooms for ceremonies, one of which has only limited wheelchair access. Ceremonies are available here on any day of the year, but must be followed by reception at the hotel.
Price guide: from £100

Reception

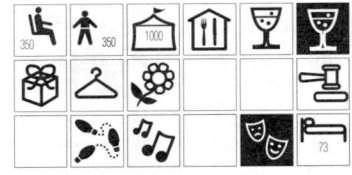

Helicopters and hot air balloons may use the grounds.
Catering: Buffets from £14.95pp Sit down from £20.70pp

STOP PRESS
St Mellons Hotel, Castleton
01633 680355
Tredegar House, Newport
01633 815880

Canolfan Pentre Ifan
Felindre Farchog
Crymych SA41 3XE
Tel: 01239 820317 Fax: 01239 820317
Contact: Carol Owen, Development Officer

Ceremony

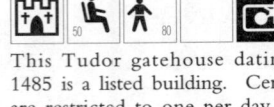

This Tudor gatehouse dating from 1485 is a listed building. Ceremonies are restricted to one per day, on any day of the year except Bank Holidays.
Price guide: £125

Reception

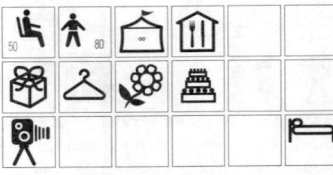

At Canolfan Pentre Ifan you may supply your own alcohol for the wedding reception but it cannot be sold on the premises. Children cannot be catered for separately. In true Welsh musical tradition a harpist can be provided if required.
Catering: £5.50pp – £10pp

Cwmwennol Country House
Swallowtree Woods
Saundersfoot SA69 9DE
Tel: 01834 813430 Fax: 01834 813430
Contact: Tony Smiles, Owner

Ceremony

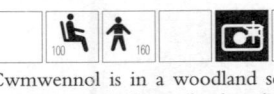

Cwmwennol is in a woodland setting, just 300 yards from the beach. The original building dates back to 1870s. The current owners took over the hotel in 1989 and have been making improvements over recent years, including the refurbishment of the restaurant in Laura Ashley designs.
Price guide: £100

Reception

The hotel uses local produce wherever

possible, and fish landed on the harbour. Barbecue weddings are a speciality.
Catering: £5.50pp (buffet) - £10pp (sit down)

St Brides Hotel
St Brides Hill
Saundersfoot SA69 9NH
Tel: 01834 812304 Fax: 01834 813303
Contact: Ian Bell, Managing Director

Ceremony

St Brides is set right by the sea, and has its own outdoor pool. Ceremonies can take place here on any day of the week except Sundays. Confetti is not permitted.
Price guide: £50 - £200

Reception

Catering: from £15 (Sit down)

Warpool Court Hotel
St Davids SA62 6BN
Tel: 01437 720300 Fax: 01437 720676
Contact: Rupert Duffin, General Manager

Ceremony

The AA and RAC Three Star, WTB Four Crown, Warpool Court Hotel enjoys sweeping views across its lawns to the coast of St Brides Bay and the off-shore islands. Inside, the hotel is decorated with 3000 hand painted tiles decorated by the lady who lived here in the early 1900s. Only one ceremony is permitted here per day on any day of the year. Confetti is not permitted.
Price guide: P.O.A.

Reception

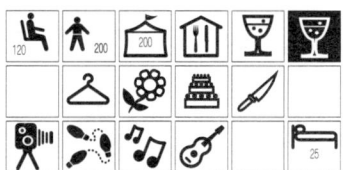

The hotel offers an extensive range of fish dishes, with smoked salmon a speciality. A choice of vegetarian dishes is always available and special diets can be catered for.
Catering: from £18.75pp (Sit down)

STOP PRESS
Castell Malgwyn, Cardigan
01239 682382
The Druidstone Hotel, Haverfordwest
01437 781221
Fourcroft Hotel, Tenby
01834 842886
Holyland Hotel & Tavern, Pembroke
01646 681444
Nantyffin Motel, Clunderwen
01437 563423
Penally Abbey, Penally
01834 843033

Caer Beris Manor
Builth Wells, Powys
Tel: 01982 552601 Fax: 01982 552586
Contact: Peter & Katharine Smith

Ceremony

This former home of Lord Swansea, set in 27 acres of parkland offers wedding ceremonies on any day of the week except Sundays.
Price guide: £50 (FOC with reception)

Reception

Cuisine at the Manor is international in style.
Catering: from £10.95pp

Castle of Brecon Hotel
The Castle Square
Brecon, Powys LD3 9DB
Tel: 01874 624611 Fax: 01874 623737
Contact: Duty Manager

Ceremony

The Castle of Brecon is a listed building with its own gardens and excellent views. It has three marriage rooms ranging in seated capacity from 35 to 150, and in standing capacity from 45 to 200. Ceremonies can take place here on any day of the year. The Castle of Brecon Hotel has set no limit on the number of ceremonies that can be held each day.
Price guide: £25

Reception

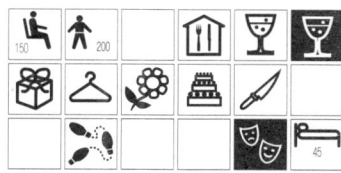

Catering: Packages from £19pp

Lake Country House Hotel
Llangammarch Wells
Powys LD4 4BS
Tel: 01591 620202 Fax: 01591 620457
Contact: Mr J P Mifsud, Proprietor

Ceremony

The Lake is a Victorian Welsh country house set in 50 acres with sweeping lawns, rhododendron lined pathways, riverside walks and a large trout lake. This is a homely sort of hotel that serves Welsh teas in front of the log fire in the drawing room every afternoon. Ceremonies can take place here any day of the year, but only one is permitted per day.
Price guide: P.O.A.

Reception

The hotel claims an award winning restaurant which uses fresh produce and herbs from its own gardens.
Catering: £22.50pp (sit-down)

Lake Vyrnwy Hotel
Lake Vyrnwy, Powys
Tel: 01691 870692 Fax: 01691 870259
Contact: Mr Jim Talbot

Ceremony

This country house hotel sits overlooking the six mile long Lake Vyrnwy. The hotel offers two marriage rooms; The Drawing Room (max 65) and the Tower Suite (max 200). Ceremonies can take place here on any day except Sundays and religious holidays, with up to four permitted per day.
Price guide: £150 - £200

Reception

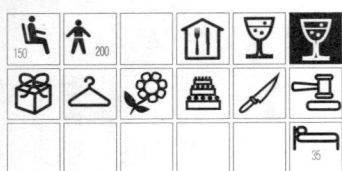

The hotel holds two AA Rosettes for its restaurant. Children cannot be catered for separately.
Catering: from £17pp

Llangoed Hall
Llyswen, Brecon LD3 0YP
Tel: 01874 754525 Fax: 01874 754545
Contact: Mrs Helen Pugh, General Manager

Ceremony

Llangoed Hall is a listed building that sits on the banks of the river Wye and was designed by Sir Clough Williams-Ellis. The atmosphere of the house is designed to be that of your own home, and is delightfully presented in the Hall's literature. Only one wedding is permitted here at any one time, and that must be followed by reception at the Hall.
Price guide: £200

Reception

The Hall can accommodate up to 50 guests in The Orangery and a maximum of 14 in the Whistler Room. Carriages should be arranged before 6pm. Should you want to party on into the evening, it would be necessary to take the Hall on an exclusive use basis. The Hall's restaurant has three AA Rosettes and four red pavilions from Michelin.
Catering: 17.50pp - £39pp

Plas Dolguog Hotel
Machynlleth, Powys SY20 8UJ
Tel: 01654 702244 Fax: 01654 702530
Contact: Mrs Pritchard, Proprietor

Ceremony

This is a listed 16th Century country house set in nine acres of garden and woodland. Ceremonies can take place here on any day except Sunday and Easter Saturday.
Price guide: £50

Reception

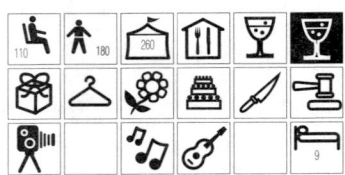

There is a site available for a large marquee.
Catering: £12.95pp

Powis Castle
Welshpool, Powys SY21 8RF
Tel: 01938 554338 Fax: 01938 554336
Contact: Caroline Sier, Property Manager

Ceremony

The ancestral home of the Herbert family since 1587, Powis Castle is perhaps best known for its wonderful gardens, which are laid out in 17th Century Italian and French styles. The Castle is now run by The National Trust, which has elected the Castle's Ballroom as the marriage room. Just one ceremony is permitted per day, and only when the Castle is closed to the public, i.e. Monday and Tuesday in April, May, June, September and October, and Mondays only in July and August (not Bank Holiday Mondays). Marriages may be held on any day during the closed season.
Price guide: £500

Reception

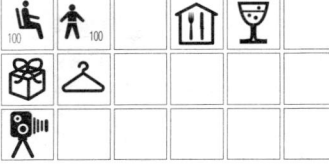

In-house catering is available at the Castle, but your own choice of contract caterer could be appointed.
Price guide: P.O.A.

Swan at Hay Hotel
Church Street
Hay on Wye, Powys
Tel: 01497 821188 Fax: 01497 821424
Contact: Mrs RG Vaughan, Proprietor

Ceremony

Cermonies at this listed Georgian building are limited to one per day on any day of the year except the 10 days over the Whitsun holiday. Wheelchair users must negotiate one step.
Price guide: £120

Reception

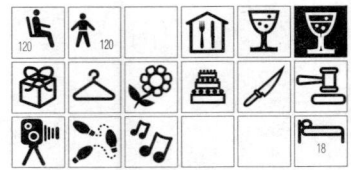

The hotel holds an AA Rosette for its food. Children cannot be catered for separately.
Catering: £12pp - £25pp

STOP PRESS
Elephant & Castle Hotel, Newtown
01686 626271
Garthmyl Hall, Montgomery
01686 640550
Gliffaes Hotel, Crickhowell
01874 730371
Greenway Manor Hotel, Llandrindod Wells
01597 851230
Llanidloes Council Chamber, Llanidloes
01686 412353
Maesmawr Hall Hotel, Caersws
01686 688255

Heritage Park Hotel
Coed Cae Road
Trehafod CF37 2NP
Tel: 01443 687057 Fax: 01442 687060
Contact: Victoria Williams, General Manager

Ceremony

The modern Heritage Park is situated 10 miles from the centre of Cardiff.

Ceremonies can take place here on any day of the year.
Price guide: £50

Reception

Bride and groom are offered a complimentary room to change in during the day, as well as overnight accommodation on their wedding night. Children under 12 years old are also catered for at half price.
Catering: from £13pp (sit down)

Miskin Manor
Pendolyn Road, Groesfaen
Pontyclun CF7 8ND
Tel: 01443 224204 Fax: 01443 237606
Contact: Joanna Kocker, Conference & Banqueting Manager

Ceremony

This four star hotel is housed in a Grade II listed building set in 20 acres of gardens. It has a Wales Tourist Board Five Crowns Highly Commended Award. There are four marriage rooms: Meisgyn, the Garden Room, the Cedar Room and the Drawing Room and Terrace Suite. These cater for a minimum of 10 guests. Ceremonies can take place here on any day except New Year's Day and Good Friday, and must be followed by a reception at the hotel.
Price guide: £275

Reception

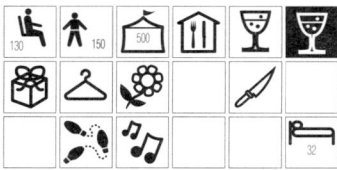

The hotel is able to offer menus to suit your requirements, including special Welsh menus. All the above services are offered in the hotel's standard wedding package, but other services can be provided. The hotel offers wedding guests a special overnight rate.
Catering: from £21.50pp

STOP PRESS
The Visitors Centre, Aberdare
01685 874672

Daw-Yr-Ogof Caves
Abercave, Swansea SA9 1GT
Tel: 01639 730049 Fax: 01639 730203
Contact: Sara Reynolds, Event Manager

Ceremony

Weddings can take place in the Cathedral Cave at this popular tourist attraction. Wheelchair access is limited. Ceremonies can take place here on any day of the year except Bank Holidays. Confetti is not permitted.
Price guide: £200

Reception

Reception facilities are not available on site, although five bedrooms are available for overnight accommodation.

Langland Court Hotel
Langland Court Road
Langland
Swansea SA34 4TD
Tel: 01792 361545 Fax: 01792 362302
Contact: Chris Hamilton-Smith, Wedding Manager

Ceremony

This Tudor style house is set in award winning gardens in a quiet residential area and boasts sea views. The Adam Lounge is licensed for ceremonies which can take place here on any day of the year except Christmas Day and Boxing Day. Helicopters and hot air balloons may use the grounds. Ceremonies here must be followed by reception at the hotel. Confetti is not permitted.
Price guide: £55

Reception

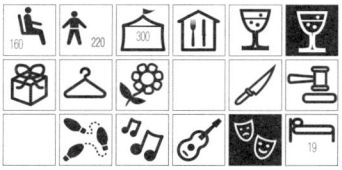

Welsh dishes and menus are a special feature of the hotel.
Catering: Buffets from £12.25pp Sit down from £15.95pp

STOP PRESS
Fairyhill Hotel, Gower
01792 390139
Swansea Marriott Hotel, Swansea
01792 642020

Parkway Hotel
& Conference Centre
Cwmbran Drive
Cwmbran, Gwent
Tel: 01633 871199 Fax: 01633 869160
Contact: Teresa Langton, Conference & Banqueting Co-ordinator

Ceremony

This privately owned hotel has AA/RAC four star status and has a five crown award from the Wales Tourist Board. Three rooms are available to hold ceremonies.
Price guide: £105

Reception

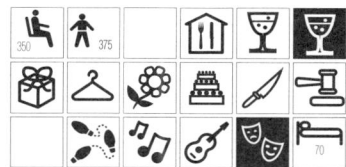

As part of the day-reception package, the hotel offers amongst other things, a choice of 12 menus and a complimentary honeymoon suite for the couple.
Catering: from £22.90pp

The Egerton Grey Hotel
Porthkerry, Nr Barry
S Glam CF62 3BZ
Tel: 01446 711666 Fax: 01446 711690
Contact: Anthony Pitkin, Proprietor

Ceremony

This former 19th Century rectory, 10 miles from Cardiff, was opened as a small luxury hotel in 1988. It is set in seven acres of gardens, with croquet lawn and tennis court, with views down to Porthkerry Park and the sea. No other habitation or road can be seen from the hotel. Weddings may take place in the Drawing Room, with views over the gardens, or in the mahogany panelled Dining Room. Ceremonies may take place here on any day except Christmas Day.
Price guide: £100

Reception

At Egerton, an alternative to the formal sit-down meal is offered: a buffet luncheon. Guests are served in the main Dining Room, but may then be seated at tables throughout the house; in the Library, the two halls, the Private Dining Room, the Drawing Room or outside.
Catering: from £17.50

The Boat Inn
Erbistock
Wrexham LL13 0Dl
Tel: 01978 780143
Contact: General Manager

Ceremony

This restaurant and public house is a Grade II listed building. One ceremony is permitted per day here, on any day of the week except Sundays and public holidays.
Price guide: £100 (£75 with reception)

Reception

The restaurant serves British/French style cuisine and has two AA Rosettes.
Catering: £8pp (buffet) - £12 pp (waited)

Hanmer Arms
Hanmer, Nr Whitchurch SY13 3DE
Tel: 01948 830532 Fax: 01948 830740
Contact: General Manager

Ceremony

The Hanmer Arms is a privately owned village hotel and restaurant. A maximum of two ceremonies are permitted per day on any day of the year. Disabled access is to the ground floor only, this room having a capacity for 40 people.
Price guide: £100

Reception

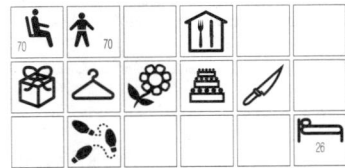

Catering: from £11pp

Rossett Hall Hotel
Chester Road, Rossett
Wrexham, Clwyd LL12 0DE
Tel: 01244 571000 Fax: 01244 571505
Contact: David Craven, Partner

Ceremony

Rossett Hall is a Grade II listed building, built in 1750. Up to two ceremonies per day are permitted here, on any day of the year.
Price guide: 500

Reception

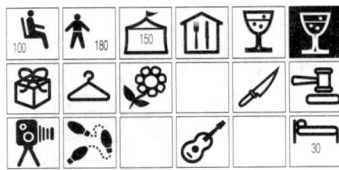

Catering: £16pp - £25pp

STOP PRESS
Cross Lanes Hotel, Wrexham
01978 780555
The Hand Hotel, Chirk
01691 773472

172